The Arab Uprisings

The Arab Uprisings

Catalysts, Dynamics, and Trajectories

EDITED BY FAHED AL-SUMAIT,
NELE LENZE, AND MICHAEL C. HUDSON

ROWMAN & LITTLEFIELD

Lanham • *Boulder* • *New York* • *London*

Published by Rowman & Littlefield
A wholly owned subsidary of The Rowman & Littlefield Publishing Group, Inc.
4501 Forbes Boulevard, Suite 200, Lanham, Maryland 20706
www.rowman.com

16 Carlisle Street, London W1D 3BT, United Kingdom

British Library Cataloguing in Publication Information Available

Library of Congress Cataloging-in-Publication Data

The Arab uprisings : catalysts, dynamics, and trajectories / edited by Fahed Al-Sumait,
Nele Lenze, and Michael Hudson.
    pages cm
    Includes bibliographical references and index.
    ISBN 978-1-4422-3900-5 (cloth : alk. paper) — ISBN 978-1-4422-3901-2 (pbk. : alk. paper)
— ISBN 978-1-4422-3902-9 (electronic) 1. Arab Spring, 2010- 2. Protest movements—
Arab countries 3. Democratization—Arab countries. 4. Arab countries—Politics and
government—21st century. I. Al-Sumait, Fahed Yahya, editor of compilation. II. Lenze,
Nele, editor of compilation. III. Hudson, Michael.
    JQ1850.A91A825 2014
    909'.097492708312—dc23

                                                                                    2014023933

♾™ The paper used in this publication meets the minimum requirements of
American National Standard for Information Sciences—Permanence of Paper for
Printed Library Materials, ANSI/NISO Z39.48-1992.

Printed in the United States of America

Contents

PART II: Dynamics

PART III: Trajectories

political system that they have lived under for the last sixty years. They have started the process of creating a new political system—underway in such a short time, with new changes emerging almost every day. They offer those of us who live in the Middle East a spellbinding spectacle. These changes are continuously present and can be seen in events related to the presidential elections, the new constitutional committees, and parliamentary elections and new political parties. There have already been significant changes in sentiments and voting patterns by Egyptians during the past few years, as evidenced in the two presidential elections, the parliamentary elections, the short rule of the Islamists, and then the Tamarrud movement and army intervention that removed the Islamists, with apparent wide popular support. This volatility will continue. Our challenge is to step back and try to understand the political changes taking place in the broader context of recent history.

My suggestion is that we should see this as the single most important moment in the history of the modern Arab world, which begins with events decades before Mohamed Bouazizi's self-immolation in December 2010. It began with the first recent wave of the Islamist movements in the 1970s, which coincided with the oil boom and the massive distortions of economic wealth and distribution. An additional influence was the cementing of the modern Arab security state, and the collapse of the Arab-Israeli conflict as a long-running military conflict among states at a regional level, after Egypt (and later Jordan) pulled out after they signed their peace treaties with Israel in 1978 and 1994, respectively. Hence, it was in the mid- to late 1970s that we find the early signs of the genesis of the Arab Uprisings that we see now. Scores of movements and formal organizations attempted to improve human rights and democracy conditions across the Arab world in the four decades before December 2010, but always to no avail—because the prevailing security-based political orders that were willing to beat down their own people and also controlled most national economic activity could not be budged by the limited activism that usually challenged these autocratic systems. Even mass uprisings, like the Kurdish and Shiite uprisings against the Baathist Iraqi government or the Muslim Brotherhood–led uprising against the Baathist Syrian government, were not able to remove or reform the security state systems. The December 2010 and January 2011 uprisings proved to be different, partly perhaps because they drew on the cumulative frustrations and humiliations that several hundred million Arab citizens had experienced in the preceding decades, and whose force was irresistible once it expressed itself in actions on the street. Another reason the Arab state orders did not give in to citizen protests (with the sole exception of the overthrow of Jaafar Numeiry in Sudan in the mid-1980s) was the significant support they received from the two superpowers during the Cold War years.

Historians will document this over time and give us a more accurate reading of this spirit of mass citizen revolt, of people in several countries rising up against their own autocratic systems, as happened first on December 17, 2010, in Sidi Bouzid in provincial Tunisia, when Mohamed Bouazizi's self-immolation proved a triggering event to this process. It also could have been anything else that started the mass revolts, for this was one of those moments—like Steve Biko and Nelson Mandela in South Africa, like Lech Walesa in Poland, or Martin Luther King Jr. or Rosa Parks in the United States, or Aung San Suu Kyi in Burma—when an individual undertakes an act, whether spontaneous or planned, of both defiance and self-affirmation, an act that simultaneously resonates with hundreds, or millions, of other people in their own country or in other countries. This is what we see happening right now across the Arab world. The movement to challenge and to change Arab authoritarian regimes is not new; the process has been going on for thirty or forty years, albeit unsuccessfully, because the powers that maintained these regimes were simply too strong to defy. As of 2014, our challenge is still to determine how we can most accurately analyze events as this process continues.

THE IGNITING SPARK

We always have to go back to the beginning in these kinds of events and transformations to better understand what is happening, and in this case we can easily identify Tunisia and Egypt as the recent catalysts—the breakthroughs that finally toppled autocratic regimes when all other activism in previous decades could not achieve this. Mohamed Bouazizi serves as a good metaphor that captures what I believe is the critical driving force for these uprisings across the region—not just uprisings in countries like Tunisia, Egypt, Libya, Syria, and Bahrain and Yemen, but also nonrevolutionary citizen demands and stirrings in other places like Jordan, Oman, Kuwait, and Morocco. There are signs all over the region that people—even if they are well-off and their basic material needs are met—have other basic political needs that are not being met, especially intangibles denominated in the language of justice, respect, and dignity. That is the critical starting point for us to understand what happened when Mohamed Bouazizi, on that day of December 17, within a span of hours, had two degrading encounters with officials of his own government—first, the policewoman who stopped him from selling fruits and vegetables, and therefore prevented his ability to meet his material needs; and second, when he went to the local governor's office to protest his mistreatment. There, he was sent away, so his inability to work and satisfy his family's material needs was compounded by the message from the local provincial governor that he also did not have any political rights. He discovered, in fact, that he did not really exist, he did not have a voice, he did not matter, and he did not count. He was an invisible person, with no rights or recourse. That combination of crucial dimensions of life help explain the uprisings to me, because they define what most Arab citizens lack: secure material needs and the intangible needs of status as a citizen—such as voice, legitimacy, participation, accountability, dignity, trust, and respect. These many words all mean essentially the same thing—that people need to feel that they are treated fairly and decently by their own power structure. This is not about invading American or British armies; we are not talking about Israeli colonization and annexation, Iranian involvement in Arab states, or other foreign interventions. Citizens are being mistreated by their own Arab countries and governments, for these uprisings are the work of disgruntled citizens who are demanding from their own societies a combination of their material rights and their intangible political rights to be given to them, at a minimum level, so that they feel that they actually do exist, that they do have rights, that they can expect their children will have reasonable opportunities to enjoy a normal, decent, and full life. Hence, going back to Mohamed Bouazizi is a useful exercise because he is a dramatic and accurate symbol of the material and the intangible political rights that Arab citizens feel they have long been denied.

The nature, extent, and consequences of the vulnerabilities experienced by tens of millions of individuals like Mohamed Bouazizi across the Arab world are better documented now and help us grasp why his lone act of desperation or defiance—we will never know his real motives—spread so quickly because it resonated so vividly with many millions of others who understood his pain because they experienced it also. Hernando de Soto at the Institute for Liberty and Democracy in Peru has done some very important work looking at informal economic actors across the Arab region, and he has spent much time in Tunisia and other Arab countries. He estimates that several hundred million Arabs basically operate in the informal sector (out of the 350 million Arabs today). In Egypt, he believes that "the extra-legal sector accounts for 84 percent of businesses and 92 percent of land parcels."[1] Several other recent studies published by his Institute for Liberty and Democracy provide considerable details about the vast scale of the informal or "shadowy" economy that defines much of the Arab region and causes so many individuals to feel vulnerable—some of whom take their lives in protest, desperation, or both.[2]

The informal entrepreneurs and workers of the Arab world mostly do not have a license or insurance, and they do not pay taxes. My conclusion from the vast scale of economic informality and social vulnerability that defines much of the Arab world is that the relationship between the citizen and the state was not based on a process of rights, registration, accountability, and management of society in a coherent way. It was based on informal relationships that were almost always greased by small bribes, payoffs, connections, and favors, without any clear set of rights or responsibilities that citizens had to deal with. In short, systems of corruption and clientelism dominated over principles of meritocracy and citizenship rights.

It is useful to step back from today's hectic changes and review the period since December 2010 in order to ask ourselves, What is it that has happened that is really meaningful and may have long-term political and national significance? To achieve this, we really need to do what was not done by most people in the last forty or fifty years—to listen really carefully to what ordinary Arab men and women are saying. The difference today (in 2014) in the Arab world since 2010 is that average people—whether they are rural farmers, urban laborers, or professional people—now have more opportunities to speak out. They can demonstrate in the street, they can hold up a sign during a protest or celebration, they can speak to Al Jazeera and dozens of other media outlets, they can vote, they can join a party, and, in places, they can participate in writing their new constitutions. The invisible, voiceless Arabs increasingly are a thing of the past, even in countries that have not experienced revolutionary upheavals and where the central government remains strong and in control, like in Jordan, Oman, Morocco, or Kuwait.

CAREFUL LISTENING

All of us—governments, academics, journalists, and civil societies—should not repeat the same mistake of ignoring a representative sample of citizens in Arab countries. When we do listen, and we hear and analyze what people have been saying since December 2010, the complexity of what is going on becomes even more daunting, because so many different groups of citizens living in a variety of conditions are making a wide range of demands and protesting an equally wide range of grievances. There is no single, unifying theme to the Arab Uprisings that take different forms in countries across the region. This is why it is important to grapple with this complexity, so that by understanding what people protest and also seek, we can identify those issues that need to be examined more thoroughly and addressed through more effective public policies. Ideally, the transitions underway in some countries will allow for two simultaneous achievements: developing more legitimate governance systems that reflect the consent of the governed and the will of the majority while protecting minority rights, and implementing public policies that more efficiently respond to citizen expectations in the realms of socioeconomic and political rights. Whatever citizens want to do with their country is up to them: they can aspire to be an Islamic republic, or a tribal confederation, or an Arab nationalist celebration, or a free enterprise part of the corporate world. The hard fact is that we do not know fully and clearly the precise balance among socioeconomic, political, rule-of-law, and security priorities that citizens speak about in different countries, because we have only been experiencing structured transformations for a short period, in erratic conditions, and in only three countries, essentially, with much more change to come.

When we listen carefully to people, we can start to get an idea of what matters to them and therefore understand better where work needs to be done to try to move societies toward citizens' aspirations. Based on what we have heard from citizens across the region since the uprisings began, we can already clearly discern the following list of issues that reflect either what people are affirming when they speak out or what they actually demand and aspire to achieve. These include, most commonly, justice, dignity, freedom, trust, legitimacy, and accountability. This is based on how citizens have expressed themselves in public in Libya, Yemen, Syria, Tunisia, Egypt, and Bahrain, but the issues raised often apply across the whole Arab world. There is no Arab country that is exempt from some dimension of citizens expressing themselves, either on the street or on the Web and through social media, about what they would like to see change or evolve.

In general, people have been expressing anger at past abuses, for which they want transitional justice. They want the crimes of the past to be dealt with, whether massive corruption, theft, jailing hundreds of thousands of people, or torturing and killing people. Arab men and women express a desire to be empowered as citizens, exercise basic citizen rights, be able to vote, share their views, debate issues, hold power accountable—in other words, to have empowerment as citizens that they have never had.

There appears to be a pervasive demand for "dignity," which is never clearly defined; dignity, like love, is hard to explain, but you know when it happens to you, and you know when it is denied you. How citizens understand "dignity" is a pressing research priority in the Arab world because understanding this concept more clearly can help shape new public policies that can lead to more stable and productive societies. A critical aspect of this is to better grasp how dignity reflects both material life needs (education, water, jobs) as well as respect for the individual's rights, such as asserting cultural or ethnic identity or participating in public life.

Closely linked to the thirst for dignity is the demand of many Arabs in the streets for "respect." As a general human trait, people want to respect each other and to be respected as individuals and as countries. One of the great areas that cries out for serious research is the link between the individual demands of people and their activism for individual rights, on the one hand, and the national configuration of countries and societies that have wider perceptions of their identities as Arabs or as Muslims, or as some other ethnic, tribal, or national identity, on the other. Respect is one of the great drivers of stable societies and countries, and it is starting to affirm itself in some Arab countries.

Justice is a leading demand of people in the uprisings. I define two kinds of justice in my analysis of the current situation. On the one hand, there is the transitional justice for the crimes of the past that I mentioned above, and on the other hand, the demand for social justice plays an important role. This is probably the most active arena where NGOs and civil society groups across the Arab world are working now.[3] They try to translate the demands for social justice into a practical set of activities, policy recommendations, or legal mechanisms to prevent the kinds of social and economic injustices that happened in the past—like poor access to clean water and decently priced food, tens of millions of workers without health or disability insurance or retirement pensions, or very poor quality public schooling that further entrenches poverty and passivity.

People are asking for the right to enjoy basic freedoms in all aspects of life. Many people express pride at living in a free society, and pride is one of the many elements on the list of intangible demands. This list of populist expressions and demands includes practical things like freedom of speech and cultural diversity, as well as many intangibles, such as being treated equitably in judicial or electoral systems. In my opinion, this suggests that we are dealing with Arabs who seek to experience life as free and full citizens and therefore express both dimensions of life—the tangible and the intangible—for the first time in many generations. They could not do so before, because in the last thirty or forty years, essentially, Arabs were told they could experience the material dimensions of life: they could go to the mall and buy as many cell phones as they wanted, or if they were among the very small minority that had some capital they could invest in real estate or stock markets as much as they wanted—but that was essentially the limit of their rights. Now, we are witnessing a change whereby many, perhaps several hundred million, Arabs cry out for more than cell phones and malls, asking for justice, rights, pride, and a normal life, and pride is one of these elements that allows mere consumers to become full citizens.

Serious issues of legitimacy shape many of the demands we hear from citizens these days. This additionally pertains to two dimensions: the legitimacy of the exercise of power and also the legitimacy of the configuration of nationhood and statehood. This is one of the interesting questions that may arise in the years ahead as countries attempt to democratize and stabilize and resume a less tumultuous historical path. Will there be any desire to reconfigure statehood, as happened for instance after the fall of the Soviet Union, when countries were divided and new ones were created? The map of the state boundaries of the former Soviet Empire before and after 1990 is very different, especially in places like former Yugoslavia and Czechoslovakia. It is hard to know if we will witness similar changes in the Arab world. We have already seen south Sudan secede, a unified Iraq sometimes appears a bit shaky in the Kurdish regions especially, as well as other Arab countries like Yemen and Libya that have strong separatist forces at play. Some Arab states like Lebanon, Palestine, or Somalia have chronic fragilities in structure and configuration. Legitimacy of the state, as well as legitimacy of the power elite, are issues to watch closely.

The twin elements of accountability and participation are common demands expressed in very different ways, including demands for more equitable electoral and parliamentary systems and wider and deeper citizen participation in creating new constitutions. People do not necessarily want to shape policy directly, but they do want to hold power accountable; they want to feel that their opinions matter and are heard in the corridors of power and policy making and that they have credible means to challenge the abuse of power, corruption, or other forms of poor governance that they experience.

The institutional anchorage for all these material and intangible demands is constitutional reform. The demand for reform is probably the single most common demand across the region, because people want a guarantee of their rights, not just promises of better days ahead. Instead of speeches with great reform

promises, people demand a rule of law that they can shape and insist on holding ruling powers accountable. Constitutional reform may be one way to fulfill
these demands. Civil society groups and politicians have learned from other
democratic transitions, such as Chile or Argentina, where significant effort went
into creating new constitutional mechanisms that guaranteed some of the newly
gained rights of citizenship or social justice.

All of the above issues—dignity, respect, accountability, social justice, and
the others—reflect a very wide range of sentiments and grievances that have
caused tens of millions of Arab men and women to take to the streets, whether
literally or figuratively, since December 2010 and try to reconfigure both their
citizenship and their statehood. These individual issues or concepts are most
meaningful to individuals, but when they are aggregated they also hold historic
meaning for entire countries.

SELF-DETERMINATION AND SOVEREIGNTY

Ultimately, all of these demands, rights, and aspirations feed into two grand
concepts that the modern Arab world has long lacked. One of them is genuine
self-determination—citizens shaping their governance system, national values,
and state policies. The second goal that is sought is true sovereignty—the ability of the state to govern itself. I would argue that we have not had genuinely
sovereign Arab countries in the last half of the century. We have had independent countries always managed by small elites but perhaps not fully sovereign
countries whose decisions fully and accurately reflect the will of the citizenry and
the consent of the governed. We may be starting on the road to approach that
goal now in several Arab countries—such as Tunisia, Egypt, and Libya—that are
going through democratic and constitutional transitions and then creating new
governance systems that are legitimate, responsive, and accountable and with
which the citizenry is comfortable.

Certainly, some Arab countries soon will be making decisions that reflect the
majority of their people's will, decisions that are made in the best interests of those
countries. So self-determination and sovereignty are the ultimate prizes that will
result from this chaotic process of change that is currently underway. I have spent
my whole adult life in the Arab world watching dysfunctional states increasingly
create marginalized, pauperized, victimized, vulnerable, and excluded people.
What is happening today for the first time ever is that we are starting to see a
more natural alignment of the citizen, the society, the government, and the state,
ideally leading to a situation of an organic, logical relationship between the citizen,

the structures of society (whether religious or tribal, civil society, professional, or political structures), and the state.

These transforming Arab countries are experiencing historical phenomena and transitions that occurred in other democratic countries, like in Western Europe or North America, over periods of one hundred to two hundred years, until national reconfigurations gave citizens equal rights and codified a general consensus on national values, principles, and policies (such as women in Europe and North America getting the vote in the early years of the twentieth century and African Americans getting their full voting and civil rights in the mid-1960s). In Egypt, Tunisia, and Libya we can see the component elements of a national transformation and definition taking place simultaneously rather than sequentially. These include processes such as a war of independence, constitutional conventions, struggles to define principles of national governance, elements of a civil war in places, ending autocratic, authoritarian regimes, and the building of democratic systems, promoting full civil rights, ensuring minority rights, and other such historic achievements. Such changes required two centuries in the United States and are still ongoing as people continue to debate the balance between state and federal rights.

In most Arab countries, I would argue, we also see the last anticolonial battle taking place in many ways, as citizens seek to do away with the lingering vestiges of power structures and family regimes whose genesis was anchored in the colonial and mandates era, ideally to be replaced by processes of self-determination that shape societies based on principles of social justice and citizenship rights. The relationship between civilian and military powers in society is one of the critical configurations of statehood that is now being addressed. The Turks went through this in recent decades, and it took them twenty years to reach the situation they are in now, where the civilian authorities more or less oversee the military. Arab countries that have embarked on constitutional reconfigurations seek to define their own balances between religious values and civil institutions; this will go on for many decades, as we see from examples of other countries. In the United States, for example, over two centuries after independence, citizens still robustly argue these issues, to judge by the debates on religious values during the last presidential election primaries. Some Arab countries, like Egypt and Tunisia, have already embarked on a similar process to define religion's role in public and political life, but they are compressing these lengthy debates into a period of months, in some cases.

Other important negotiations are taking place in countries like Yemen and Libya among the forces of Arabism, Islamism, and tribalism—the three most powerful collective identities of the modern era—to define how these three relate to each other and coexist. This includes the need to define and protect minority rights in a region that has many minorities. The quest for social justice also comprises the desire to protect society against monopolistic privileges and enforce labor rights, women's rights, and minority rights, alongside the desire to achieve a credible balance between indigenous values and international values.

I have mentioned only the most obvious of the many important issues that are being debated and negotiated simultaneously, during a period of economic stress and regional tensions. It is out of the question that any country in the world could effectively deal with all of these questions simultaneously within a few years—as Tunisia and Egypt have been attempting—but this is exactly what is going on in the Arab world. I think we need a massive dose of humility and an equally large dose of awe and respect for what the people of Tunisia, Egypt, Libya, and other countries are simultaneously doing and going through in these historic state-building processes.

We are starting to see the first significant attempt—manifested differently in every country, because the legitimacy of the ruling elite varies, different levels of anger and depravation prevail—by the indigenous people of the Arab world to define what it means to be an Arab, what it means to be a citizen of the state, and what it means to be sovereign. This process will take time—not hundreds of years, but certainly dozens of years. So I would argue for much humility and patience in trying to understand this and urge us to not fall into the entertaining but false syndrome of definitive instant analysis via television or blogging. Maybe I am an old-style journalist, but the instant blogging phenomenon that tells us, within an hour of an event, what has happened and how the world will be from now on is one of the simplistic manifestations of digitization. It has significantly demeaned and degraded our capacity to actually study such historic and complex phenomena in a serious way and to try to understand what is really happening and changing. For what is happening are a thousand different negotiations every day, in every one of these countries, at every level of life and society—the citizen, the society, the state, the neighborhood, the media, the judicial system, and the military. Every day there are negotiations going on to define our new world in a more participatory, democratic, pluralistic, accountable, and, therefore, legitimate manner. We should thank the people of Tunisia and Egypt and stand in awe before all of the people in the Arab world who are going out daily, for over two nonstop years, knowing that they are likely to be killed—but they go out nevertheless, because they want to be free, dignified, self-determinant, and, above all, sovereign citizens and normal human beings.

NOTES

1. Hernando de Soto, "What the Arab world really wants," *Spectator*, July 13, 2013, accessed March 19, 2014, http://www.spectator.co.uk/features/8959621/what-the-arab-world-really-wants/.

2. See, for example, Hernando de Soto, "The Call for Economic Liberty in the Arab World," *U.S. House Committee on Foreign Affairs Hearing*, May 21, 2013, accessed March 19, 2014, http://docs .house.gov/meetings/FA/FA00/20130521/100885/HHRG-113-FA00-20130521-SD001.pdf.

3. See, for example, the work of Arab NGO Network for Development, accessed March 19, 2014, http://www.annd.org

I

CATALYSTS

Introduction: Broadening Conversations on the Arab Uprisings

Crossing Disciplines, Approaches, and Geographies

FAHED AL-SUMAIT, NELE LENZE, AND MICHAEL C. HUDSON

The Arab Uprisings have certainly obscured the analysis of an already complex region. In 2011, these uprisings set in motion a chain of consequences that have radically altered the political, economic, and social landscapes of the Middle East and North Africa (MENA). This "Arab Spring"—as it is most commonly labeled—spread with an initial intensity and import few could have predicted, resulting in the overthrow of some long-standing autocrats and attempts at deeper entrenchment by others. Citizens too have exhibited astonishing levels of persistence and coordination in the face of grave threats to their lives and livelihoods, while the international community has demonstrated varying degrees of engagement and idleness. As the fog of the present parts to give us a clearer view of the recent past, observers are gaining ever-widening perspectives on the causes and consequences of the Arab Uprisings.

The initial euphoria (or dread) that surrounded the first years of the collective uprisings has taught us that since regional change is both highly contextual and protracted, our expectations must be appropriately calibrated. That is, as we come to terms with the realities of this transformative period, we must remain keenly focused on producing informed observations rather than hasty or generalized proclamations. Although several common factors exist across the most affected countries,[1] analyses of the Arab Uprisings must also (re)examine the unique experiences and trajectories of individual cases. Certainly, time has shown that each affected country is forming its own path, and often with different speeds and levels of "success." We suggest that this multiplicity requires equally diverse forms of analysis.

By intentionally disaggregating the analytical lenses through which we assess these Uprisings, we are also challenging the common tendency to apply the dominant metaframe of the "Arab Spring" to explanations of contemporary changes in the MENA region. Although this term serves a kind of parsimonious utility—essential for political actors and media outlets—it also elides many questions. For example, years after the catalyzing tragedy in Sidi Bouzid,[2] there is still little formal consensus on the boundaries (definitional, temporal, spatial, etc.) encapsulated by the term "Arab Spring," not to mention the host of ramifications that observers have continued to tie to it. Furthermore, there are numerous debates over the utility of the "Spring" metaphor, contesting such issues as its foreign origins or its temporal and optimistic implications. To that list of critiques, we add that referring to an "Arab Spring" has the negative and significant side effect of implying a singularity to events in a manner that often defies the varied conditions on the ground.

Rather than chiding a popular nomenclature that is unlikely to change, we raise the point to draw attention to the definitional limitations of the term "Arab Spring" from an academic perspective. This is more than simply an exercise in semantics, for herein lies one of the first—yet underexplored—obstacles to establishing functional frameworks for analysis. If the terminology we use to categorize events lacks specificity yet has temporal connotations, how then do we know what events to include under its umbrella and when to stop doing so? Is every political event and consequence in MENA since December 2010 tied to the Arab Uprisings, and, if not, what are the criteria for inclusion/exclusion? And at which stage, for instance, does Spring turn to Winter (as has been commonly expressed in both punditry and scholarship)?

Given these and other problems with the expression "Arab Spring," we instead use the term "Arab Uprisings" as the book's organizing frame. To begin with, the term is plural, not singular. Neither are the events it seeks to describe. "Uprisings" also refers to a specific type of political moment (demonstrations and revolts),[3] rather than a metaphorical season (Spring). This restricts its meaning slightly, while still maintaining the flexibility to accommodate a broad range of occurrences across countries—plus the possibility of more to come.[4] The scholars in this book span several disciplines to examine important catalyzing conditions, social dynamics, and political trajectories encapsulated by the term "Arab Uprisings." Albeit still imperfect,[5] the term is also better suited for our current purpose, which is to illustrate the value of interdisciplinary analyses organized around a particular theme—rather than concentrating on a specific academic field or writing on behalf of a single organization or institution. In so doing, we invite readers to break from individual, disciplinary, or organizational-based moorings to explore some of the commonalities of inquiry occurring across epistemological and geographical boundaries. Indeed, many of the questions our contributors frequently pose and the concerns they raise have remained central since late 2010. The result of this exercise, we hope, is greater insight into the search for such questions (and not simply answers) that will persist for some time to come.

EXPANDING PARLOR CONVERSATIONS

> Imagine that you enter a parlor. You come late. When you arrive, others have long preceded you, and they are engaged in a heated discussion, a discussion too heated for them to pause and tell you exactly what it is about. In fact, the discussion had already begun long before any of them got there, so that no one present is qualified to retrace for you all the steps that had gone before. You listen for a while, until you decide that you have caught the tenor of the argument; then you put in your oar. Someone answers; you answer him; another comes to your defense; another aligns himself against you, to either the embarrassment or gratification of your opponent, depending upon the quality of your ally's assistance. However, the discussion is interminable. The hour grows late, you must depart. And you do depart, with the discussion still vigorously in progress.
>
> —Kenneth Burke[6]

Philosopher and rhetorician Kenneth Burke (1897–1993) describes the unfolding drama of historical discourse in this metaphor of the "unending conversation." Burke's vivid portrayal touches upon inherencies of all academic analysis: we engage in "interminable" debates that are constrained by the limits of our own perceptions and the immense opaqueness of the history that precedes us. Often, scholars become so immersed in the conversations at their own "table," they miss important considerations debated elsewhere in the "parlor." In fact, in today's globally wired environment the tables are many, cacophonic, and increasing. In this volume, we invite readers on a guided tour of some of the most significant contemporary issues related to the Arab Uprisings. This exercise is akin to sampling a broad cross-section of an important parlor conversation so that we may collectively pause and reflect on the wider discussions happening at this point in history.

Much of the scholarly work on the Arab Uprisings in the past three years has traditionally come from within a singular disciplinary or institutional tradition or been confined to a specific set of events and locations.[7] This volume parts from that tradition. To provide breadth to the conversation, our authors represent several disciplinary approaches; post-positivists are contrasted with postcolonialists, traditional political science research is presented alongside literary criticism, historians weigh in beside new-media scholars, and comparative work juxtaposes individual case studies. The majority of authors are well-accomplished authorities in their respective fields, while the few younger scholars included demonstrate exceptional new research of significant import. In addition to a diversity of experience and traditions, we have also sought to prevent a US–centric perspective by including authors representing both cultural and geographical diversity, with roughly half being of Arab descent and the majority residing outside of the United States. We hope these efforts prove valuable for readers with an interest in examining a varied, but interrelated, collection of key trends and conversations happening within and across multiple disciplinary and national borders.

We have organized this book according to three unifying themes: *catalysts*, *dynamics*, and *trajectories* that roughly represent three temporal orientations in the Arab Uprisings (past, present, future). The first set of essays addresses catalyzing factors that help to explain the emergence of the Uprisings from various political, economic, and sociocultural perspectives. The possibilities of broad-based predicative indicators are explored alongside the power of specific cultural expressions. These are preceded by a helpful overview of the debates within political science that influence much of the contemporary scholarship on the Uprisings. The second section examines the functions and responses of diverse people, institutions, technologies, and ideologies during the initial years of the Uprisings. It includes an in-depth case study on the changing political situation of women in the catalyzing country of Tunisia, as well as research about the roles of political Islam, social networks, and mass media in these rapidly changing contexts. The third section assesses cross-national implications and the multitude of repercussions the Uprisings are having on the global system and its peoples. In addition, the book's foreword is by the prominent Arab journalist and public intellectual Rami Khouri, who has suggested that we take *The Long View of the Arab Uprisings*, a point oft-repeated in the following chapters.

Our selection of chapters was written to be broadly accessible to various academic and political audiences. This book will be useful to scholars and political observers of the Middle East, as well as upper-level university or graduate students with an interest in the Arab Uprisings or the general phenomenon of major social upheaval. Due to the diverse nature of contributions, it could serve as a reader for courses in political science, international relations, Middle East studies, or other topical courses on the Arab Uprisings. In addition to these areas, it has strong chapters from the perspectives of history, cultural studies, and media studies. As mentioned, we also hope this book will especially appeal to those who seek to explore intersecting disciplinary boundaries and approaches.

CHAPTER DESCRIPTIONS

In this introductory chapter, we provide an uncharacteristically detailed description of each contribution in order to illustrate the pronounced connections between them and to introduce readers who may be unfamiliar with various disciplinary approaches to some of the key points of consideration and their accompanying analytical frames. For a variety of reasons, we do not begin this exercise with a generic time line or a specific narrative about the Arab Uprisings. First, we aim to avoid the tendency to see the Uprisings as a unified concept that can be neatly explained in a single history. Second, many authors outline relevant histories for the particular subjects in their chapters, providing a more helpful and tailored approach. Third, given space constraints, we chose instead to focus attention on the interconnections between chapters, rather than cataloging the many relevant events feeding into them (or, regretfully, providing more detailed accounts of the many affected countries such as Yemen, Syria, Bahrain, or Libya, which are all unfortunately underrepresented here). Fortunately, an expansive and growing literature exists on the Arab Uprisings within several fields that can provide readers with greater depth into the topics raised here, as well as the many others we could not include. Finally, the foreword written by Rami Khouri, has drawn attention to many important touchstones in sufficient detail to provide a suitable context, and it is therefore discussed first before providing the detailed chapter descriptions.

In his foreword, Khouri has set the tone for this volume by suggesting, "We are passing through perhaps the most significant moment in the modern history of the Middle East . . . We can choose from many issues to use as a lens through which to analyze the changes taking place . . . [But] our challenge is to step back and try to understand the political changes taking place in the broader context of recent history." The journey, he has argued, is going to be long. It traces back to events decades before Mohamed Bouazizi's fatal protest in December 2010 and is characterized by the deep-rooted, but largely unmet, needs of Arab citizens.

Khouri has argued that the seeds of the recent revolts began in the 1970s with the early wave of Islamist movements, the oil boom, massive distortions of economic wealth and distribution, and the cementing of the Arab security state, as well as the collapse of the Arab-Israeli conflict at a regional level. During the ensuing years, systems of corruption and clientelism have dominated over principles of meritocracy and human rights. Furthermore, many Arab citizens have not only lacked secure material needs but also "the intangible needs of status as a citizen—such as voice, legitimacy, participation, accountability, dignity, trust, and respect." And so, the pressures continued to mount.

For decades, various movements and organizations have attempted to improve human rights and democracy across the region, but to no avail. The state's control has always been too strong. However, the Arab Uprisings proved somehow different. They resulted from a particular confluence of global, regional, and national factors that fed upon "the cumulative frustrations and humiliations that several hundred million Arab citizens had experienced in the preceding decades, and whose force was irresistible once it expressed itself in actions on the street." This new surge of empowerment manifested into two central demands across various countries: accountability and sovereignty. What remains to be seen is the degree to which states under transition can adequately satisfy such citizen demands and achieve some measure of stability.

Further complicating the reform process are influences from three of the most powerful collective identities in the modern Arab world—Arabism, Islamism, and tribalism. These forces are in constant negotiation with one another, the state, and the international community over nothing less than the region's future. In this milieu, Khouri has declared it imperative that each society form a government based on the will of the majority, with strong protections for minority rights. It is here that constitutional reform becomes critical, and under which all other formalized demands are subsumed.[8] Khouri has reminded us that such transformations occurred in Western democracies "over periods of 100 to 200 years, until national reconfigurations gave citizens equal rights and codified a general consensus on national values, principles, and policies." The challenge for journalists, academics, and others is to consider such historical lessons and not fixate on "the immediate media moment of election results, political party fragmentations, constitutional drafts, coups and counter-coups, or tribal clashes, and thus judge the political situation prematurely."

The authors in this book share many of Khouri's concerns for the historical, political, and social dimensions of the Uprisings. They, too, highlight the complex and transitional nature of the events witnessed so far, cautioning against the dangers of hasty assertions and instead offering informed research and analysis. Similarly, several of the authors address issues such as Islamist politics, tribalism, state building, and geopolitics. However, a point where Khouri has been somewhat distinct from several of the contributors is in his foregrounding of the role played by Arab citizens.[9] While Arab citizens are implied and often referenced actors (especially with regard to revolutionary moments), their occurrence as a primary subject of analysis (in this volume and more broadly) is perhaps still wanting. It may be that after decades of authoritarianism in the MENA region, many observers are not yet accustomed to according citizens a central role in Arab politics. It is here that Khouri has reminded us, "The invisible, voiceless Arabs increasingly are a thing of the past, even in countries that have not experienced revolutionary upheavals . . . [The Arab Uprisings have enabled] the first significant attempt . . . by the indigenous people of the Arab world to define what it means to be an Arab, what it means to be a citizen of the state, and what it means to be sovereign." Certainly, the Arab Uprisings have demonstrated an intense desire by the *demos* to be included in the region's political calculations. It remains to be seen how well this experiment will succeed.

PART I: CATALYSTS

The chapters in our first section examine some of the conditions that helped catalyze the Uprisings. Before providing detailed accounts of these conditions in chapters 3–5, coeditor of this volume and Middle East Institute director Michael C. Hudson provides a useful preliminary reflection on how Middle East studies (and political science in particular) have affected our preparation for, and interpretation of, the Arab Uprisings. In chapter 2, "Transition to What? Reflections on the Arab Uprisings," Hudson raises many of the core questions that we continue to grapple with nearly three years after the Uprisings began (definitional, theoretical, methodological, etc.). He specifically asks us to rethink long-held propositions about authoritarianism and democracy, which have failed to satisfactorily answer three fundamental questions. "First, what exactly were—and are—these Uprisings; how do we conceptualize them? Second, what caused them; in particular, why were most analysts surprised? Third, what will follow from them; in particular, what, if anything, do theories of transition to democracy have to offer by way of prediction?" In Hudson's view, political science (currently and historically) has ill prepared us to comprehend the Arab Uprisings.

Hudson catalogs many of the reasons why most Middle East analysts were caught off guard. Partly to blame has been a narrow focus on the "mirage" of "persistent authoritarianism," which seeks to explain why regional authoritarianism appears to work so well (by looking at things such as its well-funded military-security apparatus, state domination of the economy, Western complicity, and the like). As well, the Uprisings evidenced new expressions of Pan-Arabism and highlighted the collective shortcomings of Western dismissiveness, the "Washington consensus," aggregate economic analysis, and a tendency by regional experts to focus on the machinations of elites over the realities experienced by individual citizens. By contrast, Hudson also provides several examples where observers in fact warned of brewing change. "Journalists and pundits seemed to be more prescient than social scientists. Unencumbered by academic theories, they relied on their 'feel' for the situation." Many of these journalists, along with a handful of scholars, were perhaps surprised only by the suddenness of events in 2011 and not their imminent arrival.

As a useful entry into many of the political debates raised in this volume, Hudson provides a short history on "oscillating" currents between liberal and conservative poles in political science, as well as the subarea of transitology. "For transitologists, 'uncertainty' remains untheorized. [And] if the Arab Uprisings had one consequence, it was to generate uncertainty. . . . The main weakness of the transitology approach is its marginalization of nonelites—the masses that were the muscle of the Uprisings." He couples this critique with a description of corresponding developments in the region that continued to challenge the scholarly status quo. With the brutal arrival of militant Islam in the late 1970s, authoritarianism took on new dimensions, and the region's "liberals found themselves squeezed between two bad alternatives: dictatorial regimes and even more frightful Islamist movements. Emasculated, they reluctantly sided with regime authoritarianism." This further contributed to a reassertion of "persistent authoritarianism" in the academic debates. While this school of research did not deny the possibilities of Middle East democratization, it had the effect of reorienting analytic priorities toward explaining why the regional situation persisted. Outside of this approach, Hudson points out, useful work has been done under the rubric of "new institutionalism," which opens possibilities for a turn toward other priorities. The new institutionalism approach integrates particular social and communal sectors into the prevailing system without a preoccupation on the necessity of "democracy." Existing work in this area "has focused on how coalitions may form between regime and opposition 'soft-liners,'" the social impacts of exogenous rent income, and, importantly, the ability of authoritarian regimes to upgrade themselves. As we look at the Arab cases unfolding before us, we find no lack of important factors to examine "What we do not know is how they all fit together to foster or inhibit the political legitimacy that an eventual stable democratic order would require." Perhaps a closer look at new approaches and other disciplines can better guide our analysis of these unfolding situations.

The third chapter, "The Arab Revolts: Local, Regional, and Global Catalysts and Consequences," comes from Mark Farha, assistant professor of government at Georgetown University's School of Foreign Service in Doha, Qatar. Farha declares that "from a strictly economic perspective, the much-vaunted Arab Uprisings have been nothing short of a nightmare." Also coming from the political science tradition, he examines the economic underpinnings of these events by explaining how US and European fiscal policies following the global economic downturn contributed in 2010 to a price explosion in MENA and the subsequent outbreak of protests. "Prevalent (mis)readings by both detractors and champions of the revolutions [tend] to mystify their socioeconomic origins, whether it be by reducing the Uprisings to ideological quests for lofty ideals such as dignity and democracy . . . or by identifying nefarious agendas such as global conspiracies, militant theocracy, and terrorism as the root cause of revolt." While Farha does not suggest ignoring such considerations, he does contend "the likelihood of a revolution in any given Arab state must be weighed against a multiplicity of local and global factors, chief of which is the exposure of a critical mass of a vulnerable segment in [. . .] society to price increases in essential commodities." Farha falls short of declaring an economic determinism to the Uprisings—after all, the worst-performing member state of the Arab League, Sudan, has not yet been struck by revolution. He does, however, provide a convincing argument about the significant role economics have played in the Uprisings and will continue to play into the foreseeable future.

Because fiscal vulnerabilities are disparate across the region, Farha categorizes countries into two distinct types: (1) labor-importing, oil-exporting rentier economies, and (2) labor-abundant, oil-importing countries. Not surprisingly, we have seen the largest upheavals in this second category of countries. Rising hydrocarbon prices constituted a boon for oil-producing states and a burden for overpopulated states, which saw a growing portion of their budget being diverted for energy consumption and subsidies. In spite of the $120 billion inflow of foreign direct investment from the Gulf States to the poorer Arab states from 2003 to 2008, income disparities continued to widen as poverty was exacerbated. Many Arab states were ill situated to counter these trends. As a point of illustration, "the Arab world relies on 80 percent of imports to meet its food needs. Egypt ranks as the world's biggest consumer of bread and largest net importer of wheat and, along with Tunisia, Morocco, and Algeria, spends more on grain than any other emerging nation, at over 40 percent of total consumption per capita." Although the global recession caused GDPs to contract, the amount of subsidies in poorer Arab countries skyrocketed, further burdening the economy and—by consequence—the political status quo.

The impact of economic strife, coupled with high unemployment in the most affected countries, has also contributed to rising sectarianism in places like Lebanon and Syria. In 2010, MENA recorded the highest unemployment rate of any region in the world (though the Gulf Cooperation Council, indicatively, exhibited the lowest rate at 4 percent). In Egypt, for example, unemployment soared although GDP had doubled from 2000 to 2009. "By 2010, escalating inflation and unemployment became universally observable sources of insufferable strain . . . these pressures were refracted differently according to the characteristics of each particular state." As a result, "social and sectarian fissures in highly segmented states such as Syria and Lebanon certainly compounded what was, at its origin, an economic crisis." Farha proffers the need for economic revolutions to follow the political. With growing sectarianism, political instabilities, endemic income disparities, and spiraling unemployment, countries that experienced uprisings are now "teetering on the brink of fiscal bankruptcy," the impacts of which will spread well beyond their individual borders.

In chapter 4, the "The Political and Socioeconomic Origins of the Arab Uprisings: A Trinomial Probability Analysis," Peter Tikuisis and Anton Minkov also view economic preconditions and sectarianism as critical components in the Uprisings. Unlike Farha, though, they include these as but two of six causal indicators that they claim can be used to predict upheavals in the MENA region. Representing a policy-oriented approach consistent with their shared institutional affiliation at the Defence Research and Development Canada—the government agency that provides research and technology for the Canadian Armed Forces—Tikuisis and Minkov propose a "trinomial probability analysis" that can serve as a risk-assessment-scenario tool for policy makers. The authors explain the rationale, stating, "the rapid spread of the Uprisings among all MENA countries, regardless of the amplitude of the expression, suggests the existence of a set of common underlying factors." However, they lament that existing indicators (such as the SF-Polity 2010, the Global Peace Index, and the *Economist's* Shoe-Thrower's Index) have been unable to effectively identify the critical factors that explain the nature of the Arab Uprisings.

To address this shortfall, their proposed model utilizes the Tikuisis-Minkov (TM) composite of six primary indicators and derives a 90 percent likelihood of predictability for what they term collective political violence (CPV). CPV is a dependent variable based on three factors: the scale of protests, the type of political response, and the number of any resulting fatalities. Their trinomial probability model allows for three levels of CPV (low, medium, and high) and utilizes an empirical method for statistically testing candidate indicators. In order to characterize the environmental preconditions of the Uprisings, the authors ran their model with a wide variety of regional political, economic, social, and demographic domain data for the twelve-month period immediately preceding the Arab Uprisings (2009–2010). In their findings, "All states, except for Tunisia, [fell] on the probability curve that correspond[ed] to their observed level of CPV." In other words, the predictive value of their model appears significantly more accurate than any existing risk-assessment indicators.

It requires both well-argued logic and creativity to construct a model with the sophistication demanded by such a broad-reaching undertaking, but this approach has several strengths for consideration. For example, it utilizes a robust amount of available data sources, which makes tests of external validity and longitudinal application both possible and likely; its prospects for predictability hold significant appeal to numerous policy makers and scholars; and the model itself is custom built for the MENA region. Although the authors apply both quantitative and qualitative methodologies in building the TM composite, their research represents a post positivist orientation not found to the same degree elsewhere in this volume. In fact, its presumptions of predictability and measurement contrast sharply with many of the humanistic or historically oriented authors in several of the chapters,[10] although one area where most of our authors likely agree with Tikuisis and Minkov is in their model's confirmation "that the convergence of several interrelated, highly destabilizing factors created a 'perfect storm' that manifested into the Arab Uprisings." The difference of approach between the chapters largely boils down to the scope of factors each scholar chooses to investigate. This contrast, we hope, healthily expands the cross-disciplinary purview of this collection and introduces yet another voice into our "parlor conversation."

Rounding out this introductory section is chapter 5, from the other side of the academic spectrum, by Nouri Gana, associate professor of comparative literature and Near Eastern languages and cultures at the University of California, Los Angeles. Gana's contribution, "Dissident Tunisia: Culture and Revolt," focuses the lens of interrogation on the catalyzing country of the Arab Uprisings to underscore the longstanding rebellious instincts that Ben Ali's police state had repressed but could not eradicate. He highlights the existence of critical dissent in Tunisia by charting a counterhegemonic cultural history tracing back to the struggle against French colonialism. Dissent and frustration are expressed through numerous cultural forms, such as poetry, music, theater, and film. Nouri Bouzid, Moufida Tlatli, and Mohamed Zran, for example, directed movies that focused on the experience of defeat, which Gana says provided audiences with "the basis for fostering strategies of empowerment." They also tackled taboo topics such as homosexuality and female self-determination, illustrating that films were tools for challenging both the sociocultural status quo and the political state apparatus.

Gana points out that such expressions of discontent and hope are not confined to the spheres of poetry, theater, or cinema. "The role of hip-hop, and rap music in particular, as a vehicle of popular discontent against Ben Ali's regime before and after the revolution has become so vital that many can no longer imagine the cultural scene in Tunisia without it." Tunisian rap, he argues, has not only been a democratizing force in the field of music and arts but also in the broader public sphere where artists speak out on behalf of Tunisia's disenfranchised and frustrated people. "In the years leading up to the revolution, critique has become, surprisingly enough, more and more adventurous, vocal, and direct, particularly on YouTube and Facebook, which circulated, among other things, explosive hip-hop videos that had instantaneous effects." One well-known example is *El Général*, whose claim to national and international notoriety, "Rais Lebled" ("Head of State"), is considered by many to be the unofficial anthem of the Tunisian revolution. *Time* magazine even celebrated him as "the seventy-fourth most influential person in the world, ahead of US president Barack Obama and of FC Barcelona and Argentina soccer superstar Lionel Messi." Gana provides several other examples of influential Tunisian hip-hop artists, demonstrating a diversity of approaches and personalities—including rappers like Psyco-M, who exhibits an increasingly pronounced "regressivist-Salafist" ideology in his un-abashed criticism of Ben Ali's secular regime. As the flourishing hip-hop scene moves toward mainstream popularity, Gana muses over the effects that ensuing commoditization will have on the genre's political edge.

By exploring relationships between popular culture and public sentiment in Ben Ali's Tunisia, Gana demonstrates a more humanistic research orientation toward the Arab Uprisings, as compared to the preceding chapters. This ap-proach shifts the line of inquiry and repositions human agency. "The issue here becomes not so much how Bouazizi's suicide protest sparked a popular revolu-tion . . . but how a popular revolution sparked by Bouazizi's suicide protest is indeed the *materialization* of a cultural and critical capital that has largely been shaped by dispersed and stylized rehearsals of dissenting practices." Gana's essay concludes part I of this volume, which has presented diverse ways for exploring the contexts from which the Uprisings occurred. For the next section, we move the time frame (mostly) to the first years after the outbreak of Uprisings. Like Gana, these next four scholars are deeply interested in both historical context and the specific struggles of social actors against the state.

PART II: DYNAMICS

The chapters in this section shift the analytical lens from general contributing factors to examine some of the impacts and experiences witnessed during the first year of events. In chapter 6, "Reassessing the Recent History of Political Islam in Light of the Arab Uprisings," James Gelvin, UCLA professor of modern Middle Eastern history, looks at one of the dominating issues in the Uprisings' debates: political Islam. In particular, he examines the role of Islamists during the re-gional upheavals and subsequent elections, as well as the prior era of repression during which authoritarian states inadvertently primed Islamists to capitalize on the revolutionary moment once it came. Gelvin catalogs thirty years of Arab popular resistance to provide "a counternarrative to the predominant descrip-tion of Arab politics in which demoralized populations are cowed by autocratic regimes—that is, until the dam burst in 2010–2011." Among the key lessons of his chapter is that the Arab Uprisings have called attention to a "paradigmatic shift" that has taken place in Islamist politics. Not only are groups like the Mus-lim Brotherhood entering (and occasionally running) participatory politics, but this condition has been facilitated, in part, by both oppressive regimes and the international community's discourse on human rights and democracy.

During the 1980s and 1990s, many Arab governments undertook a campaign to eradicate violent Islamist groups. On the surface, regimes appeared successful in removing the threats and demonstrating the inefficacy of violent Islamist tactics. However, Gelvin proposes an alternative reading in which these efforts at eradication were "an unmitigated disaster" for the governments for at least three reasons. "First, the very tactics governments used to destroy those groups . . . would inspire the Uprisings that swept through the Arab world in the Winter of 2010–2011. Second, by demonstrating the inefficacy of violence, the governments' campaigns created a political opening in which mass-based, nonviolent Islamist organizations . . . might flourish. Finally, repression encouraged the creation of new 'Islamist spaces' in prisons and in exile communities that facilitated networking and strategizing among Islamists, the cross-fertilization of organizational and ideological initiatives, and the disbursement of material support for individuals and groups both domestically and transnationally." The consequences of these failings were demonstrated with potent effect when Islamist groups swept to victory in several of the post-Uprising elections.

Another significant contributor to this rise of Islamist politics was the global diffusion of international norms on human rights and democratic governance, which coincided with the Arab governments' repressive tactics. This shift created the prospect for Islamists' participation in a political order rooted in such norms, and the Islamists capitalized on these new vocabularies and opportunities. Since the 1970s, many Islamists have sharpened their skills through student politics and professional syndicates, such as those who spoke for doctors, engineers, and lawyers. "By the mid-1990s, they were firmly in control of those syndicates, and . . . they were both at ease with, and adept at, representative politics. And through their participation in syndicates, they also engaged with a culture of middle-class/entrepreneurial values congruent with an ethos of individual rights." The degree of Islamists' political success after the initial Uprisings varies by country, with verdicts far from apparent. "To be sure, the year-long Egyptian drama, which began with the inauguration of Mohamed Morsi as president on June 30, 2012, and ended with the July 3, 2013, *coup d'état*, should give pause to anyone who had looked to developments there and elsewhere in the region with even cautious optimism. Nevertheless, it would be equally mistaken to view the Egyptian experience as proving that organized Islamism as a whole is hopelessly bound by ideological and organizational fetters."

It is to the European revolutions of 1848 that Gelvin turns for an analogous lesson on the aftermaths of revolutionary upsurge. "Although none of the revolutions in that bleak year succeeded, their outbreak signaled in retrospect that the field of political contestation in Europe had opened up to include liberal and nationalist alternatives to the old order." Similarly, the political field has now opened in a handful of Arab countries. As Islamists learn to compete in these emerging spaces, they must do so carefully and in a way that at least affirms human and democratic rights (if not also their implementation). For, if Islamists are perceived as palpably violating these tenets, then their opponents can quickly capitalize on such openings for their own political advantage. In such cases, it may matter little if these opponents are only more skilled at the "game" (but not necessarily the practice) of human rights and democracy. The ascension and then banishment of the Muslim Brotherhood in Egypt is, perhaps, an illustrative case in point. After the French Revolution kick-started the modern democratic experiment (1789–1799), it still took generations for Western countries to consolidate their democracies. In the post-Uprisings context, we may be well served to expect a similar time frame before the most affected countries achieve some magnitude of political stability.

Chapter 7, "Protest Mobilization in the Age of Twitter," also maintains a deep interest in history but applies its lessons to a more unique, and very contemporary, condition. In it, Silvana Toska, doctoral candidate in political science and international relations at Cornell University, asserts that comparative historical research is required to better understand the revolutionary role of social media. She outlines key positions in current debates about the power of new media before advancing that "both sides of the debate have treated social media as an entirely new invention that is also analytically distinct." She asks, instead, how are social media similar to previous revolutionary tools, and what can history teach us about their true impact? Across time, revolutionaries and state leaders alike have sought to gain control over the means of communication in their conflicts, thus making media repression among the most common tools of authoritarianism. From the Puritan Revolution of 1640 to the Eastern European Revolutions of 1989, scholars have declared relative openings and technological innovations in the media environment to be catalysts of revolutionary unrest. Is there, however, something novel today? "Expressing the desire and plan to participate in protests in advance might well be the greatest innovation of social media and what explicitly sets them apart from other tools used in previous revolutions," she argues. The two-way flow of communication imbues social media with new capabilities for social mobilization, but in comparison with older forms of revolutionary communication, the true differences are probably just matters of degree and not kind. On this premise, the goal then becomes to carefully identify the specific conditions under which social media facilitate mass mobilization.

Toska supports her claims by testing existing theories of collective action using original Twitter data, existing research, and personal interviews with activists in Egypt and Syria. Her focus on Twitter illustrates the role played by one of the most powerful social-media platforms (at the time of protests), as it was deployed as a mobilization tool. Social media in general, she argues, served two important functions in the Uprisings: preference falsification reversal and the spotlight effect. Preference falsification is the distinction between a person's private and public beliefs. "In highly repressive regimes . . . displaying antagonism is very dangerous, and in the absence of knowledge of the preferences of others, very few dare to voice their grievances. . . . The dilemma that individuals who secretly oppose the regime face is to know how many others share their views and how many of them are willing to make these views public. This is where social media—like other media before it—were able to reverse the problem of preference falsification." The second function is termed the spotlight effect, wherein people use social media to expose and highlight regime failures, making them public knowledge and influencing perceptions of both the precarious nature of the regime and the previously hidden mass opposition to it. "Given the highly controlled media in the Arab region, social media were often the only uncensored means of communicating regime failure and personal preferences." However, looking at the flow of this sensitive information is not sufficient in itself to explain the role played by social media in the Arab Uprisings.

The other important dimension Toska highlights is the interrelationship between strong and weak social ties. "Weak ties" describes the connections between actors who are otherwise socially distant (greatly facilitated by social media), and it is through these networks that information can flow quickly and widely. But when building people's commitment to take risks, independent affirmation or reinforcement of the request is also required. These come from "strong ties," which are primarily comprised of interpersonal networks, such as those found within a social movement. In other words, social media serve as effective means for coordinating action only when digital networks mirror physical networks on the ground. "It is clear that, at least in the case of the Arab Uprisings, weak ties (online) and strong ties (social movements) developed a symbiotic relationship that had been jointly necessary for protest mobilization. As these groups started to share their physical and virtual space, their message was amplified while also becoming more reliable through multiple confirmations." Additionally, Toska points out the unintended effect of the media blackout in the midst of the Egyptian revolution, which actually encouraged more protest participation. The move not only highlighted the regime's incompetence and lack of legitimacy, it also forced people to take to the streets in the search for news and information that media could no longer supply. Therefore, it seems that both the presence and absence of social media can exacerbate revolutionary unrest under the right conditions. Perhaps autocrats will learn to avoid that temptation to "pull the plug" should revolts be upon them.

In chapter 8, Adel Iskandar, an international communication scholar teaching at Georgetown University, enters the conversation with his contribution, "Free? Not So Fast! The Fourth Estate Flourishes and Falters with the Arab Uprisings." Where Toska examined social media as a tool, Iskandar focuses on media as a type of political actor (that is, the "fourth estate"), introducing another important dimension to the post-Uprising media debates. "Prior to 2011, state media in the region never needed audience approval. Today, failing to deliver professional journalism (at least in the form of a façade) has much more serious political repercussions. Audiences now translate into citizens, active participants in public policy, and interrogators of representation." Iskandar describes 2011 to 2013 as the most tumultuous period since the advent of broadcasting in the region. As evidenced by his chapter title, two parallel but opposing currents co-exist, each representing a divergent direction in the regional media's transformation (flourishing and faltering). The title also "signifies a necessary tentativeness in a discussion dominated by research that is obsessed with forecasting, prediction, repeatability, and generalizability."

Iskandar elaborates on a variety of media phenomena characterizing the region's patchy landscape during the Uprisings, including the relationship between the medium and revolutionary discourse, fluctuating margins of freedom, the proliferation of media offerings, and the enduring obstacles of authoritarianism. Emerging from this environment were competing media discourses that complicate our perceptions of the Uprisings and their varied actors. On one hand, the proliferation of media outlets can provide alternative accounts to the simplistic protagonist-antagonist, regime-opposition, and peaceful-violent dichotomies prevalent in mainstream coverage, but emerging media sources can also emphasize these. "Given the competing agendas in the region and the vastly differentiated political emphases in coverage of the Uprisings and their ensuing milieus, the very essence of occurrence becomes contested ground." Since most observers must rely on media accounts to determine events on the ground, public memory becomes susceptible to the belief that certain occurrences took place simply on the basis of a mediated experience. For these reasons, "the communicative environment is essentially [a] battleground, with the media being among the most potent weapons employed by both sides." To illustrate, Iskandar offers the two iconic (mediated) stories: Mohamed Bouazizi's death in Tunisia and the Alexandrian man, Khaled Said, whose killing contributed significantly to the Egyptian protest movement. In both cases, "as the media actively move toward rendering these accounts into narratives—all of which are to varying degrees fictionalized—they attempt to ossify perspectives on these Uprisings. These narratives become increasingly rigid interpretations of event and actors." The ensuing situation is akin to what Jean Baudrillard has called simulacra—a version of the real when the real no longer exists or never existed.

Another major trend worth observing is the way in which Arab media have flourished since the Uprisings began. In certain cases, restrictions were lifted, media sources proliferated, and new boundaries were pushed. These openings brought their own changes, some of which also posed unique challenges. "In the case of Egypt, for instance, the state media underwent a transformation literally overnight on February 11, 2011, when Mubarak left office. Egyptians woke up the next morning, and the news media were celebrating the very revolution they had criticized the night before. . . . A renarrativization became necessary in order to report current events. This renarrativization manifested as a rejoiced enthrall-ment with the revolution and active attempts to memorialize it." Overall, the margin of media freedoms in the region has dropped from a utopian high point in 2011, but the proliferation of voices emerging from the Uprisings has been a promising development. Media are becoming more specialized, and "active audiences are not only deciphering messages and making sense of the shifting political contours in their respective countries, they are also helping challenge and shape coverage in instrumental ways."

In chapter 9, "The Arab Uprisings in Tunisia: Parity, Elections, and the Struggle for Women's Rights," we hear from the minister for Women's Affairs under Tunisia's first transitional government, Lilia Labidi, who is also a psycho-analyst and anthropologist currently at the Middle East Institute at the National University of Singapore. As a scholar who experienced, and participated in, the transformative political events in Tunisia, Labidi is well positioned to discuss the critical topic of women in the Uprisings. Like many of the authors in this book, she does so by first providing historical context. Under the Bourguiba and Ben Ali regimes, women in Tunisia had gained important rights, such as those found in the 1956 Personal Status Code, but the state had also appropriated several women's groups for cosmetic intent—creating organizations that practiced a type of "state feminism," useful for charitable events and international conferences but of limited value for advancing women's rights. The Tunisian uprising shifted the power relations between women's movements and the state, leaving previously state-sponsored organizations under question and bringing both "independent feminists" and the issue of political equality to the fore.

During Tunisia's political transition, a call for political parity (equal numbers of men and women on political lists) was initiated in order to prevent low female representation in the Constituent Assembly (the body in charge of drafting the country's constitution). The debate over this parity law "exposed unexpected divisions and alliances, and these were particularly surprising to independent feminists and to women in general." Whereas several (often liberal) political parties contested the idea on logistical grounds, the long-exiled—and eventually most successful—Islamist party, Ennahda, surprisingly voted in the affirmative and even ran a prominent female candidate who did not wear a *hijab*. Despite this progressive stance, Labidi suggests that Ennahda supported women's rights only to appeal to the masses and win the elections, not to actively engage with women. Many remained suspicious, accusing Ennahda of engaging in double-speak, being aware of the limited political space available to women in Algeria after the war of liberation, in Iran after the revolution, and in Egypt after Sadat's assassination. During the ensuing elections, women represented 46 percent of registered voters, and the parity law led to some five thousand women becoming candidates (but only 7 percent of lists had women at their head). The outcomes, though, were far from equal, with only 58 of 217 seats going to women (26.7 percent), which was proportionally close to the 2009 election results under Ben Ali. Notably, thirty-nine of the fifty-eight women were Ennahda members.

For the final part of her chapter, Labidi pulls the reader in for an even closer look at the situation by profiling two central female politicians, Bochra Belhaj Hmida and Souad Abderrahim, who each headed electoral lists for ideologically disparate political groups (the center-left Ettakatol party, and Ennahda, respectively). Both women faced a number of challenges not only from society and opposing political groups but also with respect to their own political parties. In an interview with Labidi, Hmida describes the frustrations she faced arising from the "general misogyny of the milieu." Her detractors employed tactics such as death threats, labeling her a prostitute, and associating her with the Ben Ali regime. Although the experience was different for Souad Abderrahim, who

successfully headed a list for Ennahda, she too faced her share of gender challenges. Because she did not wear a hijab, many questioned the legitimacy of her
political role in an Islamist party. Some felt she was simply a token exploited
by Ennahda to gain favor from female voters and the international community
rather than a true women's advocate. Others questioned her credentials as a
conservative Muslim, which may in part explain why she appeared to overstep
the bounds by pushing a hard-line position on the rights of single mothers that
apparently stunted her political career. While compelling fears over women's
rights remain, Labidi ultimately concludes that a net effect of the Uprisings so far
has been the growing importance of female figures in local and regional politics.

PART III: TRAJECTORIES

The chapters in this final section begin looking forward and pose many as-yet
unanswered questions about what changes we can expect to see in a region
under transformation. Chapter 10, "The Arab Uprisings: Alignments and the
Regional Power Balance," is by Raymond Hinnebusch, professor of international relations and Middle East politics at the University of St. Andrews in
Scotland. Hinnebusch attempts to discern the widely discussed and entirely
difficult terrain of the Uprisings' geopolitical implications. He asserts, "The
Uprisings have reshuffled the threats and opportunities among rival regional
powers, put identity in flux, and increased regional vulnerability to external
intervention." Coming from a realist perspective in international relations, he
describes the reshuffling of many Middle Eastern states into two categories:
(1) the rivaling regional powers of Turkey, Iran, and Saudi Arabia, from whom
emergent regimes might seek new allies, and (2) the "battleground" states of
Egypt and Syria, where old regimes are still battling uprisings, creating prime
opportunities for foreign interference. "Even if a more pacific liberal order is
the long-term effect of the Uprisings, the immediate consequence has been
to *reinforce* preexisting tendencies—that is, to *intensify* the regional power
struggle. And, far from diluting global dependencies, it has *further opened* the
region to external penetration."

Hinnebusch describes a region where at least three levels of identity—the
sub-state, state, and supra-state levels—are in a critical contest that defines
who the appropriate enemies and allies are for a given group of people. At the
supra-state level, he sees Turkey and Saudi Arabia rising, while Iran is weakened
from a constricted economy and the decline of its anti-imperialist influence due
to the conditions in Syria. Its support for the Syrian regime has also negatively

impacted the way other nations in the region might look to Iran's model of Islamic governance as compared to Turkey's. Additionally, "axis of resistance" discourse has been tempered by a more positive approach toward democracy from the many activists who generally agree its absence is a primary source of Middle Eastern problems. In a bid for Pan-Arab leadership, the Gulf Cooperation Council (GCC) has also moved to take advantage of the vacuum left by the marginalization of the key Arab republics and its bloc vote in the Arab League. Using Pan-Arab media and the league, the GCC sought to legitimize Western intervention against Gaddafi, and then again against Syria, where the council aimed to break the resistance axis that had repeatedly attacked the legitimacy of its Western alignments. The regional outcomes of the Arab Uprisings will depend on with whom the new ruling coalitions ultimately align. Between Western powers, regional nationalist-statists, and alternative global powers like Russia and China, the possibilities are many.

In his final prediction, Hinnebusch expects that the United States will be the primary benefactor of the Arab Uprisings. It is aligned with the empowered GCC, and in those states where US–friendly regimes fell (Egypt, Tunisia, Yemen) there is still a high level of dependency on the United States and its allies. With Iran, China, and Russia weakened and the resistance axis floundering, there is a possibility of a new regional order built around a coalition of Turkey-led, business-oriented, Islamist democracies working in tandem with an independent Egypt and the cash-rich GCC states. "Alternatively, a new era of disorder could be triggered by the spread of failed states and/or a US or Israeli attack on Iran, with both factors possibly exacerbating the Arab-Israel conflict, deepening sectarian polarization and sparking an anti-imperialist backlash." The reality, Hinnebusch suggests, is likely to be a mix of these scenarios as today's major powers struggle for tomorrow's dominance in the Middle East.

Following Hinnebush's discussion about the growing appeal of the "Turkish model," one of that country's foremost constitutional experts, Ergun Özbudun, from İstanbul Şehir University, provides his insights about the applicability of his country's democratic example for the broader Middle East. In chapter 11, "Turkey's Ordeal of Democratic Consolidation: A Possible Model for the Arab Uprisings?" Özbudun argues that the Turkish model ought to be approached cautiously, stating that "Turkey has not been able to fully consolidate its democracy and, in this respect, lags behind many of the 'third wave' democracies of Southern, Central, and Eastern Europe." Most observers, he states, agree that the constitution is at the heart of the problem. The current constitution of 1982 is "authoritarian, tutelarist, and statist in spirit" and is the product of the military regime of the National Security Council (NSC, 1980–1983), with almost no input from political parties and civil society. Despite seventeen amendments since 1987, the constitution has not been possible to fully eliminate this authoritarian legacy, whose goal "was to protect the state against the actions of its citizens rather than to protect the citizens against the encroachments of the state." As a result, Turkey's military still enjoys greater power and influence than its counterparts in other consolidated democracies and even beyond what is suggested by the letter of the constitution and laws.

Özbudun does not attribute Turkey's constitutional problems solely to the legacy of the NSC. Their roots trace back to the foundations of the Turkish republic—Kemalism—and its principles of nationalism, populism, and secularism that continue to create obstacles to the development of a liberal and pluralistic political system. Over the last half century, Turkey's secularist center has been locked in a power struggle with the traditional and conservative forces at its periphery. "In Egypt, the ongoing power struggle is between the Islamist parties (Muslim Brothers and the Salaffiyya), on the one hand, and a coalition of the military, the judiciary, and the secular sectors of the civil society on the other— an almost perfect replica of the 'republican alliance' in Turkey. In both countries, the close cooperation between the military and the judiciary is remarkable." Militaries in Turkey and Egypt have been eager to control the transition process and maintain important "exit guarantees" that grant them tutelary powers in the emerging regimes. Özbudun cautions that such guarantees might initially facilitate a transfer to civilian rule, but they subsequently interfere with democratic consolidation and "take a very long time to liquidate."

Across the broader Middle East, authoritarian rulers have constantly used the threat of a fundamentalist Islamist takeover to justify authoritarian policies and restrictions. By portending the possibilities of "one person, one vote, one time," they have helped to create a paradoxical situation in which liberal or secular opposition groups—normally on the side of democratic reforms—support repressive policies against the Islamist opposition. In Egypt, the long-term outcome of these power struggles will largely depend on two things: first, "the military's willingness to recede to the role of a democratic player," and, second, "Islamist groups' intention and capability to transform into moderate forces fully committed to liberal democratic procedures—a task made extremely difficult following the removal of Mohamed Morsi and increasing bans on the Muslim Brotherhood." At this point, neither goal appears easily achievable.

Özbudun concludes that, despite its shortcomings, the Turkish model does hold some positive lessons for the Arab Uprisings on how to combine a pluralist democracy, a secular system of governance, and Islamic moral values. Tunisia, he predicts, is the most likely of the severely affected countries to follow suit and join the club of Muslim democracies that exhibit moderate Islamist parties and a spirit of cooperation with secular political forces.

In chapter 12, "Democratic Contagion versus Authoritarian Resilience: Jordan's Prospects for Change," Lars Berger, senior lecturer in Middle East politics at the University of Salford in the United Kingdom, raises the prospect of an additional country yet to succumb to the Uprisings. "On the surface," he argues, "the Jordanian regime weathered the initial fallout of the democratic contagion that had begun to spread across the Arab world in early 2011," but tensions within the country have continued to simmer. His investigation into the Jordanian case illustrates some of the pressing difficulties faced—and strategies employed—by many regional leaders who have sought to inoculate their own countries against the most severe effects of wider events in the region. Berger highlights precarious economic conditions and clashing identity issues similar to those raised throughout this book. For example, in Jordan, state coffers and most citizens' pockets are strained, geopolitical players exert strong domestic influences, and new forms of communication have enabled the spread of ideas and protest memes (such as slogans and motifs) that can resonate with a broad spectrum of disenfranchised political actors. This combination of external and internal pressures has required deft moves from ruling regimes, lest they find themselves facing revolt.

In the wake of the Arab Uprisings, Berger describes a number of tried-and-true strategies taken by the Jordanian regime in an attempt to ameliorate the pressures on it. These included the flaming of real or perceived differences between Palestinian and East Bank Jordanians in order to divert political animosity away from the regime. As well, the government distributed material handouts meant to address immediate economic pains across wide sections of the Jordanian populations. These handouts were also accompanied by promises and gestures of gradual political reform, as occurred after the April 1989 bread riots in the Bedouin South that "set in motion a process of relative democratization whose defensive nature, however, never touched the fundamental power relationships within the country that were easily reverted when the regime deemed it necessary." In framing Jordan's challenges as primarily economic rather than political, the regime has attempted to restrict the corresponding corrective measures sought by citizens. Although these strategies have worked in the past, their potential limits are increasingly tested by outspoken and diverse sets of societal actors.

Intriguingly, Berger suggests that the Jordanian regime has also benefited from the Arab Uprisings in multiple ways. "First, the escalation of conflicts in Libya and Syria drove home for many Jordanians the dramatic consequences that political change in ethnically or otherwise divided countries could bring about. . . . Domestically, the regime benefits from the perception that Jordanians have more to lose in a revolution than in a gradual, albeit unsatisfactorily slow, political reform." Many Jordanians, for example, will consider themselves better off than their Egyptian and Syrian counterparts. Another benefit for King Abdullah II has been the international community's need for a stable Jordan, which has absorbed significant waves of refugees from neighboring Iraq and Syria. "On the one hand, this [influx] put enormous pressures on the country's already strained resources. On the other hand, the Iraq War had shown how Jordanian authorities are ready to instrumentalize the plight of refugees by translating inflated numbers into generous financial support from international donors." For now, Jordan's government continues to turn the country's perceived weaknesses into income-generating assets. With its scarcity of domestic resources, however, it will increasingly struggle to meet the economic demands of citizens. There is always the possibility that Jordanians will also rise above the current narrative—of gradual reform to balance its precarious economic and social situations—and band together in revolt.

And finally, in chapter 13, "Remaking the People: The Arab Uprisings and Democratization," Larbi Sadiki, associate professor of international relations at Qatar University, returns our attention to the Arab citizen—this time as represented from a postcolonial perspective. Sadiki explains how the Arab Uprisings bring into question the epistemic ways in which we create "knowledge" about events and people of the region and the often Orientalist lens through which they have been interpreted. In repudiating "the generalization and reductionism in the study of the Oriental other, the Arab Uprisings provide new opportunities, not only in the realm of direct democracy, political organization, and re-creation of community, but also in the sphere of political knowledge," argues Sadiki. "For, they introduce dynamics, practices, and thought that are bound to revise Orientalism, including prejudicial democratic transitology[11] that has written off the Arab Middle East as a region of political passivity, if not absence of active peoples endowed with democratic verve, passion, or much less know-how."[12]

Sadiki brings these two realms of "politics" and "peoplehood" together in his discussion of the Arab Uprisings, which he describes as the region's most important emancipatory moment since independence from colonialism.

In contradistinction to trends in transitology that fixate on the presence or absence of democracy, Sadiki instead compels us to examine how organizations and institutions conducive to the practice of politics are present in both democratic and nondemocratic systems. This requires a reinterpretation of "democratization as a space or realm of 'in-between' space within which power is neither competitive nor measurable by conventional means." In the Middle East, the hegemon that is the "over-stated Arab state"[13] has left little shared space for normalizing state-society relations, and even less for contesting state power. But by eliminating obvious rival political centers, these totalizing practices have paradoxically created a "void of power" that can work to undermine the state. Citizens correspondingly aim to fill this political void by using their own vocabularies and practices of subversion in an attempt to unmake power. As Sadiki describes it, "The space I am concerned with is hypothesized in terms of democratic *faragh*, or 'void'" which, as Sadiki wrote back in 2004, "is the realm of continuously searching for provisional synthesis in an ongoing contestation between thesis and antithesis." In this chapter he discusses how "It is within this void that the renegotiation of power takes place in the [Arab Middle East]." Put another way, "nonpower" is reimagined as a type of real power, which may be atomized and nonconventional yet can work to erode the state or even congeal under the right conditions with potent effect."

During the Uprisings, the power of the void received its most eloquent expression in the public squares of Tunis, Cairo, and Tripoli. Once protesters reached a critical mass, they reclaimed the very spaces meant to represent the state's authority and reorganized these into forums for democratic articulation and displays of solidarity. "What was rehearsed was the reinvention of peoplehood—without which neither state, democracy, nor democratization make sense." However, Sadiki reminds us using several examples that ousting a regime and steering a democratic state are very different endeavors. Several hurdles remain before we can expect to see transitional states effectively narrowing the gap between political ideals and practice. For now, we have witnessed an important transition for the Arab people from the periphery to the center. Even if this was only momentary (and not always egalitarian), the people have spoken and willed the downfall of the system (*al-sha'ab yureed eskaat al nazam*). In the nations where they were successful, outcomes of the transition from revolution to statecraft will be subject to conjecture for the foreseeable future.

CONCLUSION

With the chapters in this book, we have attempted to illustrate how various disciplines in the social sciences—as represented by our contributors—are attempting to make sense of emerging events in the Arab Middle East. The authors remind us of the enormity of the task at hand. Yet they also provide evidence of much common ground and the exciting possibilities for "parlor conversations" that effectively span disciplines. By way of example, the collective chapters describe how deficient economic and political orders in the region have combined with rapidly changing social conditions to set a context that was rife for catharsis but ill prepared for the challenges of transition. They portend that events on the ground are best interpreted within a broader history, even when its lessons are often highly specific. While the degree of speculation on the likely outcomes varies among contributors, the contributors do appear to agree that a multifaceted and elongated period of change has been set into motion, the implications of which are as profound as any regional event in living memory.

The authors' lenses of interrogation range from the philosophical to the geopolitical and the structural to the procedural, in order to examine topics such as the emerging interplay of authoritarianism, citizen activism, and religion in different Arab countries. Additional recurring topics include the role of media, notions of citizenship and identity, gender and income inequalities, and the importance of legal structures such as a strong constitution and equitable rule of law. Tellingly, Tunisia and Egypt receive significant consideration, albeit at the expense of other important cases such as Libya, Yemen, Bahrain, and Syria, which we could not include due to space constraints. To be clear, there are also many other important issues that a project of this scope must regrettably leave out, such as demographic challenges, security concerns, growing flows of people and weapons across borders, literary and artistic expressions, and the list goes on. Rather than attempting to present a comprehensive review of a singular event called the "Arab Spring," we have chosen instead to demonstrate multiple vantage points from which we can attempt to analyze the shifting objects that are the collective Arab Uprisings. We hope that the lessons from this volume provide insight into how we might move the conversation in some way toward a better understanding of the societal, economic, and cultural dynamics of the Uprisings rather than focus (as much of the literature does) on the state and regime or on democracy's simple presence or absence. As already stated in this introduction, this endeavor reminds us of the need to step back and focus on the search for enduring questions rather than hasty proclamations.

NOTES

1. For a discussion of many of these problems, see the 2009 *United Nations Development Programme Challenges to Human Security in the Arab Countries*, retrieved from http://ezproxy.msu .edu:2047/login?url=http://search.ebscohost.com/login.aspx?direct=true&scope=site&db=e000 xna&AN=434289.

2. "Witnesses Report Rioting in Tunisian Town," *Reuters*, December 19, 2010, retrieved from http://www.reuters.com/article/2010/12/19/ozatp-tunisia-riot-idAFJOE6BI06U20101219.

3. Most of the authors in this volume focus on specific repercussions from events in the year 2011, but, like the term "Arab Uprisings," they also leave open the possibility of more revolts to come.

4. See Hudson's chapter 2 in this volume for a further discussion on the limitations of the term "Arab Spring."

5. We recognize that problems also exist with the "Arab" part of this term, since this is not the single supra-identity for everyone who took part in the events we are describing—though arguably it is among the most salient denominators. However, to change this word as well would both broaden a lens we are trying to narrow and depart too far from the common terminology for practical purposes. Also, note that we use a capitalized term "Uprisings" to denote the collective revolts across countries, and "uprisings" lowercase when talking about the various protests that occurred within a single country (for example, "the Tunisian uprisings").

6. Kenneth Burke, *The Philosophy of Literary Form* (Berkeley: University of California Press, 1941).

7. One notable exception appears to be Fawaz Gerges in *The New Middle East: Protest and Revolution in the Arab World* (New York: Cambridge University Press, 2014).

8. See Ergun Özbudun's chapter 11 in this volume for insightful lessons about the Turkish constitutional-reform process.

9. Notable exceptions in this volume include the chapters by Gana (chapter 5), Toska (chapter 7), Berger (chapter 12), Labidi (chapter 9), and especially Sadiki (chapter13), all of whom give specific attention to the role of citizens.

10. The chapter by Toska in this book also provides a model of prediction, however her overall scope (social media) and dependent variable (political mobilization) are much more focused and restrictive in their claims.

11. See Hudson's chapter 2 in this book for an insightful history on the transitology debates in the field of political science.

12. Similarly, the foreword by Khouri as well as several other chapters in this volume explicitly call into question the long-held view of subservient Arab citizens.

13. This term is reference to the late Nazih Ayubi's influential book *Over-Stating the Arab State: Politics and Society in the Middle East* (London: I. B. Tauris, 1995), in which he challenges dominant accounts that tend to overestimate the actual power and strength of the state.

2

Transition to What? Reflections on the Arab Uprisings

MICHAEL C. HUDSON

The Arab Uprisings[1] that began at the end of 2010 have forced analysts of the Middle East to rethink long-held propositions about authoritarianism and democracy. Three fundamental questions remain to be satisfactorily answered. First, what exactly were—and are—these Uprisings; how do we conceptualize them? Second, what caused them; in particular, why were most analysts surprised? Third, what will follow from them; in particular, what, if anything, do theories of transition to democracy have to offer by way of prediction?

CONCEPTUALIZING THE "ARAB SPRING"

Without seeming overly pedantic, I think we still have a lot of work to do in defining and operationalizing our "dependent variable"—the "Arab Spring," or whatever one chooses to call it. (While I am not comfortable with "Arab Spring," it is interesting how widely this term has come into common usage, including in the Arab world itself, where "*al-rabi'a al-arabi*" seems to have taken hold.[2]) We need to fix temporal and spatial boundaries, and we need to establish the kind of "connectivity," if any, between the various Uprisings (and potential uprisings). Did it begin on December 17, 2010, in Tunisia when Mohamed Bouazizi set himself on fire? Or on June 6, 2010, with the murder of Khaled Said by Egyptian police?

Or is it part of a process, as Samer Shehata has suggested, referring mainly
to Egypt, that starts with labor protests in 2000 through 2004, followed by
protests over the US invasion of Iraq, the emergence of the *Kefaya* movement
and Egypt's growing economic difficulties in 2004, the democratizing pressures
from the Bush administration in 2003 through 2005, the Gaza war protests
of 2008 and 2009, the "farcical" elections of November 2010, and the church
bombing in Alexandria on January 1, 2011—all this before the January 25
"beginning"?[3] The sociologist Immanuel Wallerstein sees "the spirit of 1968"
flowing through the Arab Uprisings; for him the "world revolution" beginning
that year—marked by protests in France, the United States, and elsewhere—is
far from over, and the Arab Uprisings and Occupy Wall Street movement are
just its latest manifestations.[4] Whatever one may think of this alleged lineage,
he is not the only scholar to view the Arab Uprisings as a long-term historical
phenomenon whose end is not yet in sight. Contrast this view, however, with
some "realist" interpreters who are already referring to the "Arab Spring" in the
past tense.[5] In this view, there was an eruption of popular protest, but it did not
develop sufficient leadership and organization to overthrow the deeply rooted
authoritarian systems, and so authoritarianism will endure despite the recent
excitement. Nearly three years after the initial Uprisings, we are still faced with
many critical questions. For example, what of the spatial dimension? Are the
Arab Uprisings essentially Arab, or do they transcend the geographic region
from Morocco to the Gulf that we conventionally call the Arab world? Within
a year of the Uprisings, observers were attributing an influence from them to
places of protest far afield, like Israel, China, Iran, France, Britain, Greece, and
the United States. Is the discourse of protest Arab-specific, or does it touch on
apparently universal values of liberalism, democracy, participation, and human
security? What are the essential features of the Arab Uprisings, and how can
we operationalize these? How can we effectively apply quantitative analyses of
networks and connections between the protesters from Tunisia to Yemen to
Syria and other Arab countries in which overt protest has yet to occur? What
is learned from content analyses of the Uprisings' discourse; tracking of the
"Al Jazeera effect," Facebook, and Twitter; following the money trail of material
support for these sustained protests; or investigating the direct role of foreign
powers? What inferences can we draw by studying the psychology of aging
leaders too long in power and of the younger generation apparently leading
the Uprisings? And there remain several other questions about the roles of
economics, citizens, conflicting identities and ideologies, and the practice of

statecraft itself during periods of transition. This search for questions is surely an interdisciplinary endeavor and a central undertaking of this book. The authors herein address many of these topics in some detail, so for this chapter I focus primarily on the question of how well political science (currently and historically) prepares us to comprehend the Arab Uprisings.

WHY THE ANALYSTS WERE SURPRISED

The fact that so many observers were caught off guard by these dramatic upheavals suggests a failure, mainly in the academic community, to understand their causes. As one surprising uprising after another rippled across the Arab world, there arose a chorus of *mea culpas* from academics, journalists, and government experts. Blake Hounshell captured this well; he quotes flustered intelligence officials and flummoxed social scientists and even assesses the shortcomings of his own publication's (*Foreign Policy*) "Failed State Index"[6] that did not foresee the convulsions across the region.[7] Middle East sociologists like Charles Kurzman admit that revolutions are ultimately unpredictable.[8] A prominent Middle East political scientist, Gregory Gause, confessed that he and many of his colleagues were caught off base.[9] Government analysts were flummoxed as well: Andrew Shapiro, assistant secretary of state for political-military affairs, told *National Journal* in an October 2011 interview that "none of us predicted that this was going to happen."[10]

Why were the experts caught off guard? Let us count the reasons. Gregory Gause's account in *Foreign Affairs* identifies perhaps the most important ones. He finds that the Middle East studies community (mostly the political scientists) had turned their attention narrowly toward explaining why the authoritarian systems are so durable. That led to a focus on the large, well-funded, military-security apparatus so pervasive across the Arab world and its apparently tight relationship with the regime leadership. No less important was the state domination of the economy, not just in the classic pure oil-rentier manner but also in the way that, at a time of the renaissance of neoclassical market-driven economic theory, Arab regimes were still able to infiltrate and dominate the emerging private sector. Concentration on these two conditions diverted scholarly attention from the negative political effects of "the Washington consensus," which were not observed so clearly. And hardly anybody saw what Gause describes as a new cross-border Pan-Arabism.[11] While Gause is perhaps too narrow in depicting this contagion effect as a new form of Pan-Arab ideology, he is definitely onto a fundamental element of the Arab Uprisings.

Mariz Tadros, a development specialist writing in the *Guardian*, offers a little list of reasons for the failure. The West had become dismissive of the years of protest that had preceded Mubarak's fall and thus ignored an important warning sign. Scholars had underestimated the extent to which the state security forces interfere with people's ordinary lives, thus engendering a smoldering resentment that might have provided a clue. Analysts misread the economic indicators, which, at the aggregate level at least, appeared to be fairly robust, notably, the modest to impressive GDP growth. What was less noticed was structural unemployment on a massive scale. By focusing on institutionalized political actors—the top leaders and ruling elites—they neglected the growing societal disconnect from "the system" (the *nidham, le Pouvoir*). Relative inter-elite harmony was seen as a sign of overall system stability. And while social-movement theory offered—and still offers—an important new way of understanding Arab political systems, theorists did not connect these "beneath the radar" processes to the stability of the larger system.[12]

Kurt Volker, a former US Ambassador to NATO, wrote in February 2011 that there are six reasons the West has misread the Arab situation: first, an assumption that autocrats will prevail; second, European fears of migration privileged their opinion of incumbent regimes; third, fears of Islamist extremists may have encouraged their wishful thinking that everything was under control; fourth, concern for Israel encouraged the West to turn a blind eye to Arab regimes' misbehavior toward their own people; fifth, a "soft bigotry" that Arabs are not ready for democracy exists; and finally, sixth, there is a simple failure to understand emphasis on human values and ideas.[13]

Tarek Masoud, writing in the *Journal of Democracy*, observed that in hindsight the warning signs seemed like a "combustible mix" of "failing regime, aging leader, and a people increasingly willing to confront both" that would make revolution inevitable, even overdetermined. But instead scholars saw only "durable authoritarianism." Even after Tunisia, he asserts, analysts were slow to pick up on what else was to come. "Durable authoritarianism" was in fact a mirage.[14]

In fairness, not all observers were surprised; some saw the upheavals coming, and it would be interesting to ask why. Journalists and pundits seemed to be more prescient than social scientists. Unencumbered by academic theories, they relied on their feel for the situation. Tadros writes, "After all, practically every journalist who visited Egypt in the last few years seemed to mark the occasion by filing a piece warning of the regime's impending collapse."[15] David Ignatius, a columnist for the *Washington Post*—well-connected to the US intelligence establishment—wrote about the protests in Lebanon that led to the withdrawal of the Syrians and quoted Lebanese politician Walid Jumblatt: "It's strange for me to say it, but this process of change has started because of the American invasion of Iraq."[16] A month later Charles Krauthammer, a leading neoconservative syndicated columnist, wrote an article titled "The Arab Spring of 2005." Just like the 1848 revolutions in Europe, he said, the Arab world was at a turning point. His argument was based on the events in Lebanon, the women of Kuwait winning voting rights, the rise of Egyptian opposition leader Ayman Nour, and the election in Iraq.[17]

These journalists and others—and not all of them conservative—wondered whether the neocons might have been right after all and that George W. Bush's decision (short-lived, it turned out) to lend American support for Arab democracy might actually have triggered a democratic transition in that region. In Britain, the *Economist* published an article asking "Was George Bush Right?"[18] Similar pieces appeared in *Le Figaro, Der Spiegel*, and the *Toronto Star*. Gilbert Achcar wrote an editorial in *Le Monde Diplomatique* more than five years before Mohamed Bouazizi's suicide protest, under the heading "Arab Spring: Late and Cold," in which he contended that the election in Palestine of Mahmoud Abbas, a big turnout in Iraq for their January elections, and Mubarak's presidential reforms had led people to announce an "Arab Spring." But, he cautioned, the region is still far from true democracy.[19] In March 2008 an article written for *PJ Media*, a conservative blog, was titled "The Arab Spring Is Happening Now." The writer noted that the neocons who were so thrilled by an Arab Spring, citing Lebanon and Iraq, were just premature by three years.[20]

Veteran *Washington Post* journalist and long-time Middle East watcher David Ottaway published an article titled "The Arab Tomorrow" in the *Wilson Quarterly* just before the Arab Uprisings began. The article argues that the Arab world is on a precipice; Egypt in particular is in a sorry state of decline. Ottaway offers a prediction that with hindsight seems spot on: "However, this prevailing model of Arab autocracy, dependent on the *mukhabarat*[21] and a fabricated popular vote, does not seem a recipe for lasting political stability. Indeed, the Arab political cauldron contains all the ingredients for explosions in the years ahead."[22] The *Economist* did not do so badly either. In February 2011, just after the Uprisings began, it came up with its "Arab Unrest Index"—a composite of economic, social, and political indicators that places the Arab states in, or about to be in, turmoil near the top of their list of countries most likely to experience revolutions.[23] It did better than academic models of potential instability.

Not all academic observers were surprised by the Arab Uprisings, except perhaps for its suddenness. Some social scientists saw potential political upheaval arising out of an increasingly tense economic situation. As early as 2002, Arab social scientists issued the first edition of the *Arab Human Development Report*, which catalogued depressing data on the inadequacy of the "quality of life" across the Arab region. Its three famous "development deficits"—knowledge, gender, and governance—revealed a potential for political instability. And if one looks at the annual reports produced by the United Nations Economic and Social Council for West Asia and reads between the lines of bureaucratic correctness, its authors imply that there could be political fallout, especially in Egypt. Underlying many of these economic explanations was a belief that the ascendency of neoliberal economic doctrine, especially after the collapse of the Soviet Union and the communist alternative, was the decisive factor, because the policy recommendations derived from this "Washington consensus" created huge and palpable distress for ordinary people in the name of market-driven economic development.

Others pointed to political factors. The late Nazih Ayubi's magisterial work *Over-Stating the Arab State* remains perhaps the most complete exposition of the corporatist model, in which key social and economic groups are co-opted into the state. Ayubi insisted that the legitimacy and even the durability of many of these states was exaggerated, hence his useful depiction of "the strong, the weak, and the fierce" Arab states. Ayubi directs our attention to the "hollowness" of Arab authoritarian regimes.[24] Another notable analyst, the Tunisian Larbi Sadiki[25]—whose profound discussion of Arab democratization also revealed the fakery of "electoral" models and "facade" democracy—wrote an article in 2002 exposing the vulnerability of the Ben Ali regime, while most others saw it as the very model of a successful *mukhabarat* state.[26]

Perhaps the most powerful forecast from the Middle East academics was the article by Nathan Brown and Amr Hamzawy in the *National Interest* in 2007. While noting the disillusionment that had set in after the democratic stirrings in 2005, they cautiously argue that deeper changes are afoot. Egypt in particular, they assert, seems poised for some kind of democratic opening. "The wider regional scene does not look as bleak as the democratization pessimists in the United States tend to depict it. In contrast to the pessimists, we offer a sober but more hopeful view: Change has been occurring and further reform is possible. But it is neither inevitable nor bound to be purely democratic in nature."[27]

WHAT NEXT?

Almost three years into the Uprisings, scholars and policy analysts alike were attempting to assess the long-term implications. Some of the early attempts were not entirely successful, as Egyptian blogger Issandr El Amrani pointed out.[28] In Tunisia and Egypt, long-suppressed but deeply rooted Islamist parties appeared to be monopolizing the newly opened political space, raising fears of a return to authoritarianism. In Yemen, the dictator had finally relinquished the presidential palace but maintained an office just down the street, and his family-military support base was still intact. In Libya, where the old regime had been physically liquidated, an unruly collection of tribal militias and urban gangs seemed to overshadow the emerging formal political authorities. The royal authorities in Bahrain, though supported by Saudi Arabia and other Gulf monarchies, appeared both unable to snuff out a determined popular opposition movement and unwilling to deal with it seriously. But for sheer bloody violence, none of these cases could come close to Syria, where an initial nonviolent popular protest has triggered a catastrophic civil war with 150,000 deaths in two years alone and no end in sight. What had appeared as a common, Pan-Arab popular uprising in early 2011 was spinning off in different directions; and any early expectations of a transition to democracy required reconsideration two years later.

But it is the job of social scientists and area specialists to try and make sense of the unexpected, especially given the significance of this troubled region for the rest of the world. In fact, the experts have been wrestling with the question of "transitions" for a long time, and it would seem that they oscillate between liberal and conservative forecasts.

A BRIEF HISTORY OF ACADEMIC OSCILLATIONS

In their important critique of the Middle East "democracy-spotters" of the 1990s Valbjorn and Bank remind us that Middle East political science, mirroring trends and fashions in the larger field of comparative politics, took a liberal turn in the 1950s and 1960s when modernization theory in its initial version (as expressed by authors such as Lerner, Halpern, and Binderfore) saw the possibilities for democratization flowing from that basket of socioeconomic trends that Karl Deutsch labeled "social mobilization."[29] To be sure, the opening of the political arena could take an authoritarian turn (Halpern's "neo-Islamic totalitarianism"), but the prospects were still substantial that a "new middle class," including enlightened military officers, could lead this region to a stable, liberal democratic (and, hopefully, noncommunist) future. For those old enough to remember that period, there was palpable intellectual enthusiasm over dethroning the "persistent authoritarianism" of an earlier period: Orientalism, with its ahistorical cultural assumptions, and the static formal institutionalism of political science before "the behavioral revolution."

But Samuel Huntington, long before his controversial "Clash of Civilizations" thesis, recast modernization theory in a darker light, pointing out that mass mobilization could more easily lead to violence, praetorianism, or authoritarianism.[30] And the conservative movement to "bring the state back in" reminded us of the importance of restoring the state as a powerful independent variable in explaining political outcomes (correcting the formless pluralism of Bentley and Truman), of opening the "black box" of the state, and, in a Burkean sense, of myths, habit, and tradition.[31] There were sources of legitimacy other than democracy.[32] Concurrently, on the ground in the Middle East, the populist and unruly nationalism of the 1960s gave way to the "order" of the 1970s and 1980s: states were expanding dramatically, and regimes were becoming all too stable. We began to use the term "*mukhabarat* state." The "king's dilemma" gave way to a new appreciation of the seeming legitimacy of monarchies (at least those that had survived the 1950s and 1960s).

By the end of the 1980s, however, there were new stirrings of popular protest, and Middle East political scientists discovered (or rediscovered) civil society. The steady growth of NGOs was noted and tallied.[33] For an all-too-brief moment, there were democratic openings in Algeria, Jordan, Yemen, and Egypt, as well as democratic restorations in Kuwait and Lebanon. The first intifada erupted in Palestine, an extraordinary example of popular resistance. But these intimations of a liberal or even democratic "spring" were short-lived. Perhaps it was the brutal arrival of militant Islam that most contributed to the reassertion of authoritarianism. The triple "scares" of 1979—the siege of the Grand Mosque in Mecca, the Iranian Islamist revolution, and the rise of the mujahideen against the Soviet occupation of Afghanistan—laid the groundwork for the demonization of opposition forces in general; and the liberals found themselves squeezed between two bad alternatives: dictatorial regimes and even more frightful Islamist movements. Emasculated, they reluctantly sided with regime authoritarianism.

At that point a new generation of political scientists and Middle East specialists emerged with a new focus: persistent authoritarianism. Among the writers taking this tack, as Valbjorn and Bank remark, were Oliver Schlumberger, Eva Bellin, Daniel Brumberg, Raymond Hinnebusch,[34] Marsha Pripstein Posusney, and Steven Heydemann. Researchers at the Carnegie Endowment in Washington theorized about the stability of "semi-authoritarian" states. Instead of asking whether, why, and how democracy might yet emerge in this region so exceptionally immune to democratization trends elsewhere in the world, they set themselves a more manageable task: to explain why authoritarianism seems to work so well. One simple if crude answer was "brute force or the threat of it"—the *mukhabarat* pretty much explains all. Another answer was oil. Not only were the oil exporters exemplars of the rentier effect, but so also were the neighboring states, which indirectly depended on oil largesse and/or foreign economic and military assistance. Corporatism was perhaps the overarching model for authoritarian systems, which not only employed surveillance and violence but also built strategic, clientelistic relationships with key constituencies, notably the business, military, and landed elites. Furthermore, the United States, as the regional hegemon, soon discovered new security threats to "replace" (as it were) the defunct Soviet Union. With militant Islamism in its Iranian and Salafist (al-Qaeda) strains on the rise, it was no time to undermine authoritarian allies, even as the (first) Bush and Clinton administrations spoke of "a new (democratic) world order" and America as "the indispensable nation" for the coming century.[35]

It would not be fair to assert that the "persistent authoritarianism" school denied the possibilities for Middle East democratization, but it did reorient the analytic priorities toward explaining why things are the way they are. Schlumberger's edited collection illustrates some of these approaches, as does the article by Valbjorn and Bank in their discussion of the "postdemocracy" paradigm.[36] Now attention is given to the significance of small changes within regimes and oppositions, such as the shift from populist to postpopulist authoritarianism and the development of local politics and parallel networks that in a sense operate "beneath the radar" of the formal national system. And useful work has been done under the rubric of "new institutionalism." For example, pacts have been studied as mechanisms short of full democracy for integrating particular social or communal sectors into the prevailing system of governance. Other work has focused on how coalitions may form between regime and opposition "soft-liners." Applications of rentier theory focus on the extent to which regimes actually redistribute exogenous rent income to their populations. And certainly one of the most fruitful products of this approach is the notion, well-articulated by Steven Heydemann, that authoritarian regimes are capable of upgrading themselves.[37] In light of recent events, one might wonder how steep the learning curve of some of them has been, but there is no denying that ruling elites and their *mukhabarat*s, with some help from Western governments and businesses, have refined their surveillance and control abilities; and their ability to set up facade democratic institutions and processes has to some extent buffered them from genuine reform pressures. Whether it is the regimes or the oppositions that have benefited most from new information technologies and social media, however, remains to be seen.

Perhaps it is too harsh to remark that the focus has shifted from studying the forest to the trees, but it does seem that studying the mechanics of persistent authoritarianism at the expense of trying to identify dynamic factors affecting the legitimacy of the systems as a whole is a little like automotive engineers focusing on how the internal combustion engine can be upgraded instead of searching for and considering the impact of entirely new technologies.

In response to the Arab Uprisings, the academic oscillations may be poised to take a turn away from persistent authoritarianism. As dictators were displaced in Tunisia and Egypt, one political scientist, for example, discovered that "sultanistic" regimes (personal dictatorships lacking popular legitimacy), although they appear unshakeable, "are actually highly vulnerable" to overthrow.[38] The region's traditional monarchies, on the other hand, have more flexible political structures capable of adjusting to societal pressures.

And so, what goes around comes around. The question that now arises is, What next? Will we oscillate from "postdemocracy" rediscovery of authoritarianism back to a naïve anticipation of liberal-democratic nirvana or its opposite, a grim expectation of a radical Islamist dark age? Or will we be able to break out of this cycle? Let us hope so, because the evidence from the Arab Uprisings after almost three years is that neither endpoint is clearly in sight.

TRANSITOLOGY APPROACHES

One way to look at the future is through the lens of what has come to be called "transitology" approaches in political science. The distinguished comparativist Dankwart Rustow may be said to have inspired the transitions paradigm.[39] As Posusney nicely summarizes it:

> Contingency approaches stress that democracy will emerge when incumbent authoritarians opposed to change (hard-liners), as well as challengers (soft-liners, or reformists) who may themselves have antidemocratic leanings, come to see the uncertainty associated with free and fair electoral competition as the best option

among other alternatives. Thus, the contingency school emphasizes the strategic choices made by political elites, a category understood to include not only incumbent rulers but also opposition activists.[40]

Transitology is considered by some to have been an analytical advance in that it challenged the prevailing socioeconomic "modernization" paradigm that stipulated political "development" as the function of what Karl Deutsch famously called "social mobilization."[41] Instead, transitology contends that democratic transitions are made through elite bargaining, with the elites making rational choices to promote their interests. All this, they say, occurs in an atmosphere of uncertainty. Soft-liners in the challenged incumbent elite seek out soft-liners in the opposition elite. If they succeed in striking a compromise, then a democratic transition becomes possible, often through the mechanism of a pact. From this perspective cultural and economic explanations are relegated to the background; they may help explain why uprisings happen in the first place, but they do not have much to offer in explaining why transitions—democratic or otherwise—may occur.

If all this sounds a bit abstract—not to say bloodless (so to speak)—to a student of the Arab Uprisings, it may be because transitology scholars such as O'Donnell, Schmitter, and Przeworski were inspired by the wave of democracy that occurred in southern Europe and Latin America. These situations, viewed from the Middle East at least, seem to be more bounded and structured: military and business elites incorporated in the regime could deal rationally with "sensible" opposition soft-liners. Conceivably, in the pre-Uprising period, the transitology model might seem more applicable inasmuch as incremental change is all that was seriously being contemplated. Unfortunately, however, as Brumberg and others have observed, in the absence of acute uncertainty (or fear) the incumbents could bestow cosmetic crumbs of reform rather than engage seriously with the demands of comparatively powerless liberals.[42] For transitologists, "uncertainty" remains untheorized.

If the Arab Uprisings had one consequence, it was to generate uncertainty. Yet even in the face of the uncertainty engendered by mass demonstrations, there is little indication that the ruling circles around Ben Ali, Mubarak, Gaddafi, Saleh, Al-Khalifa, and Assad were negotiating a pacted transition to a democratic system with the soft-liners in the opposition. The best case for a transitology scenario is probably Egypt. Blaydes and Lo, for example, extending Przeworski's game-theoretic model, suggest that army soft-liners and Muslim Brotherhood moderates might have smoothed the way for Mubarak's departure;

yet the subsequent friction between those two parties, exemplified by President Morsi's sacking of the army chief of staff, suggests that other factors are in play.[43] In Tunisia, the neutrality of the army, rather than a pacted dialogue, seems to have hastened Ben Ali's departure. But in the other cases there is little sign of regime soft-liners rationally considering a deal. In the Assad and Gaddafi regimes, being a soft-liner at all was, to say the least, risky; in the Bahrain and Yemen cases there were soft-liners, but they were muzzled. The other big problem for the transitology model lies in the inchoateness of the oppositions: it would be oversimplified to argue that elites were driving the Uprisings. The main weakness of the transitology approach is its marginalization of nonelites—the masses that were the muscle of the Uprisings.

CONCLUSION

Nearly three years after the beginning of the Arab Uprisings, it is still unclear where the transitions are headed. Authoritarian leaders have been displaced in Tunisia, Egypt, Libya, and Yemen, and they are under pressure in Bahrain and severe pressure in Syria. The modalities of transition have been varied: popular pressures in Tunisia and Egypt, popular revolts plus massive foreign military intervention in Libya, and protracted factional violence capped by regional (Gulf Cooperation Council) diplomacy in Yemen. So have the immediate outcomes: In Tunisia and Egypt the new incumbents are Islamists legitimized to some extent by (flawed) constitutional and electoral processes. In Libya, where the *ancien régime* was essentially liquidated, leaving hardly any institutions behind, a popularly elected General National Council composed of a coalition of many parties chose a new government, but so far it exerts little authority over much of the country. In Yemen, executive authority was transferred through negotiations from the president to his vice president, but efforts to organize a comprehensive national dialogue have foundered on the unwillingness of southern politicians to participate, and the shadow of the former president and his supporters looms large. In each of these cases the consolidation of a new order is only beginning, and whether such consolidation will take a democratic rather than a new authoritarian form would seem to depend on the fostering of consensus, or at least the containment of factionalism, among the newly empowered elements.

Unfortunately, political science has so far offered little by way of enlightenment as to the future course of the Arab Uprisings. It has disappointed us in two ways: "persistent authoritarianism" did not prepare us for the Uprisings, and "transitology" seems a too-limited "fair weather" approach to what has emerged as a confusing and diverse post-Uprising environment. To be sure, some interesting insights have emerged from large-n quantitative comparative studies of the causes of instability.[44] And there has been a great deal of thoughtful analysis of how political culture, economic growth and inequality, external involvements, and political institutions might facilitate or impede democratization. As we look at the Arab cases unfolding before us, we find no lack of "important factors": political Islam, ethnosectarian configurations, a culture of cynicism, public opinion, rational incentives toward cooperation or noncooperation, the socialization of politicians, institutional durability, social movements, competing economic paradigms, foreign involvement, regional "neighborhood" effects, to name a few. What we do not know is how they all fit together to foster or inhibit the political legitimacy that an eventual stable democratic order would require. At the risk of banality, perhaps the best that can now be said is that the uprising roads will be long and convoluted and that whether they will lead to democracy, Islamist authoritarianism, or some hybrid is hard to predict at this point.

NOTES

1. This chapter is a revision of one with the same title that appeared in *Transitions to What: Reflections on the Arab Uprisings* (Instanbul: Kure Yayinlari, 2014).

2. In chapter 1 of this volume, we further problematize the term "Arab Spring" and provide our rationale for instead using the term "Arab Uprisings."

3. Samer Shehata, "The January 25 Revolution," lecture given at Georgetown University's Center for Contemporary Arab Studies on September 13, 2011. (Cited with his permission.)

4. Immanuel Wallerstein, "The Contradictions of the Arab Spring," Al Jazeera English, November 14, 2011, accessed at http://www.aljazeera.com/indepth/opinion/2011/11/20111111101711539134.html on January 22, 2013.

5. See, for example, Richard N. Haass, "The Arab Spring Has Given Way to a Long, Hot Summer," *Financial Times,* July 6, 2011, accessed at www.cfr.org/middle-east-and-north-africa/arab-spring-has-given-way-long-hot-summer/p25426 on January 22, 2013.

6. In their chapter, Tikuisis and Minkov outline problems with existing predictive indexes and propose their own model tailored for the Middle East.

7. Blake Hounshell, "Dark Crystal: Why Didn't Anyone Predict the Arab Revolutions?" *Foreign Policy,* July/August 2011, accessed at http://www.foreignpolicy.com/articles/2011/06/20/dark_crystal on January 22, 2013.

8. Charles Kurzman, *The Unthinkable Revolution in Iran* (Cambridge: Harvard University Press, 2004).

9. F. Gregory Gause III, "Why Middle East Studies Missed the Arab Spring: The Myth of Authoritarian Stability," *Foreign Affairs,* July/August 2011, accessed at http://www.foreignaffairs.com/articles/67932/f-gregory-gause-iii/why-middle-east-studies-missed-the-arab-spring on January 22, 2013.

10. Sara Sorcher, "Topsy-Turvy: The Arab Spring Has Scrambled Assumptions about U.S. Security Assistance," *National Journal,* October 6, 2011, accessed at http://www.nationaljournal.com/magazine/state-department-rethinks-the-arab-spring-20111006 on January 22, 2013.

11. Gause III, "Why Middle East Studies Missed the Arab Spring."

12. Mariz Tadros, "Arab Uprisings: Why No One Saw Them Coming," *Guardian,* February 5, 2011, accessed at http://www.theguardian.com/commentisfree/2011/feb/05/arab-uprisings-egypt-tunisia-yemen on January 22, 2013.

13. Kurt D. Volker, "Arab Revolt Is a Tidal Wave: Does the West Get What's Really behind It?" *The Christian Science Monitor (Opinion),* February 25, 2011, accessed at http://www.csmonitor.com/Commentary/Opinion/2011/0225/Arab-revolt-is-a-tidal-wave.-Does-the-West-get-what-s-really-behind-it on January 22, 2013.

14. Tarek Masoud, "The Road to (and from) Liberation Square," *Journal of Democracy* 22:3 (July 2011).

15. Tadros, "Arab Uprisings."

16. David Ignatius, "Beirut's Berlin Wall," *Washington Post,* February 23, 2005, accessed at http://www.washingtonpost.com/wp-dyn/articles/A45575-2005Feb22.html on January 22, 2013.

17. Charles Krauthammer, "The Arab Spring of 2005," *Seattle Times,* March 21, 2005, accessed at http://seattletimes.com/html/opinion/2002214060_krauthammer21.html on January 22, 2013.

18. Lexington, "Was George Bush Right?" *Economist,* February 3, 2011.

19. Gilbert Achcar, "Arab Spring: Late and Cold," *Le Monde Diplomatique,* July 2005, accessed at http://mondediplo.com/2005/07/06arabworld on January 22, 2013.

20. Abe Greenwald, "The Arab Spring Is Happening Now," *PJ Media,* April 13, 2008, accessed at http://pjmedia.com/blog/the-arab-spring-is-happening-now/ on January 22, 2013.

21. *Mukhabarat* is the common term used to denote the intelligence service or secret police.

22. David B. Ottaway, "The Arab Tomorrow," *Wilson Quarterly,* Winter 2010, accessed at http://www.wilsonquarterly.com/article.cfm?AID=1565 on January 25, 2013.

23. "Arab Unrest Index," *Economist Online,* February 9, 2011, accessed at http://www.economist.com/blogs/dailychart/2011/02/daily_chart_arab_unrest_index.

24. Nazih N. Ayubi, *Over-Stating the Arab State: Politics and Society in the Middle East* (London, New York: I. B. Tauris, 2008).

25. Sadiki is the author of the final chapter in this book, chapter 13, where he discusses a "remaking of the people" in a post–Arab Uprisings context.

26. Larbi Sadiki, "Political Liberalization in Bin Ali's Tunisia: Façade Democracy," *Democratization* 9:4 (Winter 2002): 122–41.

27. Amr Hamzawy and Nathan J. Brown, "Arab Spring Fever," *National Interest Online,* August 29, 2007, accessed at http://carnegieendowment.org/2007/08/29/arab-spring-fever/tqj on January 25, 2013.

28. Issandr El Amrani, "What to Learn—or Not—from Early Drafts of History," *Cairo Review of Global Affairs,* August 20, 2012, accessed at www.aucegypt.edu/gapp/cairoreview/Pages/article Details.aspx?aid=226 on January 25, 2013.

29. Morten Valbjorn and André Bank, "Examining the 'Post' in Post-Democratization: The Future of Middle Eastern Political Rule through Lenses of the Past," in *Middle East Critique* 19:3 (Fall 2010): 183–200.

30. Samuel P. Huntington, *Political Order in Changing Societies* (New Haven: Yale University Press, 1978).

31. Peter B. Evans, Dietrich Rueschemeyer, and Theda Skocpol (eds.), *Bringing the State Back In* (New York: Cambridge University Press, 1985), chs. 1 and 11. See also Lisa Anderson, "The State in the Middle East and North Africa," *Comparative Politics* (October 1987).

32. Michael C. Hudson, *Arab Politics: The Search for Legitimacy* (New Haven: Yale University Press, 1978).

33. See, for example, Saad Eddin Ibrahim, "The Troubled Triangle: Populism, Islam, and Civil Society in the Arab World," in *International Political Science Review* 19:4 (1998): 373–85. See also, *Political Liberalization and Democratization in the Arab World*, edited by Rex Brynen, Bahgat Korany, and Paul Noble (Boulder: Lynne Riener Publishers, 1995).

34. Hinnebusch contributes chapter 10 to this volume, "The Arab Uprisings: Alignments and the Regional Power Balance."

35. For greater detail on such discourses see, Fahed Al-Sumait, "A Rhetorical Tightrope: U.S. Political Discourse on Arab Democracy following the Cold War," in Kiran Prasad (ed.), *Transforming International Communication: Media, Culture, and Society the Middle East* (New Delhi: BRPC, 2014).

36. *Debating Arab Authoritarianism: Dynamics and Durability in Nondemocratic Regimes*, edited by Oliver Schlumberger (Stanford: Stanford University Press, 2007).

37. Steven Heydemann, "Upgrading Authoritarianism in the Arab World," Analysis Paper No. 13, October 2007, The Saban Center for Middle East Policy at the Brookings Institution.

38. Jack Goldstone, "Understanding the Revolutions of 2011: Weakness and Resilience in Middle Eastern Autocracies," *Foreign Affairs* 90:3 (May/June 2011): 8–16.

39. Dankwart A. Rustow, "Transitions to Democracy: Toward a Dynamic Model," *Comparative Politics* 2:2 (April 1970): 337–63.

40. Marsha Pripstein Posusney, "The Middle East's Democracy Deficit in Comparative Perspective," in *Authoritarianism in the Middle East: Regimes and Resistance*, edited by Marsha Pripstein Posusney and Michele Penner Angrist (Boulder: Lynne Rienner Publishers, 2005).

41. Karl W. Deutsch, "Social Mobilization and Political Development," *American Political Science Review* 55:3 (September 1961): 493–514.

42. Daniel Brumberg, "The Trap of Liberalized Autocracy," *Journal of Democracy* 13:4 (October 2002): 56–68.

43. Lisa Blaydes and James Lo, "One Man, One Vote, One Time? A Model of Democratization in the Middle East," *Journal of Theoretical Politics*, published online, November 14, 2011, at http://jtp.sagepub.com/content/early/2011/11/12/0951629811423121.

44. See, for example, Jack A. Goldstone, Robert H. Bates, David L. Epstein, Ted Robert Gurr, Michael B. Lustik, Monty G. Marshall, Jay Ulfelder, and Mark Woodward, "A Global Model for Forecasting Political Instability," *American Journal of Political Science* 54:1 (January 2010): 190–208.

3

The Arab Revolts: Local, Regional, and Global Catalysts and Consequences

Mark Farha

The unfolding uprisings across the Arab world have been viewed through a regional prism. Political scientists particularly were predisposed to view the Arab Uprisings as a long-overdue culmination of pent-up popular frustrations with corrupt and autocratic regimes. Such an exclusive focus on the democracy deficit long besetting political systems in the Arab world, however, begs the question of the particular historical moment of the outburst of 2011 and as such may not capture the full scope of the underlying dynamic. While political repression by praetorian states served as a crucial catalyst for massive street demonstrations, it is increasingly apparent that the parabolic rise of commodity prices may have kindled a politically and demographically charged situation. In its first segment, this chapter thus attempts to draw the links between monetary and fiscal policies in the United States and Europe, the ensuing contagion of global inflation, and its role in destabilizing certain Arab states, while leaving others largely insulated from the wave of revolt. I argue that the likelihood of a revolution in any given Arab state must be weighed against a multiplicity of local and global factors, chief of which is the exposure of a critical mass of a vulnerable segment in a given society to price increases in essential commodities. While Gulf rentier states—with the exception of a particularly bifurcated Bahrain—thus far have been fairly successful in staving off major street protests using direct and indirect subsidies, even seasoned autocrats such as Mubarak in Egypt or Ben Ali in Tunisia, bereft of rentier revenue, were unable to withstand the popular pressures.

Finally, the chapter examines to what degree the socioeconomic imbalances that fomented the revolutions have aggravated religious sectarianism in pluralistic Arab states such as Lebanon and Syria, thereby undermining the uprisings' declared drive for civil rights, political accountability, and social justice.

WHO LIT THE FUSE OF 2011?

"Blame the time [we live in] and not me." Thus the humiliated Tunisian street vendor Bouazizi justified his self-immolation in a farewell message to his mother. Almost instantaneously, the tragic fate of Mohamed Bouazizi seized the world's attention; yet Bouazizi's parting words warrant greater scrutiny. They challenge us to widen our focus away from this inadvertent hero of the dramatic moment to the larger stage setting: what was it in his particular "time" that impelled Bouazizi to take his life, literally setting ablaze an entire region? Despite the initial, smug dismissals by the hubristic potentates Gaddafi, Mubarak, and, later on, Bashar al-Assad,[1] the cascade of popular rebellions quickly turned out to be far more than an isolated incident contained to Tunisia. To be sure, laments of a "democratic deficit" besetting the Arab world have long been audible as an almost de rigueur refrain of academic analyses of the region. But may we go even further and view the fire that has engulfed the region as a symptom of a global dynamic? If so, what were the underlying factors at the root of the convulsions in East and West?

THE NEXUS BETWEEN THE FINANCIAL CRISIS
AND INFLATION IN THE (ARAB) WORLD

In the span of four years, two major crises shook the world: the global financial crisis after 2007 and the Arab Uprisings of 2011. This sequence of events was, it shall be argued, not entirely coincidental. For, in reaction to the credit contraction of 2007, the US Treasury and the Federal Reserve Open Market Committee followed a recipe of stimulus programs and monetary injections that was soon to be emulated by central banks and governments around the globe. As figure 3.2 illustrates, the coordinated, unprecedented expansion of the US monetary base[2] in the third quarter of 2007 would drive up dollar-denominated commodity prices, with the FAO (Food and Agriculture Organization) food-price index, soaring from 120 to 230 in 2008 and again in a second, and even more consequential, surge after 2010[3]:

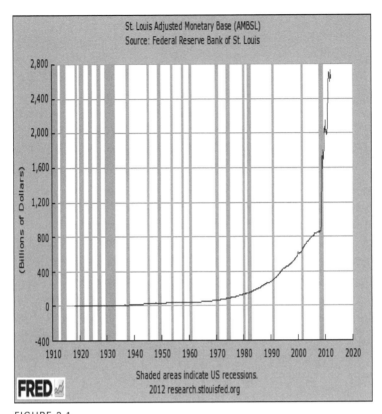

FIGURE 3.1

Source: Federal Reserve Bank of St. Louis

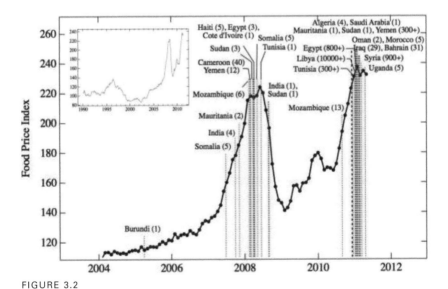

FIGURE 3.2

Source: M. Lagi, K. Z. Bertrand, Y. Bar-Yam,The Food Crises and Political Instability in North Africa and the Middle East. arXiv:1108.2455 (August 10, 2011), http://necsi.edu/research/social/foodcrises.html.

The drastic reaction of the US Fed injecting liquidity to prevent a market meltdown and freezing-up of credit markets thus carried a monumental opportunity cost as countries around the globe followed suit with monetary easing, creating a cascading inflationary ripple effect. The Arab states were no exception; many of them have currencies pegged to the dollar, and all of them must trade in dollar-denominated commodities. To be sure, the latter could also be a welcome source of surplus for select, commodity-endowed nations.

Thus, as we proceed to examine the repercussions of this 2010 price explosion for the Arab world, it behooves us to categorize the affected states into two distinct types: labor-importing, oil-exporting rentier economies (the Gulf countries plus Algeria and Libya) and labor-abundant, oil-importing countries.[4] In short, this last inflationary decade has had nearly inverse effects on the two principal subregions: the net exporters and net buyers of commodities. Even prior to the bursting of the financial bubble in 2008, the gradual expansion of global liquidity across the globe had widened preexistent, inter-Arab income disparities. Rising hydrocarbon prices constituted a boon for oil producing states and a burden for overpopulated states that saw a growing portion of the budget being diverted for energy consumption and subsidies. Just prior to the Arab Uprisings (and indeed after them), from 2003 to 2008, there was a $120 billion inflow of foreign direct investment (FDI) from Gulf states to the poorer Arab states such as Syria, Lebanon, Tunisia, and Egypt, which received more FDI from the Gulf than from anywhere else, and more investments during the brief run-up of oil prices from 2006 to 2009 than in the entire decade and a half of 1990 to 2005.[5] Yet this flow of funds proved insufficient to bridge growing intra-Arab divides; neither did it stave off the impending implosion in the overpopulated, mismanaged, corruption-infested crisis states. On the one hand, the hydrocarbon profits accumulated by oil producers could contribute to real estate bubbles in Lebanon or Egypt, enriching a thin coterie of domestic brokers but crowding out locals from an unaffordable, inflated high-end property market. On the other hand, the same petro dollars also served as absolutely vital sources of revenue for remittances, tourism, and banking in these countries. Many an investment report created by lending institutions such as the IMF, taken by double-digit growth rates, was ecstatic over the investment boom and impressive GDP growth rates in Tunisia, Lebanon, or Egypt.

Yet while GDP more than doubled from 2000 to 2009 in Egypt, so did unemployment, which leapt to 26.3 percent on the eve of the revolution in 2010.[6] As prices continued to escalate (especially after 2007), net importers of commodities found themselves increasingly strapped for cash as outlays for energy and food subsidies squeezed state budgets.[7] Extreme poverty (the inability to meet basic food needs) soared from 5.4 percent to 6.4 percent of the population between 2005 and 2009 in Egypt.[8] In 2008, demonstrations erupted on the streets of Morocco and Egypt against the mere threat of a cut to bread subsidies, while renewed strikes occurred at the Egyptian Mahalla textile factory in protest against wages failing to keep up with rampant inflation. To make matters worse, a severe series of droughts, culminating in 2010, resulted in destroyed crops in Egypt, Syria, and Russia (the latter key swing producer taking the drastic decision to ban exports)—further exacerbating an already excruciating fiscal crunch.

As Albers and Peeters note, the abrupt temporary collapse of commodity prices in the last quarter of 2008 (see figure 3.1) did not really offer much of a respite insofar as GDP also contracted with the onset of the global recession.[9] As a result, subsidies per capita could even increase in this period in certain countries like Algeria. When wheat prices returned to their meteoric rise, spiking a massive 74 percent year-to-year from October 2009 to 2010, Egypt, the world's largest wheat importer, saw its subsidy bill skyrocket in tandem. This shock was too big to absorb by any regime, let alone a sclerotic thirty-year autocracy.

PRAETORIAN STATES FACING THE REVOLT OF THE MASSES: EGYPT AND TUNISIA

> I stress that subsidy provisions in their different forms must not be tampered with and that your government just challenge all forms of corruption.
>
> —President Mubarak in a letter to his
> Prime Minister Ahmed Shafiq, January 2011.[10]

The Arab world relies on 80 percent of imports to meet its food needs. Egypt ranks as the world's biggest consumer of bread and largest net importer of wheat and, along with Tunisia, Morocco, and Algeria, spends more on grain than any other emerging nation, at over 40 percent of total consumption per capita.[11] Over half of the average Egyptian household's income is expended on food and energy. Historically, this was not always the case. Egypt transformed from a net exporter to a net importer of food staples during the era of infitah liberalization under Anwar al-Sadat. It was also under Sadat that the specter of bread riots appeared for the first time, during the famous 1977 "revolution of bread" (*thawrat al-aish*), haughtily denigrated by Sadat as a "revolt of the midgets" (*thawrat al-aqzam*). Similar protests erupted again in 1985, 1988, and 1989 in Cairo, Tunisia, Algeria, and Jordan, respectively. Only in the last decade, however, did matters come to a head, although there were several prior red flags.

The continual deterioration of mean living standards in Egypt over the past twenty years is evident in the stagnant nominal wages coupled with steadily increasing price inflation for essential staples such as food and energy. Despite possessing 1.6 percent of the world's total known gas reserves, further production is hampered by the Ministry of Petroleum's falling into more than $4 billion in debt after subsidizing local prices and buying gas (and oil) at international rates. When, just before the uprising on January 25, 2011, the Mubarak regime ignored the nation's parliament and signed a fifteen-year contract to sell Egyptian gas to Israel at well-below market prices, the extent of the political and economic surrender was made apparent. The kickback shared by Mubarak's son Gamal and businessman Hussein Salem for this backroom deal amounted to a hefty commission of $187 million.[12] Adding insult to injury was the government's staunch refusal—or inability—to allow for a rise in the minimum wage from a paltry $100 to $240 per month.[13] The Egyptian minister of finance was already suffering from dwindling currency reserves and a catch-22: any stimulus was bound to further drain the treasury and stoke inflation, which would in turn necessitate further subsidies and wage increases.

While in 2011 global wheat prices surpassed even their 2008 all-time high, the Egyptian and Jordanian governments managed to retain and even expand the subsidies (in the Egyptian case to twenty-two million additional citizens), albeit at an ever-growing cost to the public treasury as is illustrated in the gray shades of figure 3.3. In less than a decade, the expenditure for wheat imports in Egypt increased five-fold to over $3.5 billion.

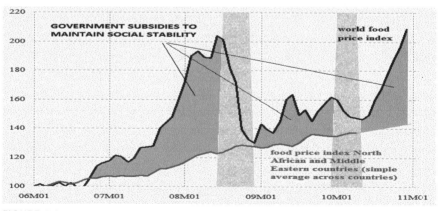

FIGURE 3.3

Source: Albers and Peeters (2011)

Aside from their tenuous fiscal sustainability, the fairness of the current subsidies has also been questioned, with smugglers trading on the black market and wealthy farmers abusing the system to feed cattle with subsidized wheat, according to the agronomist Abdel Salaam Gomaa.[14] As much as a quarter of subsidized flour ends up on the black market, where it fetches a multiple of the price.[15] Moreover, given the higher consumption patterns of the affluent, 83 percent of the bread and fuel subsidies go to the "nonpoor," and "nearly two-thirds to the rich, while a whopping 43.7 percent of Egyptians lived on less than two dollars a day in 2007."[16]

A majority of Egyptians had already been living in poverty for decades. Political pluralism had been suppressed since Nasser's one-party system. The public and educational infrastructure of the country suffered and deteriorated under Nasser's socialism, Sadat's liberalization, and Mubarak's sclerotic cronyism and oligarchy. Given the persistence of over a half century of autocratic, one-party rule in Egypt under Nasser, Sadat, and Mubarak, political repression, while certainly a source of aggravation, might not have been the primary catalyst for the uprisings. Rather than entering a, by now, hackneyed academic debate on the presumptive causes of the public insurrection of 2011, we may consider the viewpoint of the protagonists themselves.

ECONOMIC FACTORS FOMENTING THE UPRISINGS: WHAT DO THE POLLS SAY?

To emphasize the fiscal and economic factors leading up to the unrest of 2011 is not to downplay or dismiss other contributing factors. Electronic media played a role insofar as autocratic regimes could no longer control the unilateral flow of information. Yet to attribute the toppling of long-entrenched regimes to Facebook, Twitter, and Al Jazeera, or even a tragic figure like Bouazizi, is to confound the medium with the underlying message and motivation. The demographic youth bulge stands out as a much-cited common challenge across Arab states, with youth unemployment topping double digits and job creation and GDP growth unable to keep pace with new streams of graduates. In fact, in 2010, the Middle East and North Africa (MENA) region recorded the highest unemployment rate of any region in the world (though the GCC, Gulf Cooperation Council, indicatively, exhibited the lowest rate at 4 percent; see figure 3.4).

It may not strike one as the most "revolutionary" interpretation, but the conventional wisdom finds particular confirmation in the Arab world: congenial economic circumstances can mute the propensity of individuals to engage in political activities.[17] Conversely, democratic yearnings might well not be the

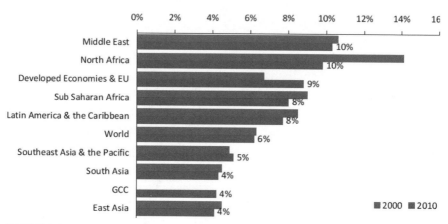

FIGURE 3.4
Unemployment rate across various regions
Source: MENA, 12

chief mainspring galvanizing mass protests. This, at least, seems to be the verdict of the available popular opinion surveys.

According to an independent poll taken in Tunisia, 13.9 percent of Tunisians identified political factors as the mainspring of the "Jasmine Revolution,"[18] while in another survey a whopping 64 percent of Egyptians cited "low living standards and lack of jobs" as the prime reason for their participation in protests.[19] A Pew study all but confirmed these findings: 82 percent of Egyptians ranked "improved economic conditions" as their top priority. Free speech and fair elections only made it to 63 percent and 55 percent, respectively, while the least-important concern was, tellingly, "uncensored access to the Internet," at only 35 and 27 percent, respectively.[20] What is more, socioeconomic issues eclipsed political concerns even more in the aftermath of the revolutions. In 2011, "living in a democratic country" was identified as a priority for 68 percent and "being paid a fair wage" for 63 percent of Arab youth. By 2012, however, fair wages were cited as "very important" by 83 percent, while democracy now was only identified by 58 percent as a prime concern (Arab youth, 14).[21] Looking to the future, 92 percent of Tunisians listed improved economic conditions as their top priority, echoing their Egyptian neighbors' preoccupation with earning a livelihood in a derelict economy.

Yet how far can we take what seems to be a strict economic determinism in interpreting political change in the Arab world? After all, revolution has thus far eluded the worst-performing member state of the Arab League in terms of runaway inflation, unemployment, and political divisions (to the degree of separatism): the Republic of Sudan. Its 40 percent inflation in the month of June 2013 alone would seem to make it an overripe candidate for an Arab Uprising, yet so far the Bashir regime has succeeded in its iron-fisted repression of any brewing revolt.[22] This raises the question of whether the Sudanese regime's showcased Islamic identity may have played a role in mollifying discontent and staving off a popular insurrection. In fact, none of the regimes toppled was explicitly an Islamic one. The subsequent ascendency of moderate and, increasingly, militant Islamist forces lends some currency to an ideological impetus driving recent events. Ironically, the chief proponent of a "Pan-Islamic revolution," Iran, stands to lose most should its vision unfold in the Sunni-majority nations in upheaval, most notably Iran's strategic ally Syria. Despite the increasingly unvarnished sectarian strife, to reduce the revolts to religious atavism is tantamount to neglecting the empirical evidence of a highly aggravated, even anarchic, socioeconomic (dis)order that even informs religious rhetoric. After all, it is the sea of despair and disorder that a more Islamic political system and the imposition of Sharia law is supposed to alleviate, according to its champions.

An empirical, graphic illustration of the comparative, inter-Arab risk assessment is provided by figure 3.5, which cross-tabulates GDP (per capita), adolescent unemployment, and the potential for unrest in Arab states. It suffers from some shortcomings, such as failing to capture intranational income disparities. Moreover, the demographic youth bulge could just as well be interpreted as an economic asset (as much as it has been bemoaned as a liability).

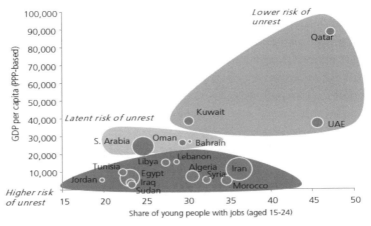

FIGURE 3.5

Source: Thomas Reuters, USB WMR as of 22 February 2011. Cited in Anderson, Reber, and Vayenas, "Global Financial Markets," Weath Management Research. UBS, February 24, 2011.

Expectedly, the above graph does place most oil-rich, "rentier" states in the lower-risk segment, with Qatar serving as the shining example due to its all-but-nonexistent unemployment, record GDP per capita, and phenomenal reserves. Yet are the Gulf-based hydrocarbon states uniformly exceptions to the rule, eternally immunized from the contagion of inflation and revolution due to their conservative facades and seemingly infinite capacity to disburse generous subsidies and preemptive payouts? This at least seemed to have been the logic behind the massive spending sprees in the oil states in the wake of the spreading unrest, with Kuwait distributing nearly 4000 USD to each family, while Algeria's and Saudi Arabia's announced stimulus programs exceeded a massive 100 billion USD each. Saudi Arabia has also made impressive strides in diversifying into a host of industries. Yet structural challenges persist in Saudi Arabia. Seventy percent of the population is under thirty, a full 92 percent of the labor force is employed in the public sector, and youth unemployment is reaching perilous proportions at 39 percent.[23] Exactly where the five million jobs deemed necessary by the Saudi Ministry of Labor by 2030 will be created remains an open question. For the moment, the Saudi state can afford to maintain this state-centric, energy-intensive, heavily subsidized, globally integrated economy, but there are signs of bottlenecks ahead. Its status as the largest oil producer in the world notwithstanding, Saudi Arabia is seeing more and more of its fuel consumed domestically, so much so that the kingdom will lose its reserve margin as soon as 2020 and consume all of its oil domestically by 2043.[24]

For the moment, the hydrocarbon cushion may postpone the day of reckoning, although several Gulf states are beginning to struggle with a dissatisfied body of citizens airing demands for freedom of expression. That the Arab Uprisings hitherto occurred almost uniformly in oil-importing nations of the Arab world should not come as a surprise. Nor should it be mistaken for a bill of immunity.

As indicated earlier, the case of Libya shows that the abundance of fossil fuels cannot be deemed the sole factor determining revolt or the absence thereof. Mismanagement, tribal and sectarian divisions, and unemployment seem to weigh more heavily. Of these, unemployment seems to be the most significant barometer. It is thus noteworthy that (revolutionary) Libya (with unemployment at 30 percent), Tunisia (18.7 percent), and Egypt (12.4 percent) were the only North African countries with double-digit unemployment, as opposed to the still status quo ante Morocco and Algeria (which, however, are not out of the woods by any means, despite mitigating macroeconomic factors such as tourism, constitutional reform, and hydrocarbon reserves). Interestingly, in Morocco the public sector accounts for only 10 percent of employment, while the labor market is somewhat better than in Egypt, Tunisia, and Jordan, perhaps shedding some light on the relative resilience of the economy there in the wake of the financial crisis.[25]

In the end, neither a showcased commitment to religion nor the surplus of a rentier state nor even the most ruthless praetorian military and security apparatus in and of itself can be deemed an iron-clad guarantee against inflation and its noxious effect on fixed wages and public welfare. After all, the rank and file of soldiers too must receive adequate salaries to obey orders, and mismanagement of oil wealth can entrench small cliques while exacerbating social divides to the degree of wreaking social havoc. Libya, Bahrain, and Algeria come to mind as cases in point. Prior to the revolt, Libya and Syria enjoyed almost zero percent debt per GDP and consistent budget surpluses. Citizens benefitted from free education, health care, and subsidized foodstuffs and energy. Yet even Gaddafi's late decision of a 150 percent increase in some public wages did little to quell the simmering anger in Benghazi and other peripheral areas of Libya. Similarly, it is by no means mere chance that popular uprisings first erupted in the rural and peripheral areas of Tunisia (Sidi Bouzid), Bahrain, and Syria (Idlib, Dera'a) while the lucrative sectors of the economy remained in the control of thin elites and nepotistic family networks.

This lack of equitable distribution of state revenue then lay at the core of the ensuing social imbalances and popular discontent. Syria's, Tunisia's, Libya's, and even Egypt's economies were growing too at a rate of 5 to 8 percent per annum, with tourism soaring in Syria by 46 percent in 2010. Tunisia's debt-to-GDP ratio stood at a modest 43 percent.[26] And yet surveys also show that by 2010 a growing number of citizens in these countries felt disenfranchised. Likewise, life expectancy and rates of education across the Arab realm over the course of a generation have outpaced almost all other regions of the world.[27] Yet Campante and Chor[28] have persuasively marshaled empirical evidence across Arab states suggesting that the combination of expanding educational levels and diminishing job opportunities in a contracting, postgraduation labor market is a particularly explosive formula for discontent, as a larger and larger segment of Arab graduates find themselves unemployed despite their degrees. Over a third of Egyptians, and over half of the unemployed in Cairo, held a university degree.[29] The jobless situation was no better in other Arab states, including Syria. And it was all too predictable that the fire of inflation and unemployment, irrespective of gross GDP growth rates, would fan intersectarian animosities in Syria, even as the political divides that came to the fore in Libya were primarily tribal-regional while Tunisia and Egypt split along largely ideological lines.

THE SECTARIAN PRISM OF SOCIAL STRATIFICATION: LEBANON, SYRIA, AND BAHRAIN

> Why is Syria stable, although we have more difficult conditions? Egypt has been supported financially by the United States, while we are under embargo by most countries of the world. We have growth although we do not have many of the basic needs for the people. Despite all that, the people do not go into an uprising. So it is not only about the needs and not only about the reform. It is about the ideology, the beliefs, and the cause that you have.
>
> —Bashar al-Assad, *Wall Street Journal*, January 31, 2011

One of the prevalent (mis)readings by both detractors and champions of the revolutions tends to mystify their socioeconomic origins, whether it be by reducing the Uprisings to ideological quests for lofty ideals such as dignity and democracy (as some Western media were prone to do) or by identifying nefarious agendas such as global conspiracies, militant theocracy, and terrorism as the root cause of revolt (as both the Libyan and Syrian regimes were wont to claim). This is not to gainsay either democratic or sectarian motivations—or even possible outcomes. Far from denying either confessional or class-based motivations, a proper analysis must consider the interplay of both elements, thus transcending the myopia of a binary lens.

Bashar al-Assad's above quotation, for instance, while conceding the plight of the people, still reflects an underestimation of the sheer extent of the economic malaise he was facing. According to the official numbers released by his own ministry, prices in Syria increased by 32.5 percent from May 2011 to May 2012, while government revenue fell by 40 percent and exports declined from twelve to four billion USD in 2012.[30] The sanctions imposed on Syria by the United States, the European Union, and the Arab League were estimated to deprive the Syrian treasury of $400 million a month.[31]

Yet even prior to the outbreak of hostilities between opposition forces and the government, the writing was on the wall. Syria's very high unemployment rate of 21 percent in 2010 stood out compared to official unemployment statistics in Bahrain, which were usually quite moderate at only 5 percent (even though this rate soars to 38 percent among Shia youth).[32] Add to that the highly unrealistic expectation of over 80 percent of Syrian graduates of finding a job in the public-sector (with a full 60 percent completely ruling out private sector employment), and one gets a stark notion of the dead end that Arab economy was like and where it was heading. Like other Arab states such as Yemen, Jordan, and Tunisia, a demographic death sentence was hovering above Syria. From a strictly demographic perspective, scholars such as George Saghir have long pointed out that Syria's growth was unsustainable. In a prescient piece published in early 2011, Saghir noted that Egypt's and Syria's fertility rate in 2010 (3.01) was far higher than Turkey's, which stood at 2.18, let alone the United States' (1.95) or Europe's (1.64). Thus, Saghir concluded, for Syria to achieve Turkey's per capita growth rate of the past twenty-five years, it had to do one of two things: (1) it had to grow its economy by a real inflation-adjusted 8.5 percent if population growth were to continue at 3.26 percent, or (2) it could grow by a real inflation-adjusted 6.5 percent if it were to succeed in slowing its population growth down to Turkey's current level of 1.25 percent. Either option presents a formidable challenge and highlights the feat that Turkey has pulled off since 1980.[33] This uphill battle notwithstanding, Syria, ironically enough, was one of the very few Arab countries that was self-sustaining in terms of its food needs. Yet in wake of the massive disruption caused by the raging violence and international sanctions, the Food and Agricultural Organization predicted two billion dollar losses in the sector, with three million Syrians in need of nutritional assistance as the escalating civil war and unaffordable fuel costs make farming impossible in swaths of the disintegrating country.[34] Moreover, Syria too was severely exposed to the price spike in essential foodstuffs such as sugar and oil, at first announcing, then quickly retracting, plans to annul subsidies in August 2011 as the rebellion started to gain momentum in the deprived, largely Sunni, rural regions of the country.

Thus emerges a key argument of this chapter: while by 2010, escalating inflation and unemployment became universally observable sources of insufferable strain, these pressures were refracted differently according to the characteristics of each particular state; both the social makeup from the "bottom" and the economic policies pursued "from the top" proved decisive. There is little doubt that social and sectarian fissures in very highly segmented states such as Syria and Lebanon certainly compounded what was, at its origin, an economic crisis. Yet while Lebanon and Syria share a multi-confessional social tapestry, their respective political systems have mediated diversity differently. If sectarian identity were always the dominant frame of analysis and criterion for political power in Lebanon's "association of minorities," the sectarian composition of the Syrian state under the Assad regime bears closer resemblance to a "veiled protectorate" of a dominant (Alawite) minority that dares not speak its name. Formally speaking, the weak, decentralized Lebanese state is at once more sectarian and more secular than its Syrian counterpart. While the Lebanese constitution does not identify any state religion, it does enshrine confessional quotas. The Assad regime (both father and son) has been judicious in its effort to publically portray its Muslim credentials while also emphasizing its paternalistic, trans-sectarian identity, albeit only indirectly by warning of a potential rise of Islamic-terrorist mayhem in the case of its demise. The increasingly shrill sectarian slogans and acts of segments of a radicalized opposition are unfortunately contributing to an eerie confirmation of this specter of fundamentalism.

A surreptitious sectarianism informs appointments to political—and even more so security-related—positions in Syria with an Alawite praetorian guard controlling key positions. Officially, however, the regime is intent to constantly downplay or deliberately ignore sectarian issues. In Lebanon, by contrast, political sectarianism is not denied but constitutionally enshrined and frequently demagogically exploited. We also find a distinct tendency in Lebanon to (over)-interpret originally economic grievances (such as those festering in the overwhelmingly destitute districts in and around Tripoli) as sectarian struggles. It is of course true that a dangerous, wide cleft between pro- and anti-Syrian and between Shia and Sunni Lebanese had already appeared immediately after the assassination of Rafiq al-Hariri. Today, the split could not be more apparent.[35]

Still, this chapter maintains that the confessional pluralism of Syria and Lebanon has only turned into violent sectarian strife in wake of severe economic stress, which is partly regional and partly global in origin. In this context, we ought to consider that food and gasoline inflation in Lebanon has outstripped all other Arab states, in part because price hikes were compounded by monopolies that dominate the Lebanese market in both the fuel and food sectors.[36] Considering its chronic social and economic deficiencies, derelict state, and fuel-dependent energy sector, Lebanon seems like an all-too-vulnerable victim: it is at once exposed to the global commodity inflation economically but has to cope additionally with the brewing regional storm arriving from Syria politically. In the end, both the "softest" and "hardest" states of the Arab world, Lebanon and Syria, are under existential threat.

THE ARAB STATE UNDER ASSAULT: PRIVATIZATION AS A PANACEA OR PERIL?

The last decade of financial integration, currency devaluation, and commodity inflation has unhinged the status quo ante balance of power in the Middle

East. Globalization has proven a double-edged sword, producing both victors and victims. Certain states—chiefly the oil-rich Gulf states—or sectors—such as the banking and tourism sector in Lebanon—were better positioned to draw benefit and, in the case of Qatar, even ascend to the status of global economic and diplomatic superpowers. Other, more populous, states—Egypt, Tunisia, Yemen, Syria—remained more exposed to the eddies of the free market. Likewise, we find that the impact of privatization differed from state to state. Economic liberalization, for instance, aggravated rather than attenuated social tensions and public debt in Egypt, Tunisia, Syria, and postwar Lebanon, while at the same time allowing Gulf states to leverage newfound wealth gained through trade and an opening to global markets.

In the run-up to the Arab Uprisings, privatization was running full steam ahead, with government companies being sold off one by one.[37] The problem was that this process was done in such a way as to benefit a very small elite of regime favorites while leaving a disgruntled group of former officials and businessmen empty-handed. In observing the last wave of privatization after 1990 across the region, we find the poorly executed free-market reform has entrenched an ever-narrowing circle of crony capitalists while all too often saddling the state with debt.[38] As Amy Chua and others have pointed out for other countries,[39] the very basic aims of the discourse of (egalitarian) democracy and (polarizing) free markets might be at loggerheads. Across the Arab world, the past decade of economic liberalization has enriched a business class of regime affiliates who benefited from preferential treatment and reaped windfall profits at the expense of the state coffers. In Syria's case, much—though not all—of this elite was Alawite (with Christian and Sunni cronies). In Bahrain, it was predominately Sunni. In Egypt, Libya, and Tunisia, cronies of the Mubarak, Gaddafi, and Ben Ali clans reaped most of the revenue, alienating broad segments of the population.

Statistically, economic reform in Egypt in the two decades resulted in the shrinking of the public sector from 67 percent in 1990 to 38 percent in 2008.[40] These numbers may be taken with a grain of salt given the blurred lines between public and private, particularly as concerns the vast network of industries owned by the military. Overall, wages in a still-bloated public sector failed to keep up with runaway inflation.[41] Therein lies the rub: the state that collapsed was, in the words of Galal Amin,[42] a "soft authoritarian state": unable to deliver on the promise of secure jobs and public infrastructure and services, state authority was further undermined by corruption and its desperate attempt to violently clamp down on any form of genuine opposition. Yet states cannot persist by the gun alone, especially once the bread becomes unaffordable. In some cases, this point of no return was symbolized by an individual act (Bouazizi in Tunisia) or by popular demonstrations in the capital (Egypt), while external intervention hastened the day of reckoning in Libya and Syria with sanctions severely aggravating an already difficult situation.

In light of the growing social stratification, it seems all the more astonishing that the regimes that have come to the fore in lieu of the previous privatizers have in general sought to work with the status quo ante international financial lending institutions such as the IMF, the United States, and the World Bank. Radical leftists, insofar as they were part of the vanguard of the January 25, 2011, demonstrations in Egypt, for instance, have been marginalized at the ballot box. The Islamist parties remain, of course, effectively involved in a host of social welfare programs, but, in the grand scheme of things, socialism in the traditional sense has not made a comeback.

This despite the fact that, from a strictly economic perspective, the much-vaunted Arab Uprisings have been nothing short of a nightmare, with costs running into the tens of billions of dollars. For the first time since 1986, the Tunisian economy contracted in 2011. Egypt is still reeling from a drying-up of foreign-currency reserves and a decline in tourism. In Morocco, one of the few countries to have eluded the wave of revolution, the king's reforms cannot forestall plummeting revenues and rising deficits. The government, albeit benefiting from a robust tourist industry, is gradually running out of resources to raise subsidies and salaries and buy social peace.

Even in the most optimistic scenarios, none of the states will be able to produce an economic growth rate necessary to supplying the jobs for an ever-growing pool of graduates. Overall, some eighty million new jobs within the next two decades were deemed necessary according to a 2007 World Bank report. This race seems to have been lost already. The situation is exacerbated in Syria by the tightening noose of sanctions and inflation, which has risen from 4.4 percent in 2010 to 12.4 percent thus far in 2012, amid a devastating civil war that also contributed to a 5.9 percent contraction of the strangled economy, a trend that no doubt has since only gained in momentum.[43] It would seem that there is no exit from the Arab states afflicted by global inflationary pressures given that some of the sources of their tribulations are external in origin. There is the example of Argentina, which, drowning in debt, attempted to decouple from global financial markets. This, however, seems like a far-fetched scenario for now.

CONCLUSION

> The task of preventing inflation has always seemed to me to be of the greatest importance, not only because of the harm and suffering major inflations cause, but also because I have long been convinced that even mild inflations ultimately produce the recurring depressions and unemployment which have been a justified grievance against the free enterprise system and must be prevented if a free society is to survive.
>
> —Friedrich von Hayek

Across the history of the Middle East, inflationary periods, along with wars, have always coincided with unprecedented profit opportunities. This was true during the World Wars, but also during wars in and between individual Arab states. Broadly speaking, the trajectory of non-oil-producing Middle Eastern economies has always dovetailed with the ups and downs of the global economy. Periods of galloping inflation usually appeared in the Middle East in the shadow of global and regional wars (examples are World Wars I and II, the Arab-Israeli War of 1973, etc.) and economic liberalization (Sadat's infitah). These eras were followed by the 1990s crony capitalism, while the twenty-first century ushered in the total financialization of economies around the globe, diverting vital capital away from production into speculative, rent-seeking investments. Given this integral historical relationship between Arab and global economies, this chapter has argued that it is misleading to view the recent dramatic political events in the region in complete isolation from the ongoing global economic stagflation.

To wit, the global competitive currency devaluation instigated by the US Fed and central banks after 2008 triggered inflationary pressures around the globe. The precipitous run-up in commodity prices, especially in 2010, was, it was argued, the proverbial straw that broke the camel's back. Ironically, the fiscal and monetary spending spree pursued by Ben Bernanke and both the Bush and Obama administrations as responses to the financial crisis after 2008 serves as a template for local regimes desperate to buy off discontent. Thus Egypt has, in a desperate attempt to stave off the inevitable, raised public-sector wages by 15 percent, but it is difficult to see how such Band-Aids can be sustained. The Egyptian central bank has repeatedly expanded the money supply (at the time of writing, the Egyptian pound had already lost almost one-quarter of its value vis-à-vis the dollar), although this begs the question of whether one can print oneself out of a fiscal and monetary crisis. History suggests this is a recipe for disaster. To be sure, the United States, the European Union, and China have pursued similar strategies, but this global competitive devaluation is, along with the speculation with easy money provided to banks by the Fed and central banks in wake of "quantitative easing," precisely one of the underlying causes for commodity inflation and the resultant social unrest.

It will be difficult for Arab states to extricate themselves completely from this vicious spiral of commodity price inflation, currency debasement, and other disruptions in global supply chains. This critical global interdependency was recently confirmed by the severe drought that afflicted the Midwestern United States in the summer of 2012, due to which the Egyptian government was forced to double the allocation for food subsidies in an already squeezed budget.[44]

In the last quarter of 2010, the Egyptian government, which relies almost exclusively on oil and gas for its energy needs, was increasingly reeling to keep fuel subsidies in line with the renewed upsurge of oil prices. The day of reckoning may have been postponed for the moment after the estimated shortfall of $11 billion over the next two years was bridged with a $4.8 billion IMF loan. But, as in the West, all this implies is that debt is being covered with more debt while debt servicing eats up growing percentages of the budget. Greater hope may be pinned on the State of Qatar's whopping $18 billion support package, which will provide investment, fiscal aid, and low-interest, one-percent loans to provide monetary reserves for the struggling Egyptian Central Bank. Similar infusions have staved off a collapse of the Lebanese and Tunisian banking systems in times of acute crisis thus far. A regional conflagration, however, is a different matter, as it would be bound to also raise borrowing costs for the creditor Gulf states.

Overall, we are, however, confronted with the bleak image of most MENA states still teetering on the brink of fiscal bankruptcy. While the media have not been keen on covering them, incidents of self-immolation have increased across the Arab world since Bouaziz's tragic precedent, with despondent youths setting themselves afire in Morocco, Tunisia, Jordan, and Bahrain without drawing due concern.[45]

Structurally, even without the added pressure of commodity price inflation and regional turmoil, there is a stark realization that the subsidy regimes across the region will have to be reformed so as to provide more incentives for the long-neglected agricultural sector while directing compensation schemes to those who need it most.[46] The Arab economies are in dire need of an economic revolution after the political upheaval, but so is the highly interdependent global economic and financial system at large.

As the testimony of one affluent Syrian businessman shows, once the social fabric frays, peace and tranquility can no longer be taken for granted, even for those wallowing in wealth. Writes Janine di Giovanni, "A few days later, I'm standing with an architect on the balcony of her elegant, Italianate villa, watching people line up for gasoline down below. (International sanctions have created severe economic problems—even for the wealthy). As we hear the ominous choppy noise of helicopters overhead, she comments, 'This is the music we live by. And I fear this will be our symphony for the next few years.'"[47]

NOTES

1. In an interview with the *Wall Street Journal* published on January 31, 2011, Assad recognized the economic impetus of the unrest across the Arab world but claimed Syria was immune to likely upheaval. "Interview with President Assad," *Wall Street Journal*, January 31, 2011, http://online.wsj.com/article/SB10001424052748703833204576114712441122894.html.

2. The gigantic expansion of the monetary base must, however, not be confounded with the increase in the money supply or currency in circulation. "The monetary base includes currency (including coin) held outside the Treasury and the Federal Reserve Banks (referred to as *currency in circulation*) plus deposits held by depository institutions at the Federal Reserve Banks." Richard G. Anderson, Robert H. Rasche, and Jeffrey Loesel, "A Reconstruction of the Federal Reserve Bank of St. Louis Adjusted Monetary Base and Reserves," *St. Louis Reserve*, September/October 2003, last accessed July 27, 2012, http://research.stlouisfed.org/publications/review/03/09/Anderson.pdf, 41.

3. Another hypothesis put forward by the World Bank identifies ethanol production and rampant speculation as the culprit for the spike in food prices. While the US government has discounted the impact of biofuels on aggregate fuel-price increases (3 percent) as negligible (Chakrabortty 2008), one might nonetheless contend that without the loose monetary policy of the Federal Reserve, the excessive leveraging that accounts for the enormous profits (and losses) of the derivative speculators (who were exempted from trading limits since 1999) would not have been possible. Aditya Chakrabortty, "Secret Report: Biofuel Caused Food Crisis," *Guardian*, July 3, 2008, http://www.theguardian.com/environment/2008/jul/03/biofuels.renewableenergy.

4. Some scholars have preferred a further disaggregation, adding sub-Saharan Arab countries such as the Sudan, Mauritania, and Yemen. James E. Rauch and Scott Kostyshak, "The Three Arab Worlds," *Journal of Economic Perspectives* 23, no. 3 (Summer 2009): 165–88.

5. Lin Noueihed and Alex Warren, *The Battle for the Arab Spring: Revolution, Counter-revolution, and the Making of a New Era* (Yale University Press, 2012), 27.

6. Hazim Kandil, "Why Did the Egyptian Middle Class March to Tahrir Square?" *Mediterranean Politics* 17, no. 2 (2012): 197–215, 210.

7. Deaton has established this ambivalence in economic theory. Angus Deaton, "Household Survey Data and Pricing Policies in Developing Countries," *World Bank Economic Review* 3, no. 2 (1989): 183–210.

8. Soheir Aboulenein, Heba El-Laithy, Omneia Helmy, Hanaa Kheir-El-Din, and Dina Mandour, "Impact of the Global Food Price Shock on the Poor in Egypt," Working Paper

157, Center for Social and Economic Research and the Egyptian Center for Economic Stud-ies, Cairo, May 2010, http://www.eces.org.eg/Uploaded_Files/%7B675AC79D-26C6-4AC3-8C69 -C6A50B2E7CD9%7D_WP%20157%20formatted%20by%20Fatma%20May%206.pdf

9. R. Albers and M. Peeters, "Food and Energy Prices, Government Subsidies, and Fiscal Balances in South Mediterranean Countries," European Commission Economic Papers, No. 437 (2011).

10. "Mubarak Orders State Subsidies," Al Jazeera, January 31, 2011, last accessed January 31, 2012, http://www.aljazeera.com/news/middleeast/2011/01/201113101237787481.html.

11. The *Wall Street Journal* notes that "the sharp rise in food prices in these countries has inevi-tably a much greater impact on living standards than the US, UK, or Japan, where food is just 7.2%, 8.7%, and 14.3% respectively." Simon Nixon, "Mideast Turmoil: Made in America?" *Wall Street Journal,* February 2, 2011, last accessed July 30, 2012, http://online.wsj.com/article/SB10001424052 748703445904576118392320337766.html.

12. The new Egyptian government canceled the skewed contract on April 22, 2012 and subse-quently sentenced Salem and former oil minister Samih Fahmi to fifteen years in prison. "Mubarak Sons Got Millions from Israel Gas Deal," *Al Arabiya*, March 7, 2011, last accessed July 30, 2012, http://www.alarabiya.net/articles/2011/03/07/140510.html.

13. Salwa Ismail, "A Private Estate Called Egypt," *Guardian,* February 6, 2011, http://www .guardian.co.uk/commentisfree/2011/feb/06/private-estate-egypt-mubarak-cronies.

14. Charles Hanley, "It's Costly to Keep Egypt's Daily Bread Cheap," *NBC News*, March 28, 2011, http://www.msnbc.msn.com/id/42303838/ns/business-world_business/t/its-costly-keep-egypts -daily-bread-cheap/#.UAWXpjFihvA.

15. Megan Detrie, "US Drought Means Egypt May Look Elsewhere for Wheat," *Egypt Inde-pendent*, July 27, 2012, last accessed July 30, 2012, http://www.egyptindependent.com/news/us -drought-means-egypt-may-look-elsewhere-wheat.

16. Soheir Aboulenein, Heba El-Laithy, Omneia Helmy, Hanaa Kheir-El-Din, and Dina Mandour, "Impact of the Global Food Price Shock on the Poor in Egypt," Working Paper 157, Center for Social and Economic Research and the Egyptian Center for Economic Studies, Cairo, May 2010, 9, http://www.eces.org.eg/Uploaded_Files/%7B675AC79D-26C6-4AC3-8C69 -C6A50B2E7CD9%7D_WP%20157%20formatted%20by%20Fatma%20May%206.pdf.

17. Kerwin Kofi Charles and Melvin Stephens Jr., "Local Labour Market Shocks and Voter Turn-out: The Role of Political Attentiveness," Mimeo, 2009.

18. Michael Robbins and Mark Tessler, "Tunisians Voted for Jobs, Not Islam," *Foreign Policy Magazine,* December 7, 2011, last accessed July 1, 2012, http://mideastafrica.foreignpolicy.com/ posts/2011/12/07/tunisians_voted_for_jobs_not_islam.

19. International Republican Institute, "Egyptian Public Opinion Survey, April 14–27, 2011, http://www.iri.org/sites/default/files/2011%20June%205%20Survey%20of%20Egyptian%20Public %20Opinion,%20April%2014-27,%202011_0.pdf.

20. Pew Research Center Global Attitudes Project, "One Year Later: Egyptians Remain Opti-mistic, Embrace Democracy, and Religion in Political Life," May 8, 2012, http://www.pewglobal .org/files/2012/05/Pew-Global-Attitudes-Project-Egypt-Report-FINAL-May-8-2012-2PM-ET.pdf.

21. Ibid.

22. Sara El Deeb, "Sudanese Struggle to Ignite Their Own Revolution," *Guardian,* July 27, 2012, http://www.guardian.co.uk/world/feedarticle/10356703.

23. Noueihed and Warren, *The Battle for the Arab Spring*, 37.

24. Jim Krane, "The End of the Saudi Oil Reserve Margin," *Wall Street Journal*, April 3, 2012, http://online.wsj.com/news/articles/SB10001424052702303816504577319571732227492.

25. Jad Chaaban, "Job Creation in the Arab Economies: Navigating through Difficult Waters," UNDP (2010), 17.

26. Noueihed and Warren, *The Battle for the Arab Spring*, 40, 66.

27. Omar S. Dahi, "Understanding the Political Economy of the Arab Revolts," *Middle East Research Information Project (MERIP)* Vol. 41, Summer 2011.

28. Filipe Campante and Davin Chor, *Journal of Economic Perspectives* 26, no. 2 (Spring 2012): 167–88.

29. Noueihed and Warren, *The Battle for the Arab Spring*, 38.

30. Sammy Ketz, "Syria's Battling Economy May Hold on with Help from Friends," *AFP*, August 19, 2012.

31. "Sanctions against Syria: As Effective as Bullets, Maybe," *Economist*, December 3, 2011, http://www.economist.com/node/21541078.

32. Hasan Tariq Alhasan, "The Socio-economic Foundations of Bahrain's Political Crisis," *Open Democracy*, February 20, 2012, last accessed July 27, 2012, http://www.opendemocracy.net/hasan-tariq-alhasan/socio-economic-foundations-of-bahrain%E2%80%99s-political-crisisof.

33. George Saghir, "What Does the Future Hold for Syria?" *Syrian Politics, History, and Religion* (blog), *Syria Comment*, February 6, 2011, http://www.joshualandis.com/blog/what-does-the-future-hold-for-syria-by-george-saghir/.

34. Food and Agriculture Organization, "Three Million Syrians Need Food, Crops, and Livestock Assistance," August 2, 2012, http://www.fao.org/news/story/en/item/153731/icode/.

35. Pew Research Global Attitudes Project, "Widespread Condemnation for Assad in Neighboring Countries," June 21, 2012, http://www.pewglobal.org/2012/06/21/widespread-condemnation-for-assad-in-neighboring-countries/.

36. *Annahar*, August 27, 2011, Beirut, 13.

37. Over one-third of the public enterprises were sold in Egypt in the 1990s. Timothy Mitchell, "*Rule of Experts: Egypt, Techno-Politics, Modernity*" (University of California Press, 2002), 280.

38. Heydemann and Leenders, "Resilient Authoritarianism in the Middle East: Lessons from Syria and Iran and Implications for Democracy Promotion," Policy Paper 2, *Knowledge Programme Civil Society in West Asia* (The Hague: Hivos and the University of Amsterdam, March 2011), 5.

39. Amy Chua, *World on Fire: How Exporting Free Market Democracy Breeds Ethnic Hatred and Global Instability* (New York: Anchor Books, 2004).

40. Noueihed and Warren, *The Battle for the Arab Spring*, 112.

41. Kandil, "Why Did the Egyptian Middle Class March," 207.

42. Quoted in Noueihed and Warren, *The Battle for the Arab Spring Revolution*.

43. "Opposition Draws on Many Groups to Fight Assad," *Deutsche Welle* (2011). Last accessed on July 21, 2011 at http://www.dw.de/dw/article/0,,16116453,00.html.

44. Megan Detrie, "US Drought Means Egypt May Look Elsewhere for Wheat," *Egypt Independent*, July 27, 2012, http://www.egyptindependent.com/news/us-drought-means-egypt-may-look-elsewhere-wheat.

45. Nada Bakri, "Self-Immolation on the Rise in the Arab World," *New York Times*, January 20, 2012.

46. Albers and Peeters, "Food and Energy Prices."

47. Janine di Giovanni, "Champagne Flows while Syria Burns," *Daily Beast*, June 7, 2012, last accessed July 30, 2012, http://www.thedailybeast.com/newsweek/2012/07/08/champagne-flows-while-syria-burns.html.

4

The Political and Socioeconomic Origins of the Arab Uprisings: A Trinomial Probability Analysis

PETER TIKUISIS AND ANTON MINKOV

The large-scale civil unrest in Tunisia that ended the twenty-four-year rule of President Zine El Abidine Ben Ali in January 2011 ignited similar movements in other countries of the Middle East and North Africa (MENA). Besides Tunisia, the most significant upheavals occurred and continue in Egypt, Libya, Syria, Bahrain, and Yemen, while smaller-scale protests have occurred in Saudi Arabia, Jordan, and Oman. These popular uprisings have initiated a process of political change in the region whose impact may take many years fully play out and be assessed.

No less important, however, is the question about the factors that contributed to the Uprisings. Few people can deny that, despite the preponderance of sophisticated forecasting tools for state instability and decades of scholarship on the modern Arab societies and politics, none successfully anticipated the ignition, the intensity, and the rapid spread of the Uprisings.[1] The massive repressive security systems established by the regimes seemed too powerful to allow the expression of popular discontent, let alone its ability to force regime change or significant political concessions.

As a result of this "surprise factor," the study of the origins of the Arab Uprisings has attracted considerable attention. According to Timo Behr, the origins discourse could be broadly placed into four different narratives.[2] One line of thought points to the structural weaknesses of the MENA authoritarian systems and economies,[3] another considers external factors borne by the increased globalization in the last decade,[4] a third focuses on the ideological dimensions of the Uprisings, and, finally, the fourth seeks explanation through the technological change that enabled the mass mobilization against the regimes.[5] To these four categories we can also add established indices that track global weaknesses—for example, the Polity IV State Fragility Index (SF-Polity),[6] the Institute for Economics' Peace Global Peace Index (GPI),[7] the Country Indicators for Foreign Policy State Fragility Index (SF-CIFP),[8] and so on. Although not specifically designed for the MENA region, these indices are often consulted by policy makers for gauging potential social upheavals.

However, a number of counterarguments could be raised against singling out factors such as globalization and ideology. For example, some of their proponents fail to acknowledge that food-price increases in countries such as Algeria are not connected with global inflation but simply with the removal of food subsidies and imposition of regulations aimed at modernizing the economy. Furthermore, "food riots" have occurred regularly through the last decade and have coincided not only with the increase of the UN's Food and Agriculture Organization (FAO) Food Price Index but also with its descent from a peak in 2008.[9] Labeling the 2011 social unrest primarily as political revolutions against "sultanistic dictatorships"[10] could also be questioned. In some instances (for example, Egypt), the protests were manipulated by factions in the elite to execute an internal coup. There, the military elite, which constitutes a business conglomerate (in control of as much as 40 percent of the Egyptian economy), had been at odds with Mubarak over his son's attempts to break this monopoly.[11] In most countries, connections to political parties were absent and protests were dominated by social and economic demands. In Saudi Arabia, for example, political demands beyond local issues did not call for more than constitutional monarchy and more rights for women.[12]

Although the social upheaval appeared to be nothing short of popular revolutions against dictatorial, oppressive regimes (and that is mostly how they have been presented in the Western media[13])—which explains the emphasis on ideological aspects of the Uprisings among some scholars—the protestors also expressed significant socioeconomic grievances, such as high levels of unemployment, rampant inflation, and lack of housing, among others.[14] The predominantly youthful characteristic of the street demonstrations was also evident, thereby pointing to MENA demographics as a contributing factor for the unrest.[15] However, it was rightfully observed that the structural factors are rather nonuniform across the region.[16] For example, with the exception of Yemen and Saudi Arabia (two countries where the Uprisings have been of very different natures), fertility rates and the corresponding youth bulge have started to recede among MENA countries.[17] Furthermore, socioeconomic conditions in Egypt and Tunisia had actually improved just before the Uprisings. Several Arab countries (Saudi Arabia, Tunisia, Algeria, Oman, and Morocco) were also among the most improved in the UN Human Development Index in 2010.[18] These differences may have contributed to the different expressions of the power and intensity of the Uprisings within the region, which leads us to another major issue of debate—whether the causes for the Arab Uprisings were "universalistic" or country-specific. In our opinion, the rapid spread of the Uprisings among all MENA countries, regardless of the amplitude of the expression, suggests the existence of a set of common underlying factors. This position does not reject arguments for country-specific factors that may have also played a role, which would add variance to the grouped common-factor analysis presented in the following.

Finally, the global fragility indices mentioned above have also turned out to be poor gauges for the events that unfolded in MENA in 2011. For example, according to the SF-Polity 2010, Syria had the same chance of stability as Saudi Arabia and Tunisia, while Libya was listed as the most stable MENA country; clearly both estimates were far from the reality of upheaval that followed in 2011. The low explanatory value of these indices will be demonstrated empirically later in the chapter. An exception is the *Economist*'s Shoe-Thrower's Index, which seems to provide a relatively accurate picture of the region, based on nine indicators of varying weights and billed as the "index of unrest in the Arab world."[19] It is designed specifically with the MENA region in mind and is intuitively appealing. However, no statistically backed rationale is disclosed for the selection of these indicators including their weights. Also absent in their assessment is a clearly defined dependent variable to test the goodness-of-fit (validity) of the index.

The objective of this chapter is to investigate the underpinnings of the contemporary sociopolitical upheaval in the MENA countries by considering aspects of the approaches identified in the previous. The chapter will examine the typology of the unrest and regime responses and will employ both qualitative and quantitative methods of assessment. The chapter proposes a dependent variable—collective political violence (CPV)—that characterizes the nature and intensity of the Uprisings, which, if sufficiently high, can threaten the security of a state (both of those governing and governed) and its political structure. It will introduce a trinomial probability analysis to address the deviation of the Uprisings' power at three levels, and it will utilize an empirical method for statistically testing candidate indicators. This method will enable the study to test the causal relation of a wide variety of political, economic, social, and demographic factors, despite their different expressions, to the rise of unrest in the region as a whole.

The geographical scope of the research includes fifteen countries: Algeria, Bahrain, Egypt, Jordan, Kuwait, Lebanon, Libya, Morocco, Qatar, Oman, Tunisia, Saudi Arabia, Syria, UAE, and Yemen. Four countries were excluded from the study—Iran, whose "Iranian Spring" may have occurred in 2009 and, although it may have been driven by similar factors, seemed somewhat disconnected from the events of 2011; Iraq, because the 2003 US invasion significantly altered the political and socioeconomic dynamics of the country; Israel, because of its political system's distinction from those of the Arab states; and the West Bank and Gaza, due to their status as occupied territories. The temporal parameters of the study are January to August 2011, inclusive.

METHODOLOGY

Data Collection

The study collected a wide variety of regional political, economic, social, and demographic domain data for the period immediately preceding the Arab Uprisings (2009–2010) in order to characterize the environmental preconditions for the Uprisings. The selection of these domains was largely driven by our objective to capture the full range of factors that may have been influential, as well as to match the types of indicators used in the Shoe-Thrower's Index and several other indices. We recognize that these domain data can be further classified under various typologies such as causal, correlational, and facilitative. We assumed that certain indicators, such as unemployment rates, may offer a direct linkage to the unrest with explanatory power and are thus highly valued not only for modelling purposes, but also for the possibility that such conditions, once identified as casual, are potentially contingent to corrective intervention to alleviate negative tensions. Correlational indicators are those that may be associated with a causal factor that cannot be directly measured and thus can serve as proxy indicators of unrest—for example, a political leader's years in power as a proxy for political legitimacy/corruption. On the other hand, factors such as those associated with media technology (for example, cell phone users' growth rates and Internet penetration) are considered enabling tools that might accelerate the unrest and/or provide real-time mood assessment. Such indicators are deemed facilitative and not causal *per se*; hence, they are hereafter ignored for the purposes of this study into the origins of the Uprisings.

Indicators such as democracy and corruption levels are regarded as within the political domain. Economic domain data include unemployment rates, inflation (including its food-prices component), the GINI coefficient (a measure of income disparity), real GDP rates, GDP growth, and GDP per capita at purchase power parity (PPP). Social indicators include literacy rates, education levels, urbanization rates, and ethnic-sectarian tensions that exist(ed) in the society. Demographic characteristics comprise data related to population density, the population under twenty-five, the fighting age cohort (fifteen to twenty-nine years old), life expectancy, infant-mortality rate, ethnicity, religious affiliation, and the ratio of the fighting-age cohort to all working adults. The data were derived from credible open sources such as the CIA World Factbook, the *Economist*'s Intelligence Unit, the World Bank, the International Monetary Fund, the UN Population Division, the UN's Food and Agriculture Organization (FAO), the Penn World Table, various official releases, and our research. Food-price inflation was sourced through the statistical reports of central banks or central statistical organizations of the individual MENA countries included in this study. Indices such as the Fund for Peace State Failure index (FSI),[20] Freedom House's Political Rights (PR) and Civil Liberties (CL) indices,[21] Polity IV State Fragility Index (SF-Polity), the Country Indicators for Foreign Policy State Fragility Index (SF-CIFP), the Institute for Economics and Peace Global Peace Index (GPI), and the Heidelberg Conflict Barometer (HCB) comprise data from several of these domains.[22]

In some instances, reliable figures were extremely difficult to obtain and only the best available estimates could be applied. Especially unreliable were data on unemployment rates. In particular, the official figures released by certain regimes seemed misleadingly low, and the gaps with the rates reported from other sources were significant. For example, the "official" unemployment rates of Syria and Yemen were 12.6 and 15.7 percent, respectively, while they were usually estimated by international agencies at 20 and 35 percent, respectively. In these situations, the independent estimates were considered as the more likely figures. In other cases, the data set was improved by a qualitative analysis of the specific situation within a country. For example, the official unemployment rate in Bahrain was reported at 3.5 percent, which is clearly not conducive to social unrest. However, considering that a significant portion of Bahrain's population is comprised of foreign workers and that the majority of the protestors came from the native Shia Arab population, it became obvious that the unemployment rate among the latter (as high as 25 percent) is the relevant figure in this case.[23] Further, the exclusion of Bahrain's foreign-workers population from the demographic figures[24] also changed the value of the country's youth bulge from 38 to 50 percent—that is, one that exerted higher pressure on the political system than official figures would have suggested.

Another variable that proved difficult to collect was data on the fluctuation of food prices in the region. Most studies that attribute the origins of the Uprisings to food-price increases use the information provided by the UN's Food and Agriculture Organization. FAO's Food Price Index, however, is global; it does not acknowledge regional or country differences and, thus, we deem it too imprecise for our use.[25] As mentioned above, we have been able to locate food-prices inflation data for the countries under this study in the statistical bulletins of their central banks or central statistical organizations.

Establishing a methodology of measuring ethnic and sectarian (ES) tensions in MENA is another instance where a mixed qualitative and quantitative approach was employed. ES tension can be a significant destabilizing factor, as, for example, in the cases of Egypt, Yemen, Syria, and Libya, where high levels of unrest can also be attributed to underlying ethnic/tribal or sectarian cleavages.[26] To measure ES tension, a two-fold approach is proposed. First, we introduce a tension scale from 1 to 5, where 1 represents none to low tensions, 2 represents the existence of tensions but no significant clashes between the opposing communities, 3 indicates violent but nonlethal clashes, 4 indicates clashes that result in some deaths, and 5 indicates major clashes that result in a high number of deaths. Second, since the region has a long history of ethnic and sectarian violence, historical levels of such violence are also considered in the estimate of the intensity of potential conflict. The overall value of ES tension is then the average of the values assigned to a particular country's 2010 ES tensions (pre–Arab Uprisings) and its historical tensions since the end of World War II, based on our knowledge. The ethnic/sectarian tensions (ES) of the MENA states are summarized below in table 4.1.

Table 4.1.

Country	2010	Propensity (Historical)	Overall Level	Major ES Fault Lines
Algeria	3	5	4	Secular/Islamist conflict
Bahrain	2	4	3	Majority Shia population, Sunnis in power
Egypt	3	5	4	Large Coptic population, Islamist—moderates conflict
Jordan	2	4	3	Significant part of the population is of Palestinian descent, conflict with descendants of Bedouin Arabs, large refugee and foreign-workers population
Kuwait	2	2	2	Tensions with stateless and foreign-workers population
Lebanon	3	5	4	Highly sectarian environment, Maronites, Shia, Sunni, Christian Orthodox, Armenians, main conflict Shia vs. the other denominations, pro-, anti-Syria clashes
Libya	2	4	3	Significant tribal and regional divisions
Morocco	1	3	2	Some Berber-Arab divisions
Oman	1	3	2	Majority Ibadi population, Sunnis in power
Qatar	1	1	1	No significant ES conflict
Saudi Arabia	2	4	3	Sunni majority, Shia population ~15%
Syria	2	5	3.5	Sunni Arabs: 60–65%; Alawi, Druze, Christians: 20–25%; Kurds: 15%; Islamism and Arab nationalism prominent, regime has predominantly secularist outlook
Tunisia	2	4	3	Berber tribal divisions
UAE	1	2	1.5	No significant ES conflict
Yemen	4	5	4.5	Houthi rebellion in the north, historical north-south division, radical Islamism

Levels of CPV

As previously introduced, collective political violence (CPV) is the dependent variable of our model. To our knowledge, there is no established definition or single measurement that could conclusively discern different levels of CPV. We define CPV as political violence exercised or threatened by the inhabitants of a state for political change and the state's political response to such action/threats. Collective action and its consequences can take several forms. Three are considered: (1) the number of deaths that occurred as a direct result of clashes between regime forces and anti-regime groups (these are distinct from the deaths associated with ES tension), (2) the scale of protests as measured by the number of

Table 4.2. Criteria for CPV Level

CPV Level	Number of Deaths	Scale of Protests	Regime Response
1 (low)	None	Limited (in the 100s)	No political concessions/subsidies
2 (medium)	<100	Major (in the 1,000s)	Limited political concessions
3 (high)	100+	Extensive (in the 10,000s)	Significant political concessions and/or violent suppression

people participating in them, and (3) the political response of the regime that can include concession making and/or violent suppression. These three form the qualitative basis of our definition of CPV; the quantification of CPV follows.

The trinomial probability model allows for three levels of CPV—low, medium, and high. The selection criteria for each component of CPV are listed in table 4.2. For example, "Regime Response" would be scored low if a regime simply extended economic benefits to their citizens; medium if promises for reform, cabinet changes, etc. were offered but none resulted in significant change; and major if either a key change in the political leadership occurred through election or otherwise or if the regime initiated a wide-scale, violent crackdown on the protests. Since each criterion could have various degrees of expression in each country, we consider the overall CPV score to be the unweighted, rounded-up average of the three criteria.

MAXIMUM LIKELIHOOD ANALYSIS

To test the different domain indicators' and standalone indices' relation to CPV, we use the statistical regression procedure of maximum likelihood (maxLL).[27] MaxLL is particularly suitable for such analyses since it can test multiple probabilistic outcomes beyond just a binary association—that is, whether CPV occurred or did not occur. In the present case, maxLL was used to estimate the probabilities of three outcomes as proposed and defined in table 4.2: low, medium, and high levels of CPV.

The functional form of the trinomial probabilities developed in this chapter is a variant of the multinomial logit function.[28] The trinomial probability model is a novel expression that is relatively intuitive and not over-parameterized. Multinomial regression for trinomial outcomes involves usually twice as many parameters (for example, a, b, g, and h in $Pr_1 = \exp[-a \cdot (IV - g)]/\{1 + \exp[-a \cdot (IV - g)] + \exp[+b \cdot (IV - h)]\}$, where IV is the independent variable) than the expression we use. Additional parameters (beyond the present two, a and b) that commercial statistical software provides cannot be justified for the few cases (n =

15) that we examine, as it would greatly inflate the standard errors of the parameter estimates. Once developed (see below), the probability functions are then calibrated using maximum likelihood. Functional constraints are such that the probability of low-level CPV is high when the causal indicator(s) of CPV suggests a low propensity toward political unrest, and vice versa. These indicators and standalone indices, when applied individually or combined as a composite, are designated as the *IV*. Henceforth, low and high *IV* values are respectively associated with a high potential for low and high levels of CPV. The mathematical form that defines the probabilities of low (Pr_1) and high (Pr_3) levels of CPV are adopted from the logistic function,[29] which describes a sigmoidal change in probability as the value of *IV* changes:

$$Pr_1 = 1 - \frac{\exp(a + IV)}{1 + \exp(a + IV)}$$

$$Pr_3 = \frac{\exp(-b + IV)}{1 + \exp(-b + IV)}$$

where a and b are offset fitting parameters that determine where the probabilities of low- and high-level CPV respectively decay and rise as the value of *IV* increases. Since all probabilities must sum to unity as a statistical necessity, the probability of medium (level 2) CPV is constrained as follows:

$$Pr_2 = 1 - Pr_1 - Pr_3$$

Collectively, the above probability functions constitute the "trinomial probability model." The probability functions can be displayed graphically whereby the actual value of *IV* will depend on the values of the candidate indicators of CPV and each country will be placed on the probability curve that corresponds to its observed level of CPV above its abscissa *IV* value (see figure 4.1 in the following). In maxLL analysis, the *IV* that yields the maximum LL value (that is, lowest negative value) is the best fit of the dependent variable (observed levels of CPV in this case).

Finally, to ensure an unbiased contribution, all indicators and indices were subjected to a standardization procedure. First, indicator and index values were valence-corrected so that increasing values correspond to an increasing risk of CPV. For example, since lower median age is associated with an increased risk of violent social upheavals,[30] this notion is captured in the data set by subtracting the median age from 100. Thus, the lower the median age, the higher its representative value in *IV*. All indicator and index values were then individually normalized on a ten-point scale from a minimum of −5 to a maximum of 5 (for display purposes), and all other values for the particular indicator/index fell linearly in between. Where indicators and/or indices are combined, they were without weight unless specified otherwise.

RESULTS

Levels of CPV

The CPV levels of individual MENA countries were based on the criteria outlined in table 4.2 and shown in table 4.3. Four countries were categorized as having experienced a high level of CPV (level 3)—Egypt, Libya, Syria, and Yemen—and four as having experienced none or low instances of CPV (level 1)—Kuwait, Lebanon, Qatar, and UAE. The remainder—Algeria, Bahrain, Jordan, Morocco, Oman, and Saudi Arabia—were categorized at the medium level of CPV (level 2).

CPV Testing of Indicators

To test the various indicators' relations to CPV, we first established the upper and lower bounds of maxLL that constitute the model's "goodness-of-fit." These boundaries were set by fixing the normalized values of *IV* to maximal values of −5, 0, and 5 for CPV levels of 1, 2, and 3, respectively, according to each state's "overall" level of CPV, which resulted in a maxLL value of −1.67 (see annex A for formulation) that represents the best possible fit. Next, the normalized value of *IV* for each state was fixed to 0, which assumes a medium level without *a priori* knowledge of the actual level of CPV. This resulted in a maxLL value of −16.28 that can be interpreted as the "null" fit of the model. Similar values can be obtained assuming random CPV levels for all cases. Hence, fits of the data with maxLL values lower than −16.28 (that is, higher negative values) are worse than one's naïve assumption, and the closer maxLL is to −1.67, the better is the fit.

Table 4.4 shows the fit of the trinomial probability model to various causal and correlational indicators singly and grouped as composites by type (political, social, economic, demographic) and to various indices. Facilitative factors were excluded, as rationalized earlier. The *Economist*'s democracy rankings[31] were selected because they measure election fairness and voter security. Corruption indices are often based on economic/business freedom, which can also implicate the level of regime corruption. In that respect, two indicators were tested: the years

Table 4.3. MENA Levels of CPV, January–July 2011[1]

Country	Number of Deaths	CPV Value	Intensity of Protests	CPV Level	Regime Response	CPV Level	Overall Level
Algeria	8	2	major	2	limited pol concessions/subsidies	2	2
Bahrain[2]	39	2	extensive	3	limited pol concessions/subsidies	2	2
Egypt	846	3	extensive	3	significant pol concessions/initial crackdown	3	3
Jordan	2	2	extensive	2	limited pol concessions/subsidies	2	2
Kuwait	0	1	limited	1	subsidies	1	1
Lebanon	0	1	major	2	no pol concessions	1	1
Libya[3]	2000+	3	extensive	3	crackdown	3	3
Morocco	5	2	extensive	2	limited pol concessions	2	2
Oman	2	2	limited	1	limited pol concessions/subsidies	2	2
Qatar	0	1	no/limited	1	subsidies	1	1
Saudi Arabia	2	2	major	2	limited pol concessions/subsidies	2	2
Syria	2000+	3	extensive	3	crackdown	3	3
Tunisia	224	3	extensive	3	extensive pol concessions/initial crackdown	3	3
UAE	0	1	limited	1	subsidies	1	1
Yemen	1000+	3	extensive	3	limited pol concessions/crackdown	3	3

Notes

1. Data provided by DRDC CORA contract research, Ivan-George Koupenov, "MENA Timeline" (September, 2011).
2. We do not consider foreign interventions as a variable because these are tied to external geopolitical and other factors that have no direct connection to the origins of the Uprisings. In the case of Bahrain, the Saudi Arabia–led intervention and subsequent crackdown of protestors was motivated to a greater degree by regional ES (Shia-Sunni) tensions and the Saudi objective to prevent the spread of unrest among its own Shia population. Thus, we do not account for the intervention in measuring Bahrain's CPV level.
3. Based on the situation before the NATO intervention on March 19, 2011.

of the leader in power as a proxy measure of political corruption[32] and the Corruption Perception index (CPI).[33] GDP per capita (PPP) as reported by the Center for International Comparisons of Production, Income, and Prices was deemed as an appropriate measure of both prosperity and inflation given that it represents converted purchasing power parity over GDP using chain series analysis.[34] Unemployment, although difficult to quantify precisely, was also included because of its importance as a destabilizing factor. Income inequality is another economic factor that was deemed important to test given the sharp economic polarization of MENA societies. The GINI coefficients were the most recently available (from 1998 for Algeria to 2008 for nine others) from several sources.[35] We also included among the economic indicators the food-prices index (FPI), given its prominence in the literature on the uprisings. FPI for individual countries was accessible from their central banks and central statistical organizations. Among the tested social indicators, we illustrate below the performance of ethnic/sectarian tensions, as well as the percent of the population urbanized and the level of education (school life expectancy from primary to tertiary).[36] Three measures of the demographic pressure on the political system were tested: the percentage of the population less than twenty-five years old, the percentage of the population fifteen–twenty-nine years old (also known as the "fighting age" cohort), and the ratio of young adults (fifteen–twenty-nine years old) to all working age adults (fifteen–sixty-five years old)—YA/WA ratio.[37] The composite scores were specific to indicator types. For example, the maxLL value of –6.67 was obtained using a single "Political" composite that comprised the normalized and unweighted indicators of "Democracy," "Years in Power," and "Corruption (CPI)."

In addition to these indicators, we also tested several established and publicly available composite indices for their predictability of CPV—namely, the Shoe-Thrower's Index, the Polity IV State Fragility Index (SF-Polity), the Country Indicators for Foreign Policy State Fragility Index (SF-CIFP), the Fund for Peace Failed States Index (FSI), Freedom House's Political Rights (PR) and Civil Liberties (CL) Indices, the Institute for Economics and Peace Global Peace Index (GPI), and the Heidelberg Conflict Barometer (HCB). Also listed are the Pearson correlation coefficients of all indicators and indices for additional statistical comparisons. All indicators and indices correlated significantly with CPV level unless indicated by "ns" (nonsignificant). Only indicators with statistically significant correlation coefficients were included in the domain composite scoring.

Table 4.4   Model Fit of Various Indicators and Indices

Indicator Type	Indicator	Correlation Coefficients	MaxLL Values (separate)	MaxLL Values (composite)
Political	Democracy	0.52	–14.64	–6.67
	Years in Power	0.63	–14.10	
	Corruption (CPI)	0.60	–13.65	
Economic	GDPpc (PPP)	0.75	–11.60	–7.64
	Unemployment (%)	0.71	–10.58	
	GINI Coefficient	0.17 (ns)	–24.06	
	Food-Prices Inflation	0.04 (ns)	–25.77	
Social	ES Tensions	0.58	–14.52	–9.82
	Urbanization	0.76	–9.60	
	Education	0.03 (ns)	–25.61	
Demographic	% < 25 yr old	0.65	–12.77	–12.40
	% 15–29 yr old	0.13 (ns)	–29.97	
	YA/WA Ratio	0.58	–15.54	
Indices	Shoe Thrower's Index	0.89		–5.95
	State Fragility— Polity IV	0.57		–15.91
	State Fragility—CIFP	0.42 (ns)		–16.10
	Failed State Index	0.53		–15.87
	Political Rights Index	0.63		–13.29
	Civil Liberties Index	0.58		–13.54
	Global Peace Index	0.18 (ns)		–23.17
	Heidelberg Conflict Barometer	0.11 (ns)		–38.30

Several conclusions can be derived from the results shown in table 4.4. First, indicators such as "GINI coefficient," "Education," and "% 15–29 yr old" that failed to surpass the null model threshold (maxLL = –16.28) also did not correlate significantly with CPV. Further, significant correlation coefficients are only suggestive, and not an assurance, of strong candidacy for CPV determinants.

It is evident that irrespective of type, causality to CPV by a single indicator is very poor. All individual political factors, especially "Education," food-prices inflation, the GINI coefficient, and the youth bulge-related "% 15–29 yr old" generated particularly low maxLL values. Indicators such as "GDPpc (PPP)," "Unemployment (%)," and "Urbanization"[38] achieved relatively higher maxLL values but were still insufficiently low to justify attributing them (individually) a power that could have caused the Uprisings. The poor performance of the food-prices indicator, especially, is noteworthy in that it casts significant doubt onto the role of food-prices inflation in the Uprisings. In some countries—for example, Egypt, where food-prices inflation was significant—the latter may have contributed to the intensity of the unrest, but on a regional basis it does not seem to be a factor.[39]

The situation changes, however, if the indicators are grouped as a composite. This is evident in the last column of table 4.4, which shows markedly higher maxLL values for composite values compared to the individual indicator's values within the same composite. Notably, the political indicators' composite with a maxLL value of –6.67 gives some merit to the proponents of the depravation of democracy in the MENA countries as the source of the contemporary upheaval. The economic indicators' composite with a maxLL of –7.64 and the social and demographic factors with respective values of –9.82 and –12.40 are close behind and thus also worthy of further exploration (that is, the possibility that combining different type indicators as composite from across domains might yield even higher maxLL).

However, there is a caveat regarding over-aggregation of indicators. Despite the higher maxLL value achieved by grouping the individual indicators by type, the indices' scores clearly demonstrate that over-aggregation does not necessarily guarantee a better fit to CPV. Most of the indices barely passed the threshold value of the null model, while some scored considerably worse, such as the Global Peace Index (GPI) and Heidelberg Conflict Barometer (HCB) with maxLL values of –23.17 and –38.30, respectively. Certain of these, such as the Political Rights (PR) and Civil Liberties (CL) indices, scored reasonably well compared to the individual political indicators but considerably worse against the composite maxLL value of the political indicators' composite. A possible deficiency of these complex indices could be tied to their global characterization that does not reflect regional issues very well and their over-aggregation. For example, the SF-Polity IV, GPI, and SF-CIFP comprise seventeen, twenty-four, and seventy-five indicators, respectively. The notable exception is the Shoe-Thrower's Index, which involves only nine indicators[40] and not only achieved the best maxLL value (–5.95) among the indices, but also compared well to the domain composites.

The reasonably good performance of the Shoe-Thrower's Index led us to conclude that a limited selection of indicators (that is, those that scored better than the null model) from among all the domain types could result in an even better fit. This comprehensive approach was also recently advocated by Timo Behr, who argued for a multivariate explanation to unravel the causation of the Arab Uprisings.[41] Although there was no a priori guidance that helped us select the best-performing mix of indicators, we tested domain indicators that are tied to the prevailing hypotheses about the origins of the Uprisings as outlined at the beginning of this study; in other words, the indicators' selection is causal in nature and grounded in the available literature. Considerable experimentation revealed that individual indicators that achieved high maxLL values such as "Urbanization" do not necessarily ensure a good composite fit, and, conversely, indicators that performed poorly when tested singly contributed positively when grouped with other indicators. Ultimately, the six indicators that collectively did achieve the highest maxLL value (–5.35) were "Democracy," "Years in Power," "GDPpc (PPP)," "Unemployment (%)," "% < 25 yr old," and "ES tension" (see annex B for values). These six indicators, hereafter termed the Tikuisis-Minkov (TM) composite, were combined with equal weight, since no theoretical basis could be applied to rationalize greater or lesser importance to any of these. This approach is a further distinction from the Shoe-Thrower's Index, where arbitrary weights were assigned to different indicators within the composite.

The TM composite best fit (maxLL = –5.34) was obtained with $a = 2.6 \pm 1.8$ (SE; standard error), $b = 1.1 \pm 1.0$ (SE), and the correlation with CPV at 0.92. All states, except for Tunisia, fall on the probability curve that corresponds to their observed level of CPV (see figure 4.1—for example, the probability for the occurrence of medium level CPV (Pr_2) for Saudi Arabia is 0.71, which is higher than for either low (Pr_1) or high level CPV (Pr_3)), for an overall postdictive accuracy of 93.3 percent (that is, 14 of 15 correctly placed cases).

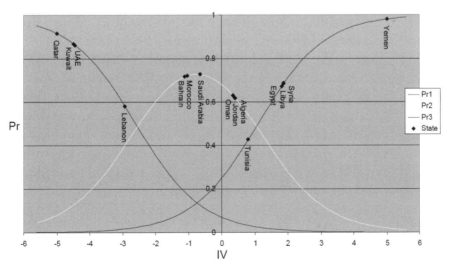

FIGURE 4.1
MENA Countries Model Fit Based on the Tikuisis-Minkov (TM) Composite Selection

As a cautionary note, the probabilities shown in figure 4.1 should be considered in a relative versus absolute sense due to the model construct. That is, the probabilities are sensitive to the IV scale, which in this case ranges from -5 to $+5$. Thus, for example, the occurrence of CPV level 3 for Egypt (shown as a probability of 69 percent in figure 4.2) should also be viewed as 2.3 times more likely than the occurrence of CPV level 2 (shown as a probability of 30 percent).

Model Validation

The robustness of the TM composite selection of indicators as a precursor of CPV was tested using split samples, also referred to as cross-validation. This is a well-accepted method for model validation, where the data are split into two subsets and the results of the first (and larger) subset are used to test (validate) the second subset.[42] In our case, three states, each with a different level of CPV, were randomly deselected from the fifteen MENA cases as the smaller subset, leaving twelve cases for model calibration (or training data). After determining the best fit, the newly regressed values of a and b were then applied to test the model's predictive accuracy of the deselected cases for model validation. This procedure was conducted ten times to confirm reproducibility. On each occasion, a different, but similar, set of a and b parameter values was generated.

All states were deselected as evenly as possible to conduct the split-sample test in as unbiased a fashion as possible. This resulted in deselecting Tunisia twice in the ten calibration data sets—that is, it was included in eight of the ten calibration trials and was one of the three states in the validation data of the other two trials. Tunisia is specifically mentioned here because it was the only state for which the model consistently underpredicted the probability of its level of CPV, both during calibration and validation. Only one other state, Lebanon, had its level of CPV narrowly underpredicted during one of the validation trials. Hence, the respective average model accuracy across all ten trials was 93.3 percent postdictive (calibration) and 90.0 percent predictive (validation). The coefficients of variation of maxLL, a, and b, were 0.08, 0.05, and 0.11, respectively, indicating close agreement across all ten trials during calibration.

Youth-Grievance Factor

The empirical findings thus far suggest that the TM composite of six equally weighted, mixed-type indicators provide good explanatory correspondence to the observed CPV levels during the Arab Uprisings. Thus, the political, economic, social, and demographic factors they represent should be considered as most probable direct contributors for the Arab Uprisings. Even by observing the raw data (annex B), it is evident that there is a clear distinction between the countries in CPV levels 1, 2, and 3 as a group. For example, the Democracy rankings' means are 3.83, 3.19, and 2.55, respectively, for level 1, 2, and 3 countries—that is, it is progressively worse for countries with higher CPV. With respect to GDPpc, it is the opposite case—lower level CPV countries have higher GDPpc means ($67,968 for level 1 and $13,272 for level 2), and the highest level CPV countries have the lowest GDPpc mean ($7,378).

What remains unsatisfactory is that it is difficult to explain how the six factors, or perhaps others, relate to each other and whether interrelation rather than weighting can further improve the maxLL score and further our understanding of the Arab Uprisings' origins. A glimpse into the possibilities that such a relational consideration could offer is to try to capture the complex links between the high number of youths in MENA, their aspirations for a better life, and political violence. Some authors have suggested that education plays a crucial role in the relationship of these factors.[43] First, there is extensive literature that connects higher education to greater political involvement and indicates that weak economic conditions lead to increased political participation among the better educated.[44] In the MENA region, the expansion of education in the last two decades has not been matched by corresponding improvement in the skilled-labor market. Campante and Chor conclude that "the low opportunity cost of political participation would thus make such individuals more likely instead to channel their efforts towards political action and political protest in particular."[45] In other words, the effects of higher education—although by itself not a direct cause for political violence (in our maxLL test, education was scored at –25.61,[46] well below the null threshold)—can be compounded by the large number of youths ("youth bulge") and a weak job market ("unemployment") in the region.

To test this possibility, we created a hybrid indicator by multiplying the normalized values of the Youth Bulge ("% pop < 25 yr") with "Unemployment (%)" and "Education" level, and termed it the Youth Grievance Factor (YGF; see annex B for values). Indeed, when YGF was combined with "GDPpc (PPP)" (probably the best indicator of a particular country's economic conditions), "Years in Power" and "Democracy" (with twice its weight)—that is, the two factors indicating political deprivation and a sense of injustice in the society—and finally, "ES tension"—that is, an indicator sensitive to the current and historical social grievances in the region—a maxLL of –4.31 was obtained (using $a = 2.6 \pm 2.1$ (SE), $b = 1.5 \pm 1.2$ (SE)) with a CPV correlation of 0.95. Most noteworthy was

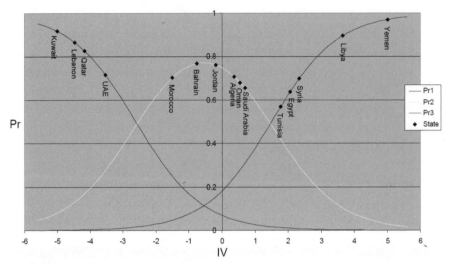

FIGURE 4.2
MENA Countries Model Fit Based on a Mixed-Weighted-Hybrid Composite of Indicators

the much-improved fit of Tunisia, which is now placed on the high CPV level curve (see figure 4.2) in concurrence with the observed level. This analysis was also validated by split-sample testing.

CONCLUSION

This chapter contributes to the discussion of the initial unrest in the MENA region and its possible causes on two levels. First, it introduces a novel methodology to study the subject quantitatively—namely, the trinomial probability model for predicting three levels of CPV, which was regressed using maximum likelihood. Second, it demonstrates that the underpinnings of the social upheaval in the MENA countries cannot be attributed to a single factor but, rather, are the result of an interrelation between political, economic, social, and demographic factors. Our findings confirm that the convergence of several interrelated, highly destabilizing factors created a "perfect storm" that manifested into the Arab Uprisings. This chapter introduces the Tikuisis-Minkov composite selection of six causal indicators (level of democracy, years of leader in power, gross domestic product per capita at purchasing power parity, unemployment rates, youth bulge, and ethnic-sectarian tension) as the best possible unbiased combination to differentiate with 90 percent prediction accuracy the different levels of CPV in the MENA region. These precursors broadly relate to the political and socio-economic origins of the Arab Uprisings put forward by other scholars; however, the Tikuisis-Minkov composite selection captures uniquely the major domains of influence by measurable indicators.

We also explored inter-factor relationships that further advance our understanding of the origins of the Arab Uprisings. The mixed-weighted-hybrid composite of indicators—namely "Years in Power," "GDPpc (PPP)," "ES tension," "Democracy" (weighted twice as much as the others), and the "YGF" (which is the hybrid product of two indicators from the TM composite plus educational levels—produced the best maxLL result. This selection suggests that dissatisfaction with political corruption and autocracy, although a dominant aspect of the Uprisings, manifested itself only when the general economic malaise, which in itself constrained some regimes' ability to react, except with violence, lowered the threshold of lost economic opportunity to the large and relatively well-educated youth cohort that confronted the regimes' security apparatus. In addition, the sharp ethnic-sectarian divisions in some MENA countries certainly compounded this situation.

These findings, though, are contingent on the acceptance of our definition of the dependent variable, which was the level of CPV based on an unweighted composite of death toll, protest intensity, and regime response. Undoubtedly, the fit of the model would yield different results using different data values even if the same independent variables were applied. However, these differences should not alter the main conclusion regarding the greater power of combining key indicators for the anticipation of CPV levels.

That the Tikuisis-Minkov combination of indicators and the mixed-weighted-hybrid version outperformed any single indicator and several global indices emphasizes the importance of addressing causation of unrest from a holistic perspective, with a judicious aggregation of factors. In its present form, the trinomial probability model has demonstrated a fusion of qualitative and quantitative methodologies that was particularly suited for a limited number of cases. Its primary attribute is the testing of causal indicators of CPV in a statistically objective manner.

From a practical perspective, the Tikuisis-Minkov composite selection makes it a leading candidate as a risk-assessment scenario tool, where future CPV levels in the MENA states can be estimated from the available data for the six indicators. Tracking the performance of the model over time will allow periodic recalibration, thus making the model a robust living tool. The model can also be reconfigured for other dependent variables of interest and thus offers the potential for further development as a risk-assessment scenario tool beyond CPV.

Future work will be directed toward testing the model's applicability of predicting CPV to other global regions. Expanding the parameterization of the model (for example, the shape of the probability curves) can eliminate the sensitivity of probabilities to the *IV* scale, but the model will require considerably more data (that is, cases) to obtain meaningful model-parameter estimations.

NOTES

1. There are some merits to give such credit to Reuel Marc Gerecht, who in his book *The Wave: Man, God, and the Ballot Box in the Middle East* (Stanford: Hoover Institution Press, 2011), completed in October 2010, asserted that "2011 might, just possibly, be decisive in democracy's regional advance" (12).

2. Timo Behr, "Talking about the Revolution: Narratives on the Origin and Future of the Arab Spring," *PapersIEMed* 9 (2012).

3. See, for example, Jack A. Goldstone, "Understanding the Revolutions of 2011," *Foreign Affairs* 90, no. 3 (May/June 2011): 8–16; and Lahcen Achy, "The Breakdown of the Arab Authoritarian Bargain," *Carnegie Commentary* (2012).

4. See Marco Lagi, Karla Z. Bertrand, and Yaneer Bar-Yam, "The Food Crises and Political Instability in North Africa and the Middle East," *New England Complex Systems Institute* (2011); Lester R. Brown, "The New Geopolitics of Food," *Foreign Policy* 186 (2011): 54–63.

5. See, for example, Marc Lynch, "After Egypt: The Limits and Promise of Online Challenges to the Authoritarian Arab State," *Reflections* 9, no. 2 (2011).

6. Available at "Polity IV Project," accessed March 19, 2014, http://www.systemicpeace.org/polity/polity4.htm.

7. Available at "Vision of Humanity," accessed March 19, 2014, http://www.visionofhumanity.org/gpi-data/#/2011/scor.

8. Available at "Country Indicators for Foreign Policy," accessed March 19, 2014, http://www4.carleton.ca/cifp/app/ffs_ranking.php.

9. See Hugh Roberts, "Algeria's National 'Protesta,'" *Foreign Policy* (2011); and Lamine Chikhi, "Algeria Army Should Quit Politics: Opposition," *Reuters*, January 21, 2011, accessed March 19, 2014, http://www.reuters.com/article/2011/01/21/ozatp-algeria-opposition-idAFJOE70K02X20110121.

10. The term "sultanistic" is terminologically problematic, since, despite its obvious Middle East connotations, Goldstone also applies it to Latin American and Asian dictatorships. Furthermore, according to Goldstone, an underlying characteristic of the sultanistic political system is its single generational character, as opposed to multigenerational monarchies. Historically, however, the term "sultan" in Islamic history has a different connotation and is often connected to long-standing dynasties rather than opportunistic power holders.

11. See Joshua Hammer and Amina Ismail, "Egypt: Who Calls the Shots?" *New York Review of Books* (2011).

12. See Ulf Laessing, "Pro-reform Saudi Activists Launch Political Party," *Reuters*, February 10, 2011, accessed March 19, 2014, http://www.reuters.com/article/2011/02/10/us-saudi-opposition-idUSTRE71942L20110210.

13. The events in MENA were even compared to the popular movements that swept the communist regimes in Eastern Europe from 1989 to 1991. See, for example, Nikolai Grozni, "The Ghost of Revolutions Past," *New York Times*, February 12, 2011.

14. It should be acknowledged that some studies emphasizing the political causes of the Uprisings also recognize the destabilizing role of other socioeconomic factors such as unemployment and demographics. However, these factors are often viewed as triggers rather than as having a causal role.

15. See, for example, Leila Austin, "The Politics of Youth Bulge: From Islamic Activism to Democratic Reform in the Middle East and North Africa," *SAIS Review* 31.2 (2011).

16. Behr, "Talking about the Revolution," 15.

17. Data were derived from the "UN World Population Prospects: 2010 Revision," accessed March 19, 2014, http://esa.un.org/unpd/wpp/unpp/panel_population.htm.

18. UNDP, *Human Development Report 2010: The Real Wealth of Nations* (New York, 2010).

19. See "The Shoe-Throwers's Index," *Economist*, February 9, 2011, accessed March 19, 2014, http://www.economist.com/blogs/dailychart/2011/02/daily_chart_arab_unrest_index.

20. See "2011 Failed States Index: Interactive Maps and Rankings," *Foreign Policy*, June 17, 2011, accessed March 19, 2014, http://www.foreignpolicy.com/articles/2011/06/17/2011_failed_states_index_interactive_map_and_rankings.

21. See http://www.freedomhouse.org/uploads/fiw10/TableofIndependentCountriesFIW2010 .pdf.

22. See "Conflict Barometer," accessed March 19, 2014, http://hiik.de/en/konfliktbarometer/.

23. As per labor-market information of Bahrain's Labour Minister Majeed al-Alawi (at www .arabianbusiness.com, accessed on April 7, 2009).

24. Based on demographic data from the "UN Population Prospects" and foreign-workers population figures from Bahrain's 2010 census, "2010 Census," accessed March 19, 2014, http://www .census2010.gov.bh/results_en.php. We were not able to apply the same methodology to the other GCC countries with large foreign-worker populations, since the lack of protests in them did not allow us to identify a specific group in the society that may have had its own demographic characteristic, as in the case of Bahrain.

25. See "FAO Food Price Index," accessed March 19, 2014, http://www.fao.org/worldfoodsituation/ wfs-home/foodpricesindex/en/.

26. In Egypt, protests with the regime overlapped with clashes between the Muslim majority and the Coptic Christian minority; in Yemen, a Shia Houthis revolt occurred in the north; in Syria, the division was between the Arab Sunni majority and the Christian, Alawi, and Druze minorities that control the political and security apparatus; while in Libya, there were significant tribal and regional cleavages as well.

27. For a description of maxLL see D. W. Marquardt, "An Algorithm for Least-Squares Estimation of Nonlinear Parameters," *Journal of the Society for Industrial and Applied Mathematics* 11, no. 2 (June): 431–41. For an example of maxLL being used for the study of conflict see Aaron Clauset, Maxwell Young, and Kristian Skrede Gleditsch, "On the Frequency of Severe Terrorist Events," *Journal of Conflict Resolution* 51, no. 1 (2007).

28. See William H. Greene, *Econometric Analysis*, 5th edition, (New Jersey: Prentice Hall, 1993), 720–23.

29. See Eric W. Weisstein, "Logistic Equation," Wolfram MathWorld, accessed March 19, 2014, http://mathworld.wolfram.com/LogisticEquation.html.

30. See, for example, Herbert Moller, "Youth as a Force in the Modern World," *Comparative Studies in Society and History* 10, no. 3 (1968): 237–60; and Henrik Urdal, "The Devil in the Demographics: The Effect of Youth Bulges on Domestic Armed Conflict, 1950–2000," *Conflict Prevention and Reconstruction Paper* 14 (2004).

31. "Democracy Index 2010: Democracy in Retreat," *Economist* Intelligence Unit, accessed March 19, 2014, http://www.eiu.com/public/topical_report.aspx?campaignid=demo2010.

32. This observation is historically well supported with respect to the MENA regimes.

33. See "Transparency International (TI) 2008 Corruption Perceptions Index (CPI)," Internet Center for Corruption Research, accessed March 19, 2014, http://www.icgg.org/corruption .cpi_2008.html.

34. Alan Heston, Robert Summers, and Bettina Aten, "Penn World Table Version 7.0," Center for International Comparisons of Production, Income and Prices at the University of Pennsylvania (June 2011), accessed March 19, 2014, http://pwt.econ.upenn.edu/php_site/pwt70/pwt70_form.php.

35. "GINI Index," The World Bank, accessed March 19, 2014, http://data.worldbank.org/indicator/ SI.POV.GINI/; "Distribution of Family Income—GINI index," CIA World Factbook, accessed March 19, 2014, https://www.cia.gov/library/publications/the-world-factbook/fields/2172.html; and "Inequality-Adjusted Human Development Index," United Nations Development Programme, accessed March 19, 2014, http://hdr.undp.org/en/statistics/ihdi/.

36. CIA World Factbook, accessed March 19, 2014, https://www.cia.gov/library/publications/ the-world-factbook/index.html.

37. For discussion of that ratio see Anton Minkov, *The Impact of Demographics on Regime Stability and Security in the Middle East* (Tech Defence R&D Canada: Center for Operational Research and Analysis, 2009), 23. Available at http://cradpdf.drdc-rddc.gc.ca/PDFS/unc87/p531870.pdf.

38. This indicator's higher score could possibly be linked to the primarily urban environment where the Arab Uprisings took place.

39. Food-prices inflation in Egypt in 2010 was 10.1 percent, while the regional average for that year was 5.6 percent. See *Annual Consumer Price Index in Urban by Main Groups (1996–2010)*, Egypt's Central Agency for Public Mobilization and Statistics, accessed march 19, 2014, http:// www.capmas.gov.eg/pdf/Static%20Book/PDF/9-%20الاسعار/9-3.pdf. Even in Egypt food-prices inflation seems to have tapered off in the second half of the year; see, *Annual Report 2009/2010*, Central Bank of Egypt (2010), 59.

40. The leader's years in power, percent of population under twenty-five, total population under twenty-five, GDP per capita, democracy ranking, corruption ranking, press-freedom ranking, adult literacy, and [number of] Internet users.

41. Behr, "Narratives," 8.

42. See, for example, S. P. O'Brien, "Anticipating the Good, the Bad, and the Ugly: An Early Warning Approach to Conflict and Instability Analysis," *Journal of Conflict Resolution* 46, no. 6 (2002): 791–811.

43. See Filipe R. Campante and Davin Chor, "Why Was the Arab World Poised for Revolution? Schooling, Economic Opportunities, and the Arab Spring," *Journal of Economic Perspectives* 26, no. 2 (2012): 167–88.

44. See ibid., 174–75, and the literature cited there.

45. Ibid., 175.

46. Not surprisingly, "Education" is the only indicator that does not lead to "clustering" of the fifteen countries (see annex B) as in the case of the other indicators. Yet, even when included in the composite of social indicators, the maxLL increased to −9.82, suggesting that education might be an important contributor when combined with other indicators.

ANNEXES

ANNEX A: METHOD OF MAXIMUM LIKELIHOOD

The likelihood (L) distribution function is given by the product of the predicted probabilities associated with the actual outcome of each case in the data set:

$$L = \prod_{n=1}^{no.cases} P_{outcome,n}$$

In the present application, $P_{outcome}$ is the probability that is predicted for the level of CPV actually observed. That is,

$$P_{outcome} = Pr_1^{outcome\ 1} \cdot Pr_2^{outcome\ 2} \cdot Pr_3^{outcome\ 3}$$

where Pr_n = predicted probability of a specific level of CPV (n = 1 = low; 2 = medium; 3 = high), and $outcome$ = 1 if the level of CPV is observed, otherwise $outcome$ = 0. For example, if the observed level of CPV is 2 (medium), then

$$P_{outcome} = Pr_1^0 \cdot Pr_2^1 \cdot Pr_3^0 = Pr_2$$

The best fit of the data is obtained when L is maximized; but given that this is the product of many numbers less than one, the maximization is performed on the more manageable logarithm of L, referred to as the log-likelihood function:

$$LL = \sum_{n=1}^{no.cases} \ln(P_{outcome,n})$$

$$= \sum_{n=1}^{no.cases} [outcome_{1,n} \cdot \ln(Pr_{1,n}) + outcome_{2,n} \cdot \ln(Pr_{2,n}) + outcome_{3,n} \cdot \ln(Pr_{3,n})]$$

MaxLL is the maximum (that is, smallest negative) attainable value of LL through the regression of the probability functions against the observed outcomes.

ANNEXES

ANNEX B

ANNEX B: Indicator Values of the TM Composite Selection with the Hybrid Youth Grievance Factor (YGF)

Country	CPV Level	Dem. Index	Yrs. Power	GDPpc (PPP)	ES Level	% < 24 Years	Edu. (yrs.)	UE (%)	YGF[1]
UAE	1	2.52	7	$52,932	3	33	13	2	10.4
Qatar	1	3.09	16	$159,368	2	28	12	1	1.7
Kuwait	1	3.88	5	$46,629	4	42	12	2	11.1
Lebanon	1	5.82	1	$12,941	8	43	14	9	55
Mean		3.83	7	$67,968	4	37	13	3.5	19.6
Algeria	2	3.44	12	$6,068	8	48	13	10	61.3
Bahrain	2	3.49	12	$23,539	6	35	14	25	122.2
Morocco	2	3.79	12	$3,294	4	48	10	10	47.6
Oman	2	2.86	41	$20,505	4	49	12	15	88.4
Saudi Arabia	2	1.84	6	$21,579	5	48	14	11	73.2
Jordan	2	3.74	12	$4,644	6	59	13	12	91.3
Mean		3.19	16	$13,272	6	48	13	13.8	80.7
Egypt	3	3.07	30	$4,956	8	51	11	10	57
Libya	3	1.94	42	$19,234	6	48	17	21	171.8
Syria	3	2.31	11	$4,002	7	57	11	20	126.1
Tunisia	3	2.79	24	$6,300	6	42	15	15	93.7
Yemen	3	2.64	33	$2,397	9	66	9	35	209.2
Mean		2.55	28	$7,378	7	53	13	20	132

NOTE
Normalized product of the three shaded columns

ernmental officers who treated him with indignity and *hope* for a better future once the wall of silence on everyday Tunisian suffering has fallen.

While both symbolic and tragic, Bouazizi's self-immolation could not by itself have triggered a revolution of such magnitude, which not only sent shock-waves throughout Tunisia but also swiftly spread to other countries in the Arab world. The fact that the many self-immolations followed suit upon Bouazizi's act in such countries as Algeria, Mauritania, and Morocco—and that have not so far resulted in revolutions in those places—makes it less likely, though, that Bouazizi's act per se should be located retrospectively at the very origin of the Tunisian revolution. Besides, Bouazizi's self-immolation could have been thrust into oblivion as has that of another street vendor before him, Abdesslem Trimech, who lit himself ablaze inside the city hall in the coastal city of Monastir on March 3, 2010, after his fruit cart had been confiscated by the police and his demand to meet with the city mayor rebuffed. This is not to say that Bouazizi's self-immolation was not inspiring and empowering, much less to say it was not an incitement to action, but rather to maintain that the protests that followed his self-immolation must have capitalized on long-standing rebellious instincts that Ben Ali's police state repressed but could not fully eradicate. *Otherwise, how could Bouazizi's act have mobilized so many, so quickly?*

The issue here becomes not so much how Bouazizi's suicide protest sparked a popular revolution (which has been so far among the most-traveled roads of inquiry about the Tunisian and Arab revolutions) but how a popular revolution sparked by Bouazizi's suicide protest is indeed the *materialization* of a cultural and critical capital that has largely been shaped by dispersed and stylized rehearsals of dissenting practices. There is no gainsaying the fact, of course, that much of what cultural critics and historians would associate with culture (including mass culture such as television, radio, and newspapers, as well as art, film, music, theater, and literature writ large) have served as tools of domination in Ben Ali's Tunisia. Both public and private media were aligned with Ben Ali's regime and invested most of their resources in perfecting their propagandistic techniques. Most writers, artists, and so-called public intellectuals were indeed state intellectuals. Most feminists have become in the name of facade modernity—and almost since Bourguiba instituted the Personal Status Code in 1957—zealous allies of his and his successor's dictatorship. A mixture of cynicism and cowardice cast its long shadow on intellectual reason.[2] Shortly after January 14, 2011, bloggers and cyber-activists published a list of all the artists and public figures who allegedly supported Ben Ali's bid for reelection in 2014. Not unexpectedly, the list included the names of iconic filmmakers Moufida Tlatli and Abdellatif Ben Ammar, actress Hend Sabri, and actor Hichem Rostom, as well as several famous singers such as Lotfi Bouchnaq, Latifa al-Arfaoui, Nabiha Karaouli, Amina Fakhit, Sonia M'barek, and Saber Reba'i.

My aim here is to study the contours (if at all) neither of this hegemonic culture of obedience and domination nor of the cultural actors whose dispositions to complicity with Bourguiba's and Ben Ali's dictatorial regimes left little room for equivocation or unproblematic interpretation. Instead, I chart a counterhegemonic cultural history whose origins are deeply steeped in the struggle against French colonialism but whose beginnings are multiple and dispersed, spanning time and space, mapping the counterintuitive formations of dissident Tunisia. It bears mentioning here that what counts as dissent is not necessarily the encoded intent of a given act, however crucial that is, but involves also the way an act is perceived in a given time and space and the effects it creates in a specific geopolitical context.[3] Dissent can possibly be direct or confrontational, and amount, therefore to subversion, which is perhaps the case with al-Shabbi's poetry and El Général's rap songs, insofar as they became the anthem of the Arab Uprisings. Oftentimes, however, and as Alan Sinfield argues, dissent "posits a field necessarily open to continuing contest, in which at some conjunctures the dominant will lose ground while at others the subordinate will scarcely maintain its position."[4] This mode of dissidence might apply in particular to the way high cultural artifacts (painting, art film, avant-garde poetry, the experimental novel, etc.) inscribe critique through rhetorical and allegorical detours. This is not generally the way that subcultural forms such as hip-hop perform dissent, even though, and as I explain in the following, the first professional Tunisian rapper, Balti, condensed and displaced his understanding of political dissidence in terms of his engagement with social issues. Perhaps because of the rigidity of censorship and the severity of self-censorship, one of the remarkable constants of Tunisian cultural products is that much of what would count for political dissidence is couched under a form of social or cognitive dissonance, in which the norms of intelligibility break up and with them all sorts of taboos. Nowhere else is this perhaps so evident as in postcolonial Tunisian film during the last three decades or so.

A COUNTERHEGEMONIC CULTURAL HISTORY

I devote much of my discussion to the Tunisian postcolonial cultural scene since the 1980s, but suffice it to mention here, however sketchily, that the tradition of cultural critique dates back at least to the decolonial struggle against French colonialism in the 1930s and 1940s and to the formation of the intellectual group called Against the Wall Group (*Jamā'it tahta al-sūr*), which brought together a heterogeneous number of intellectuals and helped raise awareness of the colonial condition through regular meetings and debates organized in popular cafés. Among the most important intellectual figures of this pre-independence period, I should name at least Tunisia's foremost national poet, Abu al-Qasim al-Shabbi, as well as Tunisia's foremost national playwright, Mahmoud al-Messadi. Both al-Shabbi and al-Messadi wrote about the human will to freedom and to a life worthy of its name. They are known for their ability to transform existential and political paralysis in their works into a basis of elaborating strategies of survival and defiance of French colonialism (euphemistically officiated as "protectorship").

It was not for nothing that the early protesters both in Tunisia and Egypt re-iterated al-Shabbi's most compelling and influential couplet from his poem "The Will to Life" ('Irādit al-Hayāt):

> *'Idhā al-sha'bu yawman 'arāda al-hayāt / fa-lā budda 'an yastajība-l-qadar*
> *Wa-lā budda lil-layli 'an yanjalī / wa-lā budda lil-qaidi 'an yankasir*
>
> Once a people reclaim their will to life / Gods must answer their call
> Their Night will have to vanish / and their chains to break and fall[5]

The resurrection of al-Shabbi's memorable lines—and their reverberations across the Arab world during and after the Tunisian revolution—should not be understood as a mere form of facile sloganeering but as an evocation of the inextricable relationship between fighting foreign *and* indigenous forms of oppression. I believe there is a repository of critical dissent that has been sustained and consolidated by the insurgency of various cultural practices in postcolonial Tunisia, not to mention the robust educational system that was put in place since independence by al-Messadi himself, the playwright who also acted as the minister of National Education in postcolonial Tunisia for a decade, from 1958 to 1968. Thanks to al-Messadi's vision, which survived even Ben Ali's onslaughts on public education, Tunisia has always boasted a high literacy rate, estimated at almost 90 percent, one of the highest in the region. Yet what bears mentioning here is that the level of literacy most Tunisians had acquired remained for decades at variance with the repressive policies of the successive regimes of Bourguiba and Ben Ali, a fact that made the popular uprising inevitable, if long overdue.[6]

But critique has not always been manifest or explicit even though some critics have quite explicitly opposed Bourguiba's and Ben Ali's regimes and paid a high price for doing so. This chapter is not merely about historical-political opponents and opposition leaders such as Rachid Ghannouchi, Hamma al-Hammami, and Moncef al-Marzouqi, among others, but about everyday Tunisians, journalists, novelists, playwrights, filmmakers, intellectuals, lawyers, and high school teachers, as well as school and university professors. Even soccer players, singers, and other popular figures have at times embraced and passed on the practices of dissent in the Tunisian public sphere whether through explicit or encoded means and intents. Sociopolitical and cultural critique is there in cinema, in theater as well as in poetry and music. Whoever studies Tunisian literature and culture since independence would not miss the latent or indirect critique it carried and disseminated.

Take, for instance, the cinematic careers of Nouri Bouzid, Moufida Tlatli, and Mohamed Zran, among others: Throughout their films, they have been preoccupied with the staging of broken and defeated individuals (both men and women, from leftist intellectuals and hip-hop artists to housekeepers, prostitutes, and misguided terrorists). By staging defeat to Tunisian audiences, Bouzid, Tlatli, and Zran not only make it possible for viewers to identify with and distance themselves from the defeated individuals on the screen, they also—and simultaneously—offer them an opportunity to immunize themselves against the psychology of defeat and the state apparatuses that perpetuate it. In the final analysis, the cinematic tendency to grapple with and visualize the experience of defeat becomes indirectly the basis for fostering strategies of empowerment. Shakespeare's meta-dramatic injunction to his readers—"through indirections find directions out"—has become one of the tactics that artists made use of to evade censorship and simultaneously keep alive the culture of critique and dissidence. Tunisian cinema had gradually developed since independence a singular reputation for its audacious treatment of controversial and taboo subjects (even for an allegedly progressive Muslim country such as Tunisia). Yet the treatment of such wide-ranging and contentious topics as Islam, imperialism, and secular modernity or variations on them is almost always infused, directly or indirectly, with a penetrating critique of the postcolonial regimes of Bourguiba and Ben Ali, their mid-term or long-term policies, and their social, economic, and political ramifications.

Férid Boughedir's *Halfaouine* and Jilani Saadi's *Tender Is the Wolf,* along with Moufida Tlatli's *The Silences of the Palace* and Mohamed Zran's *Essaïda,* as well as Moncef Dhouib's *The TV's Coming*—not to mention the half-dozen films of Nouri Bouzid, including *Man of Ashes, Golden Horseshoes*, and *Making Of*—chart a subtle genealogy of dissent from normative representations of Tunisianness in mainstream media, history, and state rhetoric. The crucial importance of these films lies in their ability to challenge the sociocultural status quo and form the basis for challenging the governmental and political state apparatus itself. The obsession with the body in Tunisian cinema bespeaks an allegorical obsession with the body politic. Dissidence is contagious: once you practice it somewhere, chances are you will be able to practice it elsewhere, even in the realm of everyday or grand politics, which had practically been something unheard of in Ben Ali's Tunisia until December 17, 2010. It bears mentioning here that Zran's 1996 *Essaïda* can be said to have arguably anticipated Bouazizi's suicide protest insofar as the character of Nidal (Chadli Bouzayen), a wretched youngster living in a popular neighborhood (Essaïda, part of the bidonville around Tunis), is driven at the end of the film to commit suicide. When chased by the police for murdering a cab driver, Nidal deserts his motorbike and climbs up a tall, high-voltage steel tower before he accidently falls or deliberately jumps to certain death. Zran's *Essaïda* paints a bleak vision of Ben Ali's Tunisia that, needless to say, has proven prophetic in the wake of Mohamed Bouazizi's self-immolation in Sidi Bouzid.

The same can be said about Jalila Baccar's most important and compelling play to date, *Khamsoun* (a.k.a. *Captive Bodies*). The starting point of *Khamsoun* is a suicidal act committed by Jouda, a young, veiled physics and chemistry teacher, on Friday, November 11, 2005, in the courtyard of her own school and, significantly enough, at the foot of a pole carrying the Tunisian flag. The play unfolds in a sequence of scenes organized along three major parts that move forward and simultaneously as far back as the early years of Bourguiba's presidency of the free republic of Tunisia. *Khamsoun*, which means "fifty" in English, was produced in 2006, fifty years after Tunisia's independence from France in 1956. Baccar wants us, therefore, to understand her play literally, not metaphorically, as an allegory of postcolonial Tunisia. This is a play in which the many individual stories Baccar weaves together are situated firmly in the canvas of national history. As a female playwright, actress, and filmmaker, Baccar's work has consistently been interested in the margins of the rhetoric of nationhood from Bourguiba to Ben Ali. Her repeated reactivation of the unassimilated histories of injustice and victimhood in postindependence Tunisia bespeaks a pedagogical and methodological investment in the psychoaffective valences of artistic and creative reckoning, thus bearing deep similarities to Nouri Bouzid's and Moufida Tlatli's early work in cinema. *Khamsoun*'s contestatory wherewithal is not the exception here but the exemplar.

Set in beylical Tunisia (the Hussein Dynasty of Beys, 1705–1957), which is technically part of the Ottoman Empire but in reality a French protectorate, Tlatli's *Silences* travels back and forth (through the cinematic economy of the flashback) between Tunisia on the eve of independence and postcolonial Tunisia, ten years after, in order to compare and contrast the fate of the nation and that of its male and female subjects—particularly Alia, the protagonist. The aim of *Silences* is not only to reclaim the lived experiences and expose the unspoken sufferings of women servants (who were practically slaves) under the Beys but also to assess the extent to which the independence of Tunisia from French colonialism has intersected with their emancipation from patriarchal bondage. The fervent and enlightened nationalist Lotfi (Sami Bouajila) had already assured the young Alia (Hend Sabri) of this promissory future before she eloped with him the night her mother died trying to abort the child resulting from the recent rape by the evil-bey-character, Si Bechir (Hichem Rostom): "You're as indecisive as our country. One word thrills you, the next scares you," Lotfi reproached the young Alia before he reassured her, "Things are going to change. A new future awaits us. You will be a great singer. Your voice will enchant everyone."

In the very same manner that many are now questioning whether anything significant has really changed after January 14, the adult Alia (Ghalia Lacroix) went through that same process of questioning in the 1960s, only to find out that postcolonial Tunisia did not offer her a fate any different from that of her mother, Khedija (Amel Hedhili). After all, Lotfi proved more conditioned by the patriarchal constrains that sealed Alia's fate as an illegitimate child than by his idealistic vision of a free Tunisia, uninhibited by the past. After presenting the viewer with a series of extended flashbacks that recapture Alia's story in screen memory style (that oscillates comparatively between past and present), the film ends ambivalently with Alia finally apprehending the extremity of her mother's suffering and addressing herself to her in a moving inner monologue, expressive of both Alia's entrapment and defiance: "I thought Lotfi would save me; I have not been saved. Like you, I've suffered, I've sweated. Like you, I've lived in sin. My life has been a series of abortions; I could never express myself; my songs were stillborn. And even the child inside me Lotfi wants me to abort. This child, however, I feel has taken root in me; I feel it bringing me back to life, bringing me back to you. I hope it will be a girl; I'll call her Khedija."

Alia's decision to keep the baby can be seen as a signal of a better and fruitful future different from the abortive past she had, but it is simultaneously a *future past* in the sense that it is in the end nothing but a reenactment of her mother's past insofar as her mother brought her up as an illegitimate child. Her choice, however, to not obey Lotfi is not something that her mother could have possibly chosen, let alone exercised. Here, it becomes clear that Alia's childhood rebelliousness against her mother's obeisance to the beys served her well in her subsequent rebelliousness against Lotfi. Not only that: her courage to break the wall of silence on what was going on outside the palace and sing the forbidden national anthem in the midst of Sara's engagement party is at once a vindication of national and female self-determination. While *Silences* embeds the conspiracy of silence and obeisance that marked colonial and postcolonial Tunisia, it embodies nonetheless the agentive ground for breaking the silence and exhorting others to do so.

Film plays for Tlatli what music in the film plays for Alia: a means of expression and empowerment. Alia's scream after she witnesses Si Bechir rape her mother comes muted not because it is less of a scream but because in order for a scream to be a scream it needs to be heard and acknowledged. The muted scream puts the viewer on the qui vive for any signals or instances of injustices that might go unnoticed because of a lack of vigilance and empathy on our part and not necessarily because of a lack of means of expression on the part of the originator of the scream. The subaltern screams, but if they are not heard, did they really scream? The organizing principle of narrative in *Silences* is the following question: Does a scream that is not heard count? What counts as a scream, and what counts less than a scream? This very same set of questions has also been broached by Nouri Bouzid in his directorial début, *Man of Ashes*, as the protagonist of the film searches in vain for an empathic ear capable of listening to the story of his childhood rape by his master carpenter.

Man of Ashes chronicles the experiences of two childhood friends, Hachemi (Imad Maalal) and Farfat (Khaled Ksouri)—the former about to tie the knot while the latter is kicked out of his father's house following the swirl of rumors, gossip, and street graffiti that calling manhood into question. When they were apprenticed youths, Hachemi and Farfat had been molested by their carpentry mentor, Ameur (Mustafa Adouani); they both grew up indelibly marked and bound up by this secret trauma. Now that that traumatic and tragic episode has come back to haunt them, they find themselves frantically scrambling for a final exit. There follows their obsessions with and anxieties over their virility, masculinity, and manhood within an allegedly heterosexual community they can neither desert nor reintegrate.

Bouzid shrewdly broaches the question of homosexuality in Tunisia (and in the entire Arab Muslim world) through the crime of child molestation. The film not only exposes the naturalized hypocrisy and moral vagaries of a society in which homosexual panic overrides pederasty but also distinguishes unequivocally between masculinity and manhood, on the one hand, and between homosociality and homosexuality, on the other. The bond between Hachemi and Farfat is homosocial and not homosexual. Bouzid is not only interested in raising the question of homosexuality to challenge sexual heteronormativity but also in underscoring the extent to which homosexual panic has come to undermine homosocial bonds in Arab societies. In the brothel scene at the end of the film, for instance, homosocial desire quickly gives way to homosexual panic, which, in turn, gives way to the reassertion of normative heterosexuality, best illustrated by the rivalry between Farfat and Azaiez (Mohamed Dhrif) to sleep with one of the two prostitutes.

While Tlatli's film stretches colonial and postcolonial times, Bouzid's film situates itself squarely in postcolonial Tunisia and in the post-1967 Arab world where the culture of defeat (and defeatism) became rampant. Bouzid's main interest is to examine how Hachemi's and Farfat's generation was penetrated by adult violence and its enduring psychic demarcations in the very same manner that Palestine was raped and dispossessed by Israel following the 1967 Six-Day War. In other words, and as Jeffrey Ruoff rightly suggests, "While Bouzid's cinema is conscious of defeat, it is not defeatist."[7] More precisely, Bouzid is interested in the privatized experience of defeat that is at once structural (pertaining to being human) and historical (pertaining to being Arab in this particular historical juncture). Bouzid argues,

> What interests me in this business of defeat is the idea that the conflict is internal. Not only internal, the conflict is borne by every individual and it cannot be settled except by each individual. *The Man of Ashes* was a notable film in this respect, it was almost a key film, and that continued with *The Golden Horseshoes*. The first film speaks of the destruction and rape of a child; the second speaks of another form of destruction and rape of an adult.[8]

Specifically, *Golden Horseshoes* retells Bouzid's own experience of torture during his imprisonment of more than five years (1973–1979) because of his political involvement in the leftist movement. *Perspectives*, Bouzid's film—which was released shortly after Bourguiba's deposition from power in 1987—is a very bold indictment of Bourguiba's clampdown on leftists and his abuse of human rights by systematic recourse to repressing, torturing, and "disappearing" his political opponents. Like the carpenter-father in *Man of Ashes*, Bourguiba saw himself as the father of Tunisia and Tunisians, a father who would not hesitate to sacrifice (in an Abrahamesque fashion) some of them. Both of Bouzid's films aspire to transform this Abrahamesque and sacrificial relation to the father of the nation (and to all the powers that be) into an oedipal relation and therefore rebellious confrontation. His revisionary approach to Tunisia's and the Arab world's postcolonial history through the lenses of defeat should be understood as an expression of discontent as well as an allegorical conjuration of a future free from injustice.[9]

Toward the end of *Man of Ashes*, Farfat kills Ameur, exacting a long-overdue vengeance on the man who "initiated" him sexually and professionally. Interestingly enough, however, while the plan to kill Ameur was premeditated, it only happened following Farfat's sexual encounter with one of the prostitutes in the brothel. After raising the question of homosexuality, the film seems to settle for normative heterosexual practice as the midwife to Farfat's manhood, revenge and freedom from the trammels of the past. Farfat has at last become what he wanted to be at the beginning of the film, "a rooftop bird": at the very same time that he is portrayed in the film's finale running away from the police, jumping in front of a moving train, and hopping across rooftops, the graffiti that called his manhood into question was being erased. While the film ends with Farfat's ultimate conformity to a conservative and patriarchal apparatus of manhood, its goal is to expose and critique it rather than to reenact and reinscribe it. The same can be said about Boughedir's *Halfaouine*, where the rituals of becoming man in patriarchal society are unraveled in greater detail and far lighter register than *Man of Ashes*.

Halfaouine is the story of Noura (Selim Boughedir), a boy going through the trials of puberty and trying to reconcile the demands of his body to those of the social body and vice versa. Not infrequently, he gets confused about what he wants and what is wanted from him by those around him, and thus he finds himself attempting to reconcile irreconcilables. For instance, his impatience to join the club of men matches only his eagerness to retain the privileges of childhood—namely, accompanying his mother to the women's *hammam* to gaze at local beauties and satisfy his growing sexual curiosity. Boughedir assembles an inventory of the different steps involved in Noura's becoming man, which include circumcision, the banishment from the women's *hammam*, and, above all, sex. Little wonder, then, that Noura's first sexual experience with an orphan-girl servant leads immediately to his revolt against his father, Si Azzouz (Mustapha Adouani), which is a signal of his triumphant resolution of the oedipal struggle and mastery of the fear of castration—really, his ascension to manhood (qua masculinity/virility).

The importance of *Halfaouine* from a postrevolutionary perspective lies not only in Noura's ability to break through all the spatial and gendered boundaries that regiment the private and the public (which is never more to be desired than in the political life of a police state in which secrecy is of the essence of governance) but also in his exposure to political dissidence as an indispensable component of responsible manhood. Noura witnesses the arrest of Salih (Mohammed Driss), an unmarried cobbler, playwright, musician, and public opponent of Bourguiba's obsolete dictatorship, particularly in the 1980s when his health deteriorated and his neurotic obsession with power bordered on psychosis. It bears mentioning here that the scene in which Noura asks Salih, "When does one become a man?" is followed immediately by the scene in which Noura helps Salih stand on an overturned bucket to cross out the graffiti on the wall that read, "Our Leader's idea is all that matters" and write above it, "Our idea is all that matters and without a Leader," which is an apt and prophetic qualification of the Tunisian revolution.

TUNISIA'S DISSIDENT RAP

In the years leading up to the revolution, critique has become, surprisingly enough, more and more adventurous, vocal, and direct, particularly on You-Tube and Facebook, which circulated, among other things, explosive hip-hop videos that had instantaneous effects. Indeed, the role of hip-hop, and rap music in particular as a vehicle of popular discontent against Ben Ali's regime before and after the revolution has become so vital that many can no longer imagine the cultural scene in Tunisia without it (despite the very fact that this genre is so novel in Tunisia and the Arab world in general). Until it came to popular attention in the early years of the new millennium with the rise of Balti as the first professional rapper, Tunisian rap remained more or less obscure (not to say absented) in the 1980s and 1990s, so much so that mizwid[10] was perceived by many as Tunisia's indigenous version of, or cultural equivalent to, Algerian raï and/or American rap music.

Despite its subsequent discomfiting complicity with Ben Ali's regime (as is variably the case with Wled Bled, Balti, Wajdi, Mascott, T-Men, DJ Costa, and others), Tunisian rap music had initially emerged as a democratizing force not only in the field of music and arts as a whole, where a great number of marginalized youth have found in it a viable career path and an accessible means to intervene in the highly commercial and competitive fiefdoms of mizwid and pop culture, but also in the public sphere, where rappers have adopted an activist agenda and spoken loudly in the name of the poor and underprivileged, conveying their political and socioeconomic malaises to the powers that be. Unlike mizwid, which foregrounded dance over lyrics, the intensely content-based form of Tunisian rap music made it immediately amenable to transparent, straightforward, and dense yet unequivocal articulations of popular sentiments, sociopolitical grievances, as well as of transformative, feasible, and perfectible futures. Only a small number of courageous Tunisian rappers, however, was adamant to turn rap into an agent of political critique (and not just a means of social criticism, as was the case with Balti, Nizar T-Men, and others).

Lak3y, Delahoja, Psyco-M, and El Général, among very few others, took rap there, where everyone else feared to tread—to the realm of sociopolitical critique (which was, it bears mentioning here, of foundational importance to the rise and prominence of American rap from Grandmaster Flash to 2Pac and Public Enemy). In 2005, the young rapper Lak3y (a.k.a. Mohamed Ben Salem), from the coastal city of Bizerte, organized an antigovernment concert in which he tore down an RCD (Constitutional Democratic Rally, Ben Ali's party) banner hung by RCD representatives over the stage. This earned him a good thrashing after the concert by a handful of Ben Ali's policemen. Lak3y went underground afterward, but he continued to be active in Tunisia's largely amateurish and obscure rap scene until he came to prominence with his December 2010 pro-revolutionary hit, "Touche Pas à Ma Tunisie" ("Don't Touch My Tunisia"). His earlier hit adopted an ironic title, "Tounes bikhayr" (that is, "Tunisia is well-off"), in order to debunk the official governmental rhetoric that Tunisia is a well-off society. Lak3y exposes socioeconomic inequality, cronyism, and the culture of corruption in a language and underground style similar to El Général's "Rais Lebled." The same can be said here about DJ Costa's "Royal Mafia" and Fami DKF's "Révolution," both of which convey searing criticisms of Ben Ali's system without naming names. Here the dissimilation of corruption and the simulation of democracy, the joined-up strategy of Ben Ali's state rhetoric, are exposed through "kynical subversion," irony and ridicule, reminiscent of

Moncef Dhouib's 2006 *The TV's Coming*.[11] The film is saturated with jokes and comic encounters, but its ultimate goal is didactic and critical. It exposes how Tunisian officialdom was able to produce and disseminate a totally falsified image of Tunisia to both Tunisians and non-Tunisians alike while unemployment, corruption, and national disillusionment were briskly thrusting the country to the brink of insurrection.

In the same year, another Tunisian rapper, Férid El Extranjero (a.k.a. Delahoja), an original member of Filozof, released a damning song titled "3bed Fi Terkina" ("People in a Prison Corner"), which exposed police brutality, the use of torture, and the overall ruthlessness of Ben Ali's criminal regime. The song begins as follows: "We live in a prison corner, our flesh is cut with a knife / Not only that, but the police insult and humiliate us / Poverty, woes and problems—it's a fish-eat-fish world." Delahoja released the song from Spain, where he has lived for quite some time now after short stops in Italy and France. He has experienced firsthand police brutality, imprisonment, and humiliation; he left Tunisia in the late 1990s following a fight with a policeman who insulted and cursed him and his family. He released the song upon his return to Spain after a short stay in Tunisia in 2005 (in which he was, not surprisingly, arrested in the airport). The song contained a few explicit words, but its language was on the whole nowhere near the explicit language of the notorious Karkadan or Mos Anif Mossa.[12] When the song reached Tunisia and became an underground hit, it drew the attention of Ben Ali's police, which exerted further pressure on rappers and left them with very limited choices. Delahoja was officially banned from reentering the country. Many went back underground, while others were more than ever convinced to stick to commercial rap and steer clear from political subjects. Chief among the latter group is Balti whose career thrived while those of others were further jeopardized.[13]

The venture of Tunisian rap music took a completely sociopolitical turn by the year 2010, the very same year that the United Nations General Assembly proclaimed, following Ben Ali's initiative, to be the International Youth Year. Little did Ben Ali know at the time that those very youth he championed would initiate his eventual deposition from power after twenty-three years of authoritarian rule. At the very same time that an orchestrated campaign calling on Ben Ali to run for the 2014 presidential elections was well underway (backed up by a petition that sixty-five Tunisian celebrities and public figures allegedly signed), rappers, along with a wide range of youth spokespersons, cyber-activists, dissident politicians, and journalists, have initiated a countercampaign calling for democratization.

Rap music has become more and more vocal and controversial in its critique of social and public issues that range from drugs, prostitution, and corruption to sound pollution (namely, the proposal that called for the reduction of the volume of *adhan*, or call to prayer, a proposal that launched a public uproar). B4 Clan decried the proposal in their song "Contre-Attaque" ("Counterattack"), and several other rappers and rap crews did the same, all the while calling for a revalorization of Islam and Islamic values. Because Ben Ali's regime denigrated everyday Islamic practices (for example, intimidation and harassment of veiled women and bearded men, mosque-goers, etc.), Tunisian rap took a more and more Islamic bent, insofar as it denounced moral bankruptcy, the loosening of traditional values, and the rampancy of corruption. Apart from El Général's "Rais Lebled," two songs in particular gave rise to public controversies and brought rap to unprecedented musical prominence in 2010.

Balti's "Passe Partout" (a damning portrait with real pictures of Tunisian girls as prostitutes and one-night-standers) provoked public responses from parents and families as well as rappers (such as DJ Costa, Emino, and Lotfi Abdelli, who collaborated on "Chawahtou som3et lebled," or "You Stained the Reputation of the Country," a response song and corrective to Balti's invective) because one version of the video clip contained the pictures of real Tunisian girls caught on camera partying in various nightclubs. The shots of the anonymous girls featured were not particularly flattering pictures, even though it was later found out that the pictures were actually picked up from Facebook pages and mounted by Balti's fans to the original clip of the song, which had not contained any such pictures. At any rate, the song provoked so much brouhaha, rage, and fury that it officially gave rise to the phenomenon of "rap clashes," long associated with the West Coast/East Coast rivalries and diatribes between Tupac Shakur and the Notorious B.I.G., and later between Nas and Jay-Z. Despite his co-option by Ben Ali's regime, Balti can be credited for writing songs that contain a measure of constructive ambiguity capable of igniting controversy and debate, which is not a negligible feat within dictatorships. *Constructive ambiguity* here means simply to raise questions indirectly about the regime's social and cultural policies, not to mention its moral values insofar as they are reflected in the video clip.

The other shock-song is "Manipulation" by Psyco-M (a.k.a. Mohamed El Jandoubi). The song was released later in the year and mounted a sweeping attack on, among others, Arab nationalists and secularists alike, accusing them of involvement in a Euro-Zionist plot against Islam. The fifteen-minute-long song included, among other things, an explicit attack on such public figures as

Sawsen Maalej, an actress who used to appear routinely on Nessma TV, and Olfa Youssef, the author of the highly contentious book *Hayrat Muslima* (The Bewilderment of a Muslim Woman). Maalej and Youssef created a public uproar, the former for making an explicit reference to the male sexual organ of her colleague on a popular TV show and the latter for pointing out that the Qur'an is inconclusive about female inheritance, homosexuality, and masturbation, among other hot-button issues. Both ended up filing a defamation suit against Psyco-M following the serious toll the song took on their reputations and the death threats they received because of its high-speed cyber-reach.

Filmmaker Nouri Bouzid had also filed a complaint against Ennahda and Psyco-M, whom he accuses of issuing a death threat against him in a public rally organized by Ennahda on April 17, 2011. The lyrics of the song at stake, "La Guerre Psychologique" ("Psychological War") express Psyco-M's passing wish to use a "Kalashnikov" against all those behind the global media campaign against Islam, including Nouri Bouzid, whose films allegedly disparage Islam and equate it with terrorism. The song, however, dates back to 2009, a time period in which Ennahda was not officially in business. In his defense, Psyco-M claimed that he used the word "Kalashnikov" metaphorically to refer to the powers and devastating effects of his rhymes. As for Bouzid, he pointed out time and again that he was not troubled by Psyco-M as an artist, whose right to artistic freedom ought to remain intact, but rather by the regressivist-Salafist ideologies that inform his songs.

Many have associated Psyco-M, who was banned from performing under Ben Ali, with extremism, fanaticism, and fundamentalist trends spearheaded by the unlicensed *Hizb al-Tahrir* (or Liberation Party), whose central political project revolves around the reinstitution of the Islamic Caliphate. Others, however, support him for his bravery and informed invectives against the equally orthodox and fundamentalist tendencies of some Francophile secularists. Psyco-M was selected the best rapper of 2010 on Facebook, where he enjoys a great reputation not only as a provocateur rapper but also as an anti-imperialist (albeit ideologically driven) artist. Notwithstanding the regressivist-Salafist tendencies of his songs, Psyco-M has clearly emerged as one of the effortless masters of the flow, oftentimes associated with the Algerian rapper Lotfi Double Kanon, who also enjoys a good reputation in Tunisia. The sheer length and scope of, not to mention the amount of information and provocation contained in, his lyrics combine to make Psyco-M easily one of the most important, albeit controversial, rappers in the entire Arab world.

It might be a contradiction in terms of rappers to adopt a nontraditional musical genre such as rap music to preach a return to traditional Islamic values, but this is for sure the logical outcome of Ben Ali's corrupt and corrupted secularist practices. Despite his notoriety and the controversial nature of his songs, the importance of Psyco-M lies in the fact that he clearly upped the ante of critique and paved the way for the emergence of raw criticisms of Ben Ali's regime. Other rappers soon followed suit, while a few others consolidated further their already contestatory credentials, including Guito'N, RTM, Weld el 15, Wistar, Gadour, L'Imbattable, Mohamed Ali Ben Jemaa, Black Eye, Sincero, Kenzi, and, above all, El Général.

El Général took on the risky task of sending direct messages to Ben Ali twice. The first was titled "Sidi Rais" ("Mr. President") and was not substantially different from his second and now greatest claim to national and international fame, "Rais Lebled" ("Head of State"). Like Psyco-M and several other rappers and rap crews, El Général called for the revalorization of Islam and Islamic values, but he went much further than most and addressed not only the sensitive question of state oppression and repression but, above all, the question of corruption. In a leaked cable, the US ambassador to Tunis, Robert F. Godec, called corruption the "elephant in the room": every Tunisian knows about it, but no one dares to address it. El Général dared the president to step down from his ivory tower in Palace Carthage and make a real field trip to the grey zones of Tunisia (and not the kind of "surprise" but elaborately planned and premeditated trips he was known for since the early years of his presidency). He addressed Ben Ali in the persona of a schoolboy, as evidenced by the opening footage from one of Ben Ali's 1990s surprise trips to two underdeveloped areas in the interior of the country.

El Général's lyrics are raw and frank, but his style is diplomatic on the whole, which is why the song worked quite well with audiences worldwide and was seductive and persuasive even to Ben Ali's supporters. The refrain of the song paints an apocalyptic picture of Tunisia and has become the rallying cry of protests from Avenue Bourguiba to Tahrir Square:

> *Rais lebled, sha'bik met*
> *Barsha 'bed mizibla klet*
> *Hek tshouf esh qā'id sāyir fil-bled*
> *Ma'āsi partout we'bed mal-qātish wīn tbet*
> *Hānī nihkī bi'sm eshsha'b illī tzalmū willī 'indāsū bissubbāt*

Mr. President, your people are dead
Many, today, on garbage fed
As you can obviously see what's going on nationwide,
Miseries everywhere and people find nowhere to sleep
I speak on behalf of those who were wronged and ground under feet

The audacity and courage of El Général's song is unmistakable, all the more so that it was uploaded to Facebook at a time when Ben Ali was celebrating the twenty-third anniversary of his ascension to power on November 7, 1987, (a.k.a., *al-Tahawul al-Mubārak*, or the Blessed Change). The song was obviously censored and El Général arrested in a dramatic manner following presidential orders on January 6, 2011. By then the song had become the anthem of the uprising throughout the country, and El Général was released three days afterward. Unlike many rap songs produced about the Arab revolutions after they unfolded, El Général's "Rais Lebled" was a leap in the dark, a sort of *cri-de-coeur* uttered way before the revolution started or took shape, at a time when very few would dare address Ben Ali publically. No wonder he was celebrated by *Time* magazine as the seventy-fourth-most influential person in the world, ahead of US president Barack Obama and of FC Barcelona and Argentina soccer superstar Lionel Messi, as well as of Israel's notorious prime minister Benjamin Netanyahu.

"Rais Lebled" has become now a classic in Tunisian and Arab rap music. It has variably been emulated by numerous wannabe MCs, and El Général's international recognition has resulted in an overdose of revolutionary and patriotic rap songs. Ben Ali and his wife, Leila Trabelsi, have excited much of the pent-up ire of postrevolutionary rappers, but, with the exception of those who were overtly or covertly the beneficiaries of Ben Ali's regime (like Balti and Mascott), most rappers hitched their wagon to the promissory train of the revolution of freedom and dignity. In postrevolutionary Tunisia, all rappers (new and old) have become vociferous claimants to revolutionary credentials. While underground contestatory rap is now being commoditized and co-opted by the market economy, it remains unclear how it will remain on target as a politically engaged musical genre, shot through with insurrection and revolt. Counting more than a hundred new rappers, the postrevolutionary Tunisian rap scene is flourishing for sure, but the political role of rap might well be in decline once its main thematic axis, the revolution, exhausts itself. Whether rap music will continue to exert pressure and garner the kind of attention it did in Tunisia during the revolution is yet to be seen, but one thing is clear for now: post–Ben Ali regimes would be well-advised to have open and perceptive ears, because, if they fail to listen, they will hardly survive the new brave voice of Tunisian youth—namely, their favorite weapon of mass insurrection, rap music.

NOTES

1. See Jacques Lacan, "The Mirror Stage as Formative of the Function of the I as Revealed in Psychoanalytic Experience," in *Literary Theory: An Anthology*, ed. Julie *Rivkin and Michael Ryan* (Oxford: Blackwell, 2004), 445. Lacan speaks of the phenomenon of suicide in relation to an overall critique of existentialism, which according to him, "must be judged by the explanations it gives of the subjective impasses that have indeed resulted from it; a freedom that is never more authentic than when it is within the walls of a prison; a demand for commitment, expressing the impotence of a pure consciousness to master any situation; a voyeuristic-sadistic idealization of the sexual relation; a personality that realizes itself only in suicide; a consciousness of the other that can be satisfied only by Hegelian murder."

2. I find the notion of the "cynical subject" applicable to the majority of state feminists and intellectuals under Bourguiba and Ben Ali. In his reading of Peter Sloterdijk's *Critique of Cynical Reason*, Slavoj Žižek defines the cynical subject as follows: "The cynical subject is quite aware of the distance between the ideological mask and the social reality, but he nonetheless still insists upon the mask." See Slavoj Žižek, "The Sublime Object of Ideology," in *Literary Theory: An Anthology*, ed. Julie Rivkin and Michael Ryan (Oxford: Blackwell, 2004), 718. State intellectuals know the emperor has no clothes. What boggles the mind, however, is not only the fact that they didn't dare say so but that they insisted on not saying so.

3. I have in mind here Alan Sinfield's definition of dissidence as "the refusal of an aspect of the dominant, without prejudging the outcome." See "Cultural Materialism, *Othello*, and the Politics of Plausibility," in *Literary Theory: An Anthology*, ed. Julie Rivkin and Michael Ryan (Oxford: Blackwell, 2004), 757.

4. See Sinfield, "Cultural Materialism, *Othello*, and the Politics of Plausibility," 757.

5. Translation mine.

6. There is no way in which Tunisians could have learned to read and understand state media that would not have enabled them, by the same token, to read and understand the underground press. There is a maxim in Tunisian culture that says, "*laou kān mush min 'amahum man en'ishush em'ahum.*" Roughly, this means, "If it were not for their blindness, we would not be able to deal with them." Ben Ali has always played the game of democracy, the game of women's rights, human rights, and the game of modernity and education for all, but he did not do that out of a belief in those rights, only to the extent they served to cast positive light on his image as the father of the nation. What he did not realize, luckily for us, is that he would be played by the game he played.

7. Jeffrey Ruoff, "The Gulf War, the Iraq War, and Nouri Bouzid's Cinema of Defeat: *It's Sche-herazade We're Killing* (1993) and *Making Of* (2006), *South Central Review* 28, no. 1 (2011): 31.

8. Nouri Bouzid, "On Inspiration," in *African Experiences of Cinema*, ed. Imruh Bakari and Mbye B. Cham (London: British Film Institute, 1996), 54.

9. For more on this, see Nouri Gana, "Bourguiba's Sons: Melancholy Manhood in Modern Tunisian Cinema," *Journal of North African Studies* 15, no. 1 (2010): 105–26.

10. *Mizwid* is Tunisia's most popular *sha'bi*, or folk music, whose name derives from the main instrument that accompanies the singing—that is, the goatskin bagpipe. See Kathryn Stapley, "Mizwid: An Urban Music with Rural Roots," *Journal of Ethnic and Migration Studies* 32, no. 2 (2006): 254.

11. According to Žižek's reading of Sloterdijk, Kynical subversion—"the plebian rejection of the official culture by means of irony and sarcasm"—undoes the cynical reason of the powers that be, their "enlightened false consciousness"—that is, their knowledge of falsehood and their attachment to it. See Žižek, *The Sublime Object of Ideology*, 718.

12. One of Karkadan's early hits curses the day the police caught the rapper by surprise at home, and, as such, the song is titled, "Zokom ak nhar" ("Fuck That Day"). Mos Anif Mossa's hit song "Tahchi Fih" ("Liar") exposes the widespread culture of hypocrisy and lying that mediates all forms of sociality in Ben Ali's Tunisia.

13. Balti claims that he was summoned to the Interior Ministry for questioning after the release of Delahoja's devastating video. The experience further convinced Balti of the entailments or potential risks of treating political subjects in his music. Both Balti and Mascott participated in concerts during Ben Ali's electoral campaigns in 2004 and 2009. In his account, David Peisner relates how Balti became a "potential revenue source" for government officials and their business associates in ways that redounded to everyone's benefit (or share of the cake). See "Inside Tunisia's Hip-Hop Revolution," *Spin*, August 24, 2011, accessed March 19, 2014, http://www.spin.com/articles/inside-tunisias-hip-hop-revolution. After the revolution Balti made a song titled "Matloumounich," in which he tries to redeem himself, explaining why he steered clear from politics and recounting how he was routinely persecuted and arrested by Ben Ali's regime.

II

DYNAMICS

6

Reassessing the Recent History of Political Islam in Light of the Arab Uprisings

James L. Gelvin

However they may play themselves out, the Arab Uprisings that began in the wake of Mohamed Bouazizi's self-immolation in December 2010 have called attention to the fact that the Arab world has not been impervious to the diffusion of international norms of human rights and democratic governance. They have also called attention to a related issue: the paradigmatic shift that had transformed Islamist politics in the region and opened up the prospect for participation by Islamists and Islamist groups in a political order rooted in those norms.

During the 1980s and 1990s, governments throughout the Arab world engaged their violent Islamist opponents, such as the Islamic Group (*al-jamaa al-islamiya*) and Egyptian Islamic Jihad (*al-jihad al-islamic al-masri*) in Egypt, the Islamic Salvation Army Armed Movement (*Armée Islamique du Salut*, or AIS) and the Armed Islamic Group (*Groupe Islamique Armé*, or GIA) in Algeria, the Muslim Brotherhood (*al-ikhwan al-muslimin*) in Syria, and the Libyan Islamic Fighting Group (*al-jamaa al-islamiyyah al-muqatilah bi-libya*), along with others, in wars of extermination. For the most part, groups targeted for elimination (rather than containment) by various governments shared a number of characteristics:

- The groups were organized in small, cadre formations, similar in structure to the cells of the early Ba'th Party. The GIA, for example, consisted of autonomous militias whose size varied from twenty or fewer members to three hundred or so.[1]
- The groups operated clandestinely, attempting to fly beneath the radar of the state's ever-expanding security apparatus.
- The groups assumed that success could only come through acts of violence. These acts were intended, variously, to eliminate leaders and regimes that were "un-Islamic," force those regimes to engage in acts of repression that would unmask their brutality to the population at large, cripple regimes by undermining tourism and financial institutions, and rouse the population through heroic acts of resistance.[2]
- The groups were Leninist, believing that change would come through the activities of devoted cadres and not through mass mobilization.
- Finally, except for calls for the replacement of the regimes against which they fought with ones committed to "Islamic governance" and rule by *sharia*, they were programmatically vague.

Ideology aside, then, the groups against which Arab governments warred during the 1980s and 1990s more closely resembled the Baader Meinhof Gang or Che's guerrillas than they did the various parties that took part in elections in the aftermath of the Arab Uprisings of 2010 and 2011.

The aforementioned groups were not the only ones against which Arab governments campaigned during this period. Governments targeted, to a greater or lesser extent, even those groups that had pledged to work within the system. Among those targeted to a greater extent were Ennahda in Tunisia and the Islamic Salvation Front (*Front Islamique du Salut*, or FIS) in Algeria. Both groups emerged during the late 1980s, when the full effects of failed economic and social policies led to popular rebellion, compelling the Tunisian and Algerian governments to flirt temporarily with more-open political systems. Leaders of Ennahda and FIS realized the tenuousness of their position and so trod carefully. But when both groups demonstrated their popularity in free elections for parliament—candidates affiliated with Ennahda officially won upward of 17 percent of the vote in 1989, and FIS candidates won close to 50 percent of the vote in 1991—the Tunisian and Algerian governments dissolved them and began jailing their members. Rachid Ghannouchi, leader of Ennahda, fled to London, from where he called for an uprising. Similarly, with the dissolution of FIS, cadres founded a plethora of armed groups that declared war on the state. The lesson learned from the brief periods of *perestroika*—that the Tunisian and Algerian regimes would never surrender their privileges peacefully—encouraged the emergence of violent cadre organizations in both cases. Gaddafi's repression of the mainstream Muslim Brotherhood in Libya during the 1980s had the similar effect of catalyzing the emergence of the Libyan Islamic Fighting Group.[3]

In Egypt, the Mubarak regime's campaign against the Egyptian Muslim Brotherhood was less dramatic but no less effective. After years of repression, the general guide of the Brotherhood renounced violence altogether in 1972, a pledge renewed in 1987.[4] Banned but tolerated and prohibited from forming its own party, the Brotherhood formed alliances with officially sanctioned parties, running candidates under their banner or as independents. In the parliamentary elections of 1987—held one year after the same sort of popular insurrection that rocked Tunisia and Algeria broke out in Egypt—opposition candidates won an unprecedented number of seats (candidates of the Brotherhood-affiliated Islamic Alliance won 60 out of a total of 458 seats), in spite of manipulation and irregularities. Then came the reaction in the 1990s—what political scientist Eberhard Kienle has called the "political deliberalization of Egypt." The regime rolled back the electoral gains made by the Brotherhood, took on the right to invalidate elections held in professional syndicates (where Brotherhood candidates had faired exceptionally well), and expanded the domain of military tribunals, among other measures. Again, a lesson was learned: The 1972 Brotherhood renunciation of violence had precipitated an organizational split and the formation of the Islamic Group and Egyptian Islamic Jihad. The deliberalization of Egypt seemingly validated their position that violence was the only effective means to bringing about political change.[5]

During the 1980s and 1990s, states undertook far-reaching measures to combat their real and perceived enemies. The Egyptian and Algerian governments cited Islamist violence as the reason to declare states of emergency in 1981 and 1992, respectively, and the Syrian government cited it as one of the reasons to maintain the state of emergency it had imposed in 1963. In all three cases, governments used states of emergency to empanel extraordinary courts and military tribunals and to suspend constitutionally guaranteed rights, such as habeas corpus. This enabled those governments to arrest suspected militants *en masse* (between 1992 and 1997, for example, the Egyptian government arrested forty-seven thousand).[6] According to the Arab Organization for Human Rights and the United Nations High Commission for Human Rights, by the early twenty-first century eleven

Arab states regularly tortured the prisoners they held. Sometimes these prisoners were interned under authorization of "state security courts," which operated with unclear jurisdictional limits, imprecise procedural guidelines, and no oversight. Eleven Arab states did not even bother putting up a facade of security courts: their constitutions allowed for extrajudicial detentions.[7]

To ensure the smooth functioning of their repressive apparatus, states relied on a pervasive security network that, as time went on, only grew more and more bloated. During the period of insurgency, the Algerian government availed itself of fifty thousand police to keep order; even as the insurgency wound down, the government kept expanding the numbers of police until they reached, by the second decade of the twenty-first century, one hundred seventy thousand.[8] A similar situation held in Libya, where Muammar Gaddafi, calling his Islamist opposition "more dangerous than AIDS," turned the entire eastern part of the country into a "security zone" from which the government extracted thousands of suspects.[9] In Syria, Egypt, Yemen, and Bahrain governments expanded their security apparatus to such an extent that they had to outsource the job to local hoodlums: *baltagiya* ("hatchet men") in the case of Egypt, Yemen, and Bahrain, *ashbah* ("ghosts") in the case of Syria, who hailed from the same sect and region as the inner circle of Syria's ruling structure. These thugs not only acted as the eyes and ears of the state, they created a threatening atmosphere to cow populations.[10] On the eve of the uprisings in Egypt, it was estimated that the security apparatus engaged approximately one million Egyptians, from interior ministry bureaucrats to agents in the field to common snitches.[11] And alongside the security apparatus throughout the region special military units were deployed when regimes felt particularly threatened by widespread insurgency, as took place in Syria in the late 1970s and early 1980s (as the story of Hama tells us) and Algeria during the 1990s, when the army's "eradicators" took on the GIA.

The measures undertaken by states to quash their Islamist opponents proved effective on a number of levels. On an individual level, some cadres—such as jailed members of the Egyptian Islamic Group—disavowed violence and pledged allegiance to the state in exchange for their release from prison.[12] In 1997, imprisoned members of the group issued an "Initiative of Cessation of Violence," which the members promoted through a government-sanctioned prison ministry initiated to convince others to follow suit (the infamous "Luxor massacre," during which other members of the group killed fifty-eight tourists and four Egyptians a few months later, demonstrated that not all were prepared, in the derisive words of future al-Qaeda leader Ayman al-Zawahiri, "to repeatedly importune corrupt secular governments to grant us permission to establish an Islamic state.")[13] Others, such as the aforementioned Rachid Ghannouchi and 'Ali Sadr al-Din al-Bayanouni, general guide of the Syrian Muslim Brotherhood, fled to Europe and North America. There were still others, not so celebrated, who simply withdrew from politics. In some cases—the most notable being Algeria— governments that had broken the backs of Islamist insurgencies offered pardons or reduced sentences to those who came in from the cold. Approximately ten thousand Algerian militants took advantage of various proposals offered by Algerian governments between 1995 and 2005. Others simply melted back into society or decamped to wage jihad in Afghanistan.[14]

The fate of groups whose memberships governments had decimated also varied. Some—Ennahda in Tunisia, the Muslim Brotherhood in Syria—were completely destroyed in their home countries, although they maintained shell organizations abroad. After two years of "reconciliation and rehabilitation" conferences involving the Libyan government and leaders and members of the Libyan Islamic Fighting Group, leaders of the group in exile recanted their beliefs and tactics in a 417-page document, "Revisionist Studies of the Concepts of Jihad, Verification, and Judgment of People," and issued an apology to Muammar Gaddafi. Soon thereafter, the group officially disbanded.[15] In June 2006, the exiled leader of the Syrian Muslim Brotherhood went even further than offering a simple apology: citing the backing of the Syrian government for the Palestinian resistance then fighting the Israelis in Gaza and for the anti-imperialist struggle in general, he withdrew his organization from the National Salvation Front, a coalition of opposition groups and figures, and declared an end to its antigovernment activities inside Syria.[16] This action did nothing to mollify the Syrian government, and membership in the Brotherhood remained a crime punishable by death.

Overall, the Arab governments' campaign against violent Islamist groups during the 1980s and 1990s might be judged a success for two reasons: it wiped out their violent opposition, and it demonstrated the inefficacy of the tactics adopted by those groups.

There is another side to the story, however: It might be argued that the Arab governments' campaigns against violent Islamist groups during the 1980s and 1990s was an unmitigated disaster for those governments. There are three reasons this might be said. First, the very tactics governments used to destroy those groups—imposing emergency laws, expanding repression and the repressive apparatus, and the like—would inspire the Uprisings that swept through the

Arab world in the Winter of 2010 and into 2011. Second, by demonstrating the inefficacy of violence, the governments' campaigns created a political opening in which mass-based, nonviolent Islamist organizations—such as those that performed so well in the 2011 and 2012 parliamentary elections held in Morocco, Tunisia, and Egypt—might flourish. Third and finally, repression encouraged the creation of new "Islamist spaces" in prisons and in exile communities that facilitated networking and strategizing among Islamists, the cross-fertilization of organizational and ideological initiatives, and the disbursement of material support for individuals and groups both domestically and transnationally.

HUMAN RIGHTS AND REVOLTS

Ironically, the Arab governments' repression of their violent opposition coincided with the diffusion of international norms of human rights and democratic governance throughout the world, including the Arab world. While the concept of human rights might be dated as far back as the eighteenth century, the contemporary human-rights movement really came into its own in the 1970s. Just why this was the case has been the subject of controversy. There is no doubt, though, that during the decade of the 1970s American policy makers found putting human rights on the international agenda useful both in its ideological confrontation with the Soviet Union and the Global South, and in advancing the cause of "economic freedom" (that is, neoliberalism *avant la lettre*) against the Global South's economic assertion (as manifested in its demand for a "New International Economic Order" and the oil-price revolution of 1973 and 1974).[17] Regardless of the reason, historian Samuel Moyn is surely correct when he states, "Over the course of the 1970s, the moral world of Westerners shifted, opening a space for the sort of utopianism that coalesced in an international human-rights movement that had never existed before."[18] But if it was utopianism, it was of a narrowly defined sort, one that promoted the primacy of individual political, civil, and personal rights over the litany of collective rights advanced in international fora by the Global South and Soviet bloc.[19]

The shift in both consequence and content of human-rights advocacy gave rise, in a very short period, to an entire apparatus devoted to the oversight of human rights that maintained, spread, and deepened it. For example, the International Criminal Court, which indicted Libyan leader Muammar Gaddafi for crimes against humanity, was founded only in 2002. And the doctrine R2P—responsibility to protect—only emerged after a series of disastrous humanitarian interventions in the 1990s.[20] R2P provided the foundation for UN Security

Council resolution 1973 calling for the establishment of a no-fly zone over Libya. International organizations founded to monitor human-rights violations also proliferated during this period. The oldest such group, Amnesty International, was founded in 1961, and Human Rights Watch dates back to just 1978.

Trends in the Arab world reflected broader trends, and while they did not affect governments' policies much, if at all, they established regional precedents. Beginning in the 1990s, for example, governments throughout the region began establishing "human-rights councils," ostensibly to review human-rights complaints. By 2008, such councils existed in ten Arab states including the Palestinian territories.[21] Although the actual purpose of the councils was to assuage international opinion, their establishment had much the same effect as had the signing of the Helsinki Declaration 1975: they catalyzed the emergence of nongovernmental bodies that kept tabs on human-rights abuses and made the discourse on rights part of a shared political vocabulary. The first such group, the *Ligue Tunisienne des Droits de l'Homme*, was founded in 1976.[22] Since that time, human-rights organizations have mushroomed throughout the region.

Beginning in the first years of the twenty-first century, Arab human rights organizations undertook a number of high-profile initiatives to promote human and democratic rights in the region.[23] In 2004, representatives from fifty-two nongovernmental Arab human-rights and prodemocracy organizations organized a civil forum in Beirut on the eve of an Arab League Summit. In its final communiqué, addressed to Arab heads of state, the representatives outlined demands for political change, ranging from ending torture and releasing political prisoners to devolving political power from bloated central governments to locally accountable councils. (For those who would attribute a starring role for the United States in the Arab drama, the declaration explicitly rejected meddlesome interference from abroad).[24] Feeling the heat, the Arab League adopted a revised version of its 1994 Arab Charter on Human Rights at its Tunis summit two months later, reaffirming the rights previously enumerated in the forum's communiqué.[25] Similar meetings of rights advocates in 2004 resulted in the Doha Declaration for Democracy and Reform, the Alexandria Charter, and the Sana'a Declaration, each expanding their predecessors' lists of enumerated rights, as well as the purview of civil-society groups.[26]

Evidence for the diffusion of international norms of human rights and democratic governance in the Arab world—in a number of cases on the popular level—might also be found in a wave of protests that began in 1988 and continued throughout the region up through the current Uprisings. Like the current Uprisings, these protests demanded social justice, democratic reform, and an end to human-rights abuses. Among their number were the following:

- The so-called "Black October" riots in Algeria in 1988 (also dubbed, dismissively, the "Couscous Riots") began as a bread riot in Algiers and quickly took a political turn as protesters targeted regime corruption, torture, and other forms of repression, and the lack of democratic institutions and rights. Protests spread throughout the country, propelled by a strike wave among students and workers and newly established civil-society groups. The ruling FLN (Front de Libération Nationale) took the protests so seriously that it offered a new constitution that guaranteed freedom of expression and association and that made no mention of the FLN at all. The FLN also issued a new electoral law that set the stage for the first truly free elections in the Arab world in which more than forty parties competed (although when the Islamic Salvation Front won close to half the vote in the first round, the military stepped in to cancel the results, precipitating Algeria's seven-year descent into violence).[27]
- The Bahraini intifada of 1994 to 1999 began with a petition movement demanding an end to emergency rule, the restoration of rights abrogated by that emergency rule, release of political prisoners, pardons for political exiles, and the expansion of the franchise to women. Petitioners also demanded a restoration of the 1973 constitution, which provided for a parliament in which two-thirds of the members were elected. Approximately one-tenth of the island's citizens signed the petitions. After the government arrested a prominent religious scholar, the population staged mass demonstrations that—after the government responded with violence—morphed into a widespread rebellion. The rebellion only subsided when Sheikh Hamad ascended to the throne and held a referendum on a National Action Charter guaranteeing basic freedoms, universal suffrage, and the rule of law (in the end, King Hamad abandoned the promises made in the charter and decreed the 2002 constitution, which suspended the democratic rights promised by the charter).[28]
- The brief "Damascus Spring" of 2000 was a period of intense political ferment that began after the death of Hafez al-Assad and the accession of his son to the presidency. The Damascus Spring began in informal salons whose participants expanded the movement first through a petition, the "Statement of the Ninety-nine," then through a second, the "Statement of a Thousand." The statements demanded, among other things, the end of the emergency law that had been in effect since 1963, the release of political prisoners, multi-party elections, and

freedom of speech, assembly, and expression. Even after the Damascus Spring turned into the Damascus Winter, aftershocks of the mobilization continued. Among those aftershocks was the Damascus Declaration Movement of 2005, which (initially) united the secular and religious opposition in a common demand for democratic rights.[29]

- Kefaya (Enough!) was formed in Egypt in 2004, shortly before the Egyptian government held a referendum to confirm a fifth term for Mubarak. Kefaya was an amalgam of political currents ranging from nationalist to communist to Islamist that united around demands for electoral reform. It was the first group ever to call for Mubarak's resignation. Not only would Kefaya make demands echoed by activists in 2011, it pioneered tactics exploited during the uprising as well. This should not be surprising: although Kefaya had faded years before the uprising, one of the founders of the April 6 Movement, which played a principal role in organizing the January 2011 Tahrir Square protests, came from Kefaya's youth movement.[30]

- Popular agitation led to the establishment of the Equity and Reconciliation Commission in Morocco, also in 2004. King Mohammed VI charged the commission to investigate human-rights abuses during the brutal "Years of Lead," a three-decades-long period of repression and extrajudicial executions that took place while his father reigned, during which hundreds of regime opponents were killed and disappeared. Once the commission had completed its work, the king apologized to Moroccans on behalf of the throne. (A similar demand for justice was made in Bahrain, where the National Committee for Martyrs and Torture Victims circulated a petition signed by thirty-three thousand demanding the repeal of a law that denied the right of victims of human-rights violations to bring suits against their persecutors.)[31]

- The well-known Cedar Revolution of 2005 (known locally as the "independence intifada") saw protesters demanding not only the removal of Syrian forces from Lebanon but parliamentary elections free from Syrian interference.

One might also add into the mix Berber protests during the so-called "Berber Spring" of 1980 in Algeria and Kurdish protests in 2004, 2008, and 2010 in Syria demanding minority rights. And the list goes on.

Overall, this catalog of popular resistance in the Arab world over the course of the past thirty years (a catalog that might also include protests and strikes demanding economic justice—from the IMF riots of the 1980s through the Egyptian strike wave from 2006 to 2008) provides a counternarrative to the predominant description of Arab politics in which demoralized populations are cowed by autocratic regimes—that is, until the dam burst in 2010 and 2011. It also calls into question the term "Arab Spring," a phrase that makes recent events appear unique and severs their connection to previous history, to describe those events.

ISLAMIST POLITICS

It would be easy to isolate the protests and uprisings enumerated above within a discrete secular realm of politics from which liberal and leftist ideologies engage Islamist politics in a zero-sum game. This, however, runs contrary to fact: a number of Islamists and Islamist groups participated in these protests alongside liberals and leftists. That they should do so should not be surprising for two reasons. First, Islamist politics is not an autonomous realm of action. It is an adjunct to a broader political sphere. Islamist politics derives its mobilizing strategies, legitimating principles, and goals from that broader sphere, which ultimately defines what sort of politics is possible and what sort is not. Second, in the wake of 9/11 a number of human-rights and prodemocracy groups and fora reached out to their Islamist counterparts in an effort not only to strengthen their political position by taking advantage of the Islamists' proven popularity but also to circumscribe what they perceived to be the rising tide of immoderate Islamism. Thus, for example, the letter sent by the Civil Forum to Arab heads of state included an open call for dialogue with Islamists who disavow violence (and the marginalization of those who do not), the participation of Islamists in an expanded political process, and a dialogue between rights advocates and religious "innovators" (*mujadadun*).[32]

This outreach on the part of human-rights activists was not without effect. By spring 2011 the conservative al-Azhar, an institution long before co-opted by the regime, responded to the Egyptian uprising by hosting meetings between prominent religious scholars and secular intellectuals. The result was the "al-Azhar Document," which highlighted areas of agreement, including constitutional rule, democratic governance (based on the Islamic notion of *shura*—consultation), equal rights for religious minorities, freedom of expression, and social justice. The document also condemned the practice of *takfir*—declaring Muslims who do not pass a religious litmus test non-Muslims—which provided the pretext for the war waged by violent Islamists in the 1980s and 1990s against their regime opponents.[33] A little more than a month after al-Azhar released the document, the Egyptian Muslim Brotherhood endorsed it.

The "al-Azhar Document" is but one example of the way changed circumstances (and, perhaps, political opportunism) shaped ideology in the aftermath of the Arab Uprisings. There have been multiple. Perhaps the most striking has to do with the transformation of fundamental attitudes toward politics and the political sphere among the previously ideologically purist Salafis in Egypt and elsewhere. Before the Egyptian uprising, Salafis, whose al-Nour Party went on to garner 20 percent of the votes in the first postuprising parliamentary elections, had foresworn participation in politics, enjoining quietism and obedience to any ruler so long as he was Muslim. The opening up of political space in post-Mubarak Egypt, however, provided an opportunity too good to be passed over, and Salafis not only abandoned their opposition to the democratic process (because it was based on *vox populi*, not *vox dei*), they also abandoned their opposition to women's participation in the public sphere (compelled by law to include women candidates on the party's parliamentary slate) and their contention that Christians in Muslim societies should be relegated to a second-class *dhimmi* status by including them as well on their electoral list (again, compelled by electoral law).[34] Their political opportunism once again trumped ideology when they endorsed the presidential candidacy of the more liberal 'Abd al-Mun'im Abu al-Futuh over the official candidate of their main rival, the Egyptian Muslim Brotherhood. Abu al-Futuh had once declared that "Freedom, in and of itself, is a central Islamic value" and that second-class status for any citizen based on religion or gender was an outmoded idea that has been "replaced by the concept of citizen-based democracy in a nation of justice and law."[35]

Whatever role opportunism might have played in encouraging decisions made by Islamists during the past several decades, the fact remains that the diffusion of international norms of human and democratic rights provided points of reference for the political field in which they have had to operate. Viewed from a slightly different angle, opportunism might be seen as the price of admission to the political sphere, which, in turn, exacts its own toll from participants. It does this in the form of shaping the practices, the expectations, and, ultimately, the ethos of those who seek inclusion. And some Islamists—at least on an individual level—adjusted well to the new political field in which they had to operate. As mentioned above, members of the Egyptian Muslim Brotherhood participated in the Kefaya movement, and exiled members of the Syrian Muslim Brotherhood participated alongside communists and liberals in the Damascus Declaration movement. In the case of Kefaya, Brotherhood members entered the coalition only months after their organization announced its "reform initiative," which, by calling for the competitive presidential elections, the curtailment of presidential powers, the revocation of the emergency law, and religious and political freedom, in fact anticipated rather than took its cue from Kefaya. (Similarly, the participation of the Syrian Muslim Brotherhood in the Damascus Declaration movement took place four years after the organization announced its "National Charter for Political Action," which called for respect for human rights and political pluralism in Syria).[36] Algerian Islamists were on the front lines during the Black October riots, and during the Bahraini intifada Shi'i Islamists from the Islamic Front for the Liberation of Bahrain (al-jabhat al-islamiya li tahrir al-bahrayn) and the Bahrain Islamic Freedom Movement (harakat ahrar al-bahrayn al-islamiya) worked side-by-side with leftists from the Bahraini National Liberation Front (jabhat al-tahrir al-watani al-bahraniya) and the Popular Front for the Liberation of Bahrain (al-jabhat al-sha'biya li tahrir al-bahrayn), first in the petition drives, then in the escalating protests.[37]

This forging of alliances joining Islamists, leftists, and liberals continued up through the Uprisings of 2010 and 2011 when, for example, the youth wing of the Egyptian Muslim Brotherhood collaborated with the April 6 Movement, the group instrumental in organizing the January 25, 2011, demonstrations that sparked the Egyptian uprising. While elder members of the Brotherhood did not endorse the demonstration, younger members turned out en masse.[38] The breakdown of those alliances in the summer of 2013—when the liberals of the Tamarrud (Rebellion!) petition movement cheered on the military coup d'état against Muslim Brotherhood rule in Egypt, and when Tunisian liberals linked up with the faloul (regime remnants) of the Nida' Tunis party to bring down a government led by Ennahda—marked a setback for a revolutionary process that had pit anti-autocrats against autocrats and their supporters, not secularists against Islamists.

The generational split within the Egyptian Muslim Brotherhood that was made manifest during the uprising of 2011 was part of a longer trend within the organization represented by the split between the so-called "old guard"—those who had cut their teeth in the Muslim Brotherhood's "Secret Apparatus" and in Nasser's jails—and those like the aforementioned 'Abd al-Mun'im Abu al-Futuh—who had begun their political careers in the 1970s as activists within student groups. Over the course of the next decade, they graduated from student politics to contesting elections in professional syndicates such as those that spoke for doctors, engineers, pharmacists, scientists, and lawyers. By the mid-

1990s, they were firmly in control of those syndicates, and, like Islamists within the Jordanian and Palestinian syndicates, they were both at ease with, and adept at, representative politics. And through their participation in syndicates, they also engaged with a culture of middle-class/entrepreneurial values congruent with an ethos of individual rights.

In 1996, this wing of the Brotherhood left the organization and founded the Wasat (Center) Party, decrying both the lack of democracy within the Brotherhood and its programmatic rigidity. Drawing a contrast between themselves and the old guard, they issued a program calling for a civil state in Egypt that would draw from "Islamic principles" but in which all citizens would enjoy equal privileges of democracy. Participation in electoral contests had thus compelled a group within the Muslim Brotherhood, like Islamists elsewhere, to master repertoires of organizational activity consistent with democratic politics. This, in turn, encouraged them to put in place new organizational structures that might support that activity and to seek new ideological underpinnings for it as well.[39]

Although the Wasat Party was the first party to receive official recognition in post-Mubarak Egypt, it did not come close to achieving the political success of the Muslim Brotherhood's Freedom and Justice Party. Abu al-Futuh, the independent candidate it supported for the presidency, came in fourth in the first round of balloting in the presidential race, trailing Mohamed Morsi of the Freedom and Justice Party 24.3 percent to 17.2 percent. Nor did the Wasat "tendency" become the predominant Islamist tendency anywhere in the Arab world in the aftermath of the Uprisings of 2010 and 2011. Its role remained marginal, and after the events of the summer of 2013 it faced the possibility of extinction. Furthermore, although the Egyptian Muslim Brotherhood *officially* shifted its doctrinal orientation, as represented by the reform initiative, during the first two years of the Egyptian uprising, it continued to manifest the structural features that had caused the future members of Wasat to bolt the organization in the first place. As a matter of fact, six months after the youth wing of the Muslim Brotherhood joined the April 6 Movement in Tahrir Square, the Brotherhood expelled the leaders of the wing for establishing the Egyptian Current Party (*hizb al-tayyar al-masri*) and for supporting Abu al-Futuh instead of working for Freedom and Justice (the Current Party's platform, calling for the separation of religion from politics, the protection of human rights, and the adoption of legislation rooted in the values of Islamic civilization rather than a strict interpretation of Islamic law, adhered closely to that of the Wasat Party).[40] If, then, there is a relationship between the rights and rules according to which organizations are governed and the attitudes such organizations bring to the public sphere, the debacle of Brotherhood rule in Egypt and its tragic dénouement in the summer of 2013 in Egypt should have been anticipated.

To be sure, the year-long Egyptian drama, which began with the inauguration of Mohamed Morsi as president on June 30, 2012, and ended with the July 3, 2013, *coup d'état*, should give pause to anyone who had looked to developments there and elsewhere in the region with even cautious optimism. Nevertheless, it would be equally mistaken to view the Egyptian experience as proving that organized Islamism as a whole is hopelessly bound by ideological and organizational fetters that were forged in a different era and that render it impervious to shifts in global norms of governance. There were far too many unique factors at play in Egypt that make its experience unsuitable for generalization. These include the interruption of the revolutionary process by a military *coup d'état* on February 11, 2011, after only eighteen days; the entrenched power of the "deep state," particularly the military, with which the Brotherhood had to contend; the incompetence of Brotherhood rule, which was exacerbated by sabotage committed by the judiciary and security services and by its own inexperience in governance; the personal inadequacies of Mohamed Morsi; the lack of structural impediments to Morsi's and the Brotherhood's high-handedness that might have saved Morsi and the organization from themselves; the structural deficiencies of the Egyptian economy; and the mutually reinforcing institutional paranoia of the military and the Muslim Brotherhood, which caused each to view the other as an existential threat and their interaction as a zero-sum game.

On the other hand, it is tempting to view the aftermath of the Arab Uprisings of 2010 and 2011 as marking another turning point in the history of contemporary Islamist politics. The army crackdown in Egypt; the collapse of the Ennahda-led government in Tunisia; the increasing radicalization of Islamist politics in Syria and Libya where jihadist groups like Jabhat al-Nusra, the Islamic State of Iraq and Syria (*ad-dawla al-Islamiyya fi al-'Iraq wal-Sham*), and Ansar al-Shari'a carved out what might prove to be permanent footholds for themselves; the sectarianization of politics in Syria, Yemen, and Bahrain; the commitment of Saudi Arabia, backed by its enormous wealth, to roll back political gains made by Egyptian Muslim Brotherhood/Ennahda–style groups throughout the region; and the secular/Islamist polarization might be the first indications that the period of mass politics, participation, and openness among Islamist groups has passed or, worse, was nothing more than an illusion.

Or it just might prove to be a setback. One need only reflect on the shape-shifting narrative of the Egyptian uprising—triumphalist if brought to a close in February 2011, tragic if brought to a close in July 2013—to appreciate the fact that even in those states where transitions are most advanced—Tunisia, Egypt, Libya, and, perhaps, Yemen—the vanishing point on the revolutionary horizon continues to recede. Likewise, the ultimate contours of the political fields engendered by those uprisings. None of this should be surprising, however. The French Reign of Terror took place more than four years after the storming of the Bastille in 1789—the event frequently used to mark the beginning of the French Revolution—and almost ten and a half years passed before Napoleon was crowned emperor—the event frequently used to mark its end. Four years after the self-immolation of Mohamed Bouazizi would bring us only to February 2014, ten and a half years, May 2020.

But while historical analogies are always deficient, there is one that might at least provide us with a suitable frame of reference to view the aftermath of the revolutionary upsurge of 2010 and 2011: 1848. Although none of the revolutions in that bleak year succeeded, their outbreak signaled in retrospect that the field of political contestation in Europe had opened up to include liberal and nationalist alternatives to the old order. An analogous lesson might be learned from the Arab Uprisings. And if Islamists should once again compete within the political sphere, they will do so in a field that affirms by inclusion (although not necessarily by implementation) human and democratic rights.

NOTES

1. Mohammed M. Hafez, "Armed Islamist Movements and Political Violence in Algeria," *Middle East Journal* 54 (2000): 576.

2. Over time, incidents of violence increased where governments were unable to suppress their violent opposition. For example, between 1970 and 1989 Islamist violence led to approximately 120 deaths in Egypt; in the five years between 1992 and 1997, there were more than ten times that amount. The list of targets also became more expansive: At the beginning of the Islamist insurgency in Algeria, Islamist groups targeted the security forces. Soon thereafter, they began assassinating government officials. By 1996, insurgents undertook wholesale massacres of villagers and targeted anyone drawing a government salary, including schoolteachers and oil workers. See Mohammed M. Hafez and Quintan Wiktorowicz, "Violence as Contention in the Egyptian Islamic Movement," in *Islamic Activism: A Social Movement Theory Approach*, Wiktorowicz (ed.), (Bloomington: Indiana University Press, 2004), 71–72; Hafez, "Armed Islamic Movements," 584–85.

3. See, *inter alia*, Fred Halliday, "Tunisia's Uncertain Future," *Middle East Report* 163 (1990): 25–27; Elbaki Hermassi, "Montée et déclin du mouvement islamiste en Tunisie," *Confluences* Médi-

terranée 12 (1990): 33–50; Robert Mortimer, "Islam and Multiparty Politics in Algeria," *Middle East Journal* 45 (1991): 575–93; Dirk Vandewalle, "At the Brink: Chaos in Algeria," *World Policy Journal* 9 (1992): 705–17; Omar Ashour, "Libya's Muslim Brotherhood Faces the Future," *Foreign Policy* (2012), accessed June 21, 2012, http://mideast.foreignpolicy.com/posts/2012/03/09/libya_s_muslim_brotherhood_faces_the_future.

4. See Carrie Rosefsky Wickham, "The Muslim Brotherhood after Mubarak: What the Brotherhood Is and How It Will Shape the Future," *Foreign Affairs* (2011), accessed January 11, 2014, http://www.foreignaffairs.com/articles/67348/carrie-rosefsky-wickham/the-muslim-brotherhood-after-mubarak. *Du'at la Qudat* (*Preachers, not Judges*), a book purportedly written by the brotherhood's imprisoned second general guide, Hasan Isma'il al-Hudaybi in 1969, also contains a denunciation of violence. Al-Hudaybi, *Du'at la Qudat* (Cairo: Dar al-taba'a wa-l-nashr al-Islamiyya, 1972).

5. Erika Post, "Egypt's Elections," *Middle East Report* 147 (1987): 17–22; Mona El-Ghobashy, "The Metamorphosis of the Egyptian Muslim Brothers," *International Journal of Middle East Studies* 37 (2005): 373–95; Joshua A. Stacher, "Parties Over: The Demise of Egypt's Opposition Parties," *British Journal of Middle East Studies* 31 (2004): 215–33; Eberhard Kienle, "More than a Response to Islamism: The Political Deliberalization of Egypt in the 1990s," *Middle East Journal* 52 (1998): 219–35.

6. Hafez and Wiktorowicz, "Violence as Contention," 78.

7. For more details, see "Arab Human Development Report 2004: Towards Freedom in the Arab World," United Nations Development Programme, accessed June 21, 2012, http://hdr.undp.org/en/reports/regional/arabstates/RBAS_ahdr2004_EN.pdf.

8. Lahcen Achy, "Why Did Protests in Algeria Fail to Gain Momentum?" *Foreign Policy* 31 (2011), accessed June 21, 2012, http://mideast.foreignpolicy.com/posts/2011/03/31/why_did_protests_in_algeria_fail_to_gain_momentum. Although the term "civil war" is commonly used, it is not entirely accurate: Most of the Algerian population served more as victims than participants in acts of violence committed by armed militias, on the one hand, and a faction of the military known as the "eradicators," on the other. That being the case, the prediction that the army *coup d'état* of July 3, 2013, in Egypt might trigger "another Algeria" might not be so far off the mark. See, *inter alia*, Rick Gladstone, "Attacks on Protesters in Cairo Were Calculated to Provoke, Some Say," *New York Times*, August 16, 2013, accessed October 31, 2013, http://www.nytimes.com/2013/08/17/world/middleeast/attacks-on-protesters-in-cairo-were-calculated-to-provoke-some-say.html.

9. "Popular Protest in North Africa and the Middle East (V): Making Sense of Libya," International Crisis Group, accessed June 21, 2012, http://www.crisisgroup.org/.

10. See Christian Caryl, "Plague of Thugs: Why Mideast Dictators Use Hoodlums to Suppress Dissent," *Foreign Policy* (2012), accessed July 13, 2012, http://www.foreignpolicy.com/articles/2012/07/18/plague_of_thugs?page=0,1.

11. Paul Amar, "Why Mubarak Is Out," *Jadaliyya*, February 1, 2011, accessed March 19, 2014, http://www.jadaliyya.com/pages/index/516/why-mubarak-is-out; Joel Beinin, "Egypt at the Tipping Point?" *Foreign Policy* (2011), http://mideastafrica.foreignpolicy.com/posts/2011/01/31/egypt_at_the_tipping_point; Harriet Alexander and Ruth Sherlock, "The Shabiha: Inside Assad's Death Squads," *Telegraph*, June 2, 2012, accessed June 21, 2012, http://www.telegraph.co.uk/news/worldnews/middleeast/syria/9307411/The-Shabiha-Inside-Assads-death-squads.html.

12. The contents of those pledges might be discerned from the "Our Understanding of Islamic Issues" section of the group's website, Al-Jamaa Al-Islamiya: Islamic Group Egypt, accessed June 23, 2012, http://www.egyptianislamicgroup.com/about/index.shtml.

13. Mustafa Kamel al-Sayyid, "The Other Face of the Islamist Movement," *Carnegie Endowment Working Papers* 33 (2003): 15–19; Amr Hamzawy and Sarah Grebowski, "From Violence to Moderation: Al-Jama'a al-Islamiya and al-Jihad," *Carnegie Papers* 20 (2010); Ayman al-Zawahiri, *Fursan tahta raya al-nabi* (*Knights under the Prophet's Banner*), 178, accessed January 18, 2012, http://www.tawhed.ws. On the difference between al-Qaeda and the Islamist groups under discussion, see James L. Gelvin, "Nationalism, Anarchism, Reform: Political Islam from the Inside Out," *Middle East Policy* 17 (2010): 118–30.

14. Rachid Tlemçani, "Algeria Under Bouteflika: Civil Strife and National Reconciliation," *Carnegie Papers* 7 (2008): 11.

15. "Libyan Islamic Fighting Group Revises Jihadist Ideology," Wikileaks, June 24, 2012, http://wikileaks.org/cable/2009/12/09TRIPOLI955.html#.

16. "Brotherhood Syria withdraw from NSF opposition," Al-Jazeera, accessed June 24, 2012, http://www.aljazeera.net/news/pages/a5cb4490-7670-490a-8395-903e0fc9ee21.

17. Daniel P. Moynihan, "The Politics of Human Rights," *Commentary* 64 (1977), accessed June 25, 2012, http://www.commentarymagazine.com/article/the-politics-of-human-rights/; Daniel P. Moynihan, "The United States in Opposition," *Commentary* 59 (1975): 31–45; James L. Gelvin, "American Global Economic Policy and the Civic Order in the Middle East," in *Is There a Middle East? The Evolution of a Geopolitical Concept*, eds. Michael Bonine, et al. (Palo Alto, CA: Stanford University Press, 2011): 191–206.

18. Samuel Moyn, *The Last Utopia: Human Rights in History* (Cambridge: Belknap Press, 2010), 1.

19. A good account of the debate at the United Nations about the nature of human rights during the organization's formative period might be found in James Frederick Green, *The United Nations and Human Rights* (Washington, D.C.: The Brookings Institution, 1956).

20. Gareth Evans, "The Responsibility to Protect Libyans," Project Syndicate, accessed June 25, 2012, http://www.project-syndicate.org/commentary/the-responsibility-to-protect-libyans.

21. The other nine are Algeria, Egypt, Jordan, Morocco, Qatar, Saudi Arabia, Sudan, Tunisia, and Yemen. See Moataz El Fegiery, "The Effectiveness of Human Rights Commissions in the Arab World," *Sada*, June 12, 2008, accessed June 25, 2012, http://carnegieendowment.org/sada/2008/08/12/effectiveness-of-human-rights-commissions-in-arab-world/6bfp.

22. Ligue Tunisienne des Droits de l'Homme, accessed June 25, 2012, http://ltdh-tunisie.org/qui-sommes-nous/.

23. A partial list of these initiatives can be found at "Partnership for Peace, Democracy and Development in the BMENA," Broader Middle East and North Africa Initiative, United States Department of State, accessed June 25, 2012, http://2005-2009-bmena.state.gov/rls/55665.htm#1.

24. See Mona Yacoubian, "Promoting Middle East Democracy II: Arab Initiatives," *Special Report* (2005): 5–6, accessed June 25, 2012, http://www.usip.org/files/resources/sr136.pdf.

25. The text of the charter can be found at "Arab Charter on Human Rights 2004," accessed June 25, 2012, http://www.acihl.org/res/Arab_Charter_on_Human_Rights_2004.pdf.

26. Yacoubian, "Promoting Middle East Democracy," 6–9.

27. See Hugh Roberts, "The Algerian State and the Challenge of Democracy," in *The Battlefield: Algeria 1988–2002, Studies in a Broken Polity*, ed. Hugh Roberts (London: Verso, 2003), 105–124; James D. Le Sueur, *Algeria Since 1989: Between Terror and Democracy* (London: Zed, 2010), 31–40.

28. Munira A. Fakhro, "The Uprising in Bahrain: An Assessment," in *The Persian Gulf at the Millennium*, ed. Gary G. Sick and Lawrence G. Potter (New York: St. Martin's, 1997), 167–88; Fred H. Lawson, "Repertoires of Contention in Contemporary Bahrain," in *Islamic Activism: A Social Movement Theory Approach*, ed. Wiktorowicz (Bloomington: Indiana University Press, 2004), 89–111.

29. Bassam Haddad, "Business as Usual in Syria?" *Middle East Report*, September 7, 2001, accessed March 19, 2014, http://www.merip.org/mero/mero090701; "The Damascus Declaration," Carnegie Middle East Center, March 1, 2012, accessed June 26, 2012, http://carnegie-mec.org/publications/?fa=48514.

30. Nadia Oweidat et al., *The Kefaya Movement: A Case Study of Grass Roots Reform Initiative* (Santa Monica, CA: Rand Corporation, 2008), accessed March 19, 2014, http://www.rand.org/content/dam/rand/pubs/monographs/2008/RAND_MG778.pdf; Tina Rosenberg, "Revolution U: What Egypt Learned from the Students Who Overthrew Milosevic," *Foreign Policy* (2011), accessed June 26, 2012, http://www.foreignpolicy.com/articles/2011/02/16/revolution_u. Three former members of Kefaya would also found Tamarrud (Rebellion!) in April 2013, which undertook a petition campaign demanding that President Mohamed Morsi of Egypt step down.

31. "Morocco's Truth Commission: Honoring Past Victims during an Uncertain Present," *Human Rights Watch* 17 (2005), accessed June 26, 2012, http://www.hrw.org/sites/default/files/reports/morocco1105wcover.pdf; "Arab Human Development Report 2004," 27.

32. Yacoubian, "Promoting Middle East Democracy," 6.

33. Nathan J. Brown, "Post-revolutionary al-Azhar," *The Carnegie Papers* (2011), accessed June 28, 2012, http://carnegieendowment.org/files/al_azhar.pdf. The original text of the "al-Azhar Document" can be found at Bouquet of Roses, accessed June 28, 2012, http://basmagm.wordpress.com/2012/01/11/.

34. Stéphanie LaCroix, "Sheikhs and Politicians: Inside the New Egyptian Salafism," *Policy Briefing* (2012), accessed March 19, 2014, http://www.brookings.edu/research/papers/2012/06/07-egyptian-salafism-lacroix; Jonathan Brown, "Salafis and Sufis in Egypt," *The Carnegie Papers* (2011), accessed June 28, 2011, http://carnegieendowment.org/files/salafis_sufis.pdf.

35. Abdul Abul Futouh, "Reformist Islam: How Gray Are the Gray Zones?" *Sada*, July 18, 2006, accessed June 28, 2012, http://carnegieendowment.org/2008/08/18/reformist-islam-how-gray-are-gray-zones/6bmh.

36. "Brotherhood Steps into the Fray," *Al-Ahram Weekly Online* 681 (2004), accessed March 19, 2014, http://weekly.ahram.org.eg/2004/681/eg3.htm; Salam Kawakibi, "Political Islam in Syria," *CEPS Working Document* 270 (2007), accessed June 29, 2012, http://papers.ssrn.com/sol3/papers.cfm?abstract_id=1338004&download=yes.

37. International Crisis Group, "Popular Protests in the Middle East and North Africa (III): The Bahrain Revolt," *Middle East North Africa Report* 105 (2011), accessed June 29, 2011, http://www.crisisgroup.org/~/media/Files/Middle%20East%20North%20Africa/Iran%20Gulf/Bahrain/105-%20Popular%20Protests%20in%20North%20Africa%20and%20the%20Middle%20East%20-III-The%20Bahrain%20Revolt.pdf.

38. James L. Gelvin, *The Arab Uprisings: What Everyone Needs to Know* (New York: Oxford University Press, 2012), 52–53.

39. Ninette S. Fahmy, "The Performance of the Muslim Brotherhood in the Egyptian Syndicates: An Alternative Formula for Reform?" *Middle East Journal* 52 (1998): 551–62; Carrie Rosefsky Wickham, "The Path to Moderation: Strategy and Learning in the Formation of Egypt's Wasat Party," *Comparative Politics* 36, no. 2 (2004): 205–28; Amr Hamzawy, "Interview with Abul Ila Al Madi, Founding Member of Egypt's Wasat (Center) Party," *Sada*, December 20, 2005, accessed June 30, 2012, http://carnegieendowment.org/2008/08/20/interview-with-abul-ila-al-madi-founding-member-of-egypt-s-wasat-center-party/44po. For the case of Jordan, see, *inter alia*, Pénélope Lazillière, "Political Commitment under an Authoritarian Regime: Professional Associations and the Islamist Movement as Alternative Arenas in Jordan," *International Journal of Conflict and Violence* 6 (2012): 11–25.

40. Salma Shukrallah, "Muslim Brotherhood Dismisses Two of Its Members, Interrogates Others," *Al-Ahram Online*, July 17, 2011, accessed March 19, 2014, http://english.ahram.org.eg/NewsContent/1/64/16625/Egypt/Politics-/Muslim-Brotherhood-dismisses-two-of-its-members,-i.aspx; "In Egypt, Youth Wing Breaks from Muslim Brotherhood," *New York Times*, June 22, 2011, accessed June 30, 2012, http://www.nytimes.com/2011/06/23/world/middleeast/23egypt.html.

7

Protest Mobilization in the Age of Twitter

Silvana Toska

"Why does every nation on Earth move to change their conditions except for us?" asked talk show host Faisal al-Qassem on Al Jazeera, seven years before many Arab nations were wracked by protests that represent one of the most impressive mass-mobilization movements in decades.[1] The belief that there is something unique about Arab politics was so embedded that, while most political scientists started examining the causes of the third wave of democratization, scholars of the Middle East were examining the causes of authoritarian durability.[2] Then, in a remote town in southern Tunisia on December 17, 2010, an unknown young man named Mohamed Bouazizi set himself on fire in protest against abusive and corrupt police and unresponsive regional government. A month later, armed only with telephones capable of accessing the Internet, hundreds of thousands of young protesters took to the streets in several Arab countries. It was all too easy for the protesters, outside observers, and regime leaders themselves to make the connection between these youths and the technology that they collectively believed was aiding their mobilization.

This raises the question, What was the role of social media in protest mobilization during the Arab Uprisings?[3] Answers to this question range from suggestions that it was largely—if not entirely—responsible for the revolts to suggestions that it was a mere facilitator to suggestions that it was entirely irrelevant.[4] This chapter addresses the same central question but provides a more coherent and effective way to assess the answers.

First, I argue that social media were important tools for protest mobilization, just like other technological novelties of the time—such as pamphlets, radio, and television—had been for other historical revolutions. Emphasis on the "novelty" of social media has impeded a proper theoretical analysis; I argue that we can understand the role of social media better by examining the mechanisms through which previous generations of revolutionaries have used technology for the dissemination of information and coordination of revolutionary protest. Specifically, like previous technological innovations, social media reinforced and further exposed the failings of the regimes (*spotlight effect*),[5] made known individuals' deep dissatisfaction with the status quo (*reverse preference falsification*),[6] and provided activists and protesters alike with a means to coordinate action (*served as a weak tie*).[7] All three are important mechanisms of protest mobilization and are present in most revolutionary periods. Further, during the Arab revolutions, social media served as platforms for many existing associations and opposition groups, whose messages were amplified through the interconnected nature of online and off-line activism, and through mainstream media's reliance on social media. The goal here is not to show that social media by themselves are necessary to protest mobilization but to demonstrate the need to identity carefully the conditions under which they can help mass mobilization.

Second, I argue that—despite its utility for mass mobilization—authoritarian leaders make a grave strategic mistake by censoring social media after protests have already started. While social media are important tools for coordination, once protests have begun, disruptions in social media seem to increase protest participation and lead to broader geographical spread. Therefore, both the *presence* and *absence* of social media can exacerbate revolutionary unrest, depending on when they occur in the time frame of protest mobilization.

Together, these arguments provide a comprehensive picture of the role of social media both before and during mass protests. In making them, I build on existing theories of collective action—especially Kuran's *preference falsification* and Granovetter's distinction between *weak* and *strong ties*—and test them through original Twitter data and existing research, as well as personal interviews with activists in Egypt and Syria.[8]

TECHNOLOGY, INFORMATION, AND COORDINATION

Technology in Context

The study of revolutions in the social sciences over the last three decades has been dominated by structural explanations as root causes of mass mobilization, and rarely have nonmaterial factors been taken into account.[9] As such, ideology and the role of ideas have largely been ignored. The study of media effects on mobilizations has suffered a similar fate, with few comprehensive studies comparing its role across revolutions. This stands in direct contradiction to the behavior of political actors with regard to the media. Both revolutionary actors and state leaders consider the control of various means of communication as central to their cause; media repression is among the most common tool of authoritarian regimes of all ages. Similarly, as a young revolutionary Lenin's first step was to establish a newspaper that would be distributed through underground cells if it were not allowed to be distributed legally.[10] A newspaper, Lenin argued, would be both substance and symbol of the revolutionary cause: "It may be said without exaggeration that the frequency and regularity with which a newspaper is printed (and distributed) can serve as a precise criterion of how well this cardinal and most essential sector of our militant activities is built up."[11]

A collection of articles that examine major historical revolutions from the Puritan Revolution of 1640 to the Eastern European Revolutions of 1989 makes precisely this point.[12] All of the chapters—with the exception of the 1989 revolutions—consider the relative opening of the media environment, in each of the revolutions they study, as catalyst of revolutionary unrest. By "relative opening," the authors imply a situation in which it became easier to establish a newspaper, to print pamphlets, or record messages. Some of these developments were intentional and a result of domestic political developments, as was the case of media freedom in France under King Louis-Philippe,[13] but others were the unintentional result of technological developments, such as the use of cassette tapes during the Iranian revolution or fax machines during the Chinese revolts of 1989.[14] The only dissenting voice in the volume is a chapter on the Eastern European Revolutions of 1989, where the author suggests that the age in which means of communication will influence revolutions has ended.[15] However, this study looks only at the domestic media environment, without considering the reach of foreign media or the diaspora, which were, at that historical moment, available in most Eastern European countries.[16] Many Eastern European countries relaxed their media restrictions toward the end of the 1980s, following President

Gorbachev's *perestroika* movement. Whereas in the earlier stages communist countries limited their media space to the Soviet bloc, in the years prior to the revolutions Western TV channels were not actively blocked, resulting in a relative opening in the media environment.

For historians, then, an emphasis on the various tools that revolutionaries use to communicate with one another and disseminate information is nothing new.[17] As early as the French Revolution, historians have discussed the role of the free press and pamphleteering for the events of their time and even suggested which method was most effective for mass mobilization and why. Pierre-Louis Roederer wrote an essay in 1796 in which he advised that, while free print journalism was an effective means of disseminating information, pamphleteering and wall posters were more important in reaching the less-educated public and in doing so quickly and furtively.[18] Writing two centuries later, Jerome Blum similarly underscores the role of media as a catalyst for the French Revolution.[19] The economic and structural conditions in France—"an explosion in population, the growth of cities, shifts in property and income among sectors of the social order, the technical and social impact of early industrialization, the emergence of new social and economic elites and an enormous increase in the uprooted and the property-less, a chronic social crisis arising from mass pauperism, and a long-lasting monetary deflation"—apply almost entirely to other European countries of the time and to Arab revolts of recent years.[20] What made France different from other European countries, however, is what makes it similar to Arab countries today: a relative opening of the media space. Due to new freedom of the media laws passed by the French King Louis-Philippe, republicans and liberal monarchists alike used the press, pamphlets, and wall posters to oppose and criticize the king. While the opening of public space is rarely an act of volition by the various regimes, and it certainly was not for King Louis-Philippe, it nevertheless gave revolutionaries the tools to highlight regime failure and organize opposition.

In order to guide and structure their political activities, each of these revolutionary groups chose the methods most readily available to them. Newspapers and pamphleteering was the method of choice in the French Revolution of 1789, European revolutions of 1848, and the Bolshevik Revolution of 1917. Radio broadcasts were used widely in the revolutions of the early part of the twentieth century. Making use of the newly available, cheap transistor radios, President Nasser of Egypt used the "Voice of Arabs" radio to create a direct, unfiltered channel from Cairo to other Arab capitals during the so-called

"Arab Cold War," while activists on the ground were circulating pamphlets and publishing op-eds in the nascent national presses.[21] Similarly, Khomeini made extensive use of mosque networks to spread his sermons and anti-regime rhetoric through prerecorded tapes and pamphlets.[22] All of these revolutionary movements drew on the new-media technologies of their times, which were used to spread information about the precarious state of the regimes and to structure political activities.

Given that revolutions occurred in other historical periods absent social media, it cannot follow that such media are a generalizable and necessary cause for revolutionary mobilization. However, once we place social media in the category of tools used by activists to spread information and coordinate with one another—like pamphlets and more traditional media—we come closer to identifying a necessary cause. It is important to note that, due to technological developments and the nature of social media, there are aspects that are novel, such as opportunities for action at different speeds and scope, and the ability to aggregate and create content on a new and more accessible scale. While the historical distance from the recent—so-called "social media"—revolutions is too short for conclusive remarks on the degree to which these distinctions amount to changed opportunities, recent research shows that, despite its novelty, social media in revolutionary situations mirror physical networks on the ground and are only as effective as those networks.[23] More specifically, actors on social media follow well-known activists who are otherwise involved with mobilization through various physical associations. Therefore, there is a degree to which these associations and activists moderate the effects of social media. This is another point of continuity with previous revolutionary media environments.

The three sections in the following use insights from studies of these previous revolutionary periods in order to examine the mechanisms through which social media have been used as mobilization tools during the Arab Uprisings.

Information: Spotlight Effect and Preference Falsification

That Arab regimes were, and many of them are, largely illegitimate in the eyes of their own citizens is a fact established long ago. Since Michael Hudson's 1977 book *Arab Politics: The Search for Legitimacy* until the end of 2010, these regimes' popularity has only decreased. With hindsight, the revolutions seem to have been inevitable given their lack of regime legitimacy, growing economic inequality, youth unemployment, corruption, and lack of personal security and political freedoms. These grievances, however, had limited outlets. Most avenues through which they could have been made public, and thereby induce political change, were blocked. All Arab countries control their media to various degrees, with some of them exhibiting total control. Elections, the token example of political change, were cosmetic and served mainly to reinforce existing regimes.[24] It is easy to perceive the "inevitability" of upheavals in retrospect, but mass discontent does not necessarily generate a popular uprising against a status quo. As Kuran argues, "to understand when it does, we need to identify the conditions under which individuals will display antagonism toward the regime under which they live."[25] In highly repressive regimes, however, displaying antagonism is very dangerous, and in absence of the knowledge of the preferences of others, very few dare to voice their grievances.

Kuran draws a distinction between a person's "true beliefs"—those held in *private*—and the "beliefs" claimed in *public*. The difference between the two is what Kuran calls *preference falsification*.[26] In a study of the Syrian regime's ability to repress dissent, Lisa Wedeen makes a similar point by demonstrating that "Assad's regime can compel people to say the ridiculous and to avow the absurd."[27] The Assad regime, it seems, was able to perfect and institutionalize individuals' preference falsification. Under such conditions overt opposition is minimal.

Moreover, a person's cost (and interest) in participating in an opposition depends on the perceived size of the opposition itself.[28] When the size of the opposition is considered small—as is the case in most authoritarian regimes—then each individual's incentive to express personal beliefs and participate in public opposition will remain small. Conversely, the larger the size of the opposition, "the smaller the individual dissenter's chances of being persecuted for his [or her] identification with the opposition" and the fewer potential dangers that person has to face.[29]

The dilemma that individuals who secretly oppose the regime face is to know how many others share their views and how many of them are willing to make these views public. This is where social media—like other media before it—were able to provide the necessary channel. In a situation of government-controlled broadcast and paper media, social media became the main venue through which individuals could—relatively anonymously and otherwise—express their dissatisfaction with the regime. By so doing, such media were able to reverse the problem of preference falsification. Furthermore, people using social media exposed and highlighted the failures of the regime. This mechanism is called the *spotlight effect,* which implies that failures of the regime—known to some and in various degrees by different sections of the population—become public knowledge.[30] Spotlighting regime failure, as was done by revolutionary groups in previous generations, changes perceptions of both the precarious nature of the regime and the previously hidden mass opposition to it.

Given the highly controlled media in the Arab region, social media were often the only uncensored means of communicating regime failure and personal preferences. A search for the hashtag "#Mubarak" on Twitter during the two weeks prior to the start of the Tunisian protests shows a long list of individuals mocking, critiquing, and bitterly denouncing the ex-president.[31] Similarly, searches for the words "Ben Ali" or "Tunisian government" reveal numerous references to Wikileaks documents highlighting the corruption of the Tunisian regime. Beforehand, individuals would have known the preferences of close kin; it was now possible to know the preferences of thousands of otherwise-disconnected Tunisians. Two important factors should be noted here: The first is that these are the most "retweeted" (shared) tweets for the period leading up to the protests. Second, individuals posting revolutionary tweets during this early period—especially from December 15 to 25—became the most followed Twitter accounts of the Arab Uprisings. Names such as @sandmonkey, @3arabawy, @GSquare86, @Ghonim, and others gained greater prominence during this early period, and they were among the Egyptian activists organizing protests on the ground at later stages.[32] Despite these activists' existing histories, it was the Uprisings that led to their popular "vetting" by the Twitter community as reliable leaders of, and speakers for, the revolutions.

Before social media, it was not as if individuals in these regimes were unaware of the failures of their governments. However, social media allowed individual citizens' knowledge of distinct failures on the part of the regime to be collected, and to be collected through a largely uncensored medium.[33] The repetition of this catalog of failures through both social media and independent foreign media working in tandem with one another made these failures harder to ignore. In some countries, like Syria, complete control of media and absolute repression a well-trained group of the younger generation from hacking past the government's protective firewalls and other easily overcome controls. This new information changed personal calculations of risk. Prior to the events of 2011, Syrians had suspected that many people opposed the regime, but it had been difficult to draw any conclusions as to how many people had done so, outside of close circles of family and friends.[34] There was considerable trepidation over the large number of Syrians who did support the regime, whether for ideological or more instrumental reasons. Activists interviewed at the early stages of the Syrian uprising were not confident that many people would join the protests, nor did they claim to have a good estimation of the potential size of the opposition.[35] In such a situation, and in the absence of free media, checking semi-anonymously with social media outlets where individuals could post opinions about the regime emboldened many youth activists. In fact, the earliest Syrian protests in Banyas started with a group of activists meeting incognito through the "Syrian Revolution" Facebook page.[36] As they witnessed the number of Syrians visiting the page grow daily, they realized that there could be a large group of potential protesters willing to take to the streets.

Exposing individuals' beliefs and regime failures, however, is a necessary but insufficient cause of mass mobilization. As many scholars have argued, despite the seemingly spontaneous and diffuse nature of mass rebellion, in order for mass revolutionary protests to occur there must also be structures of organization and coordination mechanisms that channel these grievances into organized revolts.[37] As an example, in a recent paper on Chinese social media censorship, Gary King argues that the Chinese government censors human expression very selectively.[38] Specifically, "posts with negative, even vitriolic, criticism of the state, its leaders, and its policies are not more likely to be censored. Instead, the censorship program is aimed at curtailing collective action by silencing comments that represent, reinforce, or spur social mobilization, regardless of content."[39] The Chinese government, it seems, realizes that it is calls for coordinated collective action—and not merely expressions of dissatisfaction with the regime—that represent a greater potential threat. Despite the censorship mechanism that existed in the Arab world, activists were able to use social media for both information sharing and coordination.

Coordination: Weak and Strong Ties

Malcolm Gladwell famously asserted that future revolutions "would not be tweeted" because social media function in a fundamentally different fashion from strong networks necessary to build trust and coordination in revolutionary situations.[40] Specifically, weak ties—connecting actors who are otherwise socially distant—may be useful to spread information among a large number of people, but they are less useful when the information conveyed involves situations of high risk, such as revolutionary situations.[41] Centola and Macy make a similar argument, contending that, when "behaviors are costly, risky, or controversial, the willingness to participate may require independent affirmation or reinforcement" from strong ties that connect people whose interactions are "frequent, actively charged, and highly salient to each other."[42] Unlike both Gladwell and Granovetter, Centola and Macy argue that collective action in complex situations, such as revolutions, requires independent affirmation and reinforcement from multiple sources, including both weak and strong ties.

Given that in repressive regimes—which are mostly the ones to undergo revolutionary unrest—individuals rarely know more than the beliefs of close friends and relatives, having weak ties may be precisely what is needed for information to travel. This is especially the case when information can be shared through social media by a key group of activists, who are then followed by a (relatively) large number of people on the ground. As an example, the Egyptian April 6 movement has over two hundred thousand followers, of which 50 percent are in Egypt.[43] The impact of their message is potentially many times that, as individuals share this message with their stronger network relations.

Yet there has been an understandable amount of criticism directed at arguments claiming social media are necessary tools for mobilization generally and during the Arab Uprisings specifically. There have been overgeneralizations aplenty. For example, some have described the protests in Iran and Moldova as Twitter revolutions, when the majority of individuals tweeting about these countries were outside of the countries themselves.[44] Similarly, scholars have often pointed out the fact that relatively few individuals in Middle Eastern countries subscribe to Twitter, Facebook, and other social media.[45] Most people participating in the Tahrir Square protests—sometimes nearing one million individuals—were not there because they had read Twitter or Facebook messages.[46] How, then, can the argument be made that Twitter was nevertheless an important organizational tool for protest mobilization?

First, one must acknowledge that any analysis of tools used by activists in highly repressive regimes is unlikely to lead to simple, linear, causal arguments. We can no more expect every Bolshevik to have received orders directly from Lenin than we can expect every individual in Tahrir Square to have followed Twitter or Facebook feeds regarding the revolutions. Second, we must view online and off-line activism as *weak* and *strong* ties, respectively. This implies that, per Centola and Macy's research, both have an important role to play in situations of complex contagion, like revolutionary protests.

There existed a wide distinction between these weak and strong ties prior to the summer of 2010. Looking especially at Egypt, social activists on the ground—such as *Kefaya* and the April 6 Movement—were deeply connected to unions and associations and have had a growing membership for years. They did not, however, have an extensive online presence and were disconnected from the growing numbers of youth voicing their dissatisfaction against the regime online. Meanwhile, young activists who were not affiliated with official groups—such as bloggers and the now symbolic Wael Ghonim—were divorced from physical groups on the ground and operated mainly online. The Muslim Brotherhood maintained an on-the-ground and online presence for years. It was not until the Facebook page "We Are All Khaled Said," organized by Wael Ghonim and others in July 2010, that both online and on-the-ground activism began to merge.[47] During the period leading the January 25 protest, this Facebook page was coordinating with the April 6 Movement on the ground to organize protests. It is clear that, at least in the case of the Arab Uprisings, weak ties (online) and strong ties (social movements) developed a symbiotic relationship that had been jointly necessary for protest mobilization. As these groups started to share their physical and virtual space, their message was amplified while also becoming more reliable through multiple confirmations.

Ironically, it could well be that mistakenly calling the Iranian and the Moldovan protests "Twitter revolutions"—as well as many instances of extolling the virtues of online social activism for mobilization—had a large impact in shifting the discourse on social media; such media came to be perceived as important and useful because they were mistakenly considered necessary in previous protest movements.[48] In other words, what was mistakenly perceived as an important cause was collectively willed into being one. During the second part of 2010, many Egyptian opposition parties and movements started participating in online activism due to this belief in the utility of social media, and activists previously uninvolved with protests started organizing physical protests through Facebook pages.[49] Hence, "We Are All Khaled Said" became both the forum for discussion of the ills of Egyptian politics—although falling short of calling for regime change—and an organizational tool for the future revolution. The earliest protests in Alexandria that resulted from complaints against police brutality on the Facebook page commemorating Khaled Said were only a prelude to the revolution.

Given the interconnected nature of online and off-line activism, Gladwell and others' criticism of social media as merely "weak ties"—and as therefore insignificant for mobilization under repression—does not hold. As mentioned above, weak ties are complementary to strong ties when information needs to be confirmed by multiple sources and when strong ties have limited spatial reach. Social media as weak ties was not divorced from strong ties on the ground; rather, they reinforced one another. When weak ties develop between individuals who are otherwise embedded in strong ties and there are many such connections, the spread of information increases, and credibility is enhanced.

As a result, one would have a partial understanding of the role of social media, if we focus entirely on the fact that not everyone on the ground received their information through social media. They did, however, receive such information either directly from activist leaders of various groups or indirectly through mainstream media. Activists, on the other hand, often made plans to organize and share these plans via social media, which were then picked up by mainstream media. Al Jazeera and major Western media sources were constantly reporting tweets from visible online activists. It would be erroneous to discuss the role of social media through the lens of a linear causality. If, however, we allow for the symbiotic relationship between online activism, on-the-ground activism, and their echoes through mainstream media, we can see the utility of social media during the Egyptian revolution.

Online activity, however, does not necessarily have to translate into on-the-ground action, and it is necessary to examine the content of this online activity in order to establish any degree of correlation between social media and protest mobilization. Using Twitter data collected between December 1, 2010, and March 30, 2011, tweets with "revolutionary content"—tweets that specifically mentioned "down with Mubarak," "Egypt revolution," and "January 25"—appeared as early as January 15.[50] These tweets were also picked up by Al Jazeera and other news media, which made it possible for people unable to communicate via the Internet to receive this information.[51] More importantly, by January 18, over eighty thousand individuals had signed up for the planned January 25 protest on the Facebook page titled "We Are All Khaled Said."[52] According to protesters I have interviewed, knowing that this many people were planning to attend emboldened more to participate.[53] A similar situation is taking place in Sudan at the time of writing, where activists are starting to use social media as tools of protest organization, bypassing President Bashir's extensive censorship.[54]

Expressing the desire and plan to participate in protests in advance might well be the greatest innovation of social media and what explicitly sets them apart from other tools used in previous revolutions. While all revolutionaries used pamphlets or illicit radio and television broadcasts to spread information about both the regime and impending protests, social media are the only tools that allow for individuals to directly express their intent to participate. Through the expression of this intention the relation becomes two-way; no longer are activists the main ones who control the message, but individuals may add to it and express their own opinions and plans. Looking at social media through the theoretical lens examined above—namely, the spotlight effect, expressing preferences and protest coordination—it seems that the role of older tools of revolutionary communication and the new social media are similar, but there may be a change in *degree* between the effectiveness of social media and these older tools. Future research may well highlight this difference of degrees in productive ways.

SOCIAL MEDIA *AFTER* MOBILIZATION

A Lesson for Dictators?

As discussed in King et al., the Chinese government censors social media and blogs with political content.[55] Specifically, it censors only those that include words that could pertain to coordination of protests, and it does not completely black out social media. Many other regimes in revolutionary situations, however, often make the misguided decision to completely censor social media or any other means of communication used by revolutionaries. It seems that Mubarak made precisely this "error." The Mubarak regime was well equipped to arrest (and often torture) bloggers and activists, and it had done so since social media had become a venue through which the regime was criticized. However, media were never entirely blocked. Following three days of unrest in January 2011, the Mubarak government decided to shut down the majority of Internet service providers, which led to a shutdown of 93 percent of Internet connections in the country, and, additionally, Al Jazeera's TV station was closed down. What followed was precisely what the regime had been trying to avoid: an increase in protest participation as well as more spatial spread of protest location.

At first, this seems like a surprising result. If social media were so central to protest mobilization, why should their absence *increase* mobilization? In a recent paper, Hassanpour argues that media presence is detrimental to mobilization, whereas their absence can incite protests.[56] He puts forth various explanations for this argument, but ultimately his main point—that media absence exacerbates revolutionary unrest—relies on selecting cases where revolutionary movements have already taken place, whereas the argument applies to every situation where media disruptions have, or may, occur regardless of the presence or absence of revolutionary unrest. The error is in not distinguishing between the *initial* stages of protest mobilization and later ones. I argue that media disruptions seem to play a positive role in increasing and diffusing mass mobilization *after* the population is already highly mobilized.

Additionally, not only did the number of protesters increase, but their spatial dispersion grew as well. Between January 25 and January 27, activists made extensive use of the Internet with their cell phones in order to communicate with one another, share information about police presence, and suggest alternative routes to reach Tahrir Square. These messages were then amplified through Al Jazeera and personal communication.[57] As a result, protests occurred exclusively in the square. Once the Internet was effectively shut down, however, and cell phones of main activists were shut down by presidential order by the end of the day on January 27, information could no longer be dispersed in as effective and streamlined a fashion.

Between January 28 and February 1, protests occurred in various areas across Cairo, including different neighborhoods, official buildings, bridges, and mosques.[58] Once the Internet was restored during the night of February 1, the protests reemerged in Tahrir Square. As Mona El Ghobashy argues, this dispersion and the large number of protesters (by that date) completely overwhelmed the police.[59] Ironically, because of the thousands of protests that Egypt had witnessed in the last decade alone, anti-riot police were fairly well trained to contain them. However, previous protests had been smaller and represented only one section of the population at a time in a given location. The combination of various social groups, various locations, and larger numbers was not something they were prepared for.

This flare-up in participation goes against conventional wisdom on the role of media, and it seems to militate against my contention about the importance of social media. However, it underscores the specifically organizational role of social media: absent social media, protests were no longer centralized and far less organized. The dispersion of protests during the days of media blackout seems to be directly related to media blackout. In the following, however, I briefly argue why this increase in participation and dispersion might not have occurred absent an already mobilized population.

This situation seems to be generalizable to at least a few other revolutionary periods where disruptions in the tools of communication used by revolutionaries led to similar exacerbation of revolutionary unrest. In the midst of revolutionary unrest, Petrograd newspapers ceased production as a result of Duma's dissolution on February 27, 1917, and the next few days saw the largest demonstrations and their greatest spatial spread. Similarly, the largest demonstration of the Iranian Revolution took place on December 10 and 11, 1978, in the midst of complete media blackout. In this case, journalists protested against the Shah by going on an industry-wide hiatus.[60] Shutting down media in the midst of protests in these cases resulted in the opposite effect of the intentions of the regime. While the cases of a media blackout during revolutions are few, they uniformly resulted in similar reactions from the revolutionaries—increased activities. Interviews with Egyptian activists provide preliminary explanations as to why this is the case.

Possible Causes

First, media disruptions signal that the regime may be weaker than anticipated. According to activists from the April 6 Movement, revolutionaries knew that "the regime was really scared."[61] Censuring social media is a drastic measure taken to stop protests a regime has been otherwise unable to control, and it shows that mass mobilization has already made a large impact. Second, in a context where the legitimacy of the regime is already eroded, this is seen as an act that further delegitimizes the regime. Even individuals who might have otherwise been indifferent to revolutionary unrest may be pushed into the opposition as a result of further infringement on personal freedoms and fears of what may lie ahead if the regime increases repression. Third, disruptions in social media and independent media—which leave only the discredited regime media available—make the regime ignorant of the opposition's next move. In other words, media disruptions leave the regime blind and unable to plan future repressions because it cannot properly anticipate where they might be necessary. Whereas the Mubarak government could attempt to control Tahrir Square and anticipate the revolutionaries' moves by following the opposition's debates online, once it enforced a blackout it became blind to the opposition's plans. As a result, it was caught unprepared when the protests dispersed throughout the city. Fourth, once protests have already started and the regime has shown itself as weaker and more illegitimate, and when protest organizers are not able to communicate with one another and with their targeted population, protests—rather than stopping—will become more diffuse. Disenfranchised individuals will concentrate in local squares and places that are focal points for their respective areas since they lack information on protests in other, central, locations. During the three days of media blackout, many protests originated in local mosques and remained local, because the uncertainty of what was happening in the center was too large in the absence of information. As a result, protests proliferated and became more difficult to repress.

Fifth, people who would not have participated in revolution—such as individuals who support the revolution but are free-riding and could receive their news online or through TV channels—can no longer do so and, hence, may become willing to participate. Participation of this group of people, however, is dependent on revolt having already occurred. Finally, whereas a number of people will withdraw from protests in the absence of coordinating information, others will be motivated by fear for the safety of family and friends with whom they can no longer communicate as a result of the blackout. They therefore may choose to participate in protests as a means of looking after the safety of their kin.[62]

Most of these possible mechanisms for increased and dispersed mobilization (one through four) rest on the precondition that revolutionary unrest is already taking place. It is only when protesters have already shown their resilience and coordination, and when the regime has been shown as both precarious and illegitimate, that disruptions in media seem to lead to an exacerbation in revolutionary unrest. These arguments have implications both for a debate in the social sciences as to whether social media help[63] mass mobilization as well as, perversely, policy implications for dictators who may shut down means of communication as a way of quelling unrest.

CONCLUSION

There has been a degree of historical blindness when discussing the impact of social media on revolutionary events. Both sides of the debate have treated social media as an entirely new invention that is also analytically distinct. Whether one is arguing that social media are irrelevant to mass mobilization—as Gladwell asserts—or that they are important factors behind the Arab revolutions, the common ground is that social media deserve to be treated as their own, unique variable. Due to their speed and access, they do indeed stand apart from other means of communication. But, we must ask, were not the invention of print and radio as technologically and socially distant from their predecessors as social media are from television? Because there seem to be more similarities than differences between these means of communication—in fact the differences are only a matter of degree—in this chapter I turn the question around and ask instead, How are social media *similar* to other tools used by previous revolutionaries and what can historical lessons teach us about the impact of social media?

Using this comparative-analytical lens, I looked at three main mechanisms through which various means of communication have abetted mass mobilization. The first, *spotlight effect*, highlights the way in which means of communication expose regime failures and opposition to the regime and then make such information public. Since most revolutions occur in periods of relative openings of media space and greater accessibility to information, media have historically been credited with spotlighting regime failure. In most Middle Eastern countries—including the ones with major anti-regime protests—media are tightly controlled, and criticism of the regime is generally absent. Social media became the uncensored (or, rather, censored but still accessible) platforms through which individuals could read about the failures of the regime. They also made public the degree of dissatisfaction toward the regime, which would have otherwise been limited to the closest of kin. This mechanism is a reversal of *preference falsification,* which refers to the act of an individual's hiding true beliefs due to fear of repercussions as well as ignorance of others' private beliefs. Studies of historical revolutions examine how a mass mobilization reaches a "tipping point" when individuals become aware of others' preferences and intentions to participate in rebellion, and media can serve to provide that information.[64] Social media act similarly.

Scholars who reject the utility of social media are too focused on their novelty and ignore the fact that social media do not operate in a vacuum: in fact, social media are often a mirror of events and actors on the ground. Therefore, while critics point to social media as merely "weak ties," this description is both partly accurate and fully misleading. Social media may serve as weak ties, but such ties include and extend to networks and associations on the ground whose message can become amplified and reinforced through social media. During the Egyptian and Syrian revolutions, social media acted symbiotically with social movements to organize events on the ground. Just as importantly, media have never been anything more than weak ties, yet in all previous revolutions they have proved invaluable tools for mobilization.

Finally, while means of communication understood broadly seem effective for mobilization, there are at least three historical cases—the Bolshevik, Iranian, and Egyptian revolutions—when a complete media blackout during unrest led to greater and more geographically dispersed mobilization. While this question is not widely studied, I put forth hypotheses as to why this may be the case and leave it to future research to test these claims.

There still remains a valid concern that, because of the opportunities they offer through greater speed and access, social media may differ in degrees—if not in essence—from previous revolutionary tools. This is yet another potentially fruitful avenue for comparative historical research. As this chapter argues, there is more to learn from history by examining it than there is by ignoring it.

NOTES

1. Faisal al-Qassem, "The Arab People and Revolutions," *The Opposite Direction*, Al Jazeera, aired December 23, 2003, transcript, Al Jazeera, accessed March 20, 2014, http://www.aljazeera.net/channel/archive/archive?ArchiveId=92550.

2. See, for example, Jason Brownlee, "Low Tide after the Third Wave: Exploring Politics under Authoritarianism," *Comparative Politics* 34, no. 4 (2002): 477–98; Marsha Pripstein Posusney, "Enduring Authoritarianism: Middle East Lessons for Comparative Theory," *Comparative Politics* 36, no. 2 (2004): 127–38; and M. Steven Fish, "Islam and Authoritarianism," *World Politics* 55, no. 1 (2002): 4–37.

3. While the title of the chapter refers to the "age of Twitter" and much of the data referenced does come from Twitter, social media here refers broadly to all avenues of online social interactions, such as blogs, Facebook, and Twitter.

4. See, for example, Marc Lynch, *The Arab Uprising: The Unfinished Revolutions of the New Middle East* (New York: Public Affairs, 2012); Malcolm Gladwell, "Why the Revolution Will Not Be Tweeted," *New Yorker,* October 4, 2010.

5. Jason Lyall, "Paths of Ruin: Why Revisionist States Arise and Die in World Politics," (dissertation, Cornell University, 2005), 30.

6. Timur Kuran, "Now Out of Never: The Element of Surprise in the East European Revolution of 1989," *World Politics* 44, no. 1 (1991).

7. Mark Granovetter, "The Strength of Weak Ties," *American Journal of Sociology* 78 (1973): 1360–80.

8. Kuran, "Now Out of Never"; Granovetter, "The Strength of Weak Ties."

9. The most prominent structural theories that dominated the social scientific study of revolutions follow: Theda Skocpol, *States and Social Revolutions: A Comparative Analysis of France, Russia, and China* (New York: Cambridge University Press, 1979); and Jack Goldstone, *Revolution and Rebellion in the Early Modern World* (Los Angeles: University of California Press, 1991).

10. Jeremy D. Popkin, ed., *Media and Revolution* (Lexington: University of Kentucky Press, 1995), 13.

11. Ibid., 14.

12. Ibid., 13.

13. See Jerome Blum, *In the Beginning: The Advent of the Modern Age* (New York: Macmillan Publishing, 1994); Keith Baker, *Inventing the French Revolution* (Cambridge: Cambridge University Press, 1990).

14. Jeffrey Wasserstrom, "Mass Media and Mass Actions in Urban China, 1919–1989," in *Media and Revolution*, ed. Jeremy D. Popkin (Lexington: University of Kentucky Press, 1995). See also Annabelle Sreberny-Mohammadi and Ali Mohammadi, *Small Media, Big Revolution: Communication, Culture, and the Iranian Revolution* (Minneapolis: University of Minnesota Press, 1994).

15. Owen Johnson, "Mass Media and the Velvet Revolution," in *Media and Revolution*, ed. Jeremy D. Popkin (Lexington: University of Kentucky Press, 1995).

16. For data on the reach of foreign media in Eastern European countries (with an emphasis on East Germany) during the late 1980s, see Holger Kern and Jans Hainmueller, "Opium for the Masses: How Foreign Media Can Stabilize Authoritarian Regimes," *Political Analysis* 17, no. 4 (2009): 377–99.

17. For a more detailed look at major historians examining the role of media in revolutionary processes, see François Furet, *Interpreting the French Revolution*, trans. Elborg Forster (Cambridge: Cambridge University Press, 1981); Keith Baker, *Inventing the French Revolution* (Cambridge: Cambridge University Press, 1990); Carla Hesse, *Publishing and Cultural Politics in Revolutionary Paris, 1789–1810* (Oakland: University of California Press, 1991); Jeremy Popkin, *Revolutionary News: The Press in France, 1789–1799* (Durham: Duke University Press, 1990); James W. Carey, *Communications as Culture: Essays on Media and Society* (Cambridge: Harvard University Press, 1988); and Louise McReynolds, *The News under Russia's Old Regime* (New Jersey: Princeton University Press, 1991).

18. Reviewed in Popkin, *Media and Revolution*, 14.

19. Jerome Blum, *In the Beginning: The Advent of the Modern Age* (New York: Macmillan Publishing, 1994), 10.

20. Ibid.

21. Lynch, *The Arab Uprising*, 33.

22. Charles Kurzman, *The Unthinkable Revolution in Iran* (Cambridge: Harvard University Press, 2004).

23. Silvana Toska et al., "Social Media: A Panopticon in the Arab Spring," paper presented at the Department of Sociology Colloquium, Cornell University, September 2012.

24. See, for example, Lisa Blaydes, *Elections and Distributive Politics in Mubarak's Egypt* (Cambridge: Cambridge University Press, 2010).

25. Timur Kuran, "Now Out of Never: The Element of Surprise in the East European Revolution of 1989," *World Politics* 44, no. 1 (1991): 16.

26. Ibid. 17.

27. Lisa Wedeen, *Ambiguities of Domination: Politics, Rhetoric, and Symbols in Contemporary Syria* (University of Chicago Press, 1999), 13.

28. For more details on theories of the logic of critical mass, see Michael Macy, "Learning Theory and the Logic of Critical Mass," *American Sociological Review* 55, no. 6 (1990): 809–26; William Gamson, *The Strategy of Social Protest* (Belmont, CA: Wadsworth, 1990); Mancur Olson, *The Logic of Collective Action* (Harvard University Press, 1965); and Carole Uhlaner, "Rational Turnout: The Neglected Role of Groups," *American Journal of Political Science* 33 (1989).

29. Kuran, "Now Out of Never," 18.

30. Lyall first mentioned the "spotlight effect" in his dissertation, but he conceptualized it as an opposition using the regime's own rhetoric as a focal point to facilitate collective action ("Paths of Ruin," 30). In this case, I am not implying that the opposition necessarily uses the regime rhetoric; on the contrary, the opposition may use universal democratic principles to criticize the regime. The ultimate result is the same, however: putting the regime on the spot by highlighting its failures.

31. Twitter data from December 2010 to May 2011 were collected by Michael Macy, Shaomei Wu, and me, using API locations to create a dataset of all messages originating from the Middle East for this period. The data from this project will be released shortly after publication of this book. For more information on this data, please contact me.

32. Using the retweet mechanism, we examined which were the most followed members. Interestingly, the most followed members are also real-life activists, as well as more major media outlets.

33. While many Middle Eastern countries—especially Syria and Saudi Arabia—put up firewalls that were supposed to make access to social media such as Facebook and Twitter impossible, in re-

ality these firewalls were easily broken. During field research in Syria from May to August of 2009, I had easy access to these mediums in all Internet-cafés visited around the country.

34. Interview with a group of five Syrian activists in June 2009, Damascus. Further interviews with fifteen Syrian activists were also conducted in January 2012, Beirut, Lebanon. The interviews were semi-structured, but all interviewees responded to the following questions: (1) Did you use social media prior to the revolution? (2) Did you use them during the revolution? (3) Who was your audience when using social media? (4) Do you feel that they helped in your efforts? (5) Were you aware that many other Syrians were dissatisfied with the regime?

35. Skype interview with two activists from Banyas, March 24, 2011.

36. Interviews with fifteen activists from Banyas and Homs, January 10–15, 2012, Tripoli, Lebanon. Names are kept anonymous for their safety.

37. On the role of organizations for social mobilization, see Granovetter, "The Strength of Weak Ties"; Gladwell, "Why the Revolution Will Not Be Tweeted"; and Damon Centola and Michael Macy, "Complex Contagions and the Weakness of Long Ties," *American Journal of Sociology* 113, no. 3 (2007): 702–34.

38. Gary King, Jennifer Pan, and Molly Roberts, "How Censorship in China Allows Government Criticism but Silences Collective Expression," *American Political Science Review* 107, no. 2 (2012), accessed March 20, 2014, http://j.mp/LdVXqN.

39. Ibid., 1.

40. Gladwell, "Why the Revolution Will Not Be Tweeted."

41. Granovetter was first in emphasizing the "strength of weak ties" by arguing that "whatever is to be diffused can reach a larger number of people, and traverse a greater social distance, when passed through weak ties rather than strong." Granovetter, "The Strength of Weak Ties," 1,366.

42. Centola and Macy, "Complex Contagions and the Weakness of Long Ties," 703.

43. Identified through API location.

44. For criticism on the case of Iran, see Golnaz Esfandiari, "The Twitter Devolution," *Foreign Policy*, June 7, 2010.

45. See, for example, Dina Shehata, Hossam El-Hamalawy, and Marc Lynch, "Youth Movements and Social Media: Their Role and Impact," in *From Tahrir: Revolution or Democratic Transition*, video, June 4–6, 2011, accessed March 20, 2014, http://bit.ly/pOy1QJ.

46. Ibid.

47. See also Iskandar's chapter 8 in this volume for details about the "We Are All Khaled Said" site.

48. For a list of major political and scholarly figures emphasizing the crucial role of social media for mobilization, see Gladwell's critique.

49. Interviews with three activists from the April 6 Movement, July 2011, Cairo, Egypt.

50. For more information on this data, please contact me.

51. In the days leading up to January 25, 2011, Al Jazeera was regularly putting on the screen and reporting tweets from Egyptian activists.

52. See "We Are All Khaled Said," Facebook, accessed March 20, 2014, https://www.facebook.com/elshaheeed.co.uk/info; for news reports in protests outside of Egypt, see Basem Osama," Expatriate Egyptians Protest around the World on Anniversary of Revolution," *Ahramonline*, January 26, 2012, accessed March 20, 2014, http://english.ahram.org.eg/NewsContent/1/114/32842/Egypt/-January-Revolution-continues/Expatriate-Egyptians-protest-around-the-world-on-a.aspx.

53. Interview with ten protesters who were present on January 25; July, 2011, Cairo, Egypt.

54. See the developing conversation under the hashtag at "#SudanRevolts" Twitter (http://www.twitter.com).

55. King, Pan, and Roberts, "How Censorship in China Allows Government Criticism."

56. Navid Hassanpour, "Media Disruption Exacerbates Revolutionary Unrest: Evidence from Mubarak's Natural Experiment," *American Political Science Association (APSA)* Annual Meeting, September 2011, Seattle, WA, accessed March 20, 2014, http://papers.ssrn.com/sol3/papers .cfm?abstract_id=1903351&download=yes.

57. Interview with April 6 activists, July 2011, Cairo, Egypt.

58. Data from the Interactive Timeline of the Arab Protests, available at "Arab Spring: An Interactive Timeline of Middle East Protests," *Guardian*, January 5, 2012, accessed May 20, 2012, http://www .guardian.co.uk/world/interactive/2011/mar/22/middle-east-protest-interactive-timeline.

59. Mona El Ghobashy, "The Praxis of the Egyptian Revolution," MERIP (Middle East Research and Information Project), accessed August 3, 2012, http://www.merip.org/mer/mer258/praxis -egyptian-revolution.

60. For this information, see Historical *New York Times. New York Times.*

61. Interview with the author, July 2011, Cairo, Egypt.

62. Activists in Tahrir Square in July 2011 often pointed to their relatives who were there to provide them with support and protection. Interviews with the author, July 2011, Cairo, Egypt.

63. For arguments that they will not, see Gladwell, "Why the Revolution Will Not Be Tweeted"; Kern, "Opium for the Masses," 377–99; Laurie Penny, "Revolts Don't Have to Be Tweeted," *New Statesman*, February 14, 2011. For arguments that they help mobilization, see Dr. Sahar Khamis and Katherine Vaughn, "Cyberactivism in the Egyptian Revolution: How Civic Engagement and Citizen Journalism Tilted the Balance," *Arab Media and Society*, June 2011, accessed March 20, 2014, http://www.arabmediasociety.com/?article=769; and Jose Vargas, "Spring Awakening: How an Egyptian Revolution Began on Facebook," *New York Times*, February 17, 2012, accessed March 20, 2014, http://www.nytimes.com/2012/02/19/books/review/how-an-egyptian-revolution-began -on-facebook.html?pagewanted=all.

64. For more information on the literature on the "tipping point," see Granovetter 1973, 1978; Thomas C. Schelling, *Micromotives and Macrobehavior* (New York: Norton, 1978); Kuran 1991; and Centola and Macy 2007.

mutiny, a civil war, or some other category? Is it necessary for this convulsion to be seen and examined in unison or even as a singular event across the expanse of geographic terrain, cultural incongruence, socioeconomic particularity, and political inconsistency? Keeping in mind the role that media play in drafting, documenting, archiving, and giving meaning to events on the ground, the popular lexicon of revolution is largely devised and reinforced by media institutions generally and their journalistic narrations specifically. That is, the words most commonly used in the media often become the lexicon to describe events in broader social discourse.

Competing discourses in the regional media serve to complicate perceptions of the Uprisings and their various actors beyond the simplistic protagonist-antagonist, regime-opposition, and peaceful-violent dichotomies. So rather than attempt to parse out and deconstruct these dichotomies, a critically important task, I have instead chosen to focus on cross-cutting patterns in the region's media vis-à-vis the Uprisings that are of import and help us comprehend the overall scene without effacing divergent specificities. The inability to categorize or develop a nomenclature to comprehend the media raises the question of whether the recent eruption of activism can be seen as having affected the media's configuration in the region. Did these Uprisings have a profound impact on the prevailing media landscape in the region? Did they shift the environment enough so as to transcend the authoritarian and tyrannical milieus that previously allowed the region's regimes to control messages effectively and use these to exploit their people? Alternatively, is it possible that the opposite may have occurred whereby the preexisting media structures and practices, dominated by governments, states, and influential moguls, not only prevailed against popular interrogation but also were responsible for shifts in the Uprisings themselves?

I address these questions by characterizing several regional phenomena, which, with varying degrees of salience, are evident in the way media function. The first is what I argue as the integral and sometimes synonymous relationship between the medium and the revolutionary discourse. The second is a trend evident in some countries' media systems in the revolutionary milieu that represents a widening of the margins of freedom. The third addresses a recent trend that complicates the operations, reach, and appeal of transnational media in light of recent developments and the proliferation of local media offerings. And, finally, I argue that despite prevailing optimism in the transformations of the media scene in the Arab world since the Uprisings, and against the backdrop of diversification and liberalization, preexisting conditions of authoritarianism, state oversight, populist intimidation, and other obstacles remain significant.

THE MEDIUM IS THE UPRISING

One of the most fundamentally problematic axioms in the examination of the revolutionary movements in the Arab world is the "claim to authenticity" made by competing positions. Journalistic coverage of the Uprisings has demonstrated a fetishistic obsession with the authentication of experience and the corroboration of events. Mediated content has become the only prism, outside of experience, that shapes our understanding of the conditions, occurrences, and actors in these protracted struggles. In the absence of facilitative mediation via Al Jazeera, Al Arabiya, BBC, Facebook, Twitter, YouTube, Bambuser, mobile phones, and the like, how would these dissident movements and their daily manifestations have been relayed, amplified, and iconized? How would the stories of Mohamed Bouazizi and Khaled Said have been told?[1] Or would they have been told at all? Alternatively, had it not been for the comparative neglect of the Bahrain uprising on the regional and global media landscapes, would the progress of the uprising have proceeded differently? Hence, can we argue that the way in which a protest movement is reported can have an effect on the movement itself, its efficacy, and its prospects? Fundamentally, most of our interactions with these Uprisings, as communities of international scholars as well as curious global publics outside the sites of confrontation, are facilitated and mediated. With an inability to have testimonial and anecdotal vignettes from firsthand interactants and witnesses relayed to us through channels of communication, these revolutions may have followed different courses and produced alternate outcomes. Working through these various channels of communication whether they are mobile technology, television, or the social media, our experience and understanding of these revolutions is almost entirely mediated.

One way to problematize the Uprisings is to interrogate the way they are represented, which means that we have to begin understanding what the revolutionary nomenclature represents. Certain terms such as "narrativizing," "historicizing," and "archiving" must each be comprehended in relation to the didactic, because nonlinear stories are reported from the sites of revolt and conflict. In the current configuration of public memory of the Uprisings, it is not uncommon to assume that certain occurrences took place because we have been told that they happened. For instance, if Al Jazeera is reporting that Syrian rebels have taken over the road between Damascus and Aleppo, such an occurrence is assumed to have occurred. Alternatively, if a protest in Bahrain were to not be reported on the same network, then it is assumed to have not occurred at all. This of course belongs to the agenda-setting function of media in general, but, given the competing agendas in the region and the vastly differentiated political emphases in coverage of the Uprisings and their ensuing milieus, the very essence of occurrence becomes contested ground. For example, it is not uncommon for Egyptian private stations to avoid reporting or refute the existence of pro-Morsi protests since his removal on July 3, 2013. Conversely, it is not uncommon for Al Jazeera to wildly exaggerate the size of pro-Morsi protests in Egypt or to air dated footage of such protests as "live feeds" around the clock. The same applies to virtually all the ongoing conflicts in the region and their narrativization and documentation.

Researchers and journalists appeared to have started historicizing immediately after events occurred that, in my opinion, results in an outcome of analysis of recent events in the Arab world that stands on extremely shaky historical ground. Precisely for the reasons surrounding mediated narrativity and documentation, the ability of broadcast coverage to appear real and to present actualized occurrences has rendered it sufficient for scholarship to study the representation of the phenomenon rather than the phenomenon itself. The number of scholarly treatises written in varying fields of inquiry about the Uprisings that are anchored solely on the evidence presented through mediated production is astonishingly high. In some instances, the constructions surrounding the protest movements and their adversaries are akin to what Jean Baudrillard called *simulacra*.[2] By supplanting the reified with the imaginary, the stories not only fill the place of reality, they sometimes exist where the reality never did. Being able to understand and explain the extent to which there are elements of the imaginary, the hyperbolic, and the embellished in the stories of all actors in these conflicts is often impossible. On one hand, the authoritarian regimes try to reinforce, reimagine, and rearticulate their power in hope of sustaining themselves and creating longevity in this battle for attrition. On the other hand, the protest movements are themselves engaged in the process of purging any negative perceptions and portrayals for fear of jeopardizing a delicate moral high ground. In both circumstances, the communicative environment is essentially the battleground, with the media being among the most potent weapons employed by both sides.

This is further complicated when, as in the case of Egypt between the toppling of Mubarak in February 2011 and early 2014, the revolutionaries support the regime at various junctures, effectively obliterating the moral and perspectival consistency of the protest movements. Alternatively, as media coverage of the Syrian conflict shifts, the Baathist regime of Assad itself has undergone a mediated facelift, allowing it to appear counter-hegemonic on a geostrategic level against international powers such as the United States and recast its rebel adversaries as radical al-Qaeda-aligned "terrorists."

On the "revolutionary" side, it is extremely important to narrativize and commemorate these protests by transforming them into symbols—turning the dead into martyrs and the temporal junctures into iconic moments. These categories are plenty, with some of these disseminated and, in the case of strongly partisan media, even composed wholesale by mainstream media, journalism, and social media. The one iconic moment with the greatest social capital, historical weight, and widest media footprint is the story of Mohamed Bouazizi, a story reduced to a simple dichotomy pitting a disadvantaged youth against a malevolent state. Despite the seemingly unanimous and unambiguous story circulating widely among the international media, the details of what happened to Bouazizi are not very clear or coherent. The sequence of events that led to his self-immolation remains a source of debate in local community circles in his town of Sidi Bouzid. The more one investigates behind the headlines, the more one realizes the widely accepted story is varnished and significantly revised so as to deify Bouazizi.[3] As soon as the mediated stories are revised historically, one realizes there are a lot of inconsistencies that are capitalized on by particular movements for functional political reasons and rationale. Hence, the questions that remain salient include, Who was the woman whose altercation with Bouazizi kick-started the dissent? Was she a police officer? What authority did she possess? Did she really slap him across the face? Did she actively humiliate him? Who began the incident? Did he push her first? In the case of this story, the protagonist, a representative of the subaltern, must be supported, and he must succeed, and we have to be on the side of anyone who is challenging the government. This mediated historicization deserves close examination to ensure that iconization is neither grounded in simulacra nor is a product of the amplification of politicized messaging.

Another story worth revisiting is that of the young Alexandrian man, Khaled Said, whose killing contributed significantly to the protest movement that led to the January 25, 2011, uprising in Egypt. While the conditions and details of his killing became a topic of public debate with the state and the family and activists on opposite ends of the day's accounts, with the uprising in full swing, one story prevailed—that of the blemish-free heroic martyr whose dignity infused Egyptian opposition politics with purpose and drive. With the help of a highly successful online accountability campaign created anonymously on Facebook, called "We Are All Khaled Said," Khaled had been articulated. Once articulated and reified, revisionist history is hard to come by. Nevertheless, many have tried to piece together the story of Khaled Said, including Alexandrian scholar and writer Amro Ali, who was able to investigate and retell Khaled's story without all of its otherwise exaggerated plots, revealing a more human and humane Khaled. Ali had effectively demythologized the Egyptian revolution's greatest martyr.[4]

The iconic stories of Bouazizi and Said are but singular instances in the now-perennial cascade of revolutionary myth making perpetuated by both regimes and their antagonists. As the media actively move toward rendering these accounts into narratives—all of which are to varying degrees fictionalized—they attempt to ossify perspectives on these Uprisings. These narratives become increasingly rigid interpretations of event and actors. In some narratives, the Assad regime is a nationalist anti-imperial government fighting off international terrorism, and in others Bahrain protestors are Iranian operatives trying to bring down the government. Their oppositional narratives—equally ossified—present the Assad regime as a bloodthirsty, genocidal, and sectarian one waging war against its own people and its righteous rebellion. On Bahrain, the government is seen as a tyrannical sectarian one, adamant about suppressing rights, undermining political equality, and actively reversing the Shiite majority in the country. It is only when we pan out and see what these revolutions have come to mean to media organizations and institutions from a broader historical view that we are able to glean valuable insight into the transformations over the past four years.

FREEDOM TO FLOURISH

As is evident from this chapter's title, the two parallel but opposing currents that signify the divergent directions of media's transformation in the region are coexisting. From the optimistic standpoint, one must start examining the perspective of state broadcasters. We have always known and understood these institutions in the Arab media as governed, funded, and supported by extremely top-down, hierarchical, authoritarian regimes.[5] They have been deeply committed to state policy irrespective of whether or not these are beneficial for the public at large. However, with all the turmoil in the national and regional political landscape, we began witnessing interesting examples of unique progress. For instance, there is decentralization of the state media in many of the countries that have experienced protest movements.[6] While the state media's initial response was denial, suppression, and obfuscation of the very existence of the protest movements, with time—and given the consistent and unrelenting nature of the protests despite the use of brute force against them—it became impossible for the broadcasters to ignore them completely.

In the case of Egypt, for instance, the state media underwent a transformation literally overnight on February 11, 2011, when Mubarak left office. Egyptians woke up the next morning, and the news media were celebrating the very revolution they had criticized the night before. Keep in mind that the same broadcasters, the same anchors, and the same newscasters faced the challenge of working in the same institution that was run by the Ministry of Information since its establishment. A renarrativization became necessary in order to report current events. This renarrativization manifested as a rejoiced enthrallment with the revolution and active attempts to memorialize it. As of 2014, more than three years after the toppling of Mubarak, state media—and to a greater extent private media—are describing this period as a fundamental turning point in Egyptian history. However, in the summer of 2013, following mass protests calling for early presidential elections on June 30 and the ensuing military removal of Mohamed Morsi, the renarrativization itself became further complicated. Today, in Egypt's convoluted political milieu, the commemoration of revolution is contested, not between revolutionaries and their adversaries, but rather between camps of self-proclaimed revolutionaries. I discuss this battle for revolutionary narrative between the state, the military, the Muslim Brotherhood, Islamist groups, secular parties, and revolutionaries in Egypt elsewhere in greater depth.[7]

The renarrativization of the revolution in Tunisia, while similar, has been far more sustained. The state media have gone through such a remarkable facelift, beyond the change in title—from *i'lam hokoomy* (government media) to *i'lam 'omoomi* (central media). As opposed to its predecessor, this media outfit, cut from the cloth of state programming, now effectively presents news from what might be described as a watchdog role toward the elected government—something that is extremely uncanny and probably unlikely.[8]

In many instances, we also see an increased public delegitimization of authority. With the advent of mass public mobilization and widespread uprising in several countries in the region, any failure on the part of the state media to relay accurate, even-handed, and professional journalistic content can only further entrench mistrust in these channels. For this reason, in the majority of countries, audience numbers for state media are dwindling significantly. Prior to 2011, state media in the region never needed audience approval. Today, failing to deliver professional journalism (at least in the form of a facade) has much more serious political repercussions. Audiences now translate into citizens, active participants in public policy, and interrogators of representation. For the first time ever, the media's popularity is related to viewer ratings instead of the regime's mandates. Ratings have not been crucial to a TV channel's success before; in fact, there were very few institutions that did any ratings in the Arab world as far as media are concerned.[9] In today's media environment, state broadcasts are actively competing with private stations for viewers now that there are high political stakes. Most private news networks, now thrown into the maelstrom of political competition, have become embroiled in the new milieu and often reflect the ambitions, agendas, and interests of their owners. Even networks like Al Jazeera Arabic (and other Arabic language subsidiaries), once journalistically firewalled from the Qatari state that funds it, have since April 2011 shifted to become predictably reflective in discourse and emphasis to the Gulf country's foreign policy. Unlike its earlier iteration, which garnered significant professional and academic acclaim, Al Jazeera Arabic has become unabashedly supportive of anti-regime rebels in Syria and Libya, Islamist political parties in Tunisia and Egypt, and proregime forces in Bahrain.[10]

At a time when state media seem either passé relics or demonized entities, ministries of information and similar surrogate authorities were expected to become extinct. Take the case of Egypt, where the Ministry of Information was technically described as having been dissolved or disbanded shortly after the fall of Mubarak. However, two years later, and under the administration of all three governments (the SCAF-run, Muslim Brotherhood–run, and now military-backed authority),[11] the ministry has been fully resuscitated. For some time, the military and government censors had become obsolete in the most dramatic renaissance of the press in decades. However, with the arrival of a Muslim Brotherhood government under Mohamed Morsi, campaigns of intimidation from the politicized Minister of Information began to undermine this opening. Since the removal of the brotherhood from office, and with the military back at the helm of politics in the country, the armed forces use both coercion and appeasement to ensure conformity in the Egyptian state and private news media. Censors are back to active duty, and the Ministry of Information is just one of several authorities imposing on the media environment. That does not mean there will be no resistance within these institutions, but it will be difficult to gauge its tenacity and prospects.[12] As it stands, in Egypt and throughout the Arab world, it appears the infrastructure of state-controlled media may be shifting in its political-economic structure, but not discursively or ideologically.

The private media entities too are in an unprecedented situation. In Egypt, for instance, there are the old channels in the private media that now have to distance themselves publicly from the discourse of the former regime. The changing political situation also allowed new media outlets to be approved in Egypt. The SCAF, in one of the very few signs of good faith, allowed the licensing of sixteen satellite networks.[13] This change by the authorities increased the amount of options available to Egyptians. In my analysis, this decision was made in order to control the media, but it ended up backfiring, as many of these channels became instruments in the hands of competing political forces that could no longer be controlled by the government. At varying points, these channels became hostile to the ruling military government in 2011, and others later took an adversarial stance toward the Muslim Brotherhood. In the end, with the military intervention in politics on July 3, 2013, the new government took aggressive steps to rewind time and shut down newly licensed Islamist stations and drive out pro-brotherhood platforms like Al Jazeera Mubasher Misr.[14]

Nevertheless, licensing sixteen new satellite channels opened up the media scene. However, the mixed interests on the part of the media entrepreneurs in the region led to a fragmentation of the media. The more fragmentation there is, the more pluralistic the messages are, the more complicated and cacophonous the media scene becomes, and the more interesting politically this is likely to become.

Until recently, Egypt had a plethora of channels that were clearly politically affiliated. One example is the Salafi channels Al-Hafiz and Al-Nas, which in some cases (before closure) advocated for the political party al-Nour and some of its candidates. There were also channels affiliated with the Muslim Brotherhood, such as satellite station Masr 25, which was taken off the air in July 2013 and would have been inconceivable a year and a half prior. ONTV, which belongs to Naguib Sawiris, one of the richest entrepreneurs in the Arab world, aligns to a large extent with the liberal front and sometimes specifically with his Free Egyptians Party. And so on.

One of the more interesting manifestations of the Arab Uprisings, as far as how they translated to media, is the role of transnational media. Of course viewers have grown accustomed to Al Jazeera receiving most of the accolades as far as being able to cover the revolutions. Additionally, audiences have become accustomed to Al Jazeera's perspective of representing Tahrir square in Cairo as well as to the coverage of Tunisia.

CROSSING BORDERS

The rise of satellite television in the Arab world—chronicled and analyzed by numerous scholarly works over the past two decades—was said to have disrupted the state's monopoly on information and made it possible for messages emanating from one country to more easily influence publics in another. The Arab Uprisings, considered by popular commentators to have at least been facilitated by regional transnational media, have taken a toll on the popularity of these media. Today, many of these stations—such as Al Jazeera, Al Arabiya, MBC, and others—are losing the battle for audiences as local viewers become more focused on domestic concerns and their local national media offerings more diverse and segmented. For instance, since the Uprisings, there has been a dramatic rise in the number of local and specialized news stations in Tunisia, Egypt, Libya, Yemen, and Syria. Not only are the regional transnational stations less able to compete effectively given the revival of state media and the rise of local private networks, they are also struggling in their delivery of content. At the end of the day, Al Jazeera was able to create a significant market for itself, specifically as far as the English-language channel is concerned. Their online traffic alone has skyrocketed and remains extremely high, whereas the Arabic network has dwindled.

Al Jazeera is no longer the only go-to network for local news in media-rich countries. As a single regional station, Al Jazeera Arabic could not produce sufficient dedicated local programming for every country experiencing political turmoil in the region. Instead, the Qatari government, which funds Al Jazeera, also launched and bankrolled anti-regime networks such as Libya TV[15] and Orient TV, which supports the opposition in Syria. In the case of countries like Egypt, where the loss of audiences due to media specialization and segmentation are coupled with a very sizeable population, stations like Al Jazeera needed to have focused targeted content for this market. This was the reason behind the launching of Al Jazeera Mubasher Misr ("Al Jazeera Live Egypt"). Despite the agenda-driven nature of these networks, their emergence adds to the diversity of media offerings in the region and contributes to the flourishing of the overall landscape.

As far as journalistic performance goes, the margin of freedom appears to be broader, because many previously taboo topics can be openly discussed. Topics such as revolt, dissidence, and counterhegemony are appealing to audiences and have become standard fare on many of the region's newscasts and talk shows. Even under the most dire circumstances, with journalists being targeted, newspaper licenses retracted, copy confiscated, and offices raided, the seemingly unstoppable proliferation in both number and diversity of media outlets in each country has made it possible for there to be lively debate on pressing and controversial issues. In some instances, this is done with subtlety, such as in Egypt post-Morsi. In other circumstances, the approach is more confrontational, as in the Tunisian media.

Alternatively, given the abundance and accessibility of most media in the region, adversarial, oppositional content often comes from outside each nation-state. For example, it is almost impossible for criticism of the state to air on Syrian government television or on Qatari outlets such as Al Jazeera and Qatari national television. Nevertheless, in the wider spectrum of regional media, there are numerous Syrian anti-regime outlets and a growing number of media critical of the Qatari government. This "reciprocal oppositional" media condition is certainly not an outcome of the Uprisings but dates back to the early days of broadcasting in the region. However, each state's inability to successfully shield their citizens from these oppositional media is a contemporary development that highlights the end of absolute hegemony over domestically accessible media content.

In this milieu, journalists who push the boundaries (as far as they possibly could given their respective circumstances) have become celebrities or have developed a cult following. This development can be observed in Tunisia, in Egypt, and in other countries where adversarial coverage garners attention and following. In Egypt, the likes of Ibrahim Eissa, Yosri Fouda, and Reem Maged, as well as comedian Bassem Youssef, have built massive followings as a result of their critical stances toward the National Democratic Party of Mubarak, the SCAF, and the Muslim Brotherhood in the two years after Mubarak's toppling. In the post-Morsi period, with the military calling the shots, many of these media personalities have curbed their criticism of de facto ruler General Abdel-Fattah el-Sisi and the military establishment, calling into question their commitment to journalistic values, which may take a toll on their popularity. Those who continue to be critical of the current regime at best risk becoming *personae non gratae* and at worst are the targets of arrest and sentencing at the hands of the interim government.[16] So while the margin of freedom across the region may have dropped somewhat since the near-utopian expectations of 2011, the plethora and proliferation of contrarian voices in the Arab world's cacophonous media environment should be seen as an overwhelmingly positive outcome of the Uprisings.

As media become more specialized in the increasingly crowded regional landscape, active audiences are not only deciphering messages and making sense of the shifting political contours in their respective countries, but also helping challenge and shape coverage in instrumental ways. The advent of social media and the rapid rise in Internet penetration has not only made online platforms a critical dimension in the protest movements (though not a causal effect as some writings suggest),[17] but also helps shape mainstream programming about news. Without being tempted to gravitate too far toward one end of the technological/ sociological-determinism spectrum, one can ascertain the value of social media. Technology scholar Clay Shirky and writer Malcolm Gladwell anchor the spectrum, but the reality is likely somewhere in the middle.[18] Social media are tools, albeit instrumental tools. Protest movements become increasingly adept at social media. Beyond their use by activists, social-media platforms remain predominantly used for otherwise-frivolous, self-referential entertainment and collective relational maintenance and interpersonal upkeep. Yet, since the Uprisings, Arab states have strategically shifted their approach toward social media. Rather than resorting to blatant and often unsuccessful curbing of access and reprimand or persecution of contrarian transgressors, governments in the region have become more sophisticated in their use of these platforms for outreach, popular appeal, and propagandizing. In the case of competitive politics (such as in Egypt, Tunisia, Morocco, Libya, Iraq, and elsewhere), parties and candidates have come to rely heavily on social media for publicity, recruitment, and vote mobilization.

FALTERING TOWERS

As far as the descent of Arab media, how have they failed their publics and citizens since the Uprisings? The state media of course have an incredible ingenuity at reinventing themselves. They are repeating some of the old approaches and are becoming subservient to new powers. In the case of Egypt, the military-backed interim government and the ensuing elected authority will have guaranteed, if not enshrined, conformity and cooperation from the national media—public and private. In Syria, state media have become further encamped and exclusive, engaging in an all-out war against their adversaries. The Tunisian media—despite pushing the boundaries against al-Nahda—are slowly succumbing to the binary of a new state undergoing reformation: either submit to the ruling government agenda or become so entrenched in opposing it that it espouses Ben Ali–era loyalties and commitments.

Typically journalistic unprofessionalism on these broadcasters and media manifests in the form of blatantly one-sided representation of events. Since the commencement of the Arab Uprisings, these have become characteristic. Take, for example, the coverage of Baba Amro[19] or events in Egypt after the revolution, such as the coverage of Maspero,[20] that involved Christian protesters who were attacked by the military. In the latter, many of the protesters were run over or shot by live ammunition. However, the state media reported that these protesters had attacked the military and additionally asked that honorable citizens help defend the military against these "barbaric, unarmed protesters." This type of fictional reporting contributes to the idea of the simulacra, has a remarkable appeal with politicized audiences, and should not be underestimated on the grounds of sounding unreasonable. It is not unlike some of the fantastic charges brought in the Egyptian private media against the Muslim Brotherhood members following the removal of Morsi.[21]

The private media, which I have described earlier as extremely open, cacophonous, and pluralistic compared with their pre-Uprising conditions, are beginning to succumb to infringement by state power and intrusion by state institutions. At any moment, their autonomy, independence, latitude, and very existence could be in jeopardy when the wrath of the state is unleashed. In countries whose state observes a semblance of good governance (and at least tokenistic commitment to the rule of law), intrusion and infringement come in the form of legislative and judicial curbs. In the case of Egypt, for example, after the invasion/storming of the Israeli embassy in Cairo, the Egyptian military found it entirely irresponsible that Al Jazeera Mubasher Misr presented them in a disagreeable manner. So the state was able to find justification for the retraction of the channel's ratification and license. Moreover, the staff had to leave, and the studios were closed.[22] Even a network with the clout and fame of Al Jazeera was punished in Egypt in a post-revolutionary environment, as evidenced, for example, by the high-profile arrest and trial of three of its journalists.[23] This action sends a clear signal to any of the small Egyptian-based channels.

What does this tell us? It tells us that the state did not disappear in the Arab world. Many have imagined what media might look like if the state had withered or was no longer the determinant of how media cover events. However, the state does not simply collapse as easily as was assumed. Although some presumed that Egypt had become an anarcho-syndicalist, self-governing territory, the central state with all of its bureaucratic weight has proven its resilience. The state still wields a significant amount of power. In fact, not only is the state's media narrative propagated by the state itself, even in cases where editorial autonomy was assumed, the nexus of politics and media falls squarely into the preexisting configuration of state dynamics. Networks like Al Jazeera Arabic, treated as an independent voice divorced of government control, today has metamorphosed into a foreign-policy tool of the Qatari government. This has been met with chagrin not simply from hostile governments but also from publics in the Arab world, which explains why their numbers are dwindling significantly.[24]

Nevertheless, many states in the region have started to exert great broadcasting influence through private media outfits as opposed to public networks. Egypt, a country that, as far as its media influence in the region goes, had basically fallen off the map since the mid 1970s, is now starting to wield significant influence, largely through private networks beaming from the country—such as Al-Hayat, ONTV, CBC, Al-Mehwar, Al-Qahera, Al-Naas, etc. With state broadcasting possessing limited appeal, Arab governments have found private media, in most instances bankrolled by regime loyalists, to be useful surrogates to state media. They are committed to the regimes' systems of governance but are cosmetically augmented to appear independent. That means that, while on the surface it appears the regional media map is being redrawn, the political economic infrastructure of broadcasting and news production in the region, as well as its political configuration, has not changed significantly.

MEDIA, THE INTERNET, AND ISLAM

The growing contestation between ascendant Islamic political forces in the region and their entrenched adversaries in the security-establishment ranks (liberal political groups, non-Islamist revolutionaries, and supporters of the pre-uprising regimes) has had an adverse effect on freedom of the press and information. With 75 percent of the first Egyptian parliament dominated by Islamists, they waged a war on the media, calling for curbs on the grounds of decency and sharia compliance. Alternatively, once the Muslim Brotherhood was removed from power in the summer of 2013, most of the country's Islamist networks had their licenses retracted and operations shut down. So, while political diversification following the Uprisings was expected to shepherd a liberalized, pluralistic media system in each country, instead it has produced political brinksmanship, intolerance, and a winner-takes-all approach to media.

In Tunisia, freedom of speech was assaulted when Salafis attacked a theater for the screening of a film that was deemed questionable or blasphemous and attacked a newspaper for publishing the photo of a near-nude woman, among various other violations since the fall of Ben Ali.[25] Another attack was on a television network that broadcasted the animated French-Persian film *Persepolis*, which featured a scene where the protagonist had a face-to-face conversation with "God."[26]

More than any time in recent memory, the Arab media have become embroiled in the growing cultural schisms over what is permissible and what is not. What is sharia compliant and what is not. What offends societal norms and sensibilities and what does not. What can be uttered on air, viewed on television, or published in print and what cannot. These are content-related dilemmas that touch on sensitive issues of identities, literacies, ideologies, and individual particularities and often go unresolved. With media serving as the platforms for such contestations, they have become parties in the struggle for basic freedoms, particularly those of expression and the press.

While the proliferation of Internet access is happening across the region and is significantly impacting citizen journalism and news reporting, it has also produced some deleterious results. International reporting from the Arab world and even local and regional media has developed an almost fetishistic obsession with online communities of activists and thereby amplify their often-narrow interpretation of events, perspectives, and worldviews. In many cases, these online echo chambers challenge the status quo and promote a more-accommodating view of press freedoms and other rights. Despite this, the disproportionately high levels of attention they often receive from some media leads to their views supplanting a wider base of discordant public opinion. Hence, it should come as no surprise that, since the commencement of the 2011 Uprisings, activists and citizen-journalists have made significant strides in setting the news agenda across the region in struggles often depicted as "David versus Goliath." The greatest complication in this formulaic dynamic is the assumption that patterns of expression online mirror societal patterns of public option.

A good example of this is the recent Egyptian electoral system. While the majority of people online seemed to be voting against the constitutional amendment, on March 19, 2011, the majority of people in Egypt voted for it.[27] While it appeared, based on online surveys, that the majority of people online would vote in the first round of the presidential elections for either Abdel Moneim Aboul Fotouh or Hamdeen Sabbahi, the actual outcome for Mohamed Morsi was quite the contrary. In the most recent electoral round (at the time of writing), the constitutional referendum held in January 2014, less than 40 percent of eligible voters cast their ballots, and the majority of young people did not participate at all.[28] Social-media indicators suggested the turnout might be at least twice this number with the Internet generation comprising a significant proportion. We have seen this happening quite consistently, as social media occasionally end up being false gauges largely because of Internet penetration and segmented variable online communities. It is critical not just to acknowledge the growing capacity for mediation online but to also factor in the extent to which much of the big-data research is often divorced of experiential qualitative dimensions of new-media usage. Very often, such research falters in delivering accurate readings and forecasts for political activity between the online and off-line spaces.

Further complicating the picture is a nebulous space of opaque political activity. From the Syrian regime's electronic army to Egyptian state security service's minders, the state and other groups with substantial resources and capacity are capable of obfuscating information, creating fictional stories and news, and leaking material to fragment their opponents' fronts and turn public opinion against them, among other strategies. In some instances, such activity may be attributed to the "deep state," institutions of the state, high-level political groups, competing corporate giants, and others with proximity to the loci of power.

Perhaps a short vignette about dissent in Egypt's recent history might offer some collective insights. In February 1954, a young journalist named Ihsan Abdul Kuddous wrote for a prominent, then-independent Egyptian magazine called *Roz al Youssef*. Less than two years after the toppling of the monarchy of King Farouk by the Free Officers, Abdul Kuddous posed the critical question: Who are these Free Officers? The best way to know who they were was for Abdul Kuddous to meet with each of the members of the Free Officers and ask the same series of questions.[29] He sat down with every member of the revolutionary council and inquired, What is your ideology? Background? What vision do you have for the country? He realized that none of them agreed on anything, that there was no common vision and no common ideology. He concluded that the only institution that allows for this much diversity in opinion and mutual interest is a mafia institution. This article ran in an editorial titled, "The Mob that Rules Egypt." He was jailed for three months. By the time he was released, the media environment had changed and was run by the military. The military became a Pandora's box for sixty years. Fast-forward to eighteen months after the toppling of Mubarak, when Ahmad Shafiq, one of the most prominent members of the military and one of the closest to the SCAF and a presidential candidate (and Mubarak's last prime minister), went out to vote in his area. He was confronted by hordes of individuals opposed to him who confronted him and chased him out of the polling station with shoes and slippers after he cast his ballot. If Ahmad Shafiq had won and became president (according to the polls), at the very least one thing might have been accomplished: he would not have been above the law or scrutiny. Instead, he was the target of ridicule and media criticism, which itself is a major accomplishment despite all of the losses along the way. Today, with the fall of the Muslim Brotherhood in Egypt, and despite a heavy-handed crackdown against political opposition in the media, the military-backed government is incapable of silencing dissent. With varying degrees of impact, humor on television and online, as well as cyberdissidence, remain staples of contemporary politics across the region and shift dramatically the ability of the state and political actors to monopolize discourses.

Almost four years since the eruption of the Uprisings in the Arab world, with the political landscape being redrawn (despite the continuation and perseverance of the traditional actors), there is much to rejoice over in the area of media liberalization. Nevertheless, as we have seen in many a circumstance, these gains are not irreversible and face significant challenges as conformity and dissence collide across platforms. Without succumbing to the zero-sum game of prognostication and abbreviated forecasting, one could at least confidently assert that, if anything, these past four years are likely the most tumultuous since the advent of broadcasting in the region.

NOTES

1. The stories of both men are explored in more detail later in this chapter.

2. Jean Baudrillard described a simulacra as a version of the real when the real no longer exists or never existed, effectively supplanting the real with a representation, but not as replica or replacement. Jean Baudrillard, *Simulacra and Simulations* (Ann Arbor: University of Michigan Press, 1994).

3. Reporters have traveled to Sidi Bouzid in an attempt to piece together the intricacies of the Bouazizi story and many have come back with more questions than answers. Competing versions of the same story offer both Bouazizi and the inspector who allegedly "slapped" him, Fedia Hamdi, as victims of both the incident and Ben Ali's state. One such account comes from Wyre Davies, "Doubt over Tunisian 'Martyr' Who Triggered Revolution," *BBC*, June 17, 2011, accessed March 19, 2014, http://www.bbc.co.uk/news/world-middle-east-13800493.

4. Amro Ali, "Saeeds of Revolution: De-mythologizing Khaled Saeed," in *Mediating the Arab Uprisings*, ed. Adel Iskandar and Bassam Haddad (Tadween Publishing, 2012).

5. See Naomi Sakr, *Satellite Realms: Transnational Television, Globalization and the Middle East* (London: I. B. Tauris, 2002); William A. Rugh, *Arab Mass Media: Newspapers, Radio, and Television in Arab Politics* (Santa Barbara: Praeger, 2004); Mohammed el-Nawawy and Adel Iskandar, *Al-Jazeera: The Story of the Network that Is Rattling Governments and Redefining Modern Journalism.* (Boulder: Westview, 2003)

6. Iskandar. *Mediating the Arab Uprisings.*

7. Adel Iskandar, *Egypt in Flux: Essays on an Unfinished Revolution* (Cairo: American University in Cairo Press, 2013).

8. For more on the transformation of state media in Tunisia following the removal of Ben Ali's government, see Fatima el-Issawi, "Tunisian Media in Transition," *Carnegie Papers* (2012), accessed March 20, 2014, http://carnegieendowment.org/files/tunisian_media.pdf.

9. Media audience ratings have always been difficult to conduct, ascertain, and verify across the Arab world. In many instances, these numbers were closely guarded to avoid the ramifications of public admission of failure on the part of state media and competition between private media investors. For more information about these, see Sakr, *Satellite Realms*; Rugh, *Arab Mass Media*; el-Nawawy, *Al Jazeera.*

10. Vivian Salama, "Al-Jazeera's (R)Evolution?" *Jadaliyya,* May 20, 2012, accessed March 20, 2014, http://www.jadaliyya.com/pages/index/5610/al-jazeeras-(r)evolution.

11. The SCAF is Egypt's Supreme Council of the Armed Forces.

12. For a review of the majority transformative media moments in the first year of the Egyptian revolution and the push-pull dynamics between state and protesters, see Adel Iskandar, "A Year in the Life of Egypt's Media: A 2011 Timeline," *Jadaliyya.* January 26, 2012, accessed March 20, 2014, http://www.jadaliyya.com/pages/index/3642/a-year-in-the-life-of-egypts-media_a-2011-timeline.

13. Emad Mekay, "TV Stations Multiply as Egyptian Censorship Falls," *New York Times,* July 13, 2011, accessed March 20, 2014, http://www.nytimes.com/2011/07/14/world/middleeast/14iht-M14B -EGYPT-MEDIA.html?pagewanted=all.

14. Sarah El Deeb (AP), "Egypt Court Bans Al-Jazeera TV Affiliate," Yahoo, September 3, 2013, accessed March 20, 2014, http://news.yahoo.com/egypt-court-bans-al-jazeera-tv-affiliate-102148247 .html.

15. Jason Burke, "Libyan Opposition Set to Launch TV Channel from Qatar," *Guardian,* March 30, 2011.

16. For more information about the state of journalism in Egypt and the campaigns of arrest and intimidation facing journalists under the post-Morsi regime, visit "Egypt," Committee to Protect Journalists (CPJ), accessed March 20, 2014, http://cpj.org/mideast/egypt/.

17. See Toska's chapter 7 in this volume.

18. The very public debate between Clay Shirky, who asserts that social media and technology are instrumental in the Arab Uprisings, and Malcolm Gladwell, who refutes this, became a salient part of the comprehension of the Uprisings, their organization, and overall capacity. For more information, see Malcolm Gladwell and Clay Shirky, "From Innovation to Revolution: Do Social Media Make Protests Possible?" *Foreign Policy* (2011).

19. Sam Dagher, "Arab Media Clash Over Syria," *Wall Street Journal,* March 24, 2012, accessed March 20, 2014, http://online.wsj.com/news/articles/SB10001424052970203961204577269081450 598296.

20. For a detailed account of media coverage of the incident, see the entries for October 9 and subsequent days in Iskandar, "A Year in the Life of Egypt's Media."

21. Hani Shukrallah, "The Continued Descent of Egyptian Media," Middle East Institute, October 8, 2013, accessed March 20, 2014, http://www.mei.edu/content/continued-descent-egyptian-media.

22. Noah El-Hennawy, "Military Rulers Activate Mubarak Repressive Media Policies," *Egypt Independent*, September 15, 2011, accessed March 20, 2014, http://www.egyptindependent.com/news/military-rulers-activate-mubarak%E2%80%99s-repressive-media-policies.

23. "Egypt Crisis: Al-Jazeera Journalists Arrested in Cairo," *BBC*, December 30, 2013, accessed March 20, 2014, http://www.bbc.com/news/world-middle-east-25546389.

24. "Al-Jazeera on Decline in Arab Spring Countries," *Peninsula*, April 25, 2013, accessed March 20, 2014, http://thepeninsulaqatar.com/news/qatar/234386/al-jazeera-on-decline-in-arab-spring-nations.

25. Available at AFP, "Tunisian Alarm at Salafi Assault on 'un-Islamic' Culture," *Al Arabiya*, August 17, 2012, accessed March 20, 2014, http://english.alarabiya.net/articles/2012/08/17/232793.html.

26. "Protesters Attack TV Station over Film *Persepolis*," *BBC*, October 9, 2011, accessed March 20, 2014, http://www.bbc.co.uk/news/world-africa-15233442.

27. "Egypt Referendum Strongly Backs Constitution Changes," *BBC*, March 20, 2011, accessed March 20, 2014, http://www.bbc.co.uk/news/world-middle-east-12801125.

28. Mona Salem and Jay Deshmuck (AFP), "Egypt Charter Opens Road for Sisi but Youths Alienated," Google, January 19, 2014, accessed March 20, 2014, http://www.google.com/hostednews/afp/article/ALeqM5gyHKhTuTBwX8P7P-87bNEuwkMpVw?docId=f685f753-7d68-4c45-92cf-eb69a9711598.

29. Iskandar, *Egypt in Flux*, 129–131.

9

The Arab Uprisings in Tunisia: Parity, Elections, and the Struggle for Women's Rights

Lilia Labidi

After the euphoria of January 14, 2011, when youth-led uprisings succeeded where political parties and national organizations had failed—that is, forcing Ben Ali's abscondment to Saudi Arabia—fear seized many women who were concerned with the future of their rights gained in 1956 and subsequently amended on a number of occasions. In the ensuing debates, discussions, and actions of women's movements and organizations during 2011 and 2012, I saw this distress expressed on two striking occasions, each time in different circumstances and taking distinct forms. On the first occasion, women and feminists—paralyzed by the fear of seeing secularist political parties and national organizations dominate—paradoxically did not vote for political parity between men and women. They were simultaneously witness to the Islamic-oriented *Ennahda* Party as it voted in favor of parity but did not publicly discuss this apparent contradiction. The second occasion arose at the opening of the National Constituent Assembly on November 22, 2011—following Ennahda's victory in the country's first free elections since independence—where a young woman shed tears as she recounted her fears about the future of Tunisia's Personal Status Code, which had guaranteed women's rights since 1956. After each case, both trauma and triumphs followed.

During this period and subsequently, several Tunisian psychiatrists observed an increase in the frequency of depression, psychological disturbances, and symptoms of anxiety among the general population,[1] as well as an increase in the number of people experiencing trauma.[2] Others invoked the notion of a "collective depression."[3] According to psychiatrist Anissa Bouasker, women were more affected by trauma than men, and she attributed this to deep concerns for their children[4] and family economic difficulties. Certainly, unemployment among university graduates has been increasing rapidly—55,800 (2005), 139,000 (2010), and 175,000 of a total of 700,000 unemployed (2012)[5]—as has the number of strikes. In October 2013, the number of strikes was 71 percent greater than in September 2013, with 93 percent of these led by the main Tunisian labor union, the UGTT (Union Générale Tunisienne du Travail).[6] In the three years following the revolution, psychiatrists estimated that 25 to 30 percent of patients with psychological problems had become mentally ill.[7] Some practitioners would like to see political figures intervene to reassure the population, others hope that political and socioeconomic security will set in, and many warn the government of the long-term costs for the country's public health and security. For example, the Tunisian Psychiatric Association appealed for a multidisciplinary approach, calling for a rapprochement with "nonpsychiatric colleagues" and with specialists in the human sciences.[8]

On the surface, women's rights in Tunisia after the uprising appeared to be growing: the number of women's associations created in a few months during 2011 equaled the total number formed during twenty-three years of the Ben Ali regime; women gained the right to have their national identification photographs taken wearing the *hijab*; the law on political parity between men and women was adopted; and Tunisia lifted its reservations concerning the Convention on the Elimination of all forms of Discrimination Against Women (CEDAW). Even on the regional level, women became more numerous in the parliaments of Morocco, Algeria, and Libya (though in Egypt the opposite occurred). Therefore, the question that runs through my discussion in this chapter is, Why, despite these apparent improvements, did women and feminists express such fears?

To answer this question, let me begin with a few clarifications. The Personal Status Code (PSC), promulgated in 1956, gave numerous rights to women, including outlawing polygamy and divorce by repudiation, mandating that divorce be judicially approved, ensuring women's right to work, and declaring public life open to both sexes; and the PSC was even later amended on several occasions to give such rights as Tunisian nationality to a child with a foreign father. The PSC was the product of a reformist approach where *ijtihad* (interpretation) was the expression of the will of both women and men. In my earlier writings, I have shown how the PSC was the fruit of the efforts of women who had engaged in political activism against colonialism and patriarchy—an activism that, according to political context, was at times emphasized, at times neglected.[9] These women activists found support among intellectuals, journalists, lawyers, Zeitounian theologians, and political figures, giving more power to the desire for change.

The most significant figure to support this desire for change was Habib Bourguiba, who ruled Tunisia from 1957 to 1987. He recognized women's suffering in his immediate environment as well as among women who struggled against colonialism and patriarchy more broadly. Bourguiba's powerful charisma (*heibat*) involved customary authority based on cultural traditions. His personal authority and individual manner arose from his effective and persuasive speaking power. In addition, he held legal and rational authority as the founder of the modern state and its central political party, from which he was able to keep the traditional and religious elites from blocking the promulgation of the new Personal Status Code.

In the transition from colonialism to independence during Bourguiba's ascendancy, society was subsequently restructured, and new psychological problems appeared as well. These were captured in the works of Carmel Camilleri on Tunisia and Fadéla M'Rabet on Algeria—to cite just a few—and concerned the status of women and youth in transitional situations. The difficulties encountered by such groups in adapting to new circumstances may be useful for understanding the current situation.[10]

The passage from a totalitarian system under Ben Ali (Bourguiba's successor)—where the source of fear was known—to a context of political transition brought on by the revolutionary process of 2010 and 2011 was made more unsettling by an environment where information was easily deformed and threats could be abstract or virtual.[11] In this context, both familiar and new fears emerged. A review of the international literature shows how, in a context of such fragmentation, individual and environmental factors may contribute to the psychopathological characteristics that have been described by psychiatrists in Tunisia.[12]

To elaborate on the specific conditions feeding these social insecurities, I begin my discussion with a description of the political condition for women under the

Bourguiba and Ben Ali Regimes. I examine the issue of political parity and the government's lifting of Tunisia's reservations concerning CEDAW (the Convention on the Elimination of All Forms of Discrimination against Women) that arose after the uprising. I also discuss how the parity law played out in practice during the elections and what implications this has had for the political status of women in the country that catalyzed the Arab Uprisings. To illustrate the impacts, I profile two central female political actors, Souad Abderrahim and Bochra Belhaj Hmida, who each headed electoral lists for ideologically disparate political groups. I conclude with an assessment of the conditions now emerging out of the disruptions caused by the Tunisian uprising. While the compelling fears of many women remain in this new, uncertain chapter, the net effect so far has been a growing importance of female figures in local and regional political domains.

WOMEN'S MOVEMENTS DURING THE BOURGUIBA AND BEN ALI REGIMES

Many Tunisian women have participated in the struggle against colonialism and for their rights since the beginning of the twentieth century, when they organized associations or affiliated themselves with political parties. With Tunisian independence in 1956, a new law on associations pushed a number of women's groups to join the Union Nationale de la Femme Tunisienne (UNFT), an organization that the government used to spread its policies. In order to give the UNFT political weight, its president was a member of the executive committee of the political party in power—a tradition that remained until Ben Ali came to power in 1987.

In the 1970s, the emergence of a new women's elite from national universities who kept their distance from the UNFT enabled the development of a more independent feminist discourse. After Ben Ali deposed Habib Bourguiba in 1987, the statutes of the UNFT were revised under feminist pressure, but these changes did not succeed in attracting feminists to the organization. For the independent feminists of both a "universalist" orientation (which supports full equality between men and women and sees differences between them as cultural and social) and of a "differentialist" orientation (which views the sexes as clearly different from one another, with certain occupations more appropriate for one than the other)—both of which I examine later—women's rights were not being treated independently of religious adherence.

The new regime appropriated the discourse of the independent feminist movement with its diverse currents—such as the *Association des Femmes Tunisiennes pour la Recherche et le Développement* (AFTURD, or the Association of Tunisian Women for Research and Development) and the *Association Tunisienne des Femmes Démocrates* (ATFD, or the Tunisian Association of Democratic Women)—while neglecting its social actors. In this way, it set up a "state feminism" in the context of a security policy that, during the 1990s, used the civil war in Algeria and the struggle against international "terrorism" following the 1991 Gulf War as pretexts for tightening internal security measures.[13] The authorities put cosmetic laws in place that served their own purposes but did not serve women's rights. They promoted associations such as the Association of Tunisian Mothers (ATM) and other NGOs working under the regime's umbrella. At the same time, feminists, women activists, and independent women who did not join the government's initiatives were followed, their telephones tapped, and their writings censored. Occasionally the government used insulting letters and videos to undermine them. Over these two decades these groups faced a Machiavellian policy under which they were ostensibly free but in reality were subject to surveillance and harassment.

All the official women's organizations, such as the UNFT and ATM, played no role in raising women's consciousness and fostering leadership, although they never failed to call upon women when they needed to fill a stadium for a presidential speech or to promote the first lady. These practices continued until the eve of Ben Ali's flight, when the UNFT prepared a demonstration in support of the dictator, renting buses to bring men and women to Tunis and asking supporters to wear a violet scarf, the color of Ben Ali's ruling party, so that a sign of popular support would be evident on television.[14]

After the uprising, with the population calling for the dissolution of the RCD (Ben Ali's party), the UNFT was not at first a target, until a group of independent women from cities outside the capital took up the matter in March 2011.[15] These women sent a petition to the press and to the prime minister's office with more than a thousand signatures calling for the dissolution of the UNFT. They also called for the termination of the ATM, whose principal function had been to relay the discourse of Ben Ali and his wife. Both organizations were placed under judicial supervision.

Since the 1980s, women and independent feminists had struggled for the establishment of research centers devoted to women. In the early years of Ben Ali's rule, two institutions had been set up—the Center for Research, Study, Documentation, and Information on Women (CREDIF) on the national level and the Center of Arab Women for Training and Research (CAWTAR) on the regional level. Following the Uprisings, both institutions suffered due to their ties to the authorities.

Paradoxically, while the authorities had been presenting themselves as defenders of women's rights, at the first moment of crisis during the Uprisings they offered women as a public sacrifice. For instance, according to the official version, it was the female agent who slapped Mohamed Bouazizi, which provoked his reaction of self-immolation—the act that sparked the youth revolt and subsequent Uprising(s). Fayda Hamdi, a forty-six-year-old woman who had been working as a municipal officer for eleven years and who was said to have slapped Bouazizi, spent four months in prison and started a hunger strike that lasted a month, pushing for the judicial system to take up her case. The official version of her alleged slapping of Bouazizi was designed to redirect the public's anger and turn the youth against women. Upon leaving the court after her imprisonment, she said, "Let God bless his soul; he was a victim as I was, innocent but a victim of all the injustices."[16]

POSTUPRISING CHANGES

Women's Movements and Civil Society

Following the Tunisian uprising, women were freed from the official view that the party in power was the only institution morally capable of defending the Personal Status Code and women's rights, which we might describe as the state's claim of *wassiya*, a claim of exclusive moral privilege. Strengthened by their struggles against the dictatorship and the police state, independent women and feminists within institutions and in civil society brought forth new ideas and innovative interpretations, like wearing the hijab being an individual right, the need to emphasize political parity (equal representation), and the urgency of tackling economic inequality and poor educational facilities in all of Tunisia's regions. In April 2011, the ministry of interior announced that woman would be allowed to wear a hijab for photos on identity cards, overturning Decree No. 108, in effect since 1981, and modifying article 6 of Decree No. 717 from April 13, 1993, which defines the norms for the national identity card.[17]

In addition, between January and September 2011, many so-called "citizen associations," basing themselves on "proximity" to local populations, were formed. Among them, thirty focused on women, compared to the twenty-two associations devoted to women formed during the twenty-three years of Ben Ali's rule. These associations had goals such as supporting youth, bolstering women's development, and defending rights and freedoms in the construction of democracy. Independent women's organizations, such as the ATFD and

AFTURD, excluded from political discussion for so long under the Ben Ali regime, mobilized to encourage women to vote.

The media landscape also underwent great transformation, with online media, radio, and private television stations bringing a breath of fresh air into public life. They displayed diversity and free expression never before seen in Tunisia, including the organizing of political discussions and the live broadcasting of public debates. The number of press publications expanded significantly, with 187 new additional newspapers and periodicals approved for publication. Public-opinion polling, which previously had been practiced only by governmental institutions and only with special authorization, also grew significantly.

Political Culture and the Parity Law

Parallel to the growth of civil society and media pluralism, the number of political parties increased from about ten before January 2011 to 114 in September 2011, despite 162 having been rejected. In this climate, article 16 of the electoral law on parity (which established alternation between men and women on the electoral lists—but notably not as list heads) was adopted by the High Commission for the Realization of the Objectives of the Revolution, of Political Reform, and of the Democratic Transition (formed in March 2011, hereinafter "High Instance," from the French "la *Haute* instance *pour la réalisation des objectifs de la revolution*"), with eighty-four votes (some say eighty-five) for parity and thirty-four against it.[18] Lists not respecting this alternation were to be eliminated.[19]

This vote exposed unexpected divisions and alliances, and these were particularly surprising to independent feminists and to women in general. To begin with, the Ennahda Party[20] created surprise by voting for parity, where many others voted against it. The more liberal parties representing the ideology of Arab nationalism and the trade union (the UGTT) did not vote for parity. There was also concern over a legal ruling that RCD members (individuals who had government responsibilities under the old regime or who had occupied positions in the RCD) and those referred to as Mounachidines (people who in 2010 called for Ben Ali to run again as a candidate in the 2014 elections) were ineligible for election. Some independent figures also opposed parity.[21] The Majd Party, established after the uprising by Abdelwaheb El Héni, a human-rights activist who had lived in Geneva for several years, declared that such an amendment constituted a violation of electoral freedom.[22] Various political parties and political personalities declared that they were troubled by the principle of parity, even when they voted for it, because there were not sufficient numbers of women in their parties and they felt incapable of recruiting more. Some argued that women prefer to exercise a "democracy of proximity," engaging in local matters such as those of a municipality,[23] and some families stopped women from becoming candidates out of "considerations of conservatism or personal security."[24] Maya Jribi, the first woman to be secretary-general of the PDP (Progressive Democratic Party), said, "We faced the hesitations of the women themselves; they participate but do not put themselves in the forefront."[25] Her party put only three women at the head of electoral lists.

The small political parties, whose positions were otherwise strengthened by the new election model, argued that the parity law penalized them since lists comprised of less than 50 percent women were to be eliminated. Several parties approached Béji Caïd Essebsi, the prime minister of the transitional government at that time, with their concerns. He responded by proposing a quota for women of 25 or 30 percent, because some regions would not be able to respect full parity. Feminists rejected his proposal, and many women remained suspicious. Being aware of the limited political space available to women in Algeria after the war of liberation, in Iran after the revolution, and in Egypt after Sadat's assassination, they put pressure on the prime minister and also accused Ennahda of engaging in doublespeak. Radhia Belhaj Zekri, president of AFTURD, published a declaration calling for vigilance so that Tunisian women would not suffer as had Algerian, Iranian, and Egyptian women. A petition in favor of parity was launched on the Web, and a sit-in was organized at the Kasba with slogans such as "No turning around on parity" and "Parity = equality." Eventually, the prime minister decided to support the idea.

Once the election lists were published, women became increasingly concerned with the low proportion of women as heads of the electoral lists and the low numbers that were likely to be in the Constituent Assembly. Some estimates suggested a proportion as low as 5 to 10 percent. Sometime later, the estimated proportions increased, with the journalist Nora Borsali suggesting that they would be between 15 and 20 percent.[26] Many argued for the importance of having a large number of active women in the electoral campaign move throughout the country to hold meetings and speak to the media. Hafidha Chekir further argued that a 50 percent representation of women on the electoral lists was not sufficient by itself and that the political parties should put women at the *head of their lists* in order to ensure their visibility. Salma Baccar, a filmmaker born in

Tunis in 1945 and representative of the coalition, as well as a list head for Ben Arous, said that a vote for parity without having women as list heads amounted to "shenanigans" (*entourloupettes*).[27] The Qotb (referred to as the Modernist Democratic Pole)—a secular coalition composed of four political parties and five independent groups established in May 2011 for the Constituent Assembly elections—was the only party to offer as many female list heads as male (sixteen women, seventeen men). Other political parties interpreted this as the position of a party with no hopes of winning and therefore nothing to lose. The fact that women ultimately constituted only 7 percent (110 women) of the heads of political-party electoral lists among the some 1,517 lists and 11,000 candidates for the 105 political parties came as a shock. Clearly, the political parties were not prepared to put women at the heads of their lists (see table 9.1).

Almost four and a half million people registered for the elections, of which 40 percent were women. Of the 106 parties counted, women who started a party or who occupied the position of secretary-general or spokesperson were very rare, with Maya Jribi, Neila Charchour Hachicha, and Emna Mnif among the best known. At least four other women—Essia Ben Abdallah, Fatma Ouerghi, Nadra Ben Mahfoudh, and Leila Toukabri—submitted requests for legal approval of their parties.[28]

Table 9.1. Women in Parliament by Region, 1995 and 2011

Political Party	Number of Electoral Districts	Number of Women Heading Lists	Percentage of Women Heading Lists
Libéral Maghrébin	27	1	3.7%
Afek Tounes	23	7	30.4%
Ennahda	27	2	7.4%
Pôle Démocratique Moderniste (PDM)	33	16	48.5%
Parti Démocrate Progressiste (PDP)	33	3	9.1%
Union Démocratique Unioniste (UDU)	29	6	20.7%
Parti des Verts pour le Progrès (PVP)	28	4	14.3%
Ettakatol	32	3	9.4%
Parti Communiste des Ouvriers (PCOT)	32	4	12.5%
Congrès Pour la République (CPR)	33	2	6%

Percentage of heads of political-party lists who were women in the elections for the Constituent Assembly, October 2011
http://www.ajidoo.com/actualites/divers/femmes_faible_pourcentage_de_tetes_de_liste.htm

WOMEN AND THE STRUGGLE FOR LEADERSHIP

As stated, Ennahda surprised many by voting for parity, and it surprised many again when it chose Souad Abderrahim, a pharmacist, entrepreneur, and independent who does not cover her hair, as one of its two female candidates to head a list.[29] This move upset some feminists, who saw it as a tactic to attract female voters and as the promotion of a woman who represented the elite. Rashid Ghannouchi, leader of Ennahda, argued later that his party, in naming a woman without a headscarf to head a list, showed that it accepted diversity, whereas the other parties, in not naming a woman with a headscarf for a similar position, rejected diversity. Throughout this period, the Ennahda Party continued to assert that it would not impose a hijab on women and would strengthen the Personal Status Code. It promoted women as members of its political bureau, such as lawyer Saida Akremi Bhiri, who was presented as one of Ennahda's founding figures; Leila Oueslati, who was put in charge of relations with liberation movements; Monia Brahim, who was made responsible for matters related to women and the family; and Farida Labidi,[30] who was charged with guiding judicial matters. These women and others who were tortured or spent time in prison under either Bourguiba or Ben Ali publicly discussed the ill treatment they had suffered for their ideas under the old regime.

All of these women became more visible in women's associations and national women's institutions following the results of polls that predicted Ennahda would emerge the winner. Paradoxically, rather than criticizing the UNFT, which had supported Ben Ali and his policies, they directed their criticism toward the ATFD, which had opposed Ben Ali and had been his victim when the regime "adopted" its discourse in order to minimize its impact. The group of women criticized the ATFD members for not having aided the mothers of arrested activists nor having supported women wearing a hijab nor having defended imprisoned and tortured women.[31] It became clear that Ennahda women were now involved in a struggle for the leadership of the women's movement.

Election Results and the Constituent Assembly

During the election campaign, women represented 46 percent of registered voters, and article 16 of the electoral law, which mandated parity (that is, alternating men and women on the electoral lists), led to some five thousand women becoming candidates. Seven percent of lists had women at their head, with the Tunis 2 voting district showing 17 percent, and two-thirds of Tunisia's twenty-seven election districts showing less than 5 percent.[32] Female candidates of the various political parties faced a number of challenges. Chief among them was the mystery of how women, marginalized for almost a quarter of a century, would vote in a free society.

On election day, October 23, 2011, Tunisian women of all ages were clearly happy to participate in these first free elections and waited in voting lines for hours. Official results gave 41.47 percent to Ennahda (1,501,418 of 3,702,627 votes), 13.82 percent to the *Congrès pour la République* (CPR), 9.68 percent to Ettakatol (*Forum Démocratique pour le Travail et les Libertés*), and 8.76 percent to the Popular Petition (al-Aridha, Popular Petition for Freedom, Justice, and Development), with a scattering of votes for the other parties. Thirty-five percent of the voters, or 1,250,000 people, ended up with no representation due to the "largest remainder method" employed and the large number of lists.[33]

The more than four million people who voted on October 23, 2011, represented 54 percent of the 7.5 million eligible voters. Only 2,680,000 votes were for those who were elected to the 217 seats in the Constituent Assembly (CA), with approximately one-third of the total votes for independent candidates who did not gain enough votes to be represented. While the parties who had opposed the Ben Ali regime (Ettakatol, PDP, and CPR, among others), as well as the secularly oriented parties and independents that formed following the uprising, had won 1.8 million votes—more than Ennahda's 1.5 million—these votes were scattered among a number of parties. It is worth noting that Ennahda's total vote represented about 20 percent of the total eligible votes.[34]

The proportion of women elected to the CA was 58 of a total of 217, or 26.7 percent, a proportion close to the 2009 results under Ben Ali.[35] Of this number, thirty-nine were Ennahda members. Later, when a CA member was named minister, he was replaced by a woman, which resulted in the number of women in the CA rising to sixty-two (almost 29 percent), which is slightly higher than what women had under the Ben Ali regime before the revolution. At the time of writing, Ennahda had eighty-nine seats, including thirty-nine women in the CA. Seized by panic, a portion of Tunisian women, particularly among the better-educated urban population, believed some Ennahda Party members wished to limit women's rights and became concerned about the future of the Personal Status Code.

Another study examines Ennahda voters and shows that many of its votes were drawn from the urban populations, particularly from women, youth, and the poor.[36] Its high number of votes is attributed to the general population's view that Ennahda had never been involved in the government, that it was likely to show greater morality in its affairs, and that many of its members had paid a great price for their opposition to the Ben Ali regime, suffering exile, imprisonment, and torture.

While the Islamic-based Ennahda did well in the elections, the traditional political left experienced a weak showing. Ettakatol won nineteen seats, the PDP won sixteen, and the PDM (Democratic Modernist Pole) won five with two women (Nadia Chaabane and Salma Baccar). Once the election results were tallied with Ennahda at the top, the press showed images of popular surprise, with tears of disappointment shed and with some voters expressing great discouragement and carrying banners with slogans such as "Give us back our votes." Members of a number of secularist and leftist political parties admitted that they had not understood the country's reality—essentially, that they had lost contact with the heartland. Another major problem for the left was the large percentage of independent lists, indicating a fragmentation in the political landscape—a fragmentation that, while reflecting a lack of confidence in established political parties, also reflected solidarity toward the marginalized regions of the country and toward foreign refugees arriving in the south and a desire to engage in political life after five decades of domination by the single party in power.[37]

The Impact of Women List Heads

Statistics can provide some indication of the progress achieved, but they cannot explain the problems faced by women candidates who entered into electoral battles. The experiences of two women—Bochra Belhaj Hmida, a well-known figure in Tunisia's feminist movement, and Souad Abderrahim, an activist in the Islamist-oriented student union, UGTE, during the 1980s (during which time she wore a hijab)—played an important role in the campaign of 2011. A look at their trajectories can shed some light on their personal challenges and the process more broadly.[38]

Bochra Belhaj Hmida

Bochra Belhaj Hmida (BBH) is the next-to-youngest of four children. She studied law at Tunis Law School, participated in a variety of student groups on campus, and began practicing law in 1981. Married and without children, she lives in a villa in a well-off Tunisian suburb. Much affected by her uncle Ahmed Mbarek's struggles against colonialism and her father's campaign against the collectivization of agricultural land under Bourguiba, she became committed to the independent feminist movement. She was twice elected president of the ATFD, an office she held from 1995 to 2001. She is also a member of the Tunisian Human Rights League (LTDH), founder of the human-rights section in Zaghouan in 1989, and cofounder of the Tunisian section of Amnesty International.

She was fifty-six when the 2010–2011 uprising took place in Tunisia and joined the center-left Ettakatol Party after the uprising because it seemed to be in favor of mitigating capitalism's worst aspects and promoting individual freedom—in opposition to Ennahda, which favored economic liberalism. She refused when the party[39] proposed that she occupy second place on a list in Tunis headed by Moustapha Ben Jaafar or alternatively one with Khalil Zaouia. Not wanting to be pigeonholed as a "bit player" and having fought for women to be list heads in the October 2011 elections, she judged that accepting the offer would contradict her ideals. She requested to be list head in the district of Zaghouan, the city of her birth (but not residence), and she was granted this placement.

During her campaign, BBH received the support of the party's secretary-general, Moustapha Ben Jaafar, who came to Zaghouan twice to join her in meeting the potential voters and deliver speeches. When she discovered that she was not being supported by some of the other people on her list, she said, in an interview with me, that she was dealing with what she called the "general misogyny of the milieu."[40]

Although BBH was, along with Maya Jribi (secretary-general of the PDP), the female political figure who received the most media attention, in an interview with me, she said she felt that "this was not enough to counter the practices of the other parties, which promised mountains and marvels but which did not keep these promises after the elections." She ran her campaign on such themes as social classes and political currents "living together,"[41] the idea that all are obligated to participate in finding solutions to the country's main problems, the importance of the constitution, and the necessity of decentralizing government administration so that inhabitants can take their destiny into their own hands. These themes were rather distant from the concerns of a population facing urgent daily needs.

Her detractors used two significant tactics. First, they presented the ATFD recommendations on reproductive and sexual rights that appeared in October 2010 as favoring marriage among homosexuals.[42] They also produced posters with a photo of BBH, no longer president of the ATFD but still a member and labeled as a "prostitute." Additionally, they disseminated and emphasized her televised reaction of January 13, 2011, to Ben Ali's speech that employed General de Gaulle's famous phrase, "I have understood you," when, trying to calm the situation after protesters had been killed demonstrating, she said, "I consider his speech to be a historic moment. . . . I am trusting Ben Ali."[43] BBH also noted that Ennahda's youthful activists "mounted a campaign against my list, while not fighting against any of the fifty-one other lists in the city of Zaghouan."[44] She received death threats and was accused of having collaborated with Saida Agrebi (the president of the Tunisian Association of Mothers, a group closely tied to the Ben Ali clan). Social media also became a space for the denigration of feminists such as BBH. BBH remarked that the budget she was allocated to produce posters and handouts—about $4,000—"could not counter the aggressive attacks of my adversaries."[45]

In losing the election, BBH won approximately two thousand votes and claimed that her campaign enabled her to see the realities of political life from the inside, as she discovered that the political parties were not going as far as the people had gone in the uprising. She regretted that Ettakatol's discourse was theoretical and thus not close to the population and its expectations. In addition, many perceived the feminists as "Ben Ali's orphans," implying that they no longer had the regime to protect them, whereas, in fact, they had been among its opponents.[46]

Souad Abderrahim

It is also important to examine the impact of Souad Abderrahim (SAR) on the electorate, given that she was one of only two woman list heads of Ennahda and did not fulfill the popular stereotype of the Islamist woman. Forty-seven years old, born in Sfax with her family origins in Metouia, SAR is the mother of two adolescents, a girl and a boy, and she does not wear a headscarf. A pharmacist who earned her diploma in 1992, with experience as president and director general of a company that makes pharmaceutical products, she lives in a luxurious villa in Tunis.[47] Her involvement in politics began in the 1980s when she was a student in the pharmacy faculty in Monastir and became a member for two terms of the executive bureau of the UGTE—a union formed in 1985 to defend the rights of Tunisian students. During this period, in which she wore a hijab, she was arrested and held for fifteen days while trying to end a quarrel between leftist and Islamist students. Due to the hardening of the government's struggle against Islamists, she withdrew from public life.

Ben Ali's flight on January 14, 2011, and the television images that were broadcast showing the poverty of the population in remote regions of the country inspired SAR and her family members—her mother, husband, sisters, and a friend—to organize a caravan. She gathered medicine and food amounting to approximately $50,000 and contacted Lamine Moulahi, secretary of state for

Health in the first transitional government following January 14, 2011, to coordinate the trip. He discouraged her. SAR was then convinced of the urgency of political engagement as an independent. This independent spirit is one of her characteristics, for she has at times publicly criticized Rachid Ghannouchi's declarations, such as when he declared that "Qatar is a full partner in the Tunisian revolution by virtue of Al Jazeera." She countered, "While it is true that Al Jazeera played an important media role, [it was] no more than that. . . . The revolution belongs to the Tunisian people."[48]

SAR considers Ennahda as blending modernity and Arab-Islamic civilization. When the party contacted her to propose that she be the list head in the Tunis 2 electoral district, she said,

> For me, this party's activists have a legitimacy and a long history of activism. I have spent time with them, and I know them well. . . . We have worked together. They know me well, and it is for this [reason] that they proposed that I head the list. . . . I said yes after having studied their program. Their strategy bore fruit, and they did not commit any political mistakes.[49]

SAR was aware that her candidacy constituted a message from Ennahda to Tunisians that the party was not looking to divide the country into women believers wearing a hijab and unbelieving women without a hijab. She based her campaign on the theme of the family, often displaying her children and her husband, also a pharmacist. Opposed to a strict dress code, she repeated, "It's an individual freedom. The old regime made the *mouhajabates* disappear from the landscape. I feel fine just the way I am. Perhaps one day I will wear a hijab. In any case, Ennahda will not be forcing me to."[50] She also recognized the merits of Bourguiba: "Even though I was arrested under Bourguiba, I recognize that Bourguiba deserves a lot of credit. The woman would not be what she is today if it hadn't been for Bourguiba. He opened the education doors for her . . . a model that is spreading today throughout the Arab world."[51] Women saw in her discourse and style signs of freedom and modernity within Ennahda, which was especially striking after a long period in which the authorities, by forbidding the hijab in public institutions, implied that Islamists were against modernity. A YouTube video shows SAR approaching a hijab-wearing woman in a café with her son and giving her an Ennahda pamphlet. The woman responds, "Tell me, first of all, are you going to force women to wear a hijab? Are you going to allow men to take four wives?" SAR reassures her and says that is not the case at all and that she is with Ennahda and does not wear a hijab.[52] She affirms that one can be a Muslim without exhibiting the "stereotypical" signs.[53]

SAR was perceived in a variety of ways by the media. When the Western press discussed her, rarely did it fail to mention her Western-style dress and remark on her resemblance to Sue Ellen, a character in the US television series *Dallas*, but without the alcohol. She was also referred to as "Souad Palin," evoking Sarah Palin, the former governor of Alaska, who had become the vice presidential running mate of US Republican candidate John McCain in 2008. In Tunisia, some writers called her Souad le Pen-Palin, associating her with both Palin and Marine le Pen, head of the extreme-right party in France.[54] The more neutral or positive local media, on the other hand, spoke mostly of her family and her professional success.

Her moral outlook appeared when she, for instance, criticized Tunisia's overturning of its reservations regarding CEDAW. Additionally, her position became clear when she expressed her desire to change the name of the Ministry for Women's Affairs to the Ministry of the Family and when she expressed her opinions on the subject of single mothers. This last episode occurred during an October 24, 2011, broadcast on Radio Monte Carlo, when she appeared with BBH and Nadia Chaabane of the Pôle Démocratique Moderniste (PDM). SAR seemed shocked by the question about whether a woman could choose to conceive a child outside of marriage in an Islamic society where sexuality is not to be practiced outside of marriage. She later gave an interview on Shems FM radio saying that her words had been misrepresented and that she would give aid to women who were harassed or victims of rape and to children born out of wedlock. She attributed the polemics to the opposition's wish to weaken her public image.[55]

The other guests on the Monte Carlo radio program with SAR appeared more concerned by the one thousand out-of-wedlock births per year in Tunisia. They preferred to explore the issue of how children are not responsible for these circumstances and how Tunisian law should provide nationality, protection, and health care to all children. SAR's declarations on Monte Carlo radio amounted to the mistake that the opposition was looking for, and the polemics went beyond Tunisia's borders. In France, the poet Houda Zekri and the activist Hédi Chenchabi—both members of the independent regional electoral instance (IRIE)–organized a demonstration in Paris at a symbolic square—The Fountain of Innocents. Chanting, "We are all single mothers," the demonstrators threw dolls and stuffed animals into the fountain.[56]

The trajectories of BBH and SAR—married women working in the private sector and known by their communities for their activism—show the importance of political-party support for female candidates. Whereas the other members of BBH's list abandoned her during the campaign, the Ennahda apparatus supported SAR even though she was technically an independent. Whereas BBH was attacked for her defense of liberal feminism and for her momentary support of Ben Ali, Souad Abderrahim was seen as a guarantee that Ennahda would not weaken women's rights.

BBH was strongly affected by the harshness of political life, and it appeared difficult for her to digest the fact that she represented a party in which many of its members did not support her. Being a list head in a small town where she did not live certainly did not help her establish herself as a legitimate representative of the population. But her failure is also related to the election failure of the traditional left, often called the "caviar left," referring to its relatively high living standards and the fact that it is active mostly in the capital city of Tunis.

SAR's position on the rights of single mothers certainly influenced her political destiny. Her name had been cited as a possible vice president of the Constitutional Assembly or as minister of Women's Affairs, but she did not obtain either position. The ministerial position was given to a member of the CPR and the CA vice presidency to Meherzia Labidi[57] of Ennahda, who wears a hijab.

Although SAR won 28,500 votes in her election and her list won three seats—a better performance than some of the opposition leaders who succeeded in negotiating important positions for themselves—she was able to gain only the presidency of one of the CA's seventeen commissions (only four are presided by women), the Commission on Rights, Freedoms, and External Relations. Having contributed much to broadening Ennahda's image as an open and tolerant party for citizens from all locations and walks of life (in the 1980s the party's image was strictly associated with the poor and the semi-rural), SAR was subject to attack by women's NGOs and many others critical of Ennahda. As she arrived at the Constitutional Assembly for her first day on the job, she was shaken in both a physical and figurative sense as a crowd attacked her for not defending the rights of single mothers.

WOMEN AND POLITICAL PLURALISM

The elections and the election results constituted the second phase of the uprising. Many proponents of women's rights were disappointed when Ennahda emerged as the strongest political party and then formed a coalition with two secular parties (CPR and Ettakatol) in what has become known as the Troika. As the weeks passed, many women decided to continue their struggle. On the opening day of the Constituent Assembly, young and unemployed college graduates, citizens of many different backgrounds, and the families of martyrs demonstrated in order to remind the assembly that those who did not win the elections must still be reckoned with.

In January 2012, *l'Assemblée Constitutionnelle Civile* (ACC, the Civil Constitutional Assembly) was founded and copresided by Salaheddine Jourchi, vice president of the Tunisian Human Rights League (LTDH) and member of the Islamist left, and Majida Boulila, relative of the nationalist militant Méjida Boulila and leader (since 1993) of a women's cultural group in Sfax.[58] This was a negative development in the eyes of the members of *l'Assemblée Nationale Constituante* (ANC), who feared they would be left behind. Several days after the launch of the Nida Tunis party, the ACC's preamble was addressed to the ANC. This preamble contained thirty-nine articles and called for "the sacred nature of individual rights, equality between the sexes, the right to proper employment, freedom of movement and of expression, freedom of the media, freedom of worship, the sacred nature of physical integrity and outlawing all forms of torture, abolition of the death penalty, forbidding the extradition of a person to a country where the death penalty might be imposed, and the separation of political parties from the state."[59]

Toward the end of July 2012, a polemic arose over articles proposed within the CA by the Commission on Rights, Freedoms, and External Relations, specifically article 28, which stated that "women are complementary to men," a statement open to a variety of interpretations.[60] This polemic provoked a societal crisis that covered a realignment of social forces. Among the parties that abstained in the 2011 vote for political parity were some who, in 2012, supported the position of women defending the Personal Status Code.

These crises exacerbated earlier fears that had occurred at the time of the April 2011 parity vote, when Ennahda surprised many by voting for parity. In the absence of formal commitments, Ennahda's naming of a woman without a hijab as a list head, its statement that the PSC would not be questioned, and its celebration of the August 13, 2011, commemoration of the promulgation of the PSC in 1956 were all interpreted by many Tunisian women before the October 2011 elections as possible instances of tactical doublespeak.

The vote for article 28 reinforced women's fears that women representatives in the CA had not been defending women's rights as they were supposed to—that is, they were not taking the views of women in society as a whole into account but were instead following the Ennahda party line.[61] During demonstrations that took place in several cities called by ATFD, AFTURD, and other associations and political parties, Ennahda representatives were denounced and fiercely attacked in online networks and the mass media. Salma Baccar reproached the elected Ennahda women for "follow[ing] the leadership's directives without raising an eyebrow," a view that would seem to confirm Manon Tremblay's and Réjean Pelletier's opinion that these elected women were behaving "more as women than as feminists."[62]

For SAR, "The question is settled. There is no question of a woman being against another woman. The achievements [that is, of the PSC and related legal measures concerning women's rights] cannot be touched. It is fundamental to struggle against patriarchal society and the macho mentality that dominates."[63] And she continued, asking Merherzia Labidi, vice president of the ANC, to present her apologies to an Ennahda woman member of the ANC whom she had spoken to in an abrupt manner, and Labidi did this generously. For Maya Jribi, ANC member, secretary-general of the PDP and of the Joumhouri Party, Ennahda's women ANC members are "experiencing a real division of their being. They are torn between their beliefs and their party's instructions! I wouldn't want to be in their place."[64] These observations and others—some that have been broadcast on national television transmissions of the ANC's debates—show how different Ennahda women are from the image that had been applied to them early on and how they have evolved in the context of a pluralist and critical debate.

How can we interpret the changes in Ennahda's political behavior between 1985 and 2011? Could they be due to the changes the country underwent since the movement first formed? Some of its members were in exile, others were in their homes under surveillance, and still others were trying to reconstruct their lives after prison and torture. In 2011, they were surprised to be confronting a different country from what they knew. Ennahda Party officials had perhaps seen how the young generation of protestors—peaceful, secular, and modern—aspired to freedom and dignity. The election results revealed how those who voted were seeking a framework for a universalist Islam. The policies put in place by the former regime to promote women's rights had only slightly impacted women, with "achievement [being] . . . slow, complicated, and controversial."[65] Ennahda saw an opportunity to rehabilitate its image in the parity law by distancing itself from its policies of the 1980s. In this way, the vote for political parity also enabled Ennahda's women to enter the CA via feminists' struggles. In a context of political pluralism and independent media, political parties would be obligated to choose women for their experience and competence.

In a context in which some members of the parties making up the Troika—a coalition led by Ennahda and including the CPR and Ettakatol that formed the government following the October 2011 elections—are leaving their party, in which opposition parties are realigning themselves, and in which a new party, Tunisian Call (Nida Tunis), is being founded by Béji Caïd Essebsi (the prime minister of the transitional government in 2011) and that BBH joined, Ennahda is seeking, as it did at its July 2012 congress, to present itself as centrist within a pluralist Islamist movement. Yet it is increasingly difficult for Ennahda to control its base, which often reproaches the party for its "soft Islam."

The debate over "complementarity of women" brought forward a new feminist approach—an "essentialist" one. For this essentialist feminism, there are feminine specificities that are complementary to masculine ones, and both are necessary to "humanize society." This movement traces its lineage back to women's struggles since the beginnings of Islam, to the nationalist struggle against colonialism, and to twentieth-century struggles for women's rights.[66] It stems from the reformist tradition, which considers the question of women to be central. In its support of article 22 of the proposed new constitution, which guarantees equality between men and women, the essentialist position recognized a commonality between the existing feminisms (universalist and differentialist) that dominate the political scene. Whereas the essentialists would like to see more religion in daily life, the universalist and differentialist feminists, while not opposing Islam, call for a greater role of the state and a less-prominent role for religion. All three positions oppose patriarchy. The essentialist position, when taken together with the universalist and differentialist positions, reflects the character of the debates on Tunisian feminism. Finally, the essentialist group seems to unite the universalist orientation of article 22 ("equality between men and women") in the proposed constitution with the differentialist vision ("differences between the sexes"). "Essentialist" feminism thus seeks a balance between the approaches that dominate the Tunisian feminist movement and emphasizes the notion of "complementarity."

This crisis of feminisms was a crisis over women's trust in government institutions that would be dominated by Ennahda in a fierce political environment. The inclusion of article 28 ("women are *complementary* to men") further increased the concerns of many people, both men and women, until it was finally was replaced by the term "equality."

Here it should be mentioned that the essentialist orientation needs to produce a discourse that would explain its positions in the public sphere. Souad Abderrahim carried out this effort in blending past and present or tradition and modernity. In defending women's rights and freedoms, SAR appropriates contemporary feminist discourse and contextualizes it. However, female members of the al-Nadha Party who say they support the PSC, including SAR, whose election campaign contained this theme, must make their voices clearly heard against the religious extremists who call for a return to polygamy, reducing the minimum age of marriage for girls, and even introducing excision and other measures that violate women's rights.[67]

CONCLUSION

The Tunisian uprising involved a shift in power relations between women's movements and the state authorities. On one hand, traditional organizations like the UNFT and the ATM, although they elected new management committees, no longer benefitted from the support that the state had provided in the past, and, without this support, their room for maneuver was limited. On the other hand, the independent feminist organizations like the ATFD and AFTURD must now, since this historic rupture, deal with the emergence of new associations, among them several that see themselves as feminist and as autonomous with regard to state authority. Although the legitimacy of these older feminist organizations remains intact, they also find themselves in a leadership struggle with organizations close to Islamist parties.

In addition, traditional institutions like the UGTT did not support parity, nor did the UGTT elect a woman as member of its executive committee in its December 2011 convention. This institution, even in the transitional context, remains patriarchal and unfriendly to women. However, it did demonstrate against article 28 when the context was a show of power against the government. This remark is also valid for the Ennahda Party. Although the party voted for parity, it also instrumentalized as tokens the women it put as list heads in Tunisia and abroad. In addition, explanations offered by both female and male politicians to explain the lack of women's participation in politics miss the point. The questions should now be reversed: What are the political parties doing to interest and attract women? Is the government developing policies to repair injustice regarding girls and women who were marginalized by the previous regimes?

Indeed, polls and surveys show that society as a whole seems more advanced than the political parties and the media with regard to women's activities in formal politics. Therefore, women's demands concerning parity are all the more legitimate, and when we see women's activism their demands show their full meaning. For example, in Morocco, the first government to be formed after the new constitution of 2011 was adopted—led by Abdelilah Benkirane, head of the Islamically oriented Justice and Development Party (PJD)—had only one woman in its government; the government that followed, formed in the summer of 2013 and also led by Benkirane and the PJD, increased this number to six, following pressure from Moroccan women and women's movements.

The number of women in Arab parliaments overall had progressed very slowly, from 4.3 percent in 1995 to 10.7 percent in 2011.[68] The demand for parity is reflected in the view of many women in Morocco, Algeria, Tunisia, Libya, and Egypt. They are increasingly educated, more highly qualified, living in urban areas, and expressing their refusal to be considered second-class citizens with growing frequency. In this way, women are attempting to rectify the cumulative political inequality they have experienced over the past decades.

The Arab Uprisings have provided new (though still disadvantaged) opportunities for women to make important progress in countries like Morocco, where 17 percent of parliament is now composed of women (an increase of 6.2 percent), and Algeria, where women now constitute 31.6 percent of parliament (an increase of 23.9 percent, due in large part to a quota of 30 percent).[69] In Tunisia, the numbers decreased slightly, from fifty-nine women to fifty-eight in October 2011. However, this number increased to sixty-two as women replaced men who were named to ministerial positions. In Libya, the lessons of parity in Tunisia had a substantial effect. The country's parliament applied the rule of alternating women and men on the election lists and on the level of list heads, enabling Libyan women to gain greater political visibility, advancing 8.8 percent to reach 16.5 percent, or thirty-three seats out of two hundred.[70] On the other hand, in Egypt, where political parties were obliged to include women on their lists but without any restrictions on where they would be placed, the percentage fell sharply, from 12.7 percent to 2 percent in the lower house and to 4.4 percent in the upper house. This regression compared to 2010 can be explained by the disappearance of the quota of sixty-four seats awarded to women,[71] which was replaced in 2012, after the Arab Uprisings, by obliging the parties to put at least one woman on each list.[72]

Since the Arab Uprisings, freedom of expression has benefitted all the region's women. In Tunisia, the discourse of feminists (both universalist and differentialist)—formerly limited to opposing masculine-style feminism and state feminism—today confronts the discourse of Islamist women, of an essentialist type. In the course of discussion and debates, essentialist discourse has also evolved.

Essentialist discourse—which in the Tunisian south in March 2013, on the occasion of International Women's Day, expressed opposition to lifting Tunisia's reservations concerning CEDAW—is closer to that of women in the Egyptian Islamist parties, with such women from both countries experiencing arrest and torture under the old regimes.[73] In Egypt as well as in Tunisia, the arrival of a more educated elite among Islamist women shook up accepted patterns.

Women's-rights activists, women's associations, and female academics, journalists, and artists continue to this day to apply pressure on the women who were elected to the CA, encouraging them to favor women's rights in their voting choices and to promote laws on gender equality. Confronted with the polemic generated by article 28 ("women are *complementary* to men"), women made their voices heard and succeeded in having the article modified and the term "complementary" eliminated, ensuring that the term will not be interpreted in a prejudicial manner. Souad Abderrahim let it be understood, in response to ATFD president Ahlem BelHadj, that, with so much opposition to this article, the CA members would likely expand consultation and that perhaps the article would not be adopted—which in fact turned out to be true.

Finally, BBH left Ettakatol and joined the new party, Nida Tunis. A rumor began to circulate during the summer of 2012 that SAR was leaving Ennahda; it was quickly denied. However, during the summer of 2013 she announced she would be leaving Ennahda once the CA's work had been completed.

To conclude, the discussion has highlighted three developments. First, Tunisian society suffered from manipulation by the previous regime that put in place, since the 1990s, a security policy against Islamism and other opposition forces. The regime manipulated fears, those about which women could not speak and those that were projections into the public sphere of psychopathological problems. These fears were manipulated, on the one hand, to control the opposition and the feminist movements and, on the other, to continue to gain the West's support by protecting and comforting anxieties over Islam and its compatibility with secularization and democracy.[74]

Second, while women's participation in political life is increasingly significant throughout the Arab world, the expression of this in political institutions is different in the Maghreb and the Mashreq—with women showing greater numbers and playing a much more important role in these institutions in the Maghreb.

Finally, we have witnessed the growing importance of female figures in the Tunisian political domain, even if their corporeal rights are far from guaranteed. Scholar Anoushiravan Ehteshami has suggested that we pay attention to five aspects in assessing Middle East elections: regularity and frequency, local and national impact, presidential or parliamentary systems, the nature and role of organized political forces in play, and the impact that national elections have on a prevailing political system and the wider region.[75] In the future, I would add that we must also pay close attention to the role played by women in elections, as well as the outcomes of these processes, for each is important to the construction of viable democracies in the region and for countless women the world over.

NOTES

1. Unsigned article, "Les psychiatres tunisiens ne perdent pas de temps" (27/2/2011), http://www.mensongepsy.com/fr/2011/02/les-psychiatres-tunisiens-ne-perdent-pas-de-temps/.

2. The psychiatrist Rim Ghachem has noted a rising frequency of ill temper among Tunisians. Before the revolution, police personnel would occasionally come for treatment, but, since 2012, patients are often teachers and paramedics who confront low security in the educational and health institutions. Sofiane Zribi, president of the International Francophone Federation of the Private Exercise of Psychiatry (la Fédération Internationale Francophone de Psychiatrie d'Exercice Privé), points out that an increased number of traumatized persons can also be indicated by an increase in the use of alcohol, drugs, and anti-depressants. Fadhel Mrad, president of the Medical Commission of the Razi Hospital in Tunis, notes that the number of psychiatric visits went from 139,000 in 2011 to 146,000 in 2012, with the number of hospitalizations requested by the sick person's family going from 2,560 in 2011 to 2,644 in 2012, those requested by the courts from 1,508 in 2011 to 2,220 in 2012, and those requested by the patient from 1,998 in 2011 to 2,223 in 2012. "Des psychiatres tirent la sonnette d'alarme: Le tunisien est traumatisé!" (14/2/2013), http://www.tunisienumerique.com/tunisie-des-psychiatres-tirent-la-sonnette-dalarme-le-tunisien-est-traumatise/165462; "La dépression collective," http://www.leconomistemaghrebin.com/2013/02/12/tunisie-la-depression-collective/.

3. http://www.leconomistemaghrebin.com/2013/02/12/tunisie-la-depression-collective/.

4. Laurent Ribadeau Dumas, "De l'influence de la révolution sur la santé mentale des Tunisiens," Géopolis TV (18/06/2013), http://geopolis.francetvinfo.fr/de-linfluence-de-la-revolution-sur-la-sante-mentale-des-tunisiens-17727.

5. Sarah Ben Hamadi, "Tunisie: Promotion chômage," Jeune Afrique (3/1/2013).

6. "Tunisie—Le nombre des grèves observées en octobre a augmenté de 71%," Business News (24/11/2013), http://www.businessnews.com.tn/tunisie-le-nombre-des-greves-observees-en-octobre-a-augmente-de-71,520,42434,3.

7. "Avis d'un psychiatrie: 'Les Tunisiens de plus en plus dépressifs,'" Espace Manager (06/08/2013), http://www.espacemanager.com/actualites/avis-d-un-psychiatrie-les-tunisiens-de-plus-en-plus-depressifs.html (6/8/2013).

8. Nathalie Pinta, "Y-a-t-il un psychiatre à l'hôpital?" (7/3/2013), http://psychiatrieetexclusion.blogspot.sg/2013/03/tunisie-y-t-il-un-psychiatre-lhopital.html.

9. Lilia Labidi, "The Political Role of Women during the Arab Spring in Tunisia," paper presented at the 112th Annual Meeting of the American Anthropological Association, Chicago, IL, November 2013; Lilia Labidi, *Judhur al-harakat al-nisa'iyya: riwayaat li-shakhsiyyaat tarikhiyya* [Origins of Feminist Movements in Tunisia: Personal History Narratives], 3rd edition (Tunis: Imprimerie Tunis Carthage, 2009); Lilia Labidi, *Qamus as-siyar li-lmunadhilaat at-tunisiyaat, 1881–1956* [Biographical Dictionary of Tunisian Women Militants] (Tunis: Imprimerie Tunis Carthage, 2009).

10. Carmel Camilleri, *Jeunesse, famille et développement: Essai sur le changement socio-culturel dans un pays du Tiers Monde, la Tunisie* (Paris: CNRS, 1973); Fadéla M'Rabet, *La Femme algérienne, suivi de Les Algériennes* (Paris: Maspéro, 1969).

11. Noam Chomsky, *Necessary Illusions: Thought Control in Democratic Societies* (Brooklyn: South End Press, 1989).

12. See Jai Shah, Romina Mizrahi, and Kwame McKenzie, "The Four Dimensions: A Model for the Social Aetiology of Psychosis," *British Journal of Psychiatry* 199, no. 1 (July 2011): 11–14; Peter K. Chadwick, "How Social Difficulties Produce Cognitive Problems during the Mediation of Psychosis: A Qualitative Study," *International Journal of Social Psychiatry* 52, no. 5 (Sept. 2006): 459–68.

13. Lilia Labidi, "The Nature of Transnational Alliances in Women's Associations in the Maghreb: The Case of AFTURD and ATFD in Tunisia," *Journal of Middle East Women's Studies* 3, no. 1 (Winter 2007): 6–34.

14. In January 2011, the salary of the UNFT president was equal to that of a secretary of state and was paid by the government.

15. Of the twenty members of the UNFT's directorate, one-fourth of them were employed by the MWA (Ministry of Women's Affairs), including the director of CREDIF (the Center for Research, Study, Documentation, and Information on Women).

16. "Que Dieu bénisse son âme, il était victime, tout comme moi, innocente mais victime aussi de toutes les injustices," http://www.leaders.com.tn/article/cette-gifle-qui-n-a-jamais-eu-lieu-en-hommage-a-fadia-fille-de-sidi-bouzid?id=5278.

17. From 1987 to 2011, the issue of promoting women's rights was used by the regime as a way to control the opposition. While the regime's discourse emphasized that women were present in all the professions and constituted, for example, a third of judges, lawyers, and journalists, two-thirds of pharmacists and doctors, and 40 percent of university teachers, women wearing a hijab were invisible throughout this period in the media and in public institutions.

18. The High Instance was dissolved with the elections of October 2011.

19. The High Instance was composed of seventy-one members at the beginning of March 2011. It then expanded to 120 members at the end of March and then expanded again to 155 members (thirty-seven were women) during the month of April. The members came from various political parties and civil-society organizations. There were also a variety of national figures, such as representatives from the regions and from the families of the martyrs of December 17.

20. The Ennahda Party, founded in June 1981, was legalized in March 2011. Its ideology is "political Islam," and it supports liberal economics. It is also the party that came to power following the overthrow of Ben Ali.

21. Olfa BelHassine, "Les coulisses d'un vote," *La Presse* (April 14, 2011).

22. From 2007 to 2009 Abdelwaheb El Héni was a member of the Arab Commission for Human Rights, and from 2009 to 2010 he was the spokesperson and permanent representative at the UN for the Global Network for Rights and Development.

23. A. C., "Parité mais aussi et surtout complémentarité," *L'Expert* (April 21, 2011).

24. M. H. Abdellaoui, "15% de femmes têtes de liste: la faute au conservatisme!" *La Presse* (9/9/2011).

25. http://printempsarabe.blog.lemonde.fr/2011/10/15/les-femmes-grandes-oubliees-du-scrutin -tunisien/.

26. M. H. Abdellaoui, "La faute au conservatisme," *La Presse* (September 9, 2011).

27. Salma Baccar directed *Fatma 75* (1976), in which she shows the experiences of several feminist activists during the colonial period. *La danse du feu* (1995) deals with a Jewish woman singer and her impact on Tunisian intellectual life during the 1930s. *Fleur d'oubli* (2006) addresses the question of male homosexuality. She has also directed a number of television films and documentaries.

28. The names of their political parties are, respectively, Le Parti de la Femme Tunisienne, Le Parti des Paumés, Le Parti des Républicains Démocrates, and L'Union Socialiste des Forces Populaires.

29. The other woman list head for Ennahda, representing the Americas and Europe (excluding France), was Firdaous Oueslati, who was born and grew up in Holland, holds a doctorate from Leiden University in Arabic, and literature, languages, and culture, and wears a hijab. She won 35 percent of the votes cast. (For this information, see the following: https://www.senate.mn/members/newsletter/1046_ Pappas_Sandra/OpEd%20_%20A%20Life%20of%20Karma%20for%20Women%20and%20Girls %20July%202013.pdf; http://tn.linkedin.com/pub/firdaous_oueslati/8/b5/231; and http://point debasculecanada.ca/articles/10002503_which_ennahda%E2%80%99s_candidate_will_represent_ the_americas_and_the_rest_of_europe_at_the_tunisian_constituent_assembly.html.

30. No relation to me.

31. Mona Ben Gamra, "Discussions orageuses," *Le Temps* (20/11/2011).

32. Union Européenne, Mission d'Observation Électorale en Tunisie 2011. Une première étape en-courageante vers la démocratie (Tunis, October 25, 2011), http://www.eueom.eu/files/pressreleases/ english/declaration-preliminaire-moe-ue-251011_fr.pdf.

33. "Le guide récapitulatif des résultats complets," *Le Courrier de L'Atlas* (28/10/2011), http:// www.lecourrierdelatlas.com/109328102011Tunisie_Elections_Le_guide_recapitulatif_des_resul tats_complets.html. The largest remainder method "entails the calculation of a quota based on the number of seats at stake and the number of votes cast. Each party is awarded as many seats as it has full quotas. If this leaves some seats unallocated, each party's 'remainder' is calculated by deducting from its vote total the number of votes it has already used up by winning seats. The unallocated seats are then awarded to the parties that present the largest remainders." See Michael Gallagher, "Comparing Proportional Representation Electoral Systems: Quotas, Thresholds, Paradoxes and Majorities," *British Journal of Political Science* 22, no. 4 (1992): 469–96, found on p. 271, https:// www.tcd.ie/Political_Science/staff/michael_gallagher/BJPS1992.pdf.

34. Hédia El May, "Analyse des résultats des élections du 23 octobre (Tunisie)," http://shaah-idun.wordpress.com/2012/01/22/hedia-el-may-analyse-des-resultats-des-elections-du-23-octobre -note-ajoutee-par-r-sh/.

35. Tunisia at that time had 27.57 percent women in the Chamber of Deputies and 17 percent in the Chamber of Councillors.

36. Interview with Abderrahmen Bellahgua, a teacher at the Institut Supérieur de Gestion de Tunis, "Elections du 23 octobre 2011. Le profil des électeurs," February 22, 2012, available at http://

www.mosaiquefm.net/index/a/ActuDetail/Element/18458-%C3%89lections-du-23-octobre--le
-profil-des-%C3%A9lecteurs.html.

37. Union Européenne, Mission d'Observation Électorale en Tunisie 2011. Une première étape encourageante vers la démocratie (Tunis, October 25, 2011), http://www.eueom.eu/files/press releases/english/declaration-preliminaire-moe-ue-251011_fr.pdf.

38. The UGTE and the UGET existed as two student unions until 1991, when the UGTE was legally suspended following accusations of being a wing of an Islamist group. This suspension remained in effect until 2011, after which it won elections on scientific committees with 31.3 percent of seats in 2012.

39. The Ettakatol Party is of a social-democratic orientation and was founded in 1994. It was officially legalized in 2002.

40. BBH further declared that she was in favor of equality in inheritance, a goal that has not been supported by her party.

41. http://www.youtube.com/watch?v=yUGoUawnEZc&feature=related.

42. "Les droits des femmes en Tunisie, Déclaration, Résumé des questions prioritaires soumis par l'ATFD au Comité des Nations Unies pour l'élimination de la discrimination à l'égard des femmes," 47th session, October 2010, available at http://www2.ohchr.org/english/bodies/cedaw/docs/ngos/ATFD_Declaration_fr.pdf.

43. She made this statement on the al-Tunisiyya television channel on 13/1/2011, and this can be seen at http://www.youtube.com/watch?v=khK0azNac4o.

44. Interview with the author, summer 2012.

45. Interview with the author, summer 2012.

46. Interview with the author, summer 2012. BBH's husband, shocked by the violence targeting her, formed an association called Let's Cultivate Peace to fight against this type of behavior.

47. "Souad Abderrahim, symbole ou alibi d'Ennahda?" *Le Parisien* (October 25, 2011), available at http://www.leparisien.fr/laparisienne/societe/souad-abderrahim-symbole-ou-alibi-d -ennahda-25-10-2011-1685430.php.

48. Souad Abderrahim, "Non à l'exclusion collective des ex-RCDistes," http://www.shemsfm .net/fr/actualite/actualites_shems-news/souad-abderrahim.../0.

49. The Ennahda Party, founded in June 1981, was legalized in March 2011. Its ideology is "political Islam," and it supports liberal economics.

50. She further said, "Ennahda is very open, and when nominating an independent woman the party is trying to reassure Tunisians that they are committed to preserving women's rights and freedoms." She added that women should not be afraid of Ennahda, "The proof is that they nominated me as a head of a list." See http://www.tunisia_live.net/2011/10/28/souad_abed_rahim_president_of_ the_constituent_assembly/.

51. She made these remarks on "Dhayf ElOusbou3" on Nessma TV, March 14, 2012, http:// tnreplay.tv/dhayf-el-ousbou3-tunisie-mercredi-14-mars-2012-mme-souad-abderrahim/.

52. "Voting for Freedom, http://www.youtube.com/watch?v=zwPgXqXtMFE.

53. On October 26, 2011, SAR said that "those who today are against Ennahda are opposed to democracy and seem to prefer dictatorship." "La victoire était attendue" (Mosaique FM).

54. Salah Horchani, "Souad le Pen-Palin est née!" (14/11/2011), http://www.legrandsoir.info/ tunisie-souad-le-pen-palin-est-nee.html.

55. "Interview avec Souad Abderrahim Nahda Tunisie," *FocusMagazineTN*, uploaded on November 11, 2011, http://www.youtube.com/watch?v=qQmOi2YlNnk.

56. "Flashmob, "Nous sommes toutes des mères célibataires!" (1/2), uploaded by Bernard Henry on November 27, 2011, http://www.youtube.com/watch?v=09v52rmCqXA.

57. No relation to me.

58. Driss Mohammed, "Première réunion de la Constituante Civile en présence de 170 militants de la société civile" (23/1/2012), http://www.tunisienumerique.com/tunisie-premiere-reunion-de-la-constituante-civile-en-presence-de-170-militants-de-la-societe-civile/98400.

59. "La sacralité des droits individuels, l'égalité des genres, le droit au travail décent, la liberté de se déplacer et de s'exprimer, la liberté des médias, la liberté du culte, la sacralité de l'intégrité physique et l'interdiction de toutes formes de torture, l'abolition de la peine de mort, l'interdiction d'extrader une personne dans un pays où elle sera jugée à la peine de mort et la séparation entre les partis politiques et l'Etat," in Chiraz Kefi, "La constituante civile avance son projet de constitution" (25/5/2012), http://www.gnet.tn/temps-fort/tunisie/la-constituante-civile-avance-sur-son-projet-de-constitution/id-menu-325.html.

60. "UN Working Group on Women Calls on Tunisia to Protect Achievements in Equality" August 21, 2012, http://www.un.org/apps/news/story.asp?NewsID=42712&Cr=Tunisia&Cr1=s.

61. Françoise Gaspard,"De la parité: genèse d'un concept," *Nouvelles Questions Féministes* 15, no. 4 (November 1994): 29–44.

62. See http://www.genderclearinghouse.org/upload/Assets/Documents/pdf/rapp_tunisie_final.pdf.

63. Maya Jeribi, "Les femmes d'Ennahdha vivent un déchirement reel," March 22, 2013, http://directinfo.webmanagercenter.com/2013/03/22/maya-jeribi-les-femmes-dennahdha-vivent-un-dechirement-reel/.

64. Ibid.

65. Adila Abusharaf, "Women in Islamic Communities: The Quest for Gender Justice Research," *Human Rights Quarterly* 28 (2006): 714–28.

66. See Frida Dahmani, "Saïda el-Akremi, l'avocate redoutable," *Jeune Afrique* (7/9/2011), http://www.jeuneafrique.com/Article/ARTJAJA2642p042-045-00.xml3/; and Noura Borsali, "Une autre voix—Entretien avec une avocate islamiste, Mme Saida Akremi Bhiri: 'Le CSP est un acquis à sauvegarder,'" in *Tunisie: Le défi égalitaire; Ecrits féministes* (Tunis: Arabesques, 2012), 70–78 (originally published in 1989).

67. Lilia Labidi, "Tunisian Summer 2013: A Season of Political Turmoil," http://nus_mei.theadventus.com/publications/mei-insights/tunisian-summer-2013-a-season-of-political.

68.

Table 9.2

	1995	2011
World	11.3%	19.5%
Asia	13.2%	17.9%
Arab states	4.3%	10.7%

"Regard sur l'année écoulée," *Union Parlementaire* (2011): 4.

69. Figures reflect the count at the time of writing.

70. For these figures and for the table below, see http://www.ipu.org/pdf/publications/
WIP2012e.pdf and http://www.ipu.org/pdf/publications/WIP2012F.pdf (2012).

Table 9.3.   Percentage of Women in National Parliaments in the Arab World, 2013

Country	Seats	Number of Women	Percent	Country	Seats	Number of Women	Percent
Algeria	462	146	31.6%	Jordan	148	18	12.2%
Tunisia	217	58	26.7%	Syria	250	30	12%
Iraq	325	82	25.2%	Bahrain	40	4	10%
Sudan	354	87	24.6%	Kuwait	65	4	6.2%
Mauritania	95	21	22.1%	Egypt	270	12	4.4% **for the upper house**
Saudi Arabia	151	30	19.9%	Lebanon	128	4	3.1%
UAE	40	7	17.5%	Oman	84	1	1.2%
Morocco	395	67	17%	Yemen	301	1	0.3%
Libya	200	33	16.5%	Qatar	35	0	0%

71. Eva Saenz-Diez, "Le quota de femmes au parlement égyptien. Vers une normalisation de leur statut?" in Sylvette Denèfle and Safaa Monqid (eds.), "Gouvernance locale dans le monde arabe et en Méditerranée : Quel rôle pour les femmes?" *Egypte monde arabe,* Troisième Série, no. 9 (2011), http://ema.revues.org/.

72. Dina Darwich, "Des candidates sans visage" *Ahram Hebdo,* no. 898 (November 30 to December 6, 2011).

73. During the 1960s, among the two hundred Islamist women who were arrested was Zaynab Al-Ghazali (1917–2005), founder in 1936 of the Jamaa'at al-Sayyidaat al-Muslimaat (Muslim Women's Association). In 1965 she was sentenced to twenty-five years in prison and to hard labor. Released in 1971, she wrote her memoir, *Ayyam min hayati* ("Days from My Life").

74. According to a poll carried out by Ifop (Institut français d'opinion publique), 42 percent of French citizens see Islam as a threat, and 68 percent say that Muslims are not well integrated into French society (*Le Monde,* 4/1/ 2011). Also see an Ipsos poll indicating that 74 percent believe that Islam "is not compatible with the values of French society" (*Le Monde,* Fondation Jean-Jaurès et le Cevipof, January 2013).

75. Anoushiravan Ehteshami, "Is the Middle East Democratizing?" *British Journal of Middle Eastern Studies* 26, no. 2 (November 1999): 199–217.

III

TRAJECTORIES

10

The Arab Uprisings: Alignments and the Regional Power Balance

RAYMOND HINNEBUSCH

What are the likely consequences of the Arab Uprisings for the power balance and the shape of regional order in the Middle East? Theories of democratization might expect newly mobilized public opinion to transform regional politics, reducing the security dilemma and encouraging a democratic peace. While this is possible, there is evidence that new democratizers can be *more* bellicose than authoritarian regimes, since democratic legitimacy is grounded in national identity and the nationalist card is a central component of electoral success, especially where economic prosperity cannot be swiftly delivered.[1] In any case, even if a more pacific liberal order is the long-term effect of the Uprisings, the immediate consequence has been to *reinforce* preexisting tendencies—that is, to *intensify* the regional power struggle. And, far from diluting global dependencies, it has *further opened* the region to external penetration. As such, while public opinion has undoubtedly become a newly empowered factor in foreign policy making, as realists anticipate, external constraints—the balance of power with neighbors, dependence on external patrons—will continue to substantially dilute its effect. There is no doubt that a very realist power struggle is underway among both regional and global actors to shape the post-Uprisings power balance, even if publics are now playing a greater role in this contest.

As such, a realist framework—albeit modified to include the insights of con-structivism on identity and structuralism's core-periphery division—best enables us to assess this struggle. As realists argue, a main factor in shaping the regional balance of power, especially insofar as the direct resort to war is constrained, is the competitive struggle to win allies. Middle East and North African states seek alliances to ward off threats and create spheres of influence,[2] but this struggle is affected not just by their material assets, such as military and financial capa-bility, but also by factors at the trans-state and global levels. First, in MENA's exceptionally penetrated system, global powers use intervention and patronage to create or co-opt regional clients; second, owing to the persistence of powerful supra-state identities, such as Arabism and Islam, regimes' legitimacy depends on the congruence of their alliances with these identities and is vulnerable to attack by rivals claiming a given alliance is a betrayal of such identities. Regime alliance strategies in MENA have varied chiefly between "omni-balancing" with external powers to contain regional and domestic threats[3] or "bandwagoning" with the dominant trans-state identity in order to mobilize regional alliances to balance against external powers. Which strategy states choose is shaped at the domestic level—by the identity of the state and the preferences of ruling coali-tions in their struggle with opposition over public opinion. The Uprisings have reshuffled the threats and opportunities among rival regional powers, put iden-tity in flux, and increased regional vulnerability to external intervention. This chapter assesses how this is affecting the regional power balance.

REGIONAL POWER BALANCE, TIME

Prior to the Uprisings, two coalitions were struggling over the Middle East to fashion opposing versions of regional order. A US–led coalition including the main Sunni Arab powers, Egypt, and Saudi Arabia, and tacitly including Israel, stood for *pax Americana*; an Iran-led counter coalition, heavily but not exclu-sively Shia, including Syria, Hezbollah, and Hamas, stood for anti-imperialist resistance. The power balance was tilting its way because of the decline of Egypt and Saudi Arabia, owing to their stands on the Israeli assaults on Leba-non and Gaza; the US pull-back from its interventions in Iraq and Lebanon, leaving both under Iranian influence; and the partial alignment of Turkey and Qatar toward the resistance.

The immediate effect of the Uprisings was to reshuffle regional states into two categories: (1) Three *rival regional powers*, Turkey, Iran, and Saudi Arabia, have enough power resources and enough immunity to the Uprisings to be in contention to shape the post-Uprisings regional order. They are threatened or empowered, depending on its impact on their "soft power" and on their alliances, actual or potential. They seek to shift the domestic balance in the Uprisings states so as to bring to power (or prevent the fall of) friendly forces, hence to expand (or protect) their spheres of influence. (2) *Battleground states*, those where emergent new regimes seek new allies or old regimes are still battling uprisings, are the *objects* of competitive interference. The major immediate effect of the Uprisings was to consign two previous major players, Egypt and Syria, to this category, making them the main prizes in the contest, but lesser prizes include other Uprisings states of Tunisia, Libya, Bahrain, and Yemen, and also Iraq and Lebanon, states pivotal to the regional struggle where unconsolidated regimes and fragmented societies are highly vulnerable to external penetration.

THE TRANS-STATE IDEOLOGICAL STRUGGLE

MENA states are exceptionally penetrated by supra-state identities and trans-state networks that compete with territorial states for loyalty. The states are thereby embedded in a supra-state public arena, enhanced by Arab satellite TV. Inter-Arab conflict has chiefly taken the form of political or legitimacy wars, in which one wins by gaining allies or subverting rivals; rivals in discourse wars aim to shape identity so as to legitimate their alliance choices and delegitimize those of their rivals. Trans-state networks or movements, sponsored by states or not, such as Hezbollah, the Muslim Brotherhood, and al-Qaeda, are also players in such legitimacy wars. In the "New Arab Cold War"[4] of the late 2000s, the resistance axis was winning the battle for public opinion, and its leaders—Iranian president Mahmoud Ahmadinejad, Syrian president Bashar al-Assad, Lebanon's Hassan Nasrallah, and Hamas' Khaled Mashal—were far more popular than their counterparts in US–aligned regimes that suffered substantial delegitimization of their Western alliances.[5] How have identity contests unleashed by the Uprisings reshuffled the contours of the New Arab Cold War?

The contest is over identity because it defines enemies and appropriate allies. At least three levels of identity have been in competition for the loyalties of populations in the Arab states, each having different implications for alliances: sub-state, state, and supra-state—the Arab nation or Islamic umma—with each subject, as well, to differing interpretations; complicating matters further, people can have several identities simultaneously, and, far from being fixed, they are in a constant process or construction and reconstruction.

In this process, whoever controls the media controls the agenda in the dis-course wars that shape identity.[6] If in the Pan-Arab period of the 1950s the media (Radio Cairo) was then dominated by the nationalist radicals, it is now in other hands. First, trans-state networks of Arab youth using social media have emerged as "netizens" of a virtualized Arab commonwealth[7]; these networks are dominated by the Western-educated middle classes and Arab expatriates, and Western foundations played a role in bringing Arab cyberactivists together. Sec-ond, the Pan-Arab media are dominated by countries in the Gulf Cooperation Council (GCC) and reflect their agendas. Al-Arabiyya was founded by Saudi money to counter Al Jazeera's criticism of the West and its allies; while the re-sistance axis benefited from the Al Jazeera effect when Qatar was aligned with it, notably in the 2006 Lebanon and 2008 Hamas wars, as Qatar switched sides, Al Jazeera actively encouraged revolution in the republics.[8]

The content of the post-Uprisings regional discourse suggests a shift away from the resistance-axis narrative. Thus, while the second President Bush's forced democratization, unleashing civil war in Iraq and Lebanon, seemingly discredited the notion in the 2000s, activists during the Uprisings appeared to have agreed that nondemocratic government was the chief immediate source of the Arabs' problems. The demands of the youth movements were chiefly for democracy and freedom in their *own states* rather than the traditional Pan-Arab, anti-imperialist, or anti-Zionist concerns that had dominated the New Arab Cold War.[9] Moreover, Arab nationalism suffered from association with the repressive regimes that had emerged from the Pan-Arab movements of the fifties and sixties. This could have important consequences in Syria, Arabism's traditional heartland, where the regime continued to legitimize itself in Pan-Arab terms. If Arab nationalism is marginalized, the main winners will be the West and its partners in the Arab Gulf; as Perry Anderson points out: "Without an Arabism that would redistribute the oil wealth, the region will remain disfigured by the 'monstrous opulence of the arbitrary few and the indigence of the desperate many.'"[10]

While previously regimes and publics agreed on sovereignty as a defense against Western imperialism, the discourse wars over Libya and Syria expose a major potential change to the benefit of the West. Although ambivalent on the Libyan intervention, a major portion of Arab opinion embraced the Western norm, "responsibility to protect," legitimizing intervention, although majori-ties had second thoughts after casualties soared.[11] In Syria, too, the regime and opposition engaged in wars of disinformation, with the regime claiming it faced violent terrorists that were dangerous to the West and the opposition exaggerating regime brutality, amplified by the Pan-Arab media, with the aim of legitimizing Western intervention.[12]

In the longer run, it is likely that the individual Arab states, even those initially artificial, will be more normalized by today's democratization struggles. To the degree they are democratized, citizens will be more able to identify with them as "theirs" and have less need for a supra-state Arab or Islamic identity. If the Uprisings foster identification with the individual states at the expense of supra-state identities, the West's actions in Palestine or Afghanistan may cease to inflame the region against it to the degree that has been previously seen, and those that legitimize themselves with the discourse of resistance will be weakened. Identities can, of course, coexist, and there is no *necessary* conflict between state and Pan-Arab or Pan-Islamic identity. Indeed, the uprising in Egypt was prepared by the decade of protests over the Iraq War and the Palestine cause in which publics acquired experience in organized protest and linked pro-Western foreign policies with the lack of democracy. The Uprisings have, however, pushed these issues, including Palestine, into the background, although Israeli intransigence and Washington's extremely one-sided support for it is bound to keep the Palestine issue alive, and with it anti-imperialism. Indeed, competitors for regional leadership, whether Turkey, Iran, or a reempowered Egypt, will need to champion the Palestinians.

The increased trans-state power of Islamic movements manifest in the Uprisings could heighten Islamic identity and delegitimize bandwagoning with the United States. While the Islamic movements mostly seek to Islamize the individual states, they are nevertheless linked by trans-state networks, and their simultaneous rise toward the levers of power in several states is bound to strengthen Pan-Islamic sentiments. However, there are many variants of Islam with different implications for alliance choices, and they have not been uniformly empowered.[13] The main beneficiaries are the Muslim Brotherhood from its electoral prowess and the Salafis,[14] who are often funded by GCC money—which, respectively, have affinity to the Turkish and Saudi-Islamic models. Anti-imperialist Islamic movements have been weakened. Hamas, with its Sunni constituency, could not retain its soft power without breaking with the Assad regime, but losing Syrian and Iranian support made it dependent on the pro-Western axis. Hezbollah's support for the Assad regime has debilitated its previous high standing in regional public opinion, while the defection of Hamas made it more vulnerable to Wahhabi accusations that it followed a Shia sectarian and Iranian, rather than an Arab nationalist, agenda. Al-Qaeda 's anti-imperialist Pan-Islamism targeting the Western "far enemy" that had seemed so potent in the 2000s was marginalized by the democratization movements in Tunisia and Egypt. Its new leader, Ayman Al-Zawahiri, denounced the principle of majority rule, defying the yearning of Muslim populations for democracy. While it enjoyed new opportunities to establish a presence in the failing states of Libya, Yemen, and Syria, it faced competition there from the Muslim Brotherhood and Saudi-sponsored Salafis.[15] Finally, Salafi fundamentalist currents mobilized by Riyadh against Iran as part of their geopolitical struggle are deepening the sectarian character of Islamic identity, with assistance from the Syrian and Bahraini regimes, which are using the specter of sectarianism to fight off their own Uprisings. As Dergham put it, "The smell of sectarian wars is becoming ever more redolent across the whole region,"[16] increasing insecurity and defensive sectarian solidarity in Lebanon, Syria, Bahrain, Yemen, and Iraq. Dividing Islam along Sunni-Shia lines opens it to external manipulation, allowing the United States to promote itself as a defender of Sunni Islam against Iran. Ironically, in adopting anti-Shia discourse, al-Qaeda, notably in the struggle over Syria (as earlier in Iraq), empowers the American-aligned camp.

GLOBAL COMPETITIVE INTERFERENCE

The Uprisings provide a new context in which rival global powers deploy resources to co-opt new allies or preserve old ones. After an attempt starting in the 1990s to impose a *pax Americana* on the region, US power appeared, by the mid-2000s, to be receding owing to the failure of the peace process, the widely held regional perception that the War on Terror was a war on Islam, and the invasion of Iraq, which inadvertently empowered Iran and even provoked counterbalancing by US ally Turkey. Rival powers were penetrating the region, with Russia and China developing stakes in arms sales, energy, and trade.[17]

The Uprisings constituted a threat to key US allies. Lacking ideological hegemony, the United States had to control the Arab world via alliances with key authoritarian client states, notably Egypt and Saudi Arabia. The loss of Mubarak and the possibility that al-Qaeda could benefit from failed states were immediate threats. But the West also saw opportunities to exploit the intense cleavages the Uprisings opened in Arab societies to reassert its dominance in the region. The uprising in Libya presented an opportunity for the United States to reverse perceptions that US power in the region was declining (in the face of the resistance axis) and to demonstrate the utility and low cost of military force to effect regime change after the costly failures in Iraq and Afghanistan. If the main struggle in the region was over the competing bids of the United States and Iran for regional hegemony, the uprising in Syria provided the latter with a golden opportunity to debilitate the resistance axis. The United States also sought to frame the Uprisings as heralding a democratic alternative to both al-Qaeda and Islamic Iran.[18] Washington's weak spot was its unqualified support for Israel, but the Arab Uprisings eased pressures on it, especially given the co-option of the Palestinian Authority (PA) by the West and Israel and the weakening of Hamas, which, having lost the resources formerly provided by the resistance axis, is more dependent on the pro-Western regimes.

The key leverage the West has over the region is the global political economy dominated by an unaccountable transnational financial oligarchy (in which Wall Street, the US government, International Financial Institutions—or IFIs— and the oil oligarchs of the Gulf are intimately interconnected). The subservience of local client regimes to the fundamentalist neoliberalism of this power complex, and their exploitation of its demands for privatization to seize the formerly dominant public sectors in the republics, generated crony capitalists at the power centers of most regional states who were heavily invested in relations with the West. IFIs commended Tunisia and Egypt, where the cronies of Gamal Mubarak and the Ben Ali family took advantage of their pressures for privatization to turn public-sector assets into private monopolies, as models of good economic governance.[19] The European Union also bolstered North African regimes via the Euro-Med Partnership agreements,[20] which forced open regional markets and committed North African states to control emigration. Unsurprisingly, a main target of the Uprisings was this crony capitalism, and, insofar as they were reactions to Western neoliberalism, they also threaten Western influence in the region; to address this threat, Western IFIs are reframing the Uprisings as revolts against the intrusive state and rentier monopolies, a problem to be addressed by the enhanced competition from *further opening* to global-finance capital; and they are exploiting the post-Uprisings economic crises, making loans conditional on this opening.[21] Moreover, if such external pressures are complemented by Islamist governments' adoption of the Turkish AKP model of neoliberalism legitimized by the Qur'an, the region would be penetrated not just at the level of the state but via society, too. This has domestic political implications: since the dominance of global finance capital tends to hollow out democracy, the outcome of the MENA Uprisings is likely at best to be what Robinson calls "low-intensity democracy," limited to the political sphere with countries locked into international agreements that remove the big socioeconomic issues from democratic accountability and with all political parties pursuing similar economic policies, much as in the West itself.[22]

Control of world oil markets, to which Saudi Arabia is crucial, is part of Western hegemony. Before the Arab Uprisings, the tendency of OPEC was not to increase capacity, since oil left in the ground was likely to be higher priced in the future, while, in parallel, rising MENA energy consumption was reducing exportable surpluses, threatening global supplies and increasing competition between Western states and Asian powers over energy. However, the Uprisings have altered this trend to the West's advantage. To fund the enormous handouts used to bolster the loyalty of their populations amid the Uprisings, the oil-producing monarchies had either to increase output or keep prices high; since the latter would empower Iran, Saudi Arabia opted for the former, which led to falling prices. As always, a big beneficiary of the Saudis' use of the oil weapon against Iran is the West.[23]

The Uprisings were also an opportunity for the West to roll back the growing regional influence of Russia and China, which have stakes in arms deals, energy partnerships, and trade. Russia and China also have a strong interest in defending the norm of sovereignty and the authority of the UN Security Council to constrain Western expansion into MENA and elsewhere.[24] The West's abuse of the UN resolution authorizing humanitarian intervention in Libya to effect regime change subverts the multipolar international order they seek. However, their opposition against international intervention in Syria cost them standing in the region. Insofar as Russia, China, and the norm of sovereignty are weakened, so are checks against Western domination of MENA.

THE STRUGGLE FOR THE UPRISING STATES

The Uprisings, where they succeed, change ruling coalitions and, potentially, even popular identity, hence alliance preferences. Outcomes depend on whether the new ruling coalitions are "internationalist" (foreign traders, bankers, investors oriented toward the global market) and liable to bandwagon with the Western great powers, or nationalist-statist (military, public sector managers, populist constituencies), possibly seeking to balance between them and alternative global powers (Russia, China).[25] The Uprisings have precipitated struggles among weakened statist establishments, business groups (with money and Western connections), and Islamic movements (who will be wary of the West). In the new *semi-democracies* likely to emerge, the role of the public in deciding such choices will increase, with Islamic movements best positioned to mobilize votes and hence affect the legitimacy of alliance choices. Additionally, competitive politics may stimulate consciousness of identity differences, notably religious ones, affecting conceptions of threat and of appropriate allies, notably constructing Sunni-Shia cleavages that affect the rival alliances.

Uprisings make regimes much more vulnerable to competitive interference by regional and international powers that seek to tilt these internal balances in their favor. The most pivotal states—hence the objects of the fiercest competition—are Egypt and Syria. However, Bahrain, though tiny, was also crucial, since an overthrow of the Sunni monarchy in a Shia uprising could potentially spread Shia revolt to the rest of the Gulf and empower Iran.

The Battle for Bahrain

The context of the battle over Bahrain is developments in Iraq, where, in a three-cornered struggle for power, the Maliki government had moved, in parallel with the US withdrawal, to marginalize the Sunnis, notably seeking to arrest the Sunni vice president and foster conflict with the Kurds as well. This precipitated accusations from the Saudis and Turkey that Maliki was persecuting the Sunni minority and turning Iraq into an Iranian proxy. Having lost Iraq to Shia power, the Sunni Gulf monarchies feared Iran and Iraq would benefit from the uprising in Bahrain.

Bahrain was certainly the weak spot of the GCC. Less tribal, with a bigger middle class and 90 percent literacy rate, and with less rent with which to anesthetize opposition, demands for political participation were correspondingly intense.[26] Bahrain was also vulnerable to sectarian division, ruled by a Sunni monarchy that discriminated against the large Shia majority. The Shia were excluded from the security forces and most government posts, while the lower house of parliament—in which al-Wefaq, the predominantly Shia party, won a plurality of seats—was kept in check by a royal-appointed upper house. The royal family was the richest property owner, and the neoliberal model of privatization Bahrain followed further enhanced overlapping sectarian and class inequality. The uprising, which grouped the Shia majority with secular Sunnis, began as demands for a constitutional monarchy at one point mobilized over 40 percent of the population (two hundred thousand people). The GCC military intervention and escalating repression that checked the uprising, the monarchy's use of Sunni solidarity to mobilize its supporters, and a leveling of Shia mosques that gave an overtly sectarian character to the battle were sharply criticized by Iran and Iraq and inflamed Sunni-Shia tensions across the region. Mixed up in this regional battle was the United States, whose naval bases covered a fifth of the island.[27]

The Battle for Syria

Syria was the weak spot of the resistance axis, and the uprising there turned it into a battleground between Iran, Turkey, and the GCC. The battle for Syria was being waged in several arenas: at the United Nations, in the regional media, and on the ground.

The Syrian Baath regime had traditionally used its Arab nationalist militancy and a populist social contract to build a cross-sectarian middle class and peasant constituency and legitimize its rule. However, its adoption of neoliberal policies and growing class inequality provoked protests, and the overreaction of the security forces turned demands for political reform into an uprising for regime change. To the extent sectarian identities took hold, a minority-dominated regime ruling a Sunni majority became increasingly vulnerable.

The GCC saw an opportunity to break the resistance axis. Qatar's Al Jazeera TV encouraged the uprising, and Saudi Arabia financed anti-regime tribes and Islamist factions. Amid the vacuum left by the debilitating of the republics, the GCC bloc assumed the leadership of the Arab League and deployed it against Damascus. Initially the League secretary-general Nabil al-Arabi declared that the League did not interfere in the internal affairs of its members. However, from mid-August 2011, Saudi Arabia and Qatar started contesting this position. A special committee was established to deal with the Syrian crisis headed by Qatar, although its inclusion of Algeria, Sudan, Egypt, and the secretary-general diluted the anti-Damascus tangent promoted by the GCC. On November 2, 2011, Syria agreed under external pressure to accept a disadvantageous Arab League "plan of action" that committed it to cease repression of the uprising and allow entry of Arab League observers; when the Syrian regime was deemed to renege on this, the GCC used its bloc vote to impose harsher resolutions against it than Egypt or Algeria wanted, including the suspension of Syria's League membership, economic sanctions against it, and calls for the internationalization of the crisis. While the GCC collectively withdrew its ambassadors, Algeria refused to follow suit, and Egypt did so unobtrusively but opposed internationalization. Later, Syria agreed to League observers, but the choice of Mustafa Al-Dabi, a senior Sudanese military commander, to lead it and the requirement that the observers coordinate their movements with the regime rendered the mission ineffective. This was harshly criticized in the GCC–owned Arab media, and the League halted the mission, blaming the Syrian government for escalating the repression. The League's consequent resolution to impose sanctions on Syria remained symbolic, since Syria's neighbors did not implement it; Iraq and Lebanon, having voted against it, were not bound by it, and Jordan was exempted for economic reasons. Having failed in the crisis, in February 2012, the League's Council of Foreign Ministers called on the Security Council to mandate a peacekeeping force to oversee a ceasefire in Syria and on the international community to isolate the Syrian regime and support the opposition.[28] The battle shifted to the global level.

At the United Nations, in October 2011, a European draft resolution placed blame for the crisis on the Syrian government. Nine votes favored the European resolution; Brazil, India, and South Africa (with Lebanon) abstained because the Europeans had rushed the vote, dismissing their wish for a more even-handed resolution; Russia and China vetoed it, primarily on the grounds of its violation of sovereignty and the principle of nonintervention. In blaming one side only, declared the Russian ambassador, the situation resembled the resolution on Libya, which had been used as a cover for regime change and massive bombings that did not spare civilians. Their alternative called for political dialogue between the regime and opposition and for an end to violence by both sides. After they vetoed a similar resolution in February 2012, Russia and China were subjected to vilification and a call to boycott their goods mounted by activists, the GCC media, and the Syrian opposition, which accused China and Russia of giving the Syrian regime a license to kill, which the Syrian people would not forget. When Kofi Annan was appointed special envoy to Syria on behalf of the United Nations and the Arab League, Syria agreed to the mission only under pressure from Russia and China. Thus, the crisis was "internationalized," but Annan's intervention largely conformed to Russian and Chinese preferences for a deal between regime and opposition.[29]

The Battle for Egypt

Egypt is the pivotal case, because, fully aligned with neither camp after its uprising, it is the swing power where a major change in foreign policy would be decisive for the regional power balance. Caught between external dependency and newly empowered public opinion, its orientation is sharply contested by rival domestic and external forces.

The revolution is widely seen as Egypt's chance to reassert its independence from the United States. Public opinion is highly anti-American (in 2010, 82 percent of Egyptians held an unfavorable view of the United States),[30] owing much to its long interference in Egyptian politics, its backing of Israel, and its invasion of Iraq. US aid, since it is made conditional on good relations with Israel, earns little gratitude from Egyptians. Moreover, in 2011 a mere $250 million of US aid to Egypt was economic assistance, with the great bulk of it ($1.3 billion annually) going to the military.[31] The United States relies on Egypt's dependence to maintain its influence despite the fall of Mubarak: its main leverage is its clientalization of the military and its influence over the international financial institutions on which Egypt has become dependent.

Egypt's options are sharply constrained by this dependence, which, though inherited from Mubarak, has been aggravated by the uprising: it suffered from a foreign-exchange crisis owing to the collapse in business and the tourist trade following the revolution and the level of public subsidies increased by the military to politically stabilize the county. Egypt has to import 80 percent of its basic food, much from the United States, and with global prices rising, the choice was between increased subsidies or further public hardship. Egypt's longer-term economic woes are partly rooted in its dependence on foreign loans, which have drained the country of capital, with debt repayments exceeding aid and loans by $3.4 billion, a mechanism by which Western finance capital extracts wealth from Egypt's masses. The new loans that are continuously needed to service previously accumulated debt makes the country vulnerable to the conditionality imposed by IFIs. The latter are insisting on further privatization via so-called private-public partnerships that would allow Western and Gulf investors to buy up prime parts of Egypt's infrastructure.[32] This stands to further deepen the country's dependency.

It is in this context that the country's course was subjected to a three-cornered contest pitting the revolutionary youth, the Islamists, and the army against one another. The youth movement, the main advocate of "democracy," splintered into multiple rival factions and, not organized to contest the elections, was barely represented in the postelection parliament. The army did not want to rule directly but sought to enshrine extra-constitutional guardianship, like the Turkish military used to exercise, to ensure that no future civilian government scrutinized its budget and privileges or challenged the Israel peace and the alliance with the United States.[33] The Muslim Brotherhood is, next to the army, the most organized force in society, with six hundred thousand members, an extensive social infrastructure, and considerable financial assets; in the 2011 parliamentary elections, it got 46 percent of the seats, and its candidate, Mohamed Morsi, was subsequently elected president. However, although he successfully asserted his powers against the military before his forced removal, this had been accompanied by a certain understanding that some issue areas were off limits. In parallel, the Islamist-dominated parliament was dissolved to prepare the way for new elections in which the reactivated regime network in the rural areas would contest Islamist dominance. This shifting balance of domestic power is the context in which foreign policy is shaped.

The power contenders are caught between their domestic constituencies, which expect them to assert Egypt's independence of the United States, and the dependency of the country on it. What is remarkable is that even those closest to the United States feel obliged to defy it in public. Iconic of this was the refusal of Amr Hamzawy, a leading liberal member of parliament close to Washington, to meet with visiting US senator John McCain in February 2012 because of "[McCain's] biased positions in favor of Israel and his support for invading Iraq and attacking Iran." Even the military, having assured Washington that it will not countenance challenges to the peace treaty with Israel, apparently felt empowered to play the anti-American card itself in a legitimacy contest with the Ikhwan and liberal or leftist revolutionaries. The occasion was the attack by old regime leftovers in the military-backed government on critical US–funded NGOs for taking foreign funding and interfering in Egyptian politics; most provocative was the arrest of Americans working for such NGOs, several of whom took refuge inside the US embassy in Cairo, including Sam LaHood, the son of the US Transportation secretary. The huge popularity of this move obliged all Egyptian politicians to back it. When US politicians warned Egypt's aid was at risk, Salafist preacher Mohammed Hassan campaigned for Egyptians to donate money to replace the American aid under threat. When, in order to secure an IMF loan and the release of US military aid, the military-backed government released the Americans, the Muslim Brotherhood–led parliament called for a no-confidence vote in it. Yet the Brotherhood's free-market economic policies and its potential to both drive a deeper integration into the world market while also containing the pent-up anti-capitalism of its mass constituency made its rising power at least partially congruent with US interests. Before the Brotherhood's official banning in late 2013, the United States was initially engaged in a dialogue with them, keen to commit the Ikhwan to the Israeli peace treaty, which enabled the Brotherhood's opponent to embarrass it.[34]

Israel is the biggest obstacle to good relations between the United States and Egypt. Mubarak's effort to head-off US pressures for democratization by increased collaboration with Israel, in spite of the second intifada, had cost the regime legitimacy. Egyptians resented delivery of natural gas to Israel and economic joint ventures with it believed to enrich crony capitalists around Gamal Mubarak. Mubarak's pro-Israeli policies in the 2006 and 2008 Israeli attacks on

Hezbollah and Hamas and collaboration in the siege of Gaza sparked protest movements that prepared the way for events in 2011. After the fall of Mubarak, rival politicians exploited popular anti-Israeli sentiment. Tensions with Israel rose after attacks on Israel's Cairo embassy and on the pipeline delivering gas to Israel and across the Sinai border, symptoms of a relaxation of the tight security grip over militants after Mubarak's fall. The Egyptian parliament voted unanimously to expel Israel's ambassador and halt natural-gas exports to Israel. Its Arab-affairs committee declared that it considered the Zionist entity to be the number one enemy of Egypt and the Arab nation. Yet anti-Zionism is likely to remain mere rhetoric, at least as long as the military, well aware of the costs of getting into a skirmish with a militarily dominant Israel and of alienating the US Congress, remains in charge of the issue; significantly, Egypt has only partially lifted the siege of Gaza via the Rafah crossing.[35]

Can Egypt claw back enough independence to reassert regional leadership? In parallel with the loosening of its moorings to Washington, Egypt has distanced itself from the Saudis' anti-Iranian and sectarian polarization, and the Cairo establishment is resentful of Al Jazeera's role in stirring up domestic dissent, of Qatari funding of Salafists, and what it saw as a Qatari marginalization of Egypt's traditionally preeminent role in the Arab League. Egypt will likely balance between the anti– and pro–US camps in order to maximize its value to both, and also because any Egyptian government will have to balance between the views of the public and powerful forces dependent on the United States or Gulf money—such as the army and the new capitalists.

THE UPRISINGS AND THE REGIONAL POWER BALANCE, TIME 2

Over a year into the Arab Uprisings, the power balance between the two sides of the geopolitical struggle for regional dominance had not been decisively transformed. Turkey, Qatar, and Hamas had dealigned from the resistance axis, which lost its soft power but still survived. Egypt and Iraq had been loosened from their American moorings and avoided full alignment with either side.[36]

Of the three rival contending powers, Iran—hence the resistance axis—had been most weakened. Iran suffered from greater domestic vulnerabilities, having just turned back the challenge of the Green uprising. Its economy was being constricted by international sanctions. The fall of Mubarak improved relations with Egypt, but Iran lost soft power from support for the Assad regime and the limited attractiveness of the Iranian model, compared to Turkey, for the emergent democracies. It suffered from the decline of Hezbollah's regional standing and the break of Hamas from the resistance axis. If its most important ally, Syria's Assad, were replaced by Western-installed expatriates or a hostile Salafi regime aligned with Saudi Arabia, Iran's ability to support Hezbollah and be a player in the Arab-Israeli arena—important to the regime's legitimacy—would be damaged (although any Syrian government seeking to retain leverage with the United States and Israel might quickly learn it needed Iran and Hezbollah). On the defensive, Iran sought to create via Iraq (where, post–US occupation, the move of the Maliki regime against Sunni rivals made it more dependent on Iran) a corridor linking Iran to Syria and the Lebanese coast, allowing Iran to supply Hezbollah and providing the Assad regime with a two-sided buffer that could help it survive.[37]

For the pro-Western monarchies, the loss of Mubarak's Egypt, state collapse in Yemen, and the potentially contagious Shia uprising in Bahrain offered several opportunities for Iran. But the monarchies proved more resilient than the republics in dampening the domestic threat of the Uprisings via a combination of repression, most obvious in Bahrain; political concession, most obvious in Morocco; and economic blandishments to citizens, most obvious in Saudi Arabia, where US $97 billion worth of jobs and benefits were promised, the equivalent to $5,000 per citizen. The GCC was upgraded into a "Holy Alliance" to contain the democratic threat, with the richer monarchies transferring billions to the poorer ones (Morocco, Jordan, Oman, and Bahrain) and using petro dollars to promote Salafism, for example, against the democratic youth in Egypt. For the Saudis, Yemen was becoming a failed state on their soft underbelly where al-Qaeda was finding space to operate, but they managed a controlled transfer of power in Sana'a that preserved their influence in the country. The GCC also took advantage of the vacuum left by the marginalization of the key Arab republics and its bloc vote in the Arab League in a bid for Pan-Arab leadership. It used the Pan-Arab media and the League to legitimize Western intervention against Gaddafi, an old monarchic foe, and then against Syria, where it aimed to break the resistance axis, which had repeatedly attacked the legitimacy of its Western alignments, notably in the wars in Lebanon (2006) and Gaza (2008).[38]

Turkey represented a third pole: democratic-capitalist yet more independent. Its zero-problems policy of good relations and business deals with nondemocratic neighbors initially threatened its standing in the region. The Libya crisis, where Ankara opposed Western intervention, angered the eventually triumphant opposition; the uprising in Syria, the showcase of the zero-problems policy, cost Turkey economic opportunities, the anti-Kurdish alliance with

Damascus, and good relations with Iran, as the two backed opposing sides. But as Turkey shifted its stance to back the "people" against authoritarian governments, it seemed well positioned to benefit from the Uprisings. Prime Minister Erdoğan was welcomed in Egypt as a hero (where he was by far the most popular world leader). The congruity of Turkey's political system—a democracy that incorporates Islamic forces—with regional popular aspirations, its alignment with rising business/Islamist coalitions similar to the AKP in the new Sunni democracies (Egypt, Tunisia), and the economic prowess that enables it to build interdependences with the Uprising states are factors empowering Turkey's bid for regional leadership. Ankara could be the main influence in Damascus should the opposition triumph. Far less US–dependent than the GCC, it can assert regional interests vis-à-vis the hegemon as, for example, in its opposition to the invasion of Iraq and its assertive championship of Palestine cause. [39]

CONCLUSION

The Uprisings have weakened the Arab world in debilitating two Arab powers, Egypt and Syria, with Saudi Arabia too US–dependent to promote Arab-Islamic causes. Of the three main regional powers, Turkey and Saudi Arabia are rising at the expense of Iran and the resistance axis. The US hegemon benefits from the empowerment of the GCC, while states where US–friendly regimes fell (Egypt, Tunisia, Yemen) were too dependent to turn against it, and the main checks on it, the resistance axis, and China and Russia have been weakened. These tendencies suggest the possible future emergence of a new regional order built, with the debilitation of the resistance axis, around a coalition of the Turkey-led new business/Islamist democracies, a more independent Egypt and the GCC states, with their command of money and Pan-Arab media power. It would be under Western hegemony but could possess some capacity to assert collective (Arab-Islamic) interests, notably over Palestine, particularly insofar as the power of public opinion, expressed in elections, counters US influence over decision makers. Alternatively, a new era of disorder could be triggered by the spread of failed states and/or a US or Israeli attack on Iran, with both factors possibly exacerbating the Arab-Israel conflict, deepening sectarian polarization and sparking an anti-imperialist backlash. The reality is likely to be a mix of these two scenarios, the particular outcome shaped by the effect on the balance of power of today's ongoing struggle for dominance in the Middle East.

NOTES

1. Edward D. Mansfield and Jack Snyder, "The Dangers of Democratization," *International Security* 20, no.1 (1995): 5–38.

2. Stephen M. Walt, *The Origins of Alliances* (Ithaca: Cornell University Press, 1987).

3. Steven R. David, "Explaining Third World Alignment," *World Politics* 43, no. 2 (1991): 233–56.

4. Morten Valbjorn and Andre Bank, "Signs of a New Arab Cold War: The 2006 Lebanon War and the Sunni-Shi'i Divide," *Middle East Report* 242 (2007): 6–11.

5. Shibley Telhami, "2010 Annual Arab Public Opinion Survey," presented at the Anwar Sadat Chair for Peace and Development at the University of Maryland with Zogby International, August 5, 2010, http://www.brookings.edu/%7E/media/Files/rc/reports/2010/08_arab_opinion_poll_telhami/08_arab_opinion_poll_telhami.pdf.

6. For example, see Iskandar's chapter 8 in this volume.

7. Chas W. Freeman Jr., "The Arab Reawakening and Its Strategic Implications," *Middle East Policy Council*, March 26, 2011, accessed March 20, 2014, http://www.mepc.org/articles-commentary/speeches/arab-reawakening-and-its-strategic-implications.

8. Aref Hijjawi, "The Role of Al-Jazeera (Arabic) in the Arab Revolts of 2011," *Perspectives* 2 (2011): 68–72; Magda Abu-Fadil, "Media Lives Up to Its Name as Game Changers in Spreading Arab Revolutions," *Perspectives* 2 (2011): 74–79.

9. Ahmed H. Rahim, "Whither Political Islam and the 'Arab Spring,'" *Hedgehog Review* 13, no. 3 (2011): 8–22; Yassine Temlali, "The 'Arab Spring': Rebirth or Final Throes of Pan-Arabism?" *Perspectives* 2 (2011): 46–49.

10. Perry Anderson, "On the Concatenation in the Arab World," *New Left Review* 68 (2011): 1–11.

11. Shibley Telhami, "The Striking Arab Openness to Intervention," *National Interest*, April 4, 2011, accessed 20 March, 2014, http://nationalinterest.org/commentary/the-striking-arab-openness-intervention5109%3Fpage%3Dshow?utm_medium=referral&utm_source=pulsenews.

12. William Blum, "Putting Syria into Some Perspective: The Anti-empire Report," *Dissident Voice*, April 8, 2012, accessed March 20, 2014, http://dissidentvoice.org/2012/04/putting-syria-into-some-perspective/.

13. Anissa Haddadi, "The Arab Spring and Islam: Politics, Religion, Culture and the Struggle for Identity," October, 2011, accessed March 20, 2014, http://www.ibtimes.co.uk/the-arab-spring-and-islam-politics-religion-culture-and-the-struggle-for-identity-236538.

14. The Muslim Brotherhood and Salafi currents are differentiated and often at odds owing to the more fundamentalist ultra-orthodox and often apolitical stances of the latter, which have been funded by and linked to Saudi Wahhabism. In the wake of the Uprising, however, Salafis have entered the political arena and in Egypt are, under the banner of the Nour Party, allied with the Muslim Brotherhood.

15. Gilad Stern and Yoram Schweitzer, "In Their Own Words: Al Qaeda's View of the Arab Spring," *Foreign Policy Research Institute* (September, 2011), accessed March 20, 2014, http://www.fpri.org/articles/2011/09/their-own-words-al-qaedas-view-arab-spring.

16. Raghida Dergham, "The Dangerous Upcoming Year after the Arab Spring," *Al Arabiya News* (January 1, 2012), accessed March 20, 2014, http://english.alarabiya.net/views/2012/01/01/185692.html?PHPSESSID=tf100ia5sumf4g26s3kc76b9u4.

17. Flynt Leverett and Hillary Mann Leverett, "Obama Is Helping Iran," *Foreign Policy* (February 23, 2011), accessed March 20, 2014, http://www.foreignpolicy.com/articles/2011/02/23/obama_is_helping_iran.

18. Flynt Leverett and Hillary Mann Leverett, "Iran And Syria: America's Middle East Pundits Get It Wrong (Again)," *The Race for Iran* (September 1, 2011), accessed March 20, 2014, http://www.raceforiran.com/iran-and-syria-america%E2%80%99s-middle-east-pundits-get-it-wrong-again.

19. Ibrahim Saif, "Arab Leaders and Western Countries: Swapping Democracy for Business Interests," *Perspectives* 2 (2011): 106–10; Rami Zurayk, "Feeding the Arab Uprisings," *Perspectives* 2 (2011): 119–25.

20. See "Euro-Mediterranean Partnership (EUROMED)," accessed March 20, 2014, http://www.eeas.europa.eu/euromed/index_en.htm.

21. Adam Hanieh, "Egypt's 'Orderly Transition'? International Aid and the Rush to Structural Adjustment," *Jadaliyya* (May 29, 2011), accessed March 20, 2014, http://www.jadaliyya.com/pages/index/1711/egypts-'orderly-transition'-international-aid.

22. William I. Robinson, *Promoting Polyarchy: Globalization, US Intervention, and Hegemony* (Cambridge: Cambridge University Press, 1996).

23. Paul Stevens, "The Arab Uprisings and the International Oil Markets," *Chatham House* (February, 2012), accessed March 20, 2014, http://www.chathamhouse.org/publications/papers/view/182365.

24. Stephen Blank, "Russia's Anxieties about the Arab Revolution," *Foreign Policy Research Institute* (July 2011), accessed March 20, 2014, https://www.fpri.org/enotes/2011/201107.blank russiaarabspring.html.

25. Etel Solingen, *Regional Orders at Century's Dawn: Global and Domestic Influence on Grand Strategy* (Princeton: Princeton University Press, 1998).

26. See "Arab Statistics: Adult Literacy Rate for GCC 2007," accessed March 20, 2014, http://www.arabstats.org/group.asp?gr=1&ind=128.

27. Joost Hiltermann, "Bahrain: A New Sectarian Conflict?"*New York Review of Books* (May 8, 2012), accessed March 20, 2014, http://www.nybooks.com/blogs/nyrblog/2012/may/08/bahrain-new-sectarian-conflict/; Stephen Zunes, "America Blows It on Bahrain," *Foreign Policy in Focus* (March 2, 2011), accessed March 20, 2014, http://www.fpif.org/articles/america_blows_it_on_bahrain.

28. N. Mozes, "The Decline of the Arab League—The Syrian Crisis as a Test Case," *Middle East Media Research Institute* (March 12, 2012), accessed March 20, 2014, http://www.memri.org/report/en/0/0/0/0/0/0/6164.htm.

29. Ronda Hauben, "Building a Pretext to Wage War on Syria: Hidden Agenda behind UN Security Council Resolution," *Global Research* (October 27, 2011), accessed March 20, 2014, http://www.globalresearch.ca/index.php?context=va&aid=27344; Yezid Sayigh, "China's Position on Syria," *Carnegie Endowment for International Peace* (February 8, 2012), accessed March 20, 2014, http://carnegieendowment.org/2012/02/08/china-s-position-on-syria; Y. Yehoshua, "Following Russian-Chinese Veto in Security Council, Increasing Calls in Arab World to Boycott Russian, Chinese Goods," *Middle East Media Research Institute* (February 7, 2012), accessed March 20, 2014, http://www.memri.org/report/en/print6059.htm.

30. Pew Research Center, "Egyptians Embrace Revolt Leaders, Religious Parties and Military, as Well: U.S. Wins No Friends, End of Treaty with Israel Sought," *Pew Research Global Attitudes*

Project (April 25, 2011), accessed March 20, 2014, http://www.pewglobal.org/2011/04/25/egyptians
-embrace-revolt-leaders-religious-parties-and-military-as-well/.

31. Michele Dunne, "Rethinking U.S. Relations with a Changing Egypt," *Project on Middle East Democracy* (March 22, 2012), accessed March 20, 2014, http://pomed.org/wordpress/wp-content/uploads/2012/03/POMED-Policy-Brief_Dunne.pdf.

32. Hanieh, "Egypt's 'Orderly Transition'?"

33. Mohammed Ayoob, "Beyond the Democratic Wave: A Turko-Persian Future?" *Middle East Policy* 18, no. 2 (2011): 110–19.

34. Shadi Hamid, "Beyond Guns and Butter: A U.S.–Egyptian Relationship for a Democratic Era," *Middle East Memo* 22 (2012), Saban Center for Middle East Policy at the Brookings Institute; Samuel Tadros, "The Muslim Brotherhood and Washington: Courtship and Its Discontents," *Foreign Policy Research Institute* (April, 2012), accessed March 20, 2014, http://www.fpri.org/articles/2012/04/muslim-brotherhood-and-washington-courtship-and-its-discontents.

35. Mirette F. Mabrouk, "Recalibrating a Relationship," *Middle East Memo* 20 (2011), Saban Center for Middle East Policy at the Brookings Institute; Joel Beinen, "The Israeli-Palestinian Conflict and the Arab Awakening," *Middle East Report Online* (August 1, 2011), accessed on March 20, 2014, http://www.merip.org/mero/mero080111; Anne Barnard, "Loyalty to Syrian President Could Isolate Hezbollah," *New York Times* (April 5, 2012), accessed March 20, 2014, http://www.nytimes.com/2012/04/06/world/middleeast/hezbollahs-syria-policy-puts-it-at-risk.html?_r=1&ref=annebarnard.

36. Paul Salem, "'Arab Spring' Has Yet to Alter Region's Strategic Balance," *Los Angeles Times* (May 9, 2011), accessed March 20, 2014, http://latimesblogs.latimes.com/babylonbeyond/2011/05/middle-east-arab-spring-has-yet-to-alter-regions-strategic-balance-.html.

37. Kayhan Barzegar, "Iran's Interests and Values and the 'Arab Spring,'" Belfer Center for Science and International Affairs, Harvard Kennedy School, April 20, 2011; Nazanine Metghalchi, "Is Iran Immune from the Arab Spring?—Analysis," *Fundacion para las Relaciones Internacionales y el Dialogo Exterior* (October 8, 2011), accessed March 20, 2014, http://www.eurasiareview.com/08102011-is-iran-immune-from-the-arab-spring-analysis/; Jubin Goodarzi, "Syria and Iran at the Crossroads," *Muftah* (November 30, 2011, accessed March 20, 2014, http://muftah.org/?p=2081.

38. Kristian Coates Ulrichsen, "Counterrevolution in the Gulf," *Foreign Policy* (May 6, 2011), accessed March 20, 2014, http://www.foreignpolicy.com/articles/2011/05/06/counterrevolution_in_the_gulf?page=0,1; Christian Koch, "The Gulf and the 'Arab Spring,'" *Gulf Research Center Bulletin*, November 1, 2011; Nael Shehadeh, "Economic Costs, the Arab Spring and the GCC," *Gulf Research Center Bulletin* (November 24, 2011); Bruce Maddy-Weitzman, "The Arab Regional System and the Arab Spring," in *Change and Opportunities in the Emerging Mediterranean*, ed. Stephen Calleya and Monika Wohlfeld (Malta: University of Malta, 2012), 82–94.

39. Henri J. Barkey, "Turkey and the Arab Spring," *Carnegie Middle East Center* (April 26, 2011), accessed March 20, 2014, http://carnegie-mec.org/publications/?fa=43731; Barcin Yinanc, "Arab Wave Sweeps Iran Model Out, Turkey 'In,'" *Hurriyet Daily News* (October 28, 2011), accessed March 20, 2014, http://www.hurriyetdailynews.com/default.aspx?pageid=438&n=8216arab-spring-forces-looking-to-turkey-rather-than-iran-model8217-2011-10-28; Yasser Seddiq, "Regional Complications of Arab Spring: Winners and Losers," *Al-Ahram* (January 3, 2012), accessed March 20, 2014, http://english.ahram.org.eg/NewsContent/2/8/30707/World/Region/Regional-complications-of-Arab-Spring-Winners-and-.aspx.

11

Turkey's Ordeal of Democratic Consolidation: A Possible Model for the Arab Uprisings?

Ergun Özbudun

The Arab Uprisings led to debates among scholars and policy makers in many countries about whether Turkey, the only Muslim-majority Middle Eastern country with a reasonably functioning democratic regime, can serve as a model for democratizing Arab countries. Indeed, Turkey is a "second-wave" democracy, having made its transition to a competitive political system in the mid-1940s, and it has maintained it since then despite military interruptions (those of 1960, 1971, and 1980, and the so-called "postmodern coup" of 1997) and frequent constitutional crises. Paradoxically, however, Turkey has not been able to fully consolidate its democracy and, in this respect, lags behind many of the "third-wave" democracies of Southern, Central, and Eastern Europe.[1] Thus, according to the Freedom House ratings for 2009, Turkey is still a "partially free" country with a score of 3, both with regard to civil rights and political rights.[2] Thus, by such measures it can be classified only as an "electoral democracy" but not as a fully consolidated liberal democracy.

Although this chapter concentrates essentially on the Turkish ordeal in the process of democratic consolidation, some of its features may be relevant for the countries of the Arab Uprisings. Particularly, the similarities between the Turkish and the Egyptian cases are striking. Indeed, it has been pointed out that in the

Arab world "the Egyptian case is unique, perhaps comparable among the Islamic countries of the Middle East only to Turkey, not only in its strength of statehood, but even in the resemblance to a Western-type nation-state."[3] Such similarities will be commented upon in the concluding section of this chapter.

THE TURKISH EXPERIENCE OF CONSTITUTION MAKING

Most observers, Turkish and foreign alike, agree that Turkey has a constitutional problem, which constitutes a serious obstacle on the path to democratic consolidation. The immediate cause of this situation is the authoritarian, tutelarist, and statist spirit of the current Constitution of 1982, which was the product of a military regime of the National Security Council (1980–1983) with almost no input from political parties and the civil society in general. Despite its seventeen amendments since 1987, it is generally agreed that it has not been possible to completely liquidate this authoritarian legacy.

However, the causes of this failure go deeper in history. None of the republican constitutions of Turkey (those of 1924, 1961, and 1982) were made by a freely elected, fully representative constituent or legislative assembly through genuine inter-party negotiations and compromises. The first constitution was made by an essentially single-party assembly dominated by the Kemalists, and the military played a major (in the case of the 1982 Constitution, a totally dominant) role in the making of the other two. Consequently, in the 1961 and 1982 constitution-making processes, the military was able to extract important "exit guarantees," through which it continued to exercise tutelary powers over elected bodies. The partial constitutional amendments since then brought about a considerable degree of liberalization and democratization of the political system, usually through inter-party negotiations and compromises, without, however, amounting to a complete liquidation of such tutelary controls.

The Constitution of 1982 was the product of the military regime of 1980–1983 (the National Security Council, NSC, regime). The military rulers of this period blamed what they considered the excessive liberalism of the 1961 Constitution for the breakdown of law and order in the late 1970s. Consequently, they set out to make a constitution that would strengthen the authority of the state at the expense of individual liberties and to create a set of tutelary institutions that would exercise strict control over elected civilian authorities. This meant a considerable narrowing down of the legitimate area of democratic politics. It has often been observed that the primary goal of the 1982 Constitution was to protect the state against the actions of its citizens rather than to protect the citizens against the encroachments of the state, which is what a democratic constitution should do.

On the other hand, it would be a simplification to blame Turkey's constitutional problems entirely on the NSC legacy. As I have tried to explain elsewhere in greater detail, deeper problems can be found in the incompatibility between the requirements of a truly liberal democracy and some of the principles of the founding philosophy of the republic (Kemalism).[4] Notably, three principles (nationalism, populism, and secularism—as understood during the single-party period) still create obstacles to the development of a genuinely liberal and pluralistic political system. Turkish nationalism, while never racist, nevertheless carried ethnic overtones. Thus, the Republican People's Party (RPP) program of the 1930s and 1940s defined the nation as a "body of people united in language, culture, and ideal." The insistence on linguistic and cultural unity and the goal of creating an extremely homogeneous society make it difficult, even today, to recognize a legitimate space for cultural and linguistic diversity and thus lie at the root of Turkey's Kurdish problem. Indeed, Turkey has been struggling since 1984 with an armed Kurdish separatist movement. A string of ethnic Kurdish parties, more or less in intimate relations with this organization, have gained representation in parliament, but all have been closed down by the Constitutional Court on account of activities endangering the territorial integrity of the country. Presently, the last in line of these parties, the Peace and Democracy Party (BDP), is represented in parliament. Obviously, this problem puts a severe strain on Turkey's efforts at democratic consolidation.

Similarly, populism as defined in this period was clearly synonymous with corporatist and solidarist ideologies that rejected class struggle and entrusted the paternalistic state with the duty of harmonizing the diverse but compatible interests of occupational groups. Another ideological principle of the RPP, statism (or *étatisme*), was seen as a method of accomplishing such harmonization.[5] Secularism was understood not as the separation of governmental and religious spheres, as in most Western democracies, but as a total way of life and a totalistic positivist ideology that aimed to consign religion solely to the conscience of individuals and to deny it a legitimate role in the public sphere.[6] As a corollary of this revolution from above, the state elites that spearheaded the Kemalist revolution have maintained a paternalistic and tutelary attitude toward civilian democratic politics, coupled with a deep distrust of civilian political actors. The Kemalist ideology and this tutelary mentality are strongly reflected in the 1982 Constitution, as will be spelled out in the following.

The 1982 Constitution is full of references to Kemalist ideology, particularly to its three pillars: Turkish nationalism, secularism, and a unitary and highly centralized state. Regarding the last, the territorial and national integrity of the state, or "the indivisible unity of the state with its territory and nation," in the words of the Constitution, is repeated sixteen times in the document. This phrase can be and has been used as a constitutional pretext against the claims for cultural recognition by linguistic, ethnic, and religious minorities, as is particularly evident in the Law on Political Parties that prohibited ethnically and religiously based parties. Commitment to secularism is equally strong: article 24 of the Constitution states that "no one shall use and abuse in whatsoever manner religion, or religious sentiments, or things deemed sacred by religion with the aim of even partially basing the fundamental social, economic, political, or legal orders of the State on religious rules or of obtaining political or personal benefit or influence."

The statist philosophy of the 1982 Constitution is also observed at a more symbolic, but no less significant, level. The preamble of the Constitution idealized the state (always spelled with a capital S) by describing it as the "sacred Turkish State" (deleted in 1995). Paragraph 2 of the preamble still refers to the "Sublime Turkish State." Also reminiscent of the solidarist-corporatist discourse of the 1930s are the terms "societal peace" and "national solidarity" referred to in the unamendable article 2.

More importantly, the 1982 Constitution's statist-solidarist-tutelary philosophy is not limited to such abstract and philosophical notions but is supplemented by a carefully designed and elaborate tutelary mechanism. Chief among these is the Office of the Presidency of the Republic. This office was designed to be impartial and above party, controlled by the state elites, with extensive supervisory powers over civilian politics. Through his broad powers of appointment, the president was expected to influence the composition of other tutelary agencies such as the Constitutional Court, other elements of the higher judiciary, and the Board of Higher Education (YÖK).

It is pertinent to remember here that General Kenan Evren, leader of the 1980 coup, had himself elected as the president of the republic for a period of seven years (1982–1989) through a procedure whose democratic legitimacy was extremely questionable. Thus, the election of the president was combined with the constitutional referendum, and a yes vote for the Constitution also meant a yes vote for Evren, the sole candidate. Evren frequently declared himself to be the guardian of the new constitution. Apparently, it was hoped that after his term of office, the new president would also be someone acceptable to the military from the Nationalist Democracy Party created by the NSC and expected to win the transition election of 1983. The unexpected electoral victory of Turgut Özal and his Motherland Party (ANAP) changed this picture somewhat, and the two presidents who succeeded Evren, Turgut Özal (1989–1993) and Süleyman Demirel (1993–2000), were civilian politicians and the leaders of their respective parties. However, the tutelary role of the president remained embedded in the constitution, and Ahmet Necdet Sezer (2000–2007), the former president of the Constitutional Court and a compromise candidate among political parties, used his tutelary powers even more often and more eagerly than General Evren, thus leading to frequent friction with both the coalition government of Bülent Ecevit and the AKP (Justice and Development Party) governments of Tayyip Erdoğan. The latter was also in constant conflict with the Constitutional Court and the Board of Higher Education, both strongly influenced by Sezer's appointments.

Another important tutelary agency is the National Security Council, first created by the 1961 Constitution but substantially strengthened in its 1982 counterpart. Before the constitutional amendment of 2001, military and civilian members were represented in equal numbers on the council, assuming that the president of the republic who presides over the council is a person of civilian background. Furthermore, under article 118 of the Constitution, the Council of Ministers had to give "priority consideration" to the recommendations of the NSC. The 2001 constitutional amendment gave civilian members a majority and underlined the advisory character of the NSC's recommendations. The amendment was accompanied by changes in other laws, particularly in that on the NSC secretariat. The net effect of these reforms was a significant degree of civilianization of the political system. Yet it is no secret that the military still enjoys much greater power and influence compared to the military in any consolidated democracy—and much beyond what the letter of the Constitution and the relevant laws suggest.

EXIT GUARANTEES

In many transitions from authoritarian regimes (particularly of the military type) to democracy, the outgoing military power holders are often able to extract important prerogatives and immunities as the price of relinquishing power to the newly elected civilian authorities. Such privileges, commonly called "exit guarantees," assure the military a significant share of political power in the coming civilian regime. Samuel Valenzuela distinguishes five types of such exit guarantees: tutelary powers (broad oversight over government in the name of "vaguely formulated fundamental and enduring interests of the nation-state"), reserved domains (removal of certain domains of substantive policy making from the purview of elected officials), manipulation of the electoral process, and irreversibility of certain actions of the military regime; and amnesty laws.[7]

Both the 1961 and 1982 Constitutions of Turkey are the textbook examples of such exit guarantees.[8] In addition to the tutelary roles of the President of the Republic and the NSC as referred to above, both constitutions (article 138 of the 1961 Constitution and article 145 of the 1982 Constitution) broadly defined the area of competence of military courts, putting all crimes committed in military premises under their competence and even allowing them to try civilians in certain cases. The constitutional amendment of 1971, again made under the shadow of the military intervention of March 12, 1971, created a High Military Administrative Court to deal with administrative disputes concerning military personnel, thus removing them from the competence of the civilian administrative court (the Council of State). The same constitutional amendment also exempted the military from the financial supervision of the Court of Accounts. Both arrangements were maintained by the 1982 Constitution. However, the constitutional amendment of 2010 somewhat restricted the competence of the military courts.

Again, both military regimes seriously manipulated the electoral process in the transition elections of 1961 and 1983, respectively. In the former, the leading cadres of the ousted Democrat Party (DP) were banned from all political activities, and in the latter electoral competition was limited to only three parties "licensed"by the NSC. Therefore, this election can be described only as a "limited-choice election." In both cases, the election of the leader of the coup (General Gürsel in 1961and General Evren in 1982) to the presidency of the republic was secured through means of extremely dubious democratic legitimacy. Furthermore, the 1961 Constitution granted lifetime *ex officio* Senate membership to the members of the ruling military council (National Unity Committee).

Finally, both constitutions (1961's Transitional Article 4 and 1982's Transitional Article 15) granted full amnesty to the members of the ruling military councils, ministers, members of the Constituent Assemblies, and all those who acted upon their orders and barred review of constitutionality over all laws and decrees adopted by the ruling military councils. Immunity from constitutional review was abolished by the constitutional amendment of 2001 and the amnesty provisions by the constitutional amendment of 2010.

The experience of other democratizing countries suggests that the removal of such vestiges of military regimes, or "exit guarantees," is not impossible in the long or even medium run. Two important and interrelated factors affecting the long-term viability of exit guarantees are the probability of a new military coup and the degree of unity or discord among civilian political forces with regard to the military's role in politics. In this sense, a credible threat of a coup fundamentally alters the expectations and calculations of civilian political actors, leading them to act in ways that detract from democratic consolidation—such as seeking alliances with the military or inviting them to intervene. The second factor is also very important, because disunity among civilian political forces over the proper role of the military gives the latter a powerful incentive to intervene in politics and to attempt to maintain or increase its political influence. Commenting on the Latin American experience, Agüero observes that, "by failing to display a united front, civilians have shown no common understanding of the obstacles which the military present for the prospects of democratic consolidation. A critical deterrent against the military, which would increase the costs of military domestic assertiveness, is thus given away, opening up civilian fissures for utilization by the military."[9]

This analysis seems to fit the present Turkish case. The complete civilianization of the regime and the elimination of other tutelary features are obstructed by a numerically not-so-large, but politically strong, coalition of civilian forces such as the main opposition party, the CHP (Republican People's Party), the Constitutional Court, and the higher judiciary, as well as an important part of the mainstream media and academia—a coalition that has been termed the "republican alliance."[10] The uniting factor is their deep attachment to the Kemalist legacy and their fear that the present governing party, the conservative AKP, may lead the country toward an Islamic regime.

Where such deep societal division exists, it is difficult to expect the normal functioning of democratic institutions. Thus, the conservative Justice and Development Party (AKP) government has had to face not only the parliamentary opposition but the opposition of many state institutions, including the former president, Ahmet Necdet Sezer (until the end of his term in August 2007), the military, the Constitutional Court, and the higher judiciary in general and, until quite recently, YÖK. Of these state institutions, the Constitutional Court deserves special attention, since in recent years it has become an active participant in the ongoing political conflict. The Turkish Constitutional Court was established by the Constitution of 1961 as one of the earliest and strongest constitutional courts in Europe. The Court was designed by the architects of the 1961 Constitution (essentially, the state elites and their representatives, the CHP) as a mechanism of self-protection against the unchecked power of elected parliamentary majorities (at that time represented by the Democratic Party). As such, it was viewed as the guardian of the fundamental values and interests of the state elites and their Kemalist ideology.[11] The 1982 Constitution, also the product of the state elites, did not significantly change the powers of the Constitutional Court.

It can be argued that in its practice, over close to a half century, the Turkish Constitutional Court has behaved essentially consistently with the expectations of the state elites that created and empowered it. In other words, it has acted as the guardian of the two basic pillars of the Kemalist ideology, the national and unitary state and the principle of secularism. In contrast to the practice in most Western states, fundamental rights and freedoms of the individuals were afforded lesser importance when they seemed in the eyes of the Constitutional Court judges to conflict with these values. A Turkish constitutionalist has described this attitude of the Constitutional Court as representing an "ideology-based" paradigm in contrast to a "rights-based"paradigm.[12]

The judicial activism of the Turkish Constitutional Court became more marked parallel to the rise of the moderately Islamist Welfare Party (RP) in the 1990s. The RP was closed down by the Constitutional Court on January 16, 1998, shortly after the so-called "postmodern coup" of February 28, 1997, forced the RP–led Erbakan government to resign, a clear manifestation of the cooperation between the court and the military. The court also closed down on June 22, 2001, the more moderate successor of the RP, the Virtue Party (FP).

When the AKP, even a more moderate successor to the FP, came to power as a single-party government with the 2002 parliamentary elections, the prosecularist activism of the court reached its peak point. While the entire period between 2002 and 2010 witnessed a series of clashes between the court and the government, the three most dramatic instances took place in 2007 and 2008. In the first, the court, depending on extremely dubious legal grounds, effectively stopped the parliamentary rounds of election for a new president of the Republic in order to prevent the election of the AKP candidate, Abdullah Gül. Interestingly, the court's ruling immediately followed a memorandum by the then-chief of the General Staff, Yaşar Büyükanıt, expressing strong concerns about the election of the president. In the second, the court, in a clear case of "usurpation of power," annulled a constitutional amendment designed to abolish the headscarf ban for female university students. Even though the Constitution (article 148) limited the court's review power over constitutional amendments only to procedural irregularities, the court argued that the amendment was against the secular character of the state referred to in the unamendable article 2 and therefore was null and void. The third and the most dramatic round was the closure case against the AKP, again based on legally flimsy and largely fabricated grounds. On July 30, 2008, the court decided not to close down the AKP, falling just one vote short of the required three-fifths majority, but to deprive it of half of the state funding for one year, arguing that it had become a "focal point of anti-secular activities."[13] In all these cases, the cooperation between the court and the military, as well as the other elements of the secularist establishment, is unmistakable.

The constitutional amendments of 2010 brought about certain important changes in this picture, by changing the composition of the Constitutional Court and of the High Council of Judges and Public Prosecutors (another institution that had acted as a "citadel" of the secularist establishment). The changes essentially diversified the sources of membership in these two bodies and gave them a more representative and pluralist character, in addition to limiting the area of competence of the military courts as referred to above.

CONCLUSION: SOME COMPARATIVE NOTES

Turkish politics in the last half century can be summarily described as a constant fight, sometimes particularly intense, between the secularist center and the more traditional and conservative forces of the periphery. The center was composed of the secularist Republican People's Party (CHP), which had ruled the country as the single party between 1925 and 1946, the military, much of the civilian bureaucracy, academia, and the mainstream media. The parties representing the periphery, on the other hand, have always won a clear popular majority in all of the sixteen general parliamentary elections since 1950. The tensions between the two fronts resulted in two full (1960 and 1980) and two partial (1971 and 1997) military interruptions, not to mention the countless more subtle forms of military interventions, often using the constitutional and legal tutelary mechanisms they obtained as "exit guarantees."

The similarities between the Turkish case and that of post-Mubarak Egypt are striking, without implying in any way that the situations in both countries are identical. In Egypt, the ongoing power struggle is between the Islamist parties (Muslim Brothers and the Salaffiyya), on the one hand, and a coalition of the military, the judiciary, and the secular sectors of the civil society, on the other—

an almost perfect replica of the "republican alliance" in Turkey. In both countries, the close cooperation between the military and the judiciary is remarkable, as attested by the cancellation of parliamentary elections by the Egyptian Constitutional Court, another example of a "judicial *coup d'état*" reminiscent of those by the Turkish Constitutional Court referred to in the previous.

A further similarity is the eagerness of both militaries to closely control and guide the transition process and to obtain significant exit guarantees that would guarantee them an important share of tutelary power in the emerging new regime. Reportedly, Egyptian military leaders had the 1982 Turkish Constitution translated and read it very carefully. It would not be a surprise if the new Egyptian Constitution were to contain many similar guarantees. The recent actions of the Egyptian Supreme Council of the Armed Forces (SCAF) creates a distinct sense of *déjà vu* for all those familiar with Turkish political developments. It should be born in mind that exit guarantees may facilitate the transition to a competitive civilian regime, but their persistence may prove to be a serious obstacle to the consolidation of democracy. As Valenzuela argues, "building a consolidated democracy very often requires abandoning or altering arrangements that may have facilitated the first transition (by providing guarantees to authoritarian rules and the forces backing them) but that are inimical to the second."[14] The Turkish experience suggests that it may indeed take a very long time to liquidate such guarantees.

Another striking similarity between the Turkish and the Egyptian cases is found in the composition and political positions of the bureaucratic secularist center and the conservative Islamic or Islamist periphery. Indeed, most authoritarian rulers in Turkey and in the Arab world effectively used the threat (real, exaggerated, or manipulated) of a fundamentalist Islamist takeover to justify their authoritarian and repressive policies. Thus, the security establishment sees even nonviolent Islamist groups as "wolves in sheep's clothing; they could try to infiltrate the state apparatus and key social sectors, gradually transforming the state from within. Once they gain power, it is feared, they will never relinquish it; their devotion to democratic principles can be expressed by the aphorism, 'One man, one vote, one time.' . . . The security apparatus sees pluralism as a Trojan horse. If the price for preempting radical Islam is the further reduction of the public sphere, so be it."[15]

The feeling of an Islamist threat also leads to a paradoxical situation in that liberal or secular opposition groups that should normally have been on the side of democratic reforms also support repressive policies against the

Islamist opposition. As Daniel Brumberg argues, the alliance between poten-tial democrats and the authoritarian rulers in the Middle East is the reverse of the political reform process in Eastern Europe. In the latter cases, the not-too-democratic elites nonetheless found democratic procedures useful for dealing with the opponents of the regime, thereby leading to a "democracy without democrats." In the Middle East, by contrast, fear of Islamist victories has produced an "autocracy with democrats," as potential democrats support or at least tolerate autocrats as a lesser evil than an Islamist regime.[16] This psy-chology explains the open or tacit support of many secular groups in Turkey, including the main opposition party CHP, for the military's and the judiciary's intrusions in politics, which they see as the ultimate guarantees against an Is-lamist threat. The June 2012 presidential elections in Egypt are also a case in point. The Muslim Brotherhood candidate Mohamed Morsi won a very nar-row victory, with about 52 percent of the vote, against Ahmed Shafiq, a general and Hosni Mubarak's last prime minister. With Mubarak's ouster and the ban-ning of the Muslim Brotherhood in late 2013, the depth of the Islamist-threat perceptions are clear, even within Egyptian civil society at large.

This dilemma seems to be the most crucial factor in determining the fate of the Arab Uprisings, as well as of Turkey's efforts at democratic consolidation. The relatively smooth progress toward consolidation in Turkey is due chiefly to the remarkable transformation of political Islam in the last decade and a half. The AKP replaced the Islamist RP as a moderate-conservative democratic party, at peace with pluralist democracy and a secular system of government. While it does not hide the fact that it is inspired by Islamic moral values, it has not attempted to weaken the secular foundations of the political system during its decade-long period of single-party government. Furthermore, the AKP appeals to a much broader segment of Turkish voters compared to the RP, as attested by its three consecutive electoral victories (2002, 2007, and 2011), each time increasing its share of votes and thus becoming a "predominant party." The AKP's program contains a strong commitment to secularism, which "allows people of all religions and beliefs to practice their religion convictions and to live accordingly but also allows people with no religious beliefs to organize their lives in their own direction. Therefore, secularism is a principle of freedom and social peace."[17]

Even though the ultra-secularist circles in Turkey are still not persuaded by the AKP's performance in government and continue to see it as a "wolf in sheep's clothing" engaged in dissimulation (*taqiyya*) with the "hidden agenda" of gradually introducing an Islamist regime, there are signs of the lessening of the intensity of the conflict in recent years. Thus, the major opposition party, the CHP, somewhat softened its militantly secularist stand and the constitutional amendments of 2010 significantly narrowed down the tutelary powers of the military and the judiciary over elected governments as stated above.

Thus, Turkey appears to be one of the few examples of a reasonably functioning, if not yet fully consolidated, liberal democracy in a Muslim-majority country. However, Turkey is not alone in this regard. There are other interesting examples in Bangladesh, Indonesia, Malaysia, and Pakistan. Vali Nasr describes these developments as "the rise of Muslim democracy." He argues that in these countries "the 'vital center' of politics is likely to belong neither to secularist and leftist parties nor to Islamists. More likely to rule the strategic middle will be political forces that integrate Muslim values and moderate Islamic politics into broader right-of-center platforms that go beyond exclusively religious concerns. Such forces can appeal to a broad cross-section of voters and create a stable nexus between religious and secular drivers of electoral politics." Nasr sees the rise of a Muslim bourgeoisie as one of the key factors in the rise of Muslim democracy, which "has emerged in societies where the private sector matters. The less state-dependent and more integrated into the world economy a country's private sector is, the more likely is that country to see Muslim democracy gain traction as a political force. Muslim democracy, in short, needs the bourgeoisie, and the bourgeoisie needs Muslim democracy. Muslim democracy combines the religious values of the middle and lower-middle classes with policies that serve their economic interests."[18]

Among the Arab Uprisings countries, Tunisia is the most likely candidate to follow suit and join the club of Muslim democracies, with its moderate Islamist party and the spirit of cooperation between it and the secular political forces. In Egypt, the long-term outcome will depend, on the one hand, on the military's willingness to recede into the role of a democratic player and, on the other hand, on Islamist groups' intention and capability to transform into moderate forces fully committed to liberal-democratic procedures—a task made extremely difficult following the removal of Mohamed Morsi and increasing bans on the Muslim Brotherhood. This is a tall order indeed for all Islamist parties in the Muslim world. But experience shows that it is not impossible to achieve. As stated in the *Economist*, "if Egypt goes wrong, then democratic progress elsewhere in the Arab world will be far slower. Egypt is not, however, doomed to return to dictatorship. Turkey, where the army has reached an accommodation with moderate Islamists, points to a peaceful way out."[19]

NOTES

1. Samuel P. Huntington, *The Third Wave: Democratization in the Late Twentieth Century* (Norman and London: University of Oklahoma Press, 1991), 13–26.

2. Arch Puddington, "Freedom in the World: Setbacks and Resilience," *Freedom House Survey Release* (2009), 27.

3. Gabriel Ben-Dor, *State and Conflict in the Middle East: Emergence of the Postcolonial State* (New York: Praeger, 1983), 18–20, 57.

4. Ergun Özbudun, "Turkey: Plural Society and Monolithic State," in *Democracy, Islam, and Secularism in Turkey*, ed. Ahmet T. Kuru and Alfred Stepan (New York: Columbia University Press, 2012), 61–94.

5. For a comprehensive study on this point, see Taha Parla and Andrew Davison, *Corporatist Ideology in Kemalist Turkey* (Syracuse: Syracuse University Press, 2004).

6. Ahmet T. Kuru, *Secularism and State Policies toward Religion: The United States, France, and Turkey* (Cambridge: Cambridge University Press, 2009).

7. J. Samuel Valenzuela, "Democratic Consolidation in Post-transitional Settings: Notion, Process, and Facilitating Conditions," in *Issues in Democratic Consolidation: The New South American Democracies in Comparative Perspective*, ed. Scott Mainwaring, Guillermo O'Donnell, and J. Samuel Valenzuela (Notre Dame: University of Notre Dame Press, 1992), 57–104. See also Huntington, *The Third Wave*, 238–40.

8. For details, see Ergun Özbudun, *Contemporary Turkish Politics: Challenges to Democratic Consolidation* (Boulder and London: Lynne Rienner Publishers, 2000), 103–16; Ergun Özbudun and Serap Yazıcı, "Military Regimes' Extrication from Politics: Exit Guarantees," in *Narod-Wladza-Spoleczénstwo* (Nation, Power, Society), ed. Alexandra Jasinska-Kania and Jacek Raciborski (Warszawa: Scholar, 1996), 325–40.

9. Felipe Agüero, "The Military and the Limits to Democratization in South America," in *Issues in Democratic Consolidation: The New South American Democracies in Comparative Perspective*, ed. Mainwaring, O'Donnell, and Valenzuela, 177.

10. Ceren Belge, "Friends of the Court: The Republican Alliance and Selective Activism of the Constitutional Court of Turkey," *Law and Society Review* 40, no. 3 (2006): 653–91. Also see Osman Can, "The Turkish Constitutional Court as Defender of the *Raison d'Etat*," in *Constitutionalism in Islamic Countries: Beween Upheaval and Continuity*, ed. Rainer Grote and Tilmann J. Röder (Oxford: Oxford University Press, 2012), 259–78.

11. Ergun Özbudun, "Political Origins of the Turkish Constitutional Court and the Problem of Democratic Legitimacy," *European Public Law* 12, no. 2 (2006): 213–23.

12. Zühtü Arslan, "Conflicting Paradigms: Political Rights in the Turkish Constitutional Court," *Critique: Critical Middle Eastern Studies* 11, no. 1 (2002): 9–25; also see Ergun Özbudun, "Judicial Activism v. Judicial Restraint and Collisions with the Political Elites in Turkey," in *Liber Amicorum: Antonio La Pergola*, ed. Peter van Dijk and Simona Granata-Menghini (Lund: Juritsförlaget, 2009), 261–70.

13. Ergun Özbudun, "The Turkish Constitutional Court and Political Crisis," in *Democracy, Islam, and Secularism in Turkey*, ed. Kuru and Stepan, 159–61.

14. Valenzuela, "Democratic Consolidation in Post-transitional Settings,"58.

15. Emmanuel Sivan, "Illusions of Change,"*Journal of Democracy* 11, no. 3 (2000): 77–78.

16. Daniel Brumberg, "Islamists and the Politics of Consensus,"*Journal of Democracy* 13, no. 3 (2002): 110–11; also see Daniel Brumberg, "The Trap of Liberalized Autocracy,"*Journal of Democracy* 13, no. 4 (2002): 56–68.

17. On the transformation of political Islam in Turkey, see William Hale and Ergun Özbudun, *Islamism, Democracy, and Liberalism in Turkey: The Case of the AKP* (London and New York: Routledge, 2010), *passim*, quotation from p. 21.

18. Vali Nasr, "The Rise of 'Muslim Democracy,'"*Journal of Democracy* 16, no. 2 (2005): 13–27, quotations from pp. 14–15, 18. See also Mustafa Akyol, *Islam without Extremes: A Muslim Case for Liberty* (New York and London: W. W. Norton, 2011), 237–44.

19. "Egypt in Peril," *Economist* (June 23–29, 2012): 13.

12

Democratic Contagion versus Authoritarian Resilience: Jordan's Prospects for Change

LARS BERGER

In early 2011, the Egyptian and Tunisian calls to fight corruption, unemployment, and political repression unleashed a frenzied debate among Jordanians about the extent to which their country would or should follow the revolutionary path. The broad-based social activism that swept the region from Rabat to Manama promised to initiate the kind of "contagion" effect that the comparative politics literature had previously used to describe regional waves of democratization in other parts of the world.

This chapter presents a critical assessment of the strategies that the Jordanian monarchy and its domestic and international allies employed in order to immunize Jordan as much as possible from the effects of political transitions occurring across the Arab world. It shows how the traditional mix of instrumentalizing the real or constructed differences between Palestinian and East Bank Jordanians, manipulating political institutions and processes, as well as successful appeals for additional strategic rents initially allowed the Jordanian regime to avoid making more than cosmetic concessions on political reform. At the same time, the following analysis will highlight the potential limits of this strategy in the face of an increasingly outspoken and diverse set of societal actors that demands robust action on the political, social, and economic challenges that Jordan shares with many of the Arab countries that experienced more profound political upheavals.

PATTERNS OF DEMOCRATIC CONTAGION:
INSIGHTS FROM THE COMPARATIVE POLITICS LITERATURE

While the ultimate verdict on the Arab Uprisings will take years or possibly even decades, its initial course has rather closely followed the pattern that the transition school of thought on democratization had detected in other regions of the world. Schmitter and Grugel, as well as Gleditsch and Ward, all saw the international environment as playing a crucial role in democratization processes, insofar as the successful example of a democratic transition in one country can establish a regional model for other societies and—after a number of them have followed suit—increase the pressure on the remaining regional autocracies to comply with the new democratic regional norm.[1] With regard to the actual process of democratization, Laurence Whitehead distinguishes three international dimensions: contagion within regional clusters through "neutral transmission mechanisms," the establishment of consent through national actors and international demonstration effects, and finally the exercise of control by an external actor through "sticks" and "carrots."[2]

A brief review of the Jordanian case shows how difficult it is for the Jordanian regime to inoculate the country from the effects of events in the wider region. First, across the Arab world, Whitehead's "neutral transmission mechanisms" are now more robust and extensive than ever before. Marc Lynch has shown how the two-decade-old rise of satellite television has brought the Arab world closer together by offering national publics more direct, albeit not always unbiased, access to news about political developments in other parts of the region.[3] This means that in Jordan, where 97 percent of Jordanian households own a TV set and 90 percent of these have satellite TV,[4] the wider public has ample opportunity to feel inspired or disheartened by the ups and downs of political reform across the Arab world. Possible evidence for the impact of regional narratives on raising the profile of political reform within Jordanian public opinion is provided in a Zogby poll conducted in late summer 2011. It showed that out of a list of eleven items, "political or governmental reform" had shot up from rank 9 in October 2005 to rank 4 in 2011 in terms of the number of respondents who chose this as their top priority.[5] Also, many Jordanian political activists described the inspiration they took from the events, particularly on Cairo's Tahrir Square, as well as their meetings with fellow Egyptian reformists.[6] Apparently, the powerful symbolism of events in Tunisia and Egypt was not lost on the Jordanian regime and its domestic allies: the "hegemonic discourse" as manifested in leading progovernment Jordanian newspapers was full of references to an orange-and-apples theory, according to which Jordan's problems could not, at all, be compared to those of prerevolutionary Tunisia or Egypt.[7]

Second, the specific slogans and concerns of the Arab Uprisings offered motifs that easily resonated with a broad spectrum of political actors within Jordan. As in Tunisia, early protests occurred in Jordan's poorer periphery and focused primarily on economic issues.[8] This is not surprising given that the Zogby poll mentioned above also showed that Jordan joined Tunisia, Egypt, Lebanon, Saudi Arabia, and Iraq as countries where the largest number of respondents saw the expansion of employment opportunities as the most important issue facing their country. As will be discussed in more detail in the following, the focus on widely shared economic grievances has significant implications as it makes it potentially more difficult for the Jordanian regime to employ the well-rehearsed game of liberalized autocracies, which relies on pitting the perceived interests of different social groups against each other.[9]

Third, the regime's financial dependence on external support should, theoretically, give international actors broad leverage. This raises the question about the extent to which the United States in particular has been prepared to, and is capable of, making use of "sticks or carrots" in encouraging or supporting political reform in Jordan. According to Whitehead, traditional means of such external efforts to prompt or promote democratization processes have included aid allocation, gestures of approval or disapproval, and utilizing existing networks of military and security ties.[10] The following will offer an assessment of the approach the United States and other international actors have adopted since early 2011 toward the Jordanian regime.

IMMUNIZING JORDAN FROM DEMOCRATIC CONTAGION: DAKHILIYA SQUARE AND THE RETURN OF IDENTITY POLITICS

While Jordan is undoubtedly exposed to the events in its immediate and broader neighborhood, those interested in maintaining the political status quo can count on a number of instruments at their disposal. Way and Levitsky posit that regime cohesion and regime scope explain why some authoritarian regimes are more resistant to contagion than others.[11] High-intensity measures such as the violent crackdown on large demonstrations resulting in deaths or the outright manipulation of elections require regime cohesion. Low-intensity measures to stifle opposition forces systematically rely on regime scope.[12] In the case of Jordan, general political disenchantment and protests have, for a long time, largely been at a level where the regime could rely on low-intensity measures to stifle and divide the opposition through selective harassment and general manipulation of the rules of the political game.[13]

According to Way and Levitsky, these more subtle measures only receive closer attention from outside actors in countries with strong links.[14] With Jordan's central role in the conflict between Israel and its Palestinian and Arab neighbors, attention from Western media and political elites has been assured. The stage thus appeared set for the kind of "moral pressure" that Risse and Ropp described as instrumental in "cascading" human-rights norms.[15] However, in Jordan, as elsewhere in the Middle East and beyond, nationalist and anticolonialist rhetoric has been quite successful in discrediting such external pressure and those local actors deemed in cahoots with it.[16] The events surrounding the failed protest at Amman's Dakhiliya Square in March 2011 demonstrated the ongoing ability of the Jordanian regime to instrumentalize national and subnational identity in an effort to cast those pursuing political reform as acting on behalf of "foreign" interests.

As mentioned earlier, it did not take long before prominent Jordanian political actors took up the revolutionary rhetoric put forward by their Arab brethren in Tunisia and Egypt. Zaki Bani Rusheid, head of the political bureau of the Muslim Brotherhood–affiliated Islamic Action Front, saw history in the making: "Tunisia's revolution is like the French. It will hit the Arab world and topple rulers in the same way the French Revolution did in Europe."[17] Murad Adaileh, a member of the Muslim Brotherhood executive committee, drew an even more direct link to events in Jordan:

> What happened in Tunisia and especially Egypt has brought a big hope—Egypt was the most secure and autocratic regime, and it fell. People's frustration is increasing because we have started to see a total alliance between the authority of the state and money, which has led to an unprecedented state of corruption.[18]

Worryingly for the regime, these views were equally prevalent among the leadership of the East Banker community, which has long been regarded as one of the central pillars of the Jordanian monarchy. In February 2011, three dozen tribesmen wrote a letter to King Abdullah II accusing his Palestinian wife, Queen Rania, of enriching herself and her family, and of holding an ex-

travagant fortieth birthday celebration in the Wadi Rum desert. Explicitly linking Queen Rania's lifestyle to that of the wife of former Tunisian ruler Zine El
Abidine Ben Ali, the tribesmen's letter claimed that "We are on the path where
the floods of Tunisia and Egypt will reach Jordan sooner or later, whether we
want it or not."[19] Their political demands were very clear: "Before stability and
food, the Jordanian people seek liberty, dignity, democracy, justice, equality,
human rights, and an end to corruption."[20] General Ali Habashna, member of
the National Committee of Military Veterans, added, "Soldiers are like other
citizens. They're also hurt by the government. Tunisia and Egypt have opened
their eyes."[21] The largely unprecedented challenge to Jordan's ruling family
stemmed from the fact that the king had been increasingly perceived as part of
the problem. Fariz Fayez of the Bani Sakher tribe, which blocked the highway
between Amman and Queen Alia International Airport in protest of the government taking over of tribal lands, said about King Abdullah II:

> [T]he situation is not the same as it was with his father. There's negligence in the
> state. He lets things go. It's like the shepherd that leaves his sheep to go astray. And
> for this reason, corruption has spread everywhere.[22]

At the same time, Marwan Muasher, an East Bank Christian from Al-Salt
who had served as Jordanian ambassador to Israel, deputy prime minister and
foreign minister, cautioned foreign observers not to mistake some of the 2011
protests with genuine calls for political reform. For him, they were more about
preserving rentier clientelism, which "over time and through entrenchment,
created monsters who will only acquiesce as long as the system perpetuates the
old policy of favors."[23]

The regime's initial reaction seemed to reflect this interpretation as the
government passed in quick succession a $169 million subsidy to lower fuel
and food prices and $422 million in further subsidies and pay rises in the civil
service.[24] While such gestures put Jordan's general budget outlook under further
strains, the focus on economic issues allowed the Jordanian regime to deflect
questions on the lack of progress on political reform. In an interview with a
Western journalist, King Abdullah II made the point that

> The Arab Spring didn't start because of politics; it started because of economics—
> poverty and unemployment. What keeps me up at night is not political reform
> because I am clear on where we are going. What keeps me up at night is the

economic situation, because if people are going to get back on the streets, it is because of economic challenges, not political.[25]

By framing it as a matter of tackling economic challenges, the regime made the protests that gathered pace from early 2011 onward appear as a re-run of the April 1989 bread riots in the Bedouin South. These set in motion a process of relative democratization whose defensive nature, however, never touched the fundamental power relationships within the country that were easily reverted to when the regime deemed it necessary for reasons related to domestic or foreign policy.[26] It was thus not surprising that King Abdullah II seemed to take a page from his father's playbook by dismissing Prime Minister Samir al-Rifa'i, son of former Prime Minister Zeid al-Rifa'i, whom King Hussein had sacked in response to the bread riots of 1989. This decision followed a long-established pattern in which the royal court seeks to set up domestic politics in a way that whoever leads any current government is viewed by political opposition and the wider public as ultimately responsible for the living standards of ordinary Jordanians.[27] Samir al-Rifa'i was an easy target for East Bank populists because of his Palestinian heritage (although both he and his father, former prime minister Zeid al-Rifa'i were born in Jordan), his private business interests, and his austerity measures aimed at the International Monetary Fund.[28] The appointment of Marouf al-Bakhit as Samir al-Rifa'i's successor was followed, shortly thereafter, by the appointment of Khalid al-Karaki as new chief to the royal court, a former royal court adviser, and expert on tribal politics.[29]

A second, somewhat related, measure was the announcement of what Abdullah II billed in a speech before parliament as a major effort to tackle corruption. This way, the regime hoped to portray itself as addressing widely shared concerns while at the same time playing to East Banker resentment of the Palestinian dominance of the Jordanian private sector. Specifically, he promised that "if there is any suspicion of corruption, an investigation should start promptly."[30] The campaign to tackle corruption reached its first climax in December 2011, when the former mayor of Amman, Omar Maani, was detained on corruption charges, and in February 2012, when Jordanian authorities arrested Mohammad al-Dahabi, the former director general of the General Intelligence Directorate.[31] At the same time, the king decides who can be investigated for corruption and who cannot. In his February 2011 speech, he had issued what could only be interpreted as a thinly veiled threat against those within the East Banker community who had dared to raise the issue of corruption among members of his family and close allies, declaring that "no one should be allowed to tarnish the image of this country with false and untrue claims."[32] The selective nature of Jordan's anti-corruption drive became apparent when Human Rights Watch reported that in April 2012 the state security court—whose two military judges and one civilian judge are appointed by the prime minister—charged two journalists with "subverting the system of government in the kingdom." Their "crime" consisted of a report on the Gerasa News Website based on sources from within Jordan's parliament that the royal court had instructed a parliamentary committee not to refer Sahl al-Majali, minister of housing in the 2007–2009 cabinet of Prime Minister Nader al-Dhahabi, to court over corruption charges.[33] According to amendments to the constitution approved by parliament in August 2011, the State Security Court's jurisdiction was meant to be limited to acts of terrorism, high treason, espionage, drug trafficking, and counterfeiting.[34]

Initially, the monarchy's tried-and-true ways of dealing with domestic disenchantment seemed to work. The dismissal of Samir al-Rifa'i left the organizers and participants of the early demonstration without a clear target to express their frustrations. A direct challenge to the king and monarchy was still a step too far for many. In addition, the king met with representatives of the Muslim Brotherhood for the first time since having ascended to the throne in 1999. With the movement thus withdrawing its organizational muscle, demonstrations started to fizzle out throughout February 2011.[35]

Unhappy with the apparent loss of momentum, an eclectic group of youth groups, leftists, liberals, and young Islamists sought to re-create the inspiring Tahrir Square scenario by launching a sit-in at Amman's Gamal Abdel Nasser Square on Thursday, March 24, 2011. The square is also known as Dakhiliyya Square after the nearby Ministry of Interior. Quickly, differences over the general tone and directions of the protest emerged between young Islamists who demanded a more proportional electoral law as well as the dismissal of the director of Jordan's main intelligence agency, the General Intelligence Directorate, and the significant number of East Bankers who were content with less drastic changes. Before the protests could gain any further domestic or, even more importantly due to Jordan's close reliance on international donors, global media attention, the regime did not prevent armed loyalists from attacking the protesters with the security forces joining in shortly thereafter. The successful attempt to clear the area resulted in one death and over one hundred injuries.[36] For some observers, the failure to create some momentum for street politics in Jordan had to be placed at the feet of the Muslim Brotherhood. A prominent East Banker supporter of genuine political reform blamed the movement for "hijacking" the "24 March movement" and charged it with attempting to monopolize the country's opposition at the expense of a potential competitor who "represents the silent majority of people who are ready to be organized."[37]

The violent end to the Dakhiliya Square protest indicated a new willingness by supporters of the old political order to employ tactics that many Jordanians had previously only known from watching TV reports about other Arab countries. Over the following months, violent thugs, also called *baltagiya* after similar groups in Egypt, were sent to attack protests by East Bankers and the Muslim Brotherhood as well as prominent journalists whose reports were deemed as too critical.[38] All this threatened to undermine a central narrative of the regime that King Abdullah II has skillfully employed in his appeals for Western material support and political patience:

> Two things make Jordan stand out. One is that we reached out to everybody and got a national dialogue committee. The other thing that made a major impact is that we have had demonstrations for the past eleven months but . . . nobody has been killed. It was a decision taken [from] day one that we disarmed all our police. In other countries . . . their solution was to pull out their guns and shoot.[39]

It remains to be seen to what extent such tactics can be successful in the long run. As long as the regime is unable or unwilling to address the demands expressed at these protests—whose root causes are, as mentioned above, largely identical across the Arab world—the regime's scope and cohesion will be increasingly tested. The beginning of 2012, for instance, saw a noticeable jump in labor demonstrations of 28 percent over the previous year.[40] In prerevolutionary Egypt, such events set the stage for the eventual mass demonstrations in the immediate lead-up to Hosni Mubarak's fall from power.

NATIONAL DIALOGUE AND CONSTITUTIONAL REFORM: LIMITED CHANGE FROM ABOVE

With the immediate threat of self-sustaining demonstrations at the Egyptian or Bahraini level dissipated, the Jordanian regime could engage in the usual game of making bold promises of political reform, co-opting relevant regime and opposition figures in a drawn-out process of dialogue, and finally delivering "reform" that does not change in any significant way the fundamental power structure of the state.

Here, the Jordanian regime relied on sources of influence that many other types of authoritarian regimes in the region and beyond cannot muster. This has to do with a particular combination of monarchical legitimacy and rentier clientelism. Russell Lucas sees Morocco and Jordan as exhibiting a particular sub-type of authoritarianism. In what he describes as "linchpin" monarchies, the ruling family concentrates on participating in the immediate institutions of the monarchy while keeping a distance from daily politics.[41] As Lisa Anderson put it at the beginning of the drawn-out process of negotiating political change in the post–Cold War Arab world, "The ability of a monarch to appeal to traditions, albeit often invented, to reassure the existing elite, to rely on his own kinsmen— perhaps even to hobnob with international bankers and ride horseback with presidents—is useful indeed."[42] In the context of the Arab Uprisings' ramifications increasingly engulfing and affecting Jordan, the question arises as to how long the ruling family can continue to rely on these long-established patterns.

Following his February 2011 government reshuffle, King Abdullah set out a program of reform that was meant to revamp the electoral system based on a new "comprehensive dialogue." Many Jordanian observers remained skeptical with regard to what the newly established "Committee on National Dialogue" could actually deliver.[43] Marc Lynch's summary of the Jordanian proclivity for dialogue under King Hussein apparently also applies to his son: "The king decides, but Jordan deliberates."[44]

It thus did not come as a surprise when the constitutional amendments passed in August 2011 upon recommendation by a ten-member panel chosen by the king fell short of expectations. While the establishment of a constitutional court, an independent commission to oversee elections, and the limitation of the jurisdiction of the State Security Courts were enough to attract favorable international comparisons with the constitutional reforms in Morocco, they did not address the fundamental expectation of a more equitable political representation for the different segments of Jordanian society nor the desire by many to see the country move toward a constitutional monarchy.[45]

One of King Abdullah's major promises of reform related to the electoral system. In his February 2011 speech he declared it to be his objective "that competition for Parliament takes place among parties and on the basis of programmes."[46] It is precisely this weakness of political parties that is a hallmark of liberalized autocracies in Jordan and elsewhere.[47] In Jordan, this phenomenon can be traced back to the 1956–1957 government of nationalist prime minister

Sulayman Nabulsi. King Hussein's "palace coup" by means of imposing martial law discredited membership in political parties. This explains why according to data from the Jordan Center of Social Research (JCSR) poll 98.3 percent of Jordanians had never been members of a political party.[48] The weakness of Jordan's political parties is ultimately also the result of an election law that was based on a single nontransferable vote in heavily gerrymandered multicandidate electoral districts. The 2010 electoral law did not take up the recommendation by the committee that drafted the 2005 National Agenda to introduce a measure of proportionality to help national parties grow and to counter mobilization along tribal lines. According to a 2007 survey conducted by the Center for Strategic Studies at the University of Jordan, half of all voters still based their voting decisions on tribal allegiances.[49] Jordanian elections are thus, in Ellen Lust's words, a mere "mechanism for the distribution of patronage that reduces demands for change."[50] One of the biggest beneficiaries of a system of proportional representation would be the Islamic Action Front. According to IAF deputy Abdullah al-Akaylah, such a system would produce "deputies of the nation, not deputies of the neighborhood or tribe."[51] For some Jordanians, talk about proportional representation is part of a deliberate US–led attempt to serve perceived Israeli interests; the "US agenda is to increase Palestinian representation in Jordan to lift pressure on Israel and to solve the Palestinian issue at expense of Jordan."[52]

Such concerns make the emergence of the National Front for Reform (NFR) all the more important. The NFR combines prominent Islamists, such as leading IAF figures Hamza Mansour and Zaki Bani Rusheid, leftists, East Bankers, and Palestinians. It is led by Ahmad Obeidat, former prime minister, head of intelligence, chairman of the National Charter Commission of 1990, and leading proponent of the anti-normalization drive with Israel in the 1990s. He made no secret of his views regarding the close link between high levels of corruption in Jordan and the lack of genuine democracy: "Tyranny and corruption are Jordan's main problems. Fighting corruption starts with reforming the regime itself."[53]

The NFR proposed a system in which half the seats would be elected based on proportional representation and the other half through a bloc vote at governorate level.[54] The bloc-vote system had already been used in the 1989 elections when the IAF did very well. It gave voters the same number of votes as seats allocated to an electoral district. Demonstrating flexibility, the Islamic Action Front supported the NFR proposal.

With rising popular and parliamentary opposition to Prime Minister Marouf al-Bakhit—who increasingly became the focus of corruption allegations himself—the king decided in October 2011 that it was time for another change in government.[55] In a clear sign of how important it was for King Abdullah II to portray at least a sense of reform, he chose to appoint Awn Shawkat al-Khasawneh, a judge at the International Court of Justice and former chief of the Royal Court, to be the new prime minister. The appointment of al-Khasawneh was regarded as a positive step by the Muslim Brotherhood, who nevertheless did not take up the offer of positions with the new government. Still, the king was able to recruit Salim Zoubi, a member of NFR's executive committee, as minister of Justice in al-Khasawneh's government.[56] One positive result of Al-Khasawneh's outreach was the decision by the Islamic Action Front to indicate its readiness to return to electoral politics by participating in the next parliamentary elections.[57] Ultimately, however, Awn Shawkat Al-Khasawneh's tenure as prime minister will be remembered for its brevity, ending with an unexpected resignation in April 2012, and for the presentation of an electoral law that fell significantly short of the expectations of Jordan's reformers. The new electoral law gives each citizen three votes, two for district candidates and one for national lists. The number of seats reserved for women is increased from twelve to fifteen. A limit on national lists to contest a maximum of five seats and an amendment to ban religion-based political parties were seen as direct affronts by the Muslim Brotherhood and its political arm, the Islamic Action Front.[58] All this threatens to undermine the initial cautious optimism that the Jordanian regime appeared to have engineered among the broader Jordanian populace with its carefully managed, top-down approach to limited political reform. According to Zogby International, an astounding 78 percent of respondents of a poll undertaken in September 2011 indicated their satisfaction with overall pace of change in government. In this context, the Jordanian regime also began to benefit from a changing international environment.

MOBILIZING EXTERNAL SUPPORT

The Jordanian regime benefited in multiple ways from the Arab Uprisings' eventual crisis. First, the escalation of conflicts in Libya and Syria drove home for many Jordanians the dramatic consequences that political change in ethnically or otherwise divided countries could bring about. Second, the deteriorating conditions in many parts of the Arab world made stability in the crucially-located

Jordan all the more important for many regional and international donors. Once again, Jordan's rulers could turn the country's perceived weaknesses into an income-generating asset. Just like the "dynastic monarchies" of the Gulf, Jordan enjoys the support of foreign patrons who help maintain the patronage networks that often mark "Sultanistic" and "Neopatrimonial" regimes[59] and the well-financed security apparatuses that, for a long time, served as important safeguards of autocratic stability in many Arab countries.[60]

For a regime that relies to a considerable extent on the successful pursuit of external rents,[61] 2011 was marked by what some local observers described as King Abdullah's frequent "begging trips" to Gulf and Western capitals.[62] With the specter of an escalating regional upheaval engulfing Jordan, many observers pointed out how Jordan's regime benefited from the country's perceived centrality to the interests of powerful regional and external actors.[63] The convergence of interests among the Arab world's monarchies found temporary expression in the invitation extended to Jordan and Morocco, the only remaining Arab monarchies outside the Arabian peninsula, to join the Gulf Cooperation Council thereby turning the group into a "club of monarchies." In his ultimately successful courtship of GCC rulers, King Abdullah II benefited from his smooth relationship with the ruling family in Riyadh, who appreciate the fact that he does not appear as expansionist or competitive in vying for a broader regional clout, as was his father, King Hussein, or grandfather, King Abdullah.[64] At the same time, the Arab Gulf monarchies are using their financial clout and influence to nudge the Jordanian regime away from its traditional tendency to keep all strategic options available. Some observers, for instance, linked the lack of speed with which the Arab Gulf monarchies are fulfilling their $5 billion aid package with an attempt to force Jordan to give up its initially relatively neutral position toward Syria with which it had trade ties totaling $600 million in 2011 and toward adopting a more forceful approach in confronting the regime of Bashar al-Assad.[65] Jordan already helped GCC regimes safeguard their strategic interests by sending Special Forces trainers and UAE–supplied weapons to the Yemeni regime and by allegedly sending security personnel to assist the Bahraini regime in crushing the country's protest.[66]

Syria's escalating crisis also has a number of direct implications for Jordan. It is thus not surprising that in the 2011 Zogby poll mentioned above Jordan is the country where the largest share of respondents affirmed their close interest in the events in Syria (80 percent), thereby trumping even Syria's other neighbor Lebanon (78 percent) and clearly distancing Saudi Arabia (61 percent) and Egypt (42 percent).[67] By June 2012, Jordanians (89 percent) were on par with Egyptians (89 percent) and Tunisians (88 percent) in their insistence that Bashar al-Assad had to stand down.[68] Out of those who supported the idea of Bashar al-Assad stepping down, 38 percent of Jordanians supported an Arab military intervention to achieve this as opposed to 41 percent who hoped for more sanctions to do the trick and 10 percent who even supported Western military intervention.[69] Some local observers worry that the fall of Assad could embolden calls for a wholesale change of the political system in Jordan.[70] Others suggested that the events in Syria could undermine unity within the Jordanian opposition. On the one hand, the Muslim Brotherhood has come out more strongly in support of the uprising in Syria. According to Ryan, there are also a considerable number of leftists who, on the other hand, still harbor sympathies for Bashar al-Assad for his perceived credentials as a major anti-Israel and anti–US figurehead and appear concerned about the specter of Islamist successes in the wake of the Arab Uprisings.[71]

The escalating conflict in Syria has made Jordan yet again a preferred destination of a major wave of refugees. On the one hand, this put enormous pressures on the country's already strained resources. On the other hand, the Iraq War had shown how Jordanian authorities are ready to instrumentalize the plight of refugees by translating inflated numbers into generous financial support from international donors.[72] According to Rakan Majali, a spokesman for the Jordanian government, eighty thousand Syrian refugees had fled to Jordan between the beginning of the Syrian uprising until March 2012. In contrast, Panos Moumtzis, the Syria coordinator for the UN High Commissioner for Refugees, only spoke of thirty thousand Syrian refugees across Jordan, Lebanon, and Turkey in the same period.[73]

While the European Union's February 2012 promise of three billion euros in aid over three years was certainly welcome,[74] Jordan's most reliable foreign support has come from the United States. Here, King Abdullah II has benefited from the perception of being a pro-Western monarch who is keen on reforming his country while safeguarding overall stability. It was widely reported that the United States preferred the current king over then–Crown Prince Hassan due to the former's perceived greater closeness to the United States.[75] This is why President Obama is even reported to have told King Abdullah II, "Your Majesty, we need to clone you."[76] Some US observers thus feel prompted to warn against pressing for greater democratization in Jordan. Even before the onset of the Arab Uprisings, Terrill argued in favor of a "Jordanian go-slow approach to democracy" in the face of the "limited pragmatism" a suggested Palestinian majority in

Jordan was supposed to be exhibiting.[77] In their practical application, US policies toward Jordan closely followed such views. So far, USAID funds for Jordan have never been withheld on the basis of unfulfilled conditionality. From 2004 to 2007 only 4 percent of US development assistance was used for democracy and governance assistance, mostly for the toothless parliament.[78] In September 2008, the United States pledged to provide $660 million in foreign aid per year over a five-year period, $300 million of it reserved for military aid. Almost half of the $360 million annual economic aid comes as a direct cash transfer, which Jordan uses to service its foreign debt.[79] Military aid, in particular, is dismissed by reformers as not contributing to the urgently needed development of the country and instead helping to maintain long-held practices of corruption.[80]

CONCLUSION

On the surface, the Jordanian regime weathered the initial fallout of the democratic contagion that had begun to spread across the Arab world in early 2011 by applying tried-and-true strategies of material handouts meant to address immediate economic pains across wide sections of the Jordanian populations, of promises and gestures of gradualist political reform and, finally, of instrumentalizing real or perceived differences between Palestinian and East Bank Jordanians.

At the same time, the long-term outlook for Jordan's stability hinges on a number of factors closely related to the three dimensions of immunizing Jordan's authoritarian political structures from democratic contagion that could easily turn the country into another hotspot of political upheaval.

At the level of international support, Jordan, clearly, is not a rentier state with the kind of resources that Saudi Arabia and other GCC countries enjoy. The government might thus eventually reach a breaking point over its efforts to accommodate the economic demands of East Bankers and other constituencies. While the narrative of Jordan's strategic importance makes it likely that foreign donors might come to the rescue, it is not a foregone conclusion that the regime will be as successful in adapting to economic shocks as during the early 1990s.[81] Its ongoing reliance on foreign support in addressing its budgetary woes also makes Jordan dependent on continuity in the strategic calculus of its foreign funders. A reassessment of US strategic priorities in the Middle East or domestic upheaval in GCC countries could leave Jordan's finances dramatically exposed.

Domestically, the regime benefits from the perception that Jordanians have more to lose in a revolution than in a gradual, albeit unsatisfactorily slow, political reform. This is because many Jordanians still consider themselves to be better off and less homogeneous than their Egyptian counterparts. Revolutionary upheaval is thus seen as threatening the living standards of many aspiring middle-class Jordanians and as bringing the country closer to the civil-war scenario playing itself out in similarly heterogeneous Syria.[82] Increasing instances of violence as well as the apparent rise of radical ideologies such as "Salafism" have clearly undermined the demonstration effect that proved crucial in democratic contagion processes in other regional contexts.

Ultimately, there is the chance that Jordanians will put their differences aside and follow the example set by Egypt where the years leading up to the revolution of February 2011 saw various constituencies from workers to Islamists and secular liberals launching their independent, apparently unthreatening, demonstrations only to ultimately converge under the shared banner of change at the very top. Of crucial importance is the future direction of support from East Bankers, whose representatives are increasingly willing to directly take on the regime and the king in their criticism. As General Ali Habashna put it, "for Jordanians, the Hashemite family used to be a sacred issue. But now it's the issue. If there is no real political reform and no economic change, I think people will explode one day."[83]

ACKNOWLEDGEMENT

I thank the Council for British Research in the Levant for the generous support of field research in Amman in November and December 2010 and April and May 2011.

NOTES

1. Philippe C. Schmitter, "The Influence of the International Context upon the Choice of National Institutions and Policies in Neo-Democracies," in L. Whitehead (ed.), *The International Dimensions of Democratization* (New York: Oxford University Press, 2001), 26–55. Jean Grugel, "Contextualizing Democratization: The Changing Significance of Transnational Factors and Non-state Actors," in Grugel, J. (ed.), *Democracy without Borders: Transnationalisation and Conditionality in New Democracies*, (London: Routledge, 1999), 3–22. Kristian Skrede Gleditsch and Michael D. Ward, "Diffusion and the International Context of Democratization," *International Organization* 60, no. 4 (Fall 2006): 911–33.

2. Laurence Whitehead, "The Three International Dimensions of Democratization," in Whitehead (ed.), *The International Dimensions of Democratization: Europe and the Americas* (Oxford: Oxford University Press, 2001), 3–25.

3. Marc Lynch, "Political Science and the New Arab Public Sphere," *Foreign Policy* (June 12, 2012), accessed June 14, 2012, http://lynch.foreignpolicy.com/posts/2012/06/12/political_science_and_the_new_arab_public_sphere. Marc Lynch, *Voices of the New Arab Public: Iraq, Al-Jazeera, and Middle East Politics Today*, (Columbia University Press, 2005).

4. Rana F. Sweis, "Jordanians Debate Role of Press," *New York Times* (September 14, 2011), accessed 24 March, 2014, http://www.nytimes.com/2011/09/15/world/middleeast/jordanians-debate -role-of-press.html?pagewanted=all.

5. James Zogby, "The Attitudes of Arabs 2005," *Arab American Institute* (November 7, 2005), accessed May 11, 2005, http://www.aaiusa.org/reports/attitudes-of-arabs-2005. James Zogby, "Political Concerns and Government," *Zogby Research Services* (November 2011), accessed May 11, 2012, http://aai.3cdn.net/2212d2d41f760d327e_fxm6vtlg7.pdf .

6. Interviews, Amman, April and May 2011.

7. See, for example, op-eds in *Al-Rai* newspaper on January 15 and 16, 2011; interviews, Amman, April and May 2011.

8. Nicolas Pelham, "Jordan's Balancing Act," *Middle East Review Online* (February 22, 2011), accessed July 14, 2011, http://www.merip.org/mero/mero022211. "Dallying with Reform in a Divided Jordan," *International Crisis Group*, Middle East/North African Report No. 118 (March 12, 2012).

9. Daniel Brumberg, "Sustaining Mechanics of Arab Autocracies," *Middle East Channel* (December 19, 2011), accessed June 14, 2012, http://mideast.foreignpolicy.com/posts/2011/12/19/sustaining_mechanics_of_arab_autocracies. Daniel Brumberg, "Liberalization versus Democracy, Understanding Arab Political Reform," *Carnegie Endowment for International Peace*, Democracy and Rule of Law Project, No. 37, (May 2003), accessed June 26, 2012, http://carnegieendowment .org/files/wp37.pdf.

10. Laurence Whitehead, "The Three International Dimensions of Democratization," in Whitehead (ed.), *The International Dimensions of Democratization: Europe and the Americas* (Oxford: Oxford University Press, 2001), 3–25.

11. Lucan A. Way and Steven Levitsky, "The Dynamics of Autocratic Coercion after the Cold War," *Communist and Post-Communist Studies* 39, no. 3 (2006): 387–410.

12. Ibid., 392.

13. Ellen Lust-Okar, "*Structuring Conflict in the Arab World: Incumbents, Opponents, and Institutions*" (Cambridge: Cambridge University Press, 2005).

14. Way and Levitsky, "The Dynamics of Autocratic Coercion after the Cold War," 393.

15. Thomas Risse and Stephen C. Ropp, "International Human Rights Norms and Domestic Change: Conclusions," in T. Risse, S. C. Ropp, and K. Sikkink, eds., *The Power of Human Rights: International Norms and Domestic Change* (Cambridge: Cambridge University Press, 1999), 234–78.

16. Jon Alterman, "The False Promise of Arab Liberals," *Policy Review*, no. 125, (2004), accessed June 26, 2012, http://csis.org/files/media/csis/pubs/false_promise_of_arab_liberals.pdf.

17. Pelham, "Jordan's Balancing Act."

18. Kim Murphy, "In Jordan, King Abdullah II Getting Earful from Tribal Leaders," *Los Angeles Times*, February 24, 2011, accessed March 24, 2014, http://articles.latimes.com/2011/feb/24/world/la-fg-jordan-tribes-20110225.

19. Ethan Bronner, "Tribesmen in Jordan Issue Urgent Call for Political Reform," *New York Times*, February 7, 2011, accessed March 24, 2014, http://www.nytimes.com/2011/02/08/world/middleeast/08jordan.html.

20. Ibid.

21. Pelham, "Jordan's Balancing Act."

22. Kim Murphy, "In Jordan, King Abdullah II Getting Earful from Tribal Leaders," *Los Angeles Times*, February 24, 2011, accessed March 24, 2014, http://articles.latimes.com/2011/feb/24/world/la-fg-jordan-tribes-20110225.

23. Marwan Mu'asher, "A Decade of Struggling Reform Efforts in Jordan, the Resilience of the Rentier System," *Carnegie Endowment for International Peace*, The Carnegie Papers, (May 2011), accessed July 19, 2011, http://www.carnegieendowment.org/files/jordan_reform.pdf, 4.

24. Sean Yom, "Don't Forget about Jordan: A Regime Caught between Contagion and Consent," *Foreign Policy*, February 2 2011, accessed June 20, 2012, http://mideast.foreignpolicy.com/posts/2011/02/02/don_t_forget_about_jordan_a_regime_caught_between_contagion_and_consent?hidecomments=yes.

25. Lally Weymouth, "Jordan's King Abdullah on Egypt, Syria and Israel," *Washington Post* (October 25, 2011), accessed March 24, 2014, http://www.washingtonpost.com/opinions/jordans-king-abdullah-on-egypt-syria-and-israel/2011/10/24/gIQAejhRDM_story.html.

26. Glenn E. Robinson, "Defensive Democratization in Jordan," *International Journal of Middle East Studies*, 30:3, (1998), 387–410.

27. Scott Greenwood, "Jordan's 'New Bargain': The Political Economy of Regime Security," *Middle East Journal*, 57, no. 2 (March 2003), 256–57.

28. Pelham, "Jordan's Balancing Act."

29. Jeremy Sharp, "Jordan: Background and U.S. Relations," *Congressional Research Service* (April 21, 2011), accessed July 18, 2011, http://opencrs.com/document/RL33546/2011-04-21/, 2.

30. Abdullah II, "Address by His Majesty King Abdullah II to Heads and Members of the Executive, Legislative and Judicial Authorities," *Embassy of the Hashemite Kingdom of Jordan* (February 20, 2011), accessed May 12, 2012, http://www.jordanembassyus.org/new/jib/speeches/hmka/hmka02202011.html.

31. "Dallying with Reform in a Divided Jordan," *ICG*, MENA Report No. 118 (March 12, 2012): 4.

32. Abdullah II, "Address by His Majesty," February 20, 2011.

33. "Jordan: Publisher, Journalist Charged in State Security Court," *Human Rights Watch* (April 25, 2012), accessed May 15, 2012, http://www.hrw.org/news/2012/04/25/jordan-publisher-journalist-charged-state-security-court.

34. "Dallying with Reform in a Divided Jordan," *ICG*, MENA Report No. 118 (March 12, 2012): 22.

35. Interview with liberal activist, Amman, April 2011.

36. "Dallying with Reform in a Divided Jordan," *ICG*, MENA Report No. 118 (March 12, 2012): 3.

37. Interview, Amman, April 2011.

38. "Dallying with Reform in a Divided Jordan," *ICG*, MENA Report No. 118 (March 12, 2012): 8, 14.

39. Weymouth, "Jordan's King Abdullah on Egypt, Syria and Israel," *Washington Post* (October 25, 2011).

40. "Labour Protests Increase in First Quarter of 2012," *Jordan Times* (April 8, 2012), accessed June 21, 2012, http://jordantimes.com/labour-protests-increase-in-first-quarter-of-2012-report.

41. Russell Lucas, "Monarchical Authoritarianism: Survival and Political Liberalization in a Middle Eastern Regime Type," *International Journal of Middle East Studies* 36 (2004): 108.

42. Lisa Anderson, "Absolutism and the Resilience of Monarchy in the Middle East," *Political Science Quarterly* 106, no. 1 (Spring 1991): 15.

43. Interviews, Amman, April 2011.

44. Marc Lynch, *State Interests and Public Spheres: The International Politics of Jordan's Identity* (New York: Columbia University Press, 1999), 24.

45. Sean Yom, "Don't forget about Jordan"; Sean Yom, "Jordan Goes Morocco," *Foreign Policy* (August 19, 2011), accessed August 23, 2011, http://mideast.foreignpolicy.com/posts/2011/08/19/jordan_goes_morocco.

46. Abdullah II, "Address by His Majesty," February 20, 2011.

47. Vickie Langohr, "Too Much Civil Society, Too Little Politics: Egypt and Liberalizing Arab Regimes," *Comparative Politics* 36, no. 2 (January 2004): 181–204.

48. Quoted in Andrew W. Terrill, "Jordanian National Security and the Future of Middle East Stability," *Strategic Studies Institute* (Carlisle, PA: January 2008), 75, EN 43.

49. Ellen Lust, "Competitive Clientelism in the Middle East," *Journal of Democracy* 20, no. 3, (July 2009): 127.

50. Lust, "Competitive Clientelism in the Middle East," 122.

51. Russell E. Lucas, *Institutions and the Politics of Survival in Jordan: Domestic Responses to External Challenges, 1988–2001* (Albany: State University of New York Press, 2005), 107.

52. Interview, Amman, April 2011.

53. "Islamists, Leftists Unite Over Jordan Corruption," *Al-Ahram Online* (June 2, 2011), accessed June 20, 2012, http://english.ahram.org.eg/NewsContent/2/0/13469/World/0/Islamists,-leftists-unite-over-Jordan-corruption.aspx.

54. "Dallying with Reform in a Divided Jordan," *ICG*, MENA Report No. 118 (March 12, 2012).

55. Christina Satkowski, "Fragile Hopes for Jordan's New Prime Minister," *Foreign Policy Middle East Channel* (October 24, 2011), accessed June 21, 2012, http://mideast.foreignpolicy.com/posts/2011/10/24/fragile_hopes_for_jordan_s_new_pm.

56. "Dallying with Reform in a Divided Jordan," *ICG*, MENA Report No. 118 (March 12, 2012): 20.

57. "Dallying with Reform in a Divided Jordan," *ICG*, MENA Report No. 118 (March 12, 2012): 4.

58. Rana F. Sweis, "Jordanian Vote Reform Vexes Brotherhood," *New York Times* (March 18, 2012), accessed March 24, 2014, http://www.nytimes.com/2012/04/19/world/middleeast/jordanian-vote-reform-vexes-brotherhood.html.

59. J. Brownlee, ". . . And Yet They Persist: Explaining Survival and Transition in Neopatrimonial Regimes," *Studies in Comparative International Development* 37, no. 3 (Fall 2002): 35–63. Richard Snyder, "Paths Out of Sultanistic Regimes: Combining Structural and Voluntarist Perspectives," in ed. H. E. Chehabi and J. Linz, *Sultanistic Regimes* (Baltimore: Johns Hopkins University Press, 1998), 49–81.

60. E. Bellin, "The Robustness of Authoritarianism in the Middle East: Exceptionalism in Comparative Perspective," *Comparative Politics* 36, no. 2 (January 2004): 139–57.

61. Laurie A. Brand, "*Jordan's Inter-Arab relations: The Political Economy of Alliance Making*" (New York: Columbia University Press, 1994).

62. Numerous interviews, Amman, April 2012.

63. Numerous interviews, Amman, April 2012.

64. Curtis Ryan, "'Jordan First': Jordan's Inter-Arab Relations and Foreign Policy under King Abdullah II," *Arab Studies Quarterly* 26, no. 3 (Summer 2004): 45.

65. Josh Wood, "Effects of Instability Spill Over to Syria's Neighbors," *New York Times* (March 7, 2012), accessed March 24, 2014, http://www.nytimes.com/2012/03/08/world/middleeast/effects-of-instability-spill-over-to-syrias-neighbors.html?_r=0.

66. Michael Knights, "Could the Gulf States Intervene in Syria?" *Washington Institute for Near East Policy*, Policy Watch no. 1929 (April 17, 2012), accessed May 16, 2012, http://www.washingtoninstitute.org/policy-analysis/view/could-the-gulf-states-intervene-in-syria; Pelham, "Jordan's Balancing Act."

67. James Zogby, "Arab Attitudes towards Syria," *Arab American Institute*, accessed March 24, 2014, http://aai.3cdn.net/c3bd1500d778d87ac7_ism6b92b1.pdf, 3.

68. "Widespread Condemnation for Assad in Neighboring Countries," *Pew Research Center*, Global Attitudes Project (June 21, 2012), accessed June 21, 2012, http://www.pewglobal.org/2012/06/21/widespread-condemnation-for-assad-in-neighboring-countries/.

69. Ibid.

70. Interview, Amman, April 2012.

71. Curtis Ryan, "Identity and Corruption in Jordanian Politics," *Foreign Policy, The Middle East Channel* (February 10, 2012), accessed May 16, 2012, http://mideast.foreignpolicy.com/posts/2012/02/09/identity_and_corruption_in_jordanian_politics.

72. Nicholas Seeley, "The Politics of Aid to Iraqi Refugees in Jordan," *Middle East Research and Information Project 256* (Fall 2010), accessed July 14, 2011, http://www.merip.org/mer/mer256/politics-aid-iraqi-refugees-jordan.

73. Rana F. Sweis, "Jordan Girds for Influx of Syrian Refugees," *New York Times*, March 21, 2012.

74. "Dallying with Reform in a Divided Jordan," *ICG*, MENA Report No. 118 (March 12, 2012): 26.

75. Russell Lucas, "Monarchical Authoritarianism: Survival and Political Liberalization in a Middle Eastern Regime Type," *International Journal of Middle East Studies* 36 (2004): 128; Terrill, "Jordanian National Security and the Future of Middle East Stability," 65.

76. Jillian Schwedler, "Jordan's Risky Business as Usual," *Middle East Research and Information Project* (June 30, 2010), accessed May 12, 2012, http://www.merip.org/mero/mero063010.

77. Terrill, "Jordanian National Security and the Future of Middle East Stability," 66–67.

78. Anna Mariel Peters and Pete Moore, "Beyond Boom and Bust: External Rents, Durable Authoritarianism, and Institutional Adaptation in the Hashemite Kingdom of Jordan," *Studies in Comparative International Development* 44 (July 2009): 275, 279.

79. Jeremy Sharp, "Jordan: Background and U.S. Relations," *Congressional Research Service*, (April 2011), accessed July 18, 2011, http://opencrs.com/document/RL33546/2011-04-21/.

80. Inteview, Amman, April 2011.

81. Rex Brynen, "Economic Crisis and Post-rentier Democratization in the Arab World: The Case of Jordan," *Canadian Journal of Political Science* 25, no. 1 (March 1992): 69–97.

82. Sarah Tobin, "Jordan's Arab Spring: The Middle Class and Anti-revolution," *Middle East Policy* 19, no. 1 (Spring 2012): 96–109.

83. Liz Sly, "In Jordan, Growing Discontent Over Pace of Reform," *Washington Post* (May 7, 2012), accessed March 24, 2014, http://www.washingtonpost.com/world/middle_east/jordans-stability-in-doubt/2012/05/06/gIQANINa7T_story.html.

13

Remaking the People: The Arab Uprisings and Democratization

Larbi Sadiki

[I]n the site of *faragh*, the notion of incommensurability of different readings cedes to that of inter-textuality. That is, discursive practices are never independent of each other and that they can speak to each other, making dialogism possible. *Faragh* then is the realm of continuously searching for provisional synthesis in an ongoing contestation between thesis and antithesis. Thus an ethos of democracy becomes embodied in power being permanently maintained as a place of absence—one without fixed and singular power holders.[1]

There are always highs and lows on any learning journey. However, it is the people and the epistemic communities we encounter through colearning, dialogues, discussions, and classrooms that create the greatest memories—and hopefully intellectual sparks. This chapter provides a kind of "meditation" along with some reflection on this cascading change commonly referred to as the "Arab Spring" or "Uprisings." No other event has rocked the Middle East region to its foundation as much. Its impact making equals the discovery of oil in Iran (1908) and Saudi Arabia (1938), the founding of Israel in 1948, Egypt-Israel Camp David Accords (1979), the Declaration of Principles (1993), 9/11 (2001), and the sacking of Baghdad (2003). Many Arabs are validated in thinking that only in-dependence from the yoke of colonialism shares historical parity with the Arab Uprisings of 2011. Both represent emancipatory moments separated by decades of postcolonial misrule by indigenous elites of which the likes of Ben Ali, Mo-hamed Hosni Mubarak, and Muammar Gaddafi were quintessential examples of dictators swept from power by the 2011 protest movements—unprecedented politically in the Arab Middle East (AME). Hence a good departure point is to contextualize as well as reflect on the still-unfolding fervor spawned by the "Arab Spring"—not as yet possessing the hindsight of historical *longue durée*.

Hence, I shall depart from terra firma, first, by offering a number of general observations concerning the pre–Arab Uprisings state of play in the AME. In so doing, I am hoping to tease out some creative thinking about the cascading of "peoplehood" in the context of the Arab Uprisings—or whatever term is fitting in reference to these cataclysmic sociopolitical events. There is so much in terms of general character and specificity on display across the Arab Upris-ings' geography or space. It is a compelling and at the same time challenging task, which seeks to disclose whatever "knowing" is possible. Partly, I am guided by the curiosity of an avid student of Arab democratic transitions. I am also partly motivated by the sense of wonderment and intellectual excitement that the study of this tsunami-like event is bound to induce. This in no small part relates to the sheer diversity of the "Arab Spring"; being the total sum of several "springs," some are yet to bloom, others are yet to flourish, and others which may arrive in the future.

INTRODUCTION: THE ARAB MIDDLE EAST AND TRANSITOLOGY

The nature of research confronting "transitology" in the AME calls for attention. It is a line of inquiry intended to privilege local knowledge—that is, to speak and write back, seeking to project an indigenous perspective. Similarly, it is an attempt to interrogate the dogmas of Euro-American theories of democratic transition. The idea is to enter into some kind of dialogue with dominant ap-proaches—namely, those that tend to over-state the Arab "state" and understate society. In a nutshell, the aim is to focus on society and explore how its various agents go about carving out a space for democratic struggles in the AME.

The Problematic/Problematique

The space I am concerned with is hypothesized in terms of democratic *faragh*, or "void," as noted in the epigraph. It is within this void that the renegotiation of *power* takes place in the AME. The hegemon—that is the "over-stated Arab state"[2]—has historically invested itself with all the attributes of power (coercive, financial, legal, tribal, ideological, informational, social, etc.). It has left society with little shared space for normalizing state-society relations and even less space for societal contests of state power. Since its emergence into territorial existence, the Arab postcolonial state's design of this brand of statecraft fulfills what might be called "total politics," the practice of "totalizing" political activity, hindering the rise of potentially rival centers of power—that is, a state with a notable blind spot: the "void of power." This is where society strikes back to invent the vocabulary of self-recognition and self-existence, as well as the attendant thought practice congenial to speaking back and responding to the hegemon. Therein lies the promise of negotiating the democratic *void*. In the ongoing struggle to populate the void of power, potentially and sometimes actually, Arab societies seek to convert the "void of power" into the "power of the void." In every retreat/absence by the state, there emerges the potential for advancement/presence by society, as if (state) "zero-power" equates with (societal) "positive power," at least potentially.

Thus the challenge in the enterprise at hand is twofold:

1. To reinterpret democratization as a space or realm of "in-between" space within which power is neither competitive nor measurable by conventional means.
2. To unpack and grasp the problem of transition by redesigning the "problematic" of politics, within an Arab setting, in order to think about the boundaries within which people subvert and sabotage power. To my mind, one key specificity integral to the practice of Arab politics is bottom-up struggles and attendant capacity to unmake power (as opposed to make power) as a constant feature of long-standing struggles to unhinge authoritarianism. The examples are legion (Sudan, 1985; Algeria, 1988; Egypt, Libya, and Tunisia, 2011).

This is one possible route to considering nonconventional forms of democratic mobilization and struggles from below. To this end, my approach, still in its infancy, is seeking to elaborate a critical and novel account of power as "non-power"—that is, first, as a void where the centralized body politic of the authoritarian state is corroded by nonconventional centrifugal forces and, second, as atomization and subsequent dispersion of power (from the retreating state to the advancing society), thus creating multiple viable spaces. These spaces are potentially reclaimed by a brand of noncompetitive civic bodies whose objectives are acquiring civic and ethical tool kits for enacting democratic struggles rather than competing for office or occupation of the state through conventional channels. To an extent, this is one possible reading of the Uprisings of 2011 that shook the rigid and emerging dynastic political system in three states—where clear ousters took place—to its foundation.

CONTEXTUALIZING POLITICAL ORGANIZATION: DISSOLUTION

One key idea advanced here is that the postcolonial political organization that preceded the Arab Uprisings was too ossified to be able to remedy irreversible incorrigibility and irreparability. Integral to political organization was the absence of serious safety valves that allowed society channels of venting anger. "Explosion" was a matter of time. In December 2010, a Tunisian fruit vendor, Mohamed Bouazizi, became the trigger. Thus, any narration of the context of the Arab Uprisings would be incomplete without accounting for the state of political organization in the pre–Arab Uprisings political setting, as argued in the following.

Students of politics in the Arab setting are presented with key challenges when addressing the state of political organization. There are two intertwined reasons for this. First, political organization must be accounted for in a context quite distinctive from that found in consolidated democracies, as well as newer democracies of the type that have evolved from second and third waves of democratization as explicated by Huntington.[3] In these settings, political democratization has benefited from longer stints of nation- and state-building as well as struggles that enabled civic bodies to carve out a margin of existence, generally functioning as a bulwark against the state and partaking in competitive politics. Second, by and large, from an anthropological perspective, the actual communal or societal framework within which the structure of politics takes shape is itself subject to different types of loyalty, agents, regulation, allocation of resources, and value assignment. In the AME, the organization of politics is complicated not only by authoritarianism[4] but also by deep-rooted primordial practices, making status, influence, input, leadership, and distribution in the realm of power among "citizens" within any given Arab organized political community almost irreversibly unequal. In fact, the meaning of politics, as put succinctly by Lasswell nearly eighty years ago, "who gets what, when, how," may be handicapped by the absence of fair rules of engagement and rule of law that engender equal citizenship.[5] Michels contends that even under consolidated

democratic regimes where political organization is established and professional-
ized, oligarchical tendencies do not completely disappear.[6] There is no politics
without organization. When organized, politics facilitates the business of government, framing it in ways that democratizes leader-citizen and state-society
relations. Thus it renders the whole political vocation of "who gets what, when,
how" more subject to norms of equality, transparency, accountability, and legality. Political organization is in some readings assumed to have the potential to
"be a source, in many cases and in many ways, of democratization."[7] That is, all
institutions that advance democracy by way of facilitating processes conducive
to the practice of politics pertain to the realm of political organization, which
exists in both democratic and nondemocratic systems. Specifically, in this chapter political organization refers to all institutions and units that belong either to
political society or civil society, governmental and nongovernmental, competitive and noncompetitive, local and national, formal and informal, top-down and
bottom-up, as part of pressure or interest networks, advocacy work or political
parties, and which by virtue of function are integral to the overall political process in a given state. The example of political parties is relevant here since they
are motivated by both narrow interests (for example, competing for high office
and seats in parliament) as well as national and collective goals articulated in
political programs and agendas. The chief observation to make here is that political organization contributes to the overall performance of a political system
and is itself informed by the nature of a given polity in terms of separation of
power, freedom, discipline, legality, and professionalism, and so on. These are
not features that exist in the majority of political systems in Arab MENA states,
both before and after the emergence of the Arab Uprisings. As for democracy,
the chapter uses Huntington's conventional and minimalist definition whereby
he classifies a given political system as democratic when "its most powerful collective decision makers are selected through fair, honest and periodic elections
in which candidates freely compete for votes and in which virtually all the adult
population is eligible to vote."[8] Implied within this definition is the set of civil
and political liberties needed to facilitate not only the practice of politics in general but also the electoral process.

Political Organization: Old Problems in the Pre–Arab Uprisings Setting

Almost invariably across boundaries of geography, history, local culture, and
levels of development, Arab political systems are mapped out onto postcolonial
imagined communities that have artificially grown out of two brutal historical

undertakings. Initially, colonizers vacated the center of power only to bequeath it to new sets of oppressive orders, which were hierarchically organized and centralized: tribe or clan, liberation guerrillas (for example, Algeria), so-called "free officers" (examples are Egypt, Yemen, etc.), and single-party entities. In all of these formulations, power ended being reconfigured through "national mentors" who in essence were tribal leaders (for example, Ibn Saud), army generals (in the cases of Nasser, Gaddafi, Ali Abdallah Salih), or demagogues (for example, Bourguiba). Thus, politics did not require the development of shared values, democratic norms, rules governing competition, and participation in politics. Nor did the very notion of power sharing emerge as part and parcel of the "cake of civic culture" underpinning political organization.[9] The common denominator, with varying degrees, is that of leadership acting as a national mentor. What might not be generalizable, as far as these assumptions go, is the degree and source of legitimacy that determine the nature of political leadership. Here claims can be made for and against the degree of and type of "charisma" a given leader possessed. In this context, Ibn Saud relied on a brand of traditional charisma in which tribal genealogy coupled with preference for an Islamized polity and performance legitimacy (founder of the state) helped his rise to power. The inheritors of his throne varied in terms of charisma and reputation as credible leaders (for example, King Faisal due to Pan-Arabism and Pan-Islam). Nasser's political feats in nationalizing the Suez and mounting a sustained political rhetoric noted for anticolonial (including guardianship over the Palestinian cause) and Pan-Arab substance helped solidify his stranglehold over the reins of power. Gaddafi, Saddam, and the Assads, more or less, followed suit. In North Africa, the "supreme combatant," the self-designated honorific title Bourguiba, trained as a lawyer in France during the 1940s, used to mark out his distinct political identity, pandered to notions of moderation, rational Islam, and gradual decolonization coupled with association with Western norms of development, humanism, and secular politics. Politics in the AME was reproduced as an exclusive bastion for the demi-gods whose largely self-centered tendencies left no room for society to create space for *contre-pouvoir*–type forces to emerge, much less contest power and the sets of legitimacy that evolved in the newly independent Arab states. Across the board, the organization of politics in the new realms was detrimental to the rise of rival centers of power that could, potentially and autonomously, organize, compete with, and contest politics unhindered. Struggles, however, for the creation and empowerment of civil society in most Arab states were continuous. Arabs were not passive toward authoritarian rule. Yet civil society never was allowed to grow unhampered by coercion and state intervention.[10]

From an anthropological perspective, Arab political systems tend to be "hybrid." They are at once centralized and decentralized. For, as centralized political configuration, they include primordial units such as tribes and clans and concomitantly have a measure of decentralization built within them as a result of the emergence of states and new types of leadership, which in theory, at least, suggest the introduction of "legal-rational" dimensions as opposed to "personalist" or "traditional" attributes of power and leadership. The common denominator, however, across both traditional (for example, Gulf states) and nominally legal-rational political systems is degrees of tradition and "modernization" combined in the crafting of states and the "imagining of communities" for the greater part of postcolonial political history. Put differently, and at the expense of oversimplification, tradition is thus subjected to degrees of modernization, and modernization is not fully engineered without reference to tradition (clan and tribe, religion, and other forms of primordial association). No contextualization of political organization in the Arab setting would be complete without accounting for this peculiar dynamic that tends to inform Arab politics even after the 2011 Uprisings.[11] Note the rise of religion-based political identities and the extent to which they have thus far shaped the quest for postauthoritarian politics in countries such as Egypt, Tunisia, Libya, Yemen, and Syria. In particular, one peculiarity must be flagged. Even the process of modernization of politics in republican political systems such as via the creation of political parties was itself reconfigured by reliance on quasi-traditional modes of leadership. The postcolonial fashion was to invent states, anthems, flags, and the institutions emblematic of power with little regard to modes of legitimacy.[12] Yet the very act of refashioning new polities meant that organization of power, much less its distribution, never measured up to the rigor of due process, merit, democratic competition, decentralized management, and dispersion of power and responsibility. Accordingly, political parties ended up being "mass mobilizational," the constituencies of which were primordially selected—rather than elected—the "brother-leader" (for example, the late Colonel Gaddafi of Libya), the omnipresent leader (Nasser, Sadat, etc.), and the like—Tunisia's "president for life" (the late Habib Bourguiba). The center—as the quintessential example of "*makhzen*-ite" repository of all power—amassed within it the means of coercion, providence or distribution, and propaganda. To invoke Weber, it was not only "monopoly over the legitimate use of force" that defined polity, it was also, and more importantly, monopoly of the legitimacy to organize politics that have throughout postcolonial history defined state-society relations.

What actually took place, under these zero-sum-type political arrangements was that the mass-mobilizational party partially supplanted tribe and clan where these were weakened (but not totally eliminated) such as in Arab republics (Egypt and Tunisia being very good examples); in Yemen and Libya this allowed for the interplay of tribal affiliation and political association. Tribe and clan, in these instances, became subject to patronage-clientelism practices, with their incorporation in politics limited to provision of loyalty—in exchange for fiscal benefits, other goods such as land or business concessions, and nonmaterial favors, especially recruitment into the military, security, and the bureaucracy as a whole. To accrue these benefits, these primordial entities had to surrender one thing: the right to autonomous political organization. Political parties, arguably political units of legal-rational nature, were oddly enough divested of any agency, much less legal rights, to act as independent actors. Furthermore, they too were engulfed in the overall primordial practices that framed the contours of the political game. Politics was far from what it is intended to be as conceptualized in Western systems: "who got what, when, how" took a different meaning in which neither contestation and participation, nor accountability and rule of law (all of which are associated with the practice of democracy), were intended to be normative under such systems. The center's ideology, too, secular and religious, was treated as sanctimonious, open neither to debate nor to contest. The vagaries of so-called "Bourguibism" (that is, gradual development, moderation, and the Western alliance), "Nasserism" (or so-called Arab socialism, Pan-Arabism, and decolonization), and Gaddafi's *jamahiriyyah* (republic of the masses) never produced their intended goals. More importantly, the political systems that emerged under the auspices of these rigid regimes turned out to be hindrances to the deepening of contestation and widening of participation and, most importantly, to the civic infrastructure amenable to a brand of competitive, participatory, and inclusive political communities. Those who came after Nasser and Bourguiba in Tunisia, for instance, improved on the inherited systems but only just to serve legitimation exigencies. Once in full control, as proven by Sadat, then Mubarak in Egypt, and Ben Ali in Tunisia, they reverted to consolidation of singular political practices that only selectively allowed for a margin of existence for dissidents and opposition on the whole.[13] Political organization improved mostly to respond to local and global demands for reform; but reform was not strategically adopted as serious policy preferences. They were tactics deployed for political survival, never devoid of patronage and clientelism, coercion, and primordial tendencies as dynastic politics intervened with all aspects of political organization ranging from recruitment into the state and polity to law making.[14] Statecraft across the Arab Middle East features practices inimical to good government.[15]

"DE-IMAGINING COMMUNITY": THE ONSET OF THE ARAB UPRISINGS

The linchpin of the postcolonial hegemonic order in the AME is the "total state."[16] "De-imagining" marks the onset of speaking back to the hegemon, striking back, as it were, at the state. From Haenel, in Schmitt's interpretation, we find a distinction between the "universal state" and the "total state." The former derives its mission from law and acts as one organization of many within a given society but is distinguished by its ability to rise above them for the purpose of being everyone's state. It is charged with "delimiting and organizing socially effective forces" according to the spirit of the law.[17] According to Haenel, a total state, by contrast, has the potential to exercise power in order to make "all social goals of society its goals,"[18] and this he opposes. Accordingly, and in reference to the AME, the brand of total state is one that has largely engaged society through its ambition to occupy the entirety of the field of political action, from the management of theater and football to defense-policy design. To this end, it has deployed various instruments (ranging from coercive to distributive and discursive) exclusively guarding politics as a narrow and closed bastion, thus inhibiting the rise of public arenas for the habituation of society into the skills and ethics of citizenship.

As the exclusive bastion of the few, the brand of "imagined community" that has been produced for the enactment of politics through nation- and state-building in the AME has been subject to ongoing and fierce contests. The resulting imagined community has not been all-embracing and universal in the exercise of "power over." It has relegated to a secondary class of citizenship its minorities and dissidents and even its own members who have sought to act through unimpaired free choice and voluntary judgment in many instances throughout the AME. In essence, the imagined community of the ruling few has grown unaccustomed to all forms of autonomous checks by society or legally sanctioned rival projects of imagined communities.

The fierce contests against the hegemonic imagined communities of the Arab Middle East within the realm of the void allow for imagined communities in reverse. That is, they signal the onset of the de-imagining of the existing hegemonic imagined communities, seeking their overthrow for being parochial, private-public, privatized, and primordialized while still claiming a universal nationhood of sorts and for inhibiting free choice in the exercise of "power over." To restate Benedict Anderson,[19] nations or communities are imagined through a number of processes:

1. Deprimordialization, that is, the "imagining" or "inventing" of a community, supersedes kinship ties and close knowledge and association of a clan or tribe. Hence, "all communities larger than primordial villages of face-to-face contact . . . are imagined."[20] Anderson notes how the "image of communion" is maintained in territorially vast and populous nations, and this happens not through close contact or informal ties but, rather, happens and "lives" in "the minds" of a given nation's members.[21] The syllabus, the media, and the myths erected to celebrate nationalism all contribute to the imagining and confirming of "imagined communities."

2. As for nationalization of identity and belonging, imagined nations pander to nationalist "ethnocentricity." As Anderson puts it, the image of communion is inevitably exclusionary of imagined otherness—of other nations, or for that matter, of humanity as a whole. "The most messianic nationalists do not dream of a day when all the members of the human race will join their nation in the way that it was possible, in certain epochs, for, say, Christians to dream of a wholly Christian planet."[22]

3. Concerning dedivinization of the newly imagined nations and states (owing to the ascendance of Enlightenment and revolutionary rationality, as Anderson points out), it is within the precincts of nations and territorial self-identification and imagining that religions seek their own brand of "communion" with God, as if the imagined state is a new quasi-transcendental in its own right, not in need of rival deity.[23]

4. Indeed, having dedivinized religion, the new Enlightenment-based rationality mythologized and sacralized the imagined nationalist community (a "fraternity" or association of compatriots) as a "deep, horizontal comradeship" to die for in the name of patriotism. Once recruited to the imagined community, passions take over. Self-sacrifice becomes a further baptism of patriotism, adding to the image of communion. Anderson is baffled by the firm grip imagining a myth, and dying for it holds as part of the imaginings of the edifice that is imagined nationalism. For its sake, it has been "possible, over two centuries, for so many millions of people not so much to kill as willingly to die for such limited imaginings."[24]

The imagining of the postcolonial community or nationhood has more or less followed a similar trajectory in the AME. The itinerary of the power bidders and new occupiers of the postcolonial state have, from day one at the helm, set out to dismantle primordial association and symbols of identification and anchors (and even arms in many instances) in the name of centralization and modernization. The passing of a type of traditional correctness after the postcolonial era has also relegated religion to a secondary role. Literally, to use Eric Hobsbawm's phrases, the age of postcolonialism has been at once an "age of revolutions" (by free officers, Pan-Arabists, secularists, and eventually Islamists) and of "extremes"[25] (national versus tribal, modern versus traditional, universal versus parochial, etc.). The new rallying myths through which the newly born imagined communities are to be mediated exalt the state and loyalty to its center. Patriotism has demanded loyalty, sacrifice, and modern rationality, as opposed to the rationality of religion and tradition. Just as socialism and social justice during this time furnish additional rallying myths, imperialism and backwardness lace the imagined communities' official transcripts with antitheses, necessary "enemies" to rally newly nationalized identities around the center.

Anderson's four processes that have collectively constructed and entrenched the imagined community are more or less coming unstuck. Rather, and more precisely, they were witnessing reversal, in varying degrees, throughout the AME prior to the eruption of the Arab Uprisings. Such a reversal signaled retreat in the original pristine aura and awe of nationalism. The multitude that once substituted nation for tribe, clan, family, or other primordial association is today having second thoughts. Many do already join the swelling march back from the imagined community and toward the protection, certainty, and the anchorage of these primordial associations. When the Baathist imagined community collapsed in Iraq, there were surviving sanctuaries within which counter-imagined communities could be constructed post–Saddam Hussein. In Yemen, the center's neverending duals with peripheral counterimaginings of imagined communities that embrace tribe, sect, and unruly activism (al-Qaeda) are chipping into the already limping nation-state. From Sudan to Somalia, similar manifestations are evident in various corroding imagined communities in the AME.

Briefly, prior to the Arab Uprisings, there was profusion from below of voices and forces with their own projects to de-imagine the existing imagined communities beset by the rot of moral void. Religion has been back as one source feeding counterimaginings of community. Again, this is a reversal of the process of dedivinization that coupled the rise of imagined nations in the modern era.

Perhaps nothing has reified it more than the failure of the project of modernity constructed on the pedestal of imagined community. Copts, Shiites, and Sunnis are turning in droves to faith. In the democratic moment, the intersection of the profane and sacred gives birth and nurtures liminal identities. Religious symbols, dictums, and metaphors intermingle with democratic language, infusing it with nuance. The return of religious verities seeps into politics through maverick, populist, popular, and charismatic challenges to the status quo.

These processes worked in tandem, giving anger and revolution simmering below the surface the facade, as it were, to catalyze the deluge of peoplehood and of rebellion that changed the face of politics and history. In the Arab public squares, what was rehearsed was the reinvention of peoplehood—without which neither state, democracy, nor democratization make sense. The power of the void received its most eloquent expression in the public squares. The peoples spoke and willed (*al-sha'ab yureed*) the downfall of the system (*eskaat al nazam*). They spoke as if to declare vows of enactment, of birth.

THE POST–ARAB UPRISINGS DYNAMIC: REMAKING THE "PEOPLE"

The Arab Uprisings: Enacting Empowerment

To aver that the Arab Uprisings have dealt a blow to Orientalism and Western paradigms of transitology is no exaggeration. In looking at the civility of the Arab Uprisings—values of participation, organization, mobilization, expression, and self-governance—one finds ample evidence of how the Arab Uprisings have forced contestation over how the AME has been studied by scholars of democratic transition. A look at the nexus of public space and politics in enacting people power in the revolutions of 2011 in Egypt and in Tunisia helps illustrate this.

From Cairo through Libya to Tunis, the central squares developed by the postcolonial authoritarian states' urban planners—named after political icons or iconic historical events—were part and parcel of a form of sociopolitical engineering aimed at defining the territory of power and largely of state holders. Tahrir (Liberation) Square and the *mugamma'* edifice[26] adjacent stood centrally as powerful reminders and symbols of centralized power and of the Egyptian state's authoritarian-bureaucratic clout. Tahrir as liberation is a powerful idiom that conveys messages of historicity as well as legitimacy. The *mugamma'* was the one inevitability the majority of the Egyptian citizenry could not avoid: it housed the huge bureaucracy producing their legal personas and paperwork for the construction of their identities. Under the control of autocrats, the *mugamma'* had effectively—as its name in Arabic denotes—been the collective unifying repository through which Egyptian citizenry is filtered, as if the very conception of "Egyptianness" could not be imagined outside the Interior Ministry's labyrinth of windows and clerks that formed the bureaucratic mill inside the *mugamma.'* That link to the Interior Ministry was a thread that "shackled" the collective psyche to fear of both state power and the over-bureaucratization that served as an additional device of control over the citizenry and the construction of Egyptian identity since the Free Officers' takeover in 1952.

In Tunisia, the capital's central boulevard, at the end of which stood the Interior Ministry's massive building, was named after the country's postcolonial leader and national mentor, the late Habib Bourguiba. Like him, the boulevard his urban planners named after him was an example of how the politics of space was never innocent. Bourguiba and the space—the squares, gardens, memorials, libraries, and streets—all represented value-laden signifiers of power.[27] They stood for an Ataturk-like brand of nation and state building inspired by the former colonial metropolis, Paris. Thus, following the bloodless coup of November 1987, the first thing his successor did was to rename the squares, often deleting "Habib Bourguiba" to cede to the new administration's politicosocial engineering label "7th of November," supposedly a symbol and idiom of the ousted dictator's "New Deal"—a deal that never was. The Habib Bourguiba Boulevard survived the architectural purge that saw the redesigning and relabeling of public space. Like in Cairo's Tahrir, the Interior Ministry stood as an eyesore in the Bourguiba Boulevard, a powerful reminder of the police state Ben Ali and his henchmen had built over twenty-three years of authoritarian rule. Like the *mugamma',* it evoked fear as well as indignation. It is this indignation that proved resourceful and momentous in both countries' protests in January and February of 2011.

So what is the relevance of the dimension of space in the politics of civic resistance in Cairo and Tunis in 2011?

The Tunisian and Egyptian protesters contested regime monopoly over the control, use, and manipulation of public space. When the Tunisian protesters began their build-up of a critical mass, they had first to reclaim the space the state claimed as its own, the hub of its centralized authority, as a physical edifice and politicomoral authority. A critical mass was needed to reoccupy the geography of the authoritarian state and the terrain from which it organized the lives of the citizenry. Just as the authoritarian state had purged the citizenry from the terrain on which it pitched, designed, diffused, and sustained the reproduction of its authority, the citizenry had to recover that terrain and redesign it as its own in order to navigate it as a new topography of mass resistance against state hegemony. And just as the state had purged the citizenry from its geography of power, the protesters had to purge the state from that very space. That space was thus converted into forums for mass organization and mobilization. It is within the precincts of that space that a new imagining of community and democratic politics was made possible by the protesters in both Egypt and Tunisia. The space was literally transformed from authoritarian space into popular space and reorganized into forums for democratic reticulation and displays of solidarity. Universal messages of rejection of authoritarianism were designed and rede-signed and communicated through the use of all kinds of techniques, ranging from new national anthems to communal prayers and marches. The critical mass of protesters turned the central public spaces—squares, for instance—into "gymnasiums" of civic activism in which the citizenry sharpened both its skills of anti-systemic protest and its appetite for democratic politics through sustained and creative mass protest. Thus, the masses in Egypt and Tunisia were able to reinvent themselves by contesting the authoritarian state's politics and programs openly. Ultimately, this is what led to the transformation of former spaces of reified state authority into public space for reenacting popular sovereignty and collective reownership of the state. In these reclaimed spaces—Tahrir Square in Cairo and the Habib Bourguiba Boulevard and the Kasbah in Tunis—the fight against authoritarianism was concretized, built into a critical mass, and defiantly sustained to yield eventually the tipping point that brought the authoritarian structure completely unstuck.

The transferable value of the exploration of the dimension of space as an an-gle on the Arab Uprisings is today evident in Syria. Thus far in neither Damascus nor Aleppo have protesters reclaimed public space such that they can directly display solidarity and resist hegemony through collective, direct, participatory action. This limits their ability to render the state unable to act or offer accept-able responses. Were public spaces to be reclaimed as they were in Tunisia and Egypt, the public resolve, now focused in a space it claims as its own, could shift from the former politics of accommodation with the state to total defiance and rejection of authoritarianism. In Libya, the rebels also felt the need to occupy Gaddafi's compounds and "Green Square"—which they renamed "Martyrs' Square"—in order to claim possession of their revolt and realize a kind of politi-cal closure in the wake of the overthrown political order.

One can see, then, that a critical dimension of the Arab Uprisings has been the protesters' claim over and creation of public space. Egyptians, Libyans, Tunisians, and Syrians have sought to remake both the moral and the physical worlds in which they want to thrive as free citizens. They came together to dismantle the physical worlds framed by the powers that be to restrict their potential as free agents. In the protesters' agency to change their physical world lie hints at the spatial implications of the Arab Uprisings as a potential geography of dissent, free politics, and good government.

Under authoritarianism, space and its architecture was geared toward reproduction of subjection and control. The Arab Uprisings challenged this order. By reclaiming public squares, the peoples in Egypt, Libya, and Tunisia reenacted peoplehood by reclaiming the spaces of tyrannical rule, breaking all barriers of fear, and redesigning space into a realm of *res publica*—where the public breathes life into ossified politics. More importantly, they reconciled[28] psychological space (feeling free again, reclaiming citizenship through protest and rejection of tyranny) with architectural space: Thus Gaddafi's Green Square ceded to Martyrs' Square and Tunisians unofficially, then officially, renamed many public boulevards Bouazizi Place. In doing so, they have opened up endless possibilities for self-mastery and sociopolitical spheres of freedom and dignity. Ultimately, this is a matter of political organization—that is, democratic political organization in the age of the Arab Uprisings.

TOWARD DEMOCRATIC POLITICAL ORGANIZATION?

The transition from the periphery to the center, from rebellion to formal organization and from revolution to statecraft, will remain for some time subject to conjecture. Indeed, the marginal of yesteryear seem to converge upon the center, vie for power, organize to contest it and hold it. Occupying a square and ousting a regime is not the same as occupying the state and steering the state democratically—that is, filling the void of power as the old structures of political organization collapses like a house of cards. Nonetheless, in the context of the Arab Uprisings and their aftermath, the outlook for political organization remains mixed.[29] Hence there is a need for nuanced analysis and assessment. In Egypt after the July 3, 2013, coup and counterrevolution, which ousted the elected president, Mohamed Morsi, and has taken measures to ban the Muslim Brotherhood, one of the main politically organized parties in the country, political organization may be said to be reverting to old practices typical of the authoritarian period under Nasser, Sadat, and Mubarak. The constitutional amendments suggested by the Supreme Council of the Armed Forces (SCAF), under the auspices of its chief, Abdel Fattah el-Sisi, do not encourage optimism about the prospects of political organization benefiting from supportive democratic and legal protection in the foreseeable future. Of the countries that have formed part and parcel of the Arab Uprisings' élan, only Tunisia, which has gradually, despite initial difficulties and divisions, progressed toward democratization, has moved to renew the legal basis in a way that should after the 2014 elections solidify political organization, making it responsive to the challenges of a fledgling democracy. Libya is far from coming near to anything conducive to strengthening political organization as the country's security worsens, plunging both polity and society into a state of uncertainty. More importantly, Libya's political organization faces an old problem, and the new challenge after the ouster of Gaddafi in 2011, of primordial association. As witnessed either in the political alignments, including in the 2012 elections or in the interregional divisions, clan and tribal identity is featuring as a major hurdle for equal and democratic political organization. In the Libyan context, such an identity has emerged both as a rallying cause that draws and frames parochial loyalty (for example, the internecine fighting between Warfalla, Zintan, and Misrata, among other tribes), and an organizing forum that attracts voters (voter behavior was informed by tribal, and even regional, loyalty).

As political organization concerns the very business of managing politics in a way that equalizes between citizens regardless of other personal forms of identity and notions of belonging, democratization in all of the countries hoping to democratize their systems following the 2011 Uprisings calls for laws that immure recruitment to office, regulation, distribution of power, and welfare goods by the state from sanguine and regional considerations. *Rentier* states (where rent of a single commodity, oil or gas, is the mainstay of the economy) are noted still for distribution that takes into account not only need but also tribal lineage.[30] This is where constitution framing is expected to make a difference to these processes in the Arab Uprisings' region. In this respect, Libya is trailing behind Egypt and Tunisia. However, the challenges facing the latter two are of a different nature. In the former, the army remains the most resourceful and most organized institution whose current return to power will discriminate against political forces opposing SCAF and its preference for a democratic reconstruction without the Muslim Brotherhood and religious morality as an organizing political factor. In Tunisia, there is a huge religious constituency that envisions a role for religion in politics—supporters of the moderate Islamist party, al-Nahda, and the Salafis, who have only recently experienced organized politics and legal status. Ideology on the opposite side by leftists and liberals remains undecided or hostile to mixing religion and politics. Inevitably, political organization is expected to experience a degree of ideological tension. If pushed too far, the implications for political organization could be serious, especially if ideology becomes itself reason for exclusion. In the "New Tunisia," where democracy is expected to take root, the government of the day, whether Islamist, leftist, or liberal, will be elected and therefore given a mandate to execute laws and propose them, regulate, and distribute power and goods. Like in any other country, the legal setting—and there are different trajectories as can be gleaned from Egypt and Tunisia—will determine whether discriminatory loopholes become mechanisms for ideological officers of the state to exclude foes and reward allies. Democracy and democratization are learning processes, and Tunisia will have to undergo this experience by narrowing the gap between ideal and practice. Mistakes or limitations in any incipient democracy are part and parcel of the democratic learning process. Political organization itself is subject to consolidation and improvement before fully equal citizenship becomes the norm that universalizes rights—irrespective of primordial ties or ideological color. It is true that the Arab Uprisings states are more qualified than other Arab MENA states to see tangible gains in terms of political organization. However, disappointingly, there are still hurdles that will hamper political equalization for certain segments such as minorities (in need of group rights and perhaps constitutional protection) and women (note how even the parity law of 2011 in Tunisia did not produce parliamentary parity, but the principle itself is worthwhile the effort).[31, 32]

CONCLUSION

The Arab Uprisings provide material for questioning the modes of essentialism intrinsic to Western approaches to understanding the Arab Middle East.

Historically, policy makers and scholars have tended to treat the AME, more or less, as an "empty space" in relation to democratization. Modes of pre–Arab Uprisings political democratization, management, and distribution of power seemed to corroborate the narration of the region's politics. Post–9/11, the gist of the reform "tool kit" packaged to the region—such as under the Greater Middle East Initiative—has tended to place a premium on changing the way the AME "thinks" and "knows." In this framework, when "West" meets "East," contrast and difference reign. The West is privileged as the sole source of all knowledge and knowing of democracy. The East, or Orient, is paired with the West only for the convenience of constructing opposing images. The Orient is invented to highlight and celebrate, by way of contrast, what the West is and is not. In such mirror images the "non-West" is marginal to rationality, peripheral to theory, and on the sidelines of knowledge making. Most representations of the Arab Middle East, generally, expose the persistence of this line of thinking. This glaring omission within the wide field of transitology reveals the prejudicial position of the Occident as the "knower" of democracy.

Discussion of the popular empowerment and civic engagement in the public squares in which the Arab Uprisings' own vitality was and continues to be forged shows how the Arab Uprisings are facilitating the profusion from below of civil dynamism that defies and triumphs against authoritarianism. As a new dynamic that repudiates the generalization and reductionism in the study of the Oriental other, the Arab Uprisings provide new opportunities not only in the realm of direct democracy, political organization, and re-creation of community but also in the sphere of political knowledge. For they introduce dynamics, practices, and thought that are bound to revise Orientalism, including prejudicial democratic transitology that has written off the Arab Middle East as a region of political passivity if not absence of active peoples endowed with democratic verve, passion, or much less know-how.

Good government is a good in and of itself: acquired knowledge leads to virtuous government according to the great minds of Arabo-Islamic philosophy. Notions of the common good are to be developed as the movement from the "Cave" to the outside world occurs. Knowledge accompanies this movement when the individuals who have been in the Cave venture out into the world and begin the process of the acquisition of democratic knowledge, the instrument of empowerment of the people. Time and space are needed for those individuals to gradually acclimatize to this new world. One may posit that democracy is of the same nature: a cultural universe needs to develop wherein protagonists can identify and explore a new world of senses and perceptions in the present unhindered by the false illusions and tyranny of the past. For now, the people cascade has exploded into a fountain of light, extinguishing some of the darkness of the authoritarian era . . . in Tunis, Cairo, and Tripoli. In these spaces, the peoples have spoken, restoring a degree of sovereignty and self-mastery to realms of res publica and people's politeia. May the Arab Uprisings keep shining . . . and cascading peoplehood.

NOTES

1. Larbi Sadiki, *The Search for Arab Democracy: Discourses and Counter-discourses* (New York: Columbia University Press, 2004), 90.

2. Nazih Ayubi, *Over-Stating the Arab State: Politics and Society in the Middle East* (London: I. B. Tauris, 1995).

3. Samuel P. Huntington, *The Third Wave: Democratization in the Late Twentieth Century* (Norman: University of Oklahoma Press, 1991).

4. *Authoritarianism* is succinctly defined here as forms of exclusionary power that happen under either secular or traditional rule across the Arab geography and is additionally noted for near or total absence of competitive, representative, and accountable politics. Moreover, when elections take place as was the case in countries such as Egypt, Tunisia, and Yemen before the 2011 ousters, they did not result in democratic government. This notion is described as a form of "electoral fetishism." See Larbi Sadiki, *Rethinking Arab Democratization: Elections without Democracy* (Oxford: Oxford University Press, 2009).

5. Harold D. Lasswell, *Politics: Who Gets What, When, How* (New York: McGraw-Hill, 1936).

6. See Robert Michels, *Political Parties: A Sociological Study of the Oligarchical Tendencies of Modern Democracies* (Kitchener: Batoche Books, 2001).

7. John D. May, "Democracy, Organization, Michels," *American Political Science Review* 59, no. 2 (1965): 417.

8. Huntington, *The Third Wave*, 1–30.

9. Gabriel Almond and Sydney Verba, *The Civic Culture: Political Attitudes and Democracy in Five Nations* (Boston: Little, Brown, and Co., 1965).

10. Augustus R. Norton, "The Future of Civil Society in the Middle East," *Middle East Journal* 47, no. 2 (1993): 205–16.

11. Roger Owen, *State, Power and Politics in the Making of the Modern Middle East* (London: Routledge, 2000).

12. Michael Hudson, *Arab Politics: The Search for Legitimacy* (New Haven: Yale University Press, 1977).

13. For reference on the Tunisian example, see Larbi Sadiki, "The Search for Citizenship in Bin Ali's Tunisia: Democracy versus Unity," *Political Studies* 50, no. 3 (2002): 497–513.

14. For a comparative analysis of dynastic politics in Egypt, Libya, and Yemen before the Arab Uprisings, see Larbi Sadiki, "Like Father, like Son: Dynastic Republicanism in the Middle East," *Policy Outlook* 52 (2009), Beirut and Washington: Carnegie Endowment for International Peace Middle East Center.

15. Lisa Anderson, "The State in the Middle East and North Africa," *Comparative Politics* 20, no. 1 (1987): 1–8.

16. See for instance how the German theorist Albert Haenel distinguishes between the state as being "universal" and being "total." Carl Schmitt states that Haenel "sees in the state an entity joining other organizations of society but of a 'special kind [that] rises above these and is all embracing.' Although its general purpose is universal, though only in [the] special task of delimiting and organizing socially effective forces, i.e., in the specific function of the law, Haenel considers wrong the belief that the state has, at least potentially, the power of making all the social goals of [human society] its goals too. Even though the state is for him universal, it is by no means total." See Carl Schmitt, *The Concept of the Political* (Chicago: University of Chicago Press, 1996), 24.

17. Ibid.

18. Ibid.

19. Benedict Anderson, *Imagined Communities* (London and New York: Verso, 2006).

20. Ibid., 6.

21. Ibid.

22. Ibid., 7.

23. Ibid., 7, Anderson states, "Coming to maturity at a stage of human history when even the most devout adherents of any universal religion were inescapably confronted with the living pluralism of such religions, and the allomorphism between each faith's ontological claims and territorial stretch, nations dream of being free and, if, under God, directly so. The gage and emblem of this freedom is the sovereign state."

24. Ibid., 7.

25. Eric Hobsbawm, *The Age of Revolutions, 1789–1884* (London: Abacus, 1962); Eric Hobsbawm, *The Age of Extremes: A History of the World, 1914–1991* (London: Michael Joseph, 1994).

26. Part of the interior ministry apparatus in central Cairo.

27. Gaston Bachelard, *The Poetics of Space* (New York: Beacon Press, 1994).

28. I borrow the idea of "reconcilation" from the work of the French Marxist intellectual Henri Lefebvre, who discusses reconciliation of mental and geographical spaces in *La production de l'espace* [The Production of Space] (Paris: Anthropos, 1974).

29. Larbi Sadiki, ed., *The Routledge Handbook of the Arab Spring: Reflections on Democratization* (London: Routledge, June 2014).

30. Giacomo Luciani, *The Arab State* (London: Routledge, 1993).

31. In Tunisia, women form nearly 30 percent of the Constituent Assembly as voted on October 23, 2011. This was the result of equal representation on electoral lists mandated by the parity law introduced in 2011. Not many women fared well in all of Egypt's 2012 elections for the National Assembly and the *Shura* Council, and the percentage is much lower than in Tunisia. Libya more or less adopted the Tunisian example, and this facilitated many more than 20 percent of seats in parliament going to women. In Yemen, there was a 30 percent quota adopted in order to include women in the process of the National Dialogue Conference, which is part of the embattled country's democratic transition process.

32. See also Labidi's chapter 9 in this volume, which provides an intimate perspective on Tunisia's parity law and its political context.

Index

About the Editors and Contributors

EDITORS

Fahed Al-Sumait is assistant professor of communication and department chair at the Gulf University for Science and Technology in Kuwait. He was previously a Fulbright-Hays fellow for his research into contested discourses on Arab democratization and a postdoctoral research fellow at the Middle East Institute in the National University of Singapore. Dr. Al-Sumait is founding member of the Association for Gulf and Arabian Peninsula Studies through the Middle East Studies Association. His notable publications include "Public Opinion Discourses on Democratization in the Arab Middle East" (2011), "Terrorism's Cause and Cure: The Rhetorical Regime of Democracy in the US and UK" (2009), as well as forthcoming chapters in *Transforming International Communication: Media, Culture, and Society the Middle East* (2014) and *State Power 2.0: Authoritarian Entrenchment and Political Engagement Worldwide* (2014). He is also coauthor of the book *Covering bin Laden: Global Media and the World's Most Wanted Man* (2014). Dr. Al-Sumait holds an MA and PhD both in communication from the University of New Mexico and the University of Washington, respectively.

Nele Lenze is researcher and editor at the Middle East Institute in the National University of Singapore. She obtained her MA in Arabic literature from Freie University Berlin and PhD in Middle East studies and media studies from the University of Oslo, where she also lectured on the Arab online sphere. Her research focuses on cultural online spheres in the Arabian Peninsula. Dr. Lenze's recent publications include "Aspects of Arabic Online Literature in the Gulf" (2011), "Short Stories and Interaction in Literature Online in the Gulf" (2012), and *Converging Regions: Global Perspectives on Asia and the Middle East* (forthcoming), which she edited with Charlotte Schriwer and Nele Lenze.

Michael C. Hudson is director of the Middle East Institute and professor of political science at the National University of Singapore. For many years, he was director of the Center for Contemporary Arab Studies and professor of international relations and Saif Ghobash Professor of Arab Studies at Georgetown University, where he is now professor emeritus. He holds both an MA and PhD in political science from Yale University. Among Dr. Hudson's publications are *The Precarious Republic: Political Modernization in Lebanon* (1968, 1985), *The World Handbook of Political and Social Indicators* (1972), *Arab Politics: The Search for Legitimacy* (1977), *The Palestinians: New Directions* (editor and contributor), and *Middle East Dilemma: The Politics and Economics of Arab Integration* (1999). His recent articles and chapters include "The Middle East in Flux" in *Current History* (December 2011), "The United States in the Middle East" in *International Relations of the Middle East* (2005, 2009), "Washington vs. Al-Jazeera: Competing Constructions of Middle East Realities" (2005), "U.S. Policy and the Arab-Israeli Conflict: What Should and Can the Next President Do?" in *Middle East Policy* 15, no. 4 (2008), "America's 'Palestine Fatigue'" in *Transformed Landscapes: Essays on Palestine and the Middle East in Honor of Walid Khalidi* (2009), and "The United States and West Asia" in *Perspectives on West Asia* (2012).

CONTRIBUTORS

Lars Berger received his MA and PhD in political science from the Friedrich-Schiller University of Jena in Germany. In 2006–2007, he was British Academy fellow at the department of politics at Newcastle University. Dr. Berger has studied, traveled, and researched widely in the Middle East, including a one-year study stay at the American University in Cairo, as well as further research trips to Egypt, the Moshe Dayan Center for Middle Eastern and African Studies in Tel Aviv, Israel, the King Faisal Centre for Research and Islamic Studies in Riyadh, Saudi Arabia, as well as the Council for British Research in the Levant in Amman, Jordan. In 2002–2003, Dr. Berger was one of two Germans to join the American Political Science Association's Congressional Fellowship Program, which provided him with unique insights into the foreign policy-making process in the United States. In 2007, the German Middle East Studies Association (DAVO) recognized his research with an award for the best PhD dissertation of the year. Since 2011, Dr. Berger has been a frequent commentator on various BBC TV and Radio channels regarding the political changes sweeping the Arab world.

Mark Farha (PhD Harvard, 2007) is assistant professor of government at Georgetown University's School of Foreign Service in Doha, Qatar. At Georgetown, he teaches courses on the history and politics of the modern Middle East. His publications include "Demographic Dilemmas" in *Lebanon: Liberation, Conflict, and Crisis* (2009), "From Beirut Spring to Regional Winter?" in *Breaking the Cycle: Civil Wars in Lebanon* (2007), "Historical Legacy and Political Implications of State and Sectarian Schools in Lebanon" in *Rethinking Education for Social Cohesion* (2012), and "Global Gradations of Secularism" in *Comparative Sociology* 11, no. 3 (2012). "Secularism in a Sectarian Society: The Divisive Drafting of the Lebanese Constitution" in *Constitution Writing, Religion, and Democracy* is forthcoming. Dr. Farha is currently editing a book manuscript titled "Secularism under Siege in Lebanon: Global and Regional Dimensions of a Malaise."

Nouri Gana is associate professor of comparative literature and Near Eastern languages and cultures at the University of California, Los Angeles. He published numerous articles and chapters on the literatures and cultures of the Arab world and its diasporas in such scholarly venues as *Comparative Literature Studies*, *PMLA*, *Public Culture*, and *Social Text*. He also contributed op-eds to such magazines and international newspapers as the *Guardian*, *El Pais*, the *Electronic Intifada*, *Jadaliyya*, and *CounterPunch*. He is the author of *Signifying Loss: Toward a Poetics of Narrative Mourning* (2011) and editor of *The Making of the Tunisian Revolution: Contexts, Architects, Prospects* and of *The Edinburgh Companion to the Arab Novel in English* (2013). He is currently completing a book manuscript on the politics of melancholia in the Arab world and another on the history of cultural dissent in colonial and postcolonial Tunisia.

James L. Gelvin is professor of modern Middle Eastern history at the University of California, Los Angeles. He received his BA from Columbia University, his master's in international affairs from the School of International and Public Affairs at Columbia University, and his PhD from Harvard University. He has taught at Boston College, Harvard University, MIT, and the American University of Beirut. A specialist in the modern social and cultural history of the Arab East, he is author of four books: *The Arab Uprisings: What Everyone Needs to Know* (2012, 2014), *The Modern Middle East: A History* (2004, 2007, 2011, 2015), *The Israel-Palestine Conflict: One Hundred Years of War* (2005, 2007, 2014), and *Divided Loyalties: Nationalism and Mass Politics in Syria at the Close of Empire* (1998), along with numerous articles and chapters in edited volumes. He is also coeditor of *Global Muslims in the Age of Steam and Print, 1850–1930* (2013).

Raymond Hinnebusch is professor of international relations and Middle East politics at the University of St. Andrews in Scotland and director of the Centre for Syrian Studies. He is author of *The International Relations of the Middle East* (2003); *Turkey-Syria Relations: Between Enmity and Amity*, coedited with Ozlem Tur (2013); *Sovereignty after Empire: Comparing the Middle East and Central Asia*, coedited with Sally Cummings (2011); *The Foreign Policies of Middle East States*, edited with A. Ehteshami (2001); *Syria: Revolution from Above* (2000); *Syria and Iran: Middle Powers in a Penetrated Regional System*, with A. Ehteshami (1997); *Authoritarian Power and State Formation in Ba'thist Syria: Army, Party and Peasant* (1990); *Peasant and Bureaucracy in Ba'thist Syria: The Political Economy of Rural Development* (1989); and *Egyptian Politics under Sadat* (1985).

Adel Iskandar is scholar of media and international communication. He is author and coauthor of several works including *Al-Jazeera: The Story of the Network that Is Rattling Governments and Redefining Modern Journalism*, coauthored with Mohammed el-Nawawy (2003). Iskandar's work deals with the intersections of media (print, electronic, and digital), culture, identity, and politics, and he has lectured extensively on these topics at universities worldwide. His latest publications include two coedited volumes titled *Edward Said: A Legacy of Emancipation and Representation*, coedited with Hakem Rustom

(2010), and *Mediating the Arab Uprisings* (2013), and his just-published title, the authored anthology *Egypt in Flux: Essay on an Unfinished Revolution* (2013). Iskandar is currently fellow at the Center for Contemporary Arab Studies (CCAS) and faculty member in the Communication, Culture, and Technology program at Georgetown University.

Rami G. Khouri is visiting scholar and lecturer at Princeton University and director of the Issam Fares Institute for Public Policy and International Affairs, American University of Beirut. He is also a syndicated columnist for the *Agence Global Syndicate* and the *Daily Star Beirut*.

Lilia Labidi, a Tunisian psychoanalyst-anthropologist, has been professor at the University of Tunis and is cofounder of the Association of Tunisian Women for Research and Development and the Tunisian Association for Health Psychology. She has organized numerous international conferences and documentary exhibitions on women's movements and social issues and is author of many publications on the Arab world, treating subjects such as gender issues, the feminist movement, the construction of identity, and the aftermath of the Arab Spring. From January to December 2011, Labidi was minister for Women's Affairs in the provisional Tunisian government, following the fall of the Ben Ali regime. She has held fellowships at the Institute for Advanced Study (Princeton) and the Woodrow Wilson International Center for Scholars (Washington, DC) and has been visiting professor at the American University in Cairo (Egypt) and Yale University (United States). She is currently visiting research professor at the Middle East Institute, National University of Singapore, working on Arab women scientists and on the current situation in the Arab world.

Anton Minkov has a PhD in Islamic studies, with a major in Islamic history (McGill University). He has taught history of the Middle East at Carleton University and University of Ottawa. His book *Conversion to Islam in the Balkans: Kisve Bahasi Petitions and Ottoman Social Life 1670–1730* was published in 2004. He has contributed to *Encyclopedia of Islam*, third edition, and published in *Islamic Law and Society* and other journals and volumes. Currently, Dr. Minkov works for the Centre for Operational Research and Analysis (CORA), part of Defence Research and Development Canada (DRDC). His recent work focused on the impact of demographics and other socioeconomic issues on security and regime stability in the Middle East.

Ergun Özbudun is professor of political science and constitutional law at İstanbul Şehir University, Turkey. He graduated from Ankara University law school and has taught at Bilkent University and İstanbul Şehir University. He was also research fellow at the Harvard University Center for International Affairs, the Truman Institute, and Hebrew University of Jerusalem. He has been visiting professor in Chicago, Paris, Columbia, and Princeton and is current member of the European Committee for the Prevention of Torture. His books in English include *Party Cohesion in Western Democracies: A Causal Analysis, Social Change and Political Participation in Turkey,* and *Contemporary Turkish Politics: Challenges to Democratic Consolidation.* He has also coedited five books and contributed to such international journals as *Comparative Politics, International Journal of Middle East Studies, Journal of Democracy, European Constitutional Law Review, European Public Law, South European Society and Politics,* and *Representations.*

Larbi Sadiki is Arab-Australian of Tunisian origin. He is specialist in Arab democracy and democratization, currently serving as associate professor of international relations at Qatar University. He was previously scholar at the Carnegie Middle East Center and has taught at Australian National University, University of Exeter, and University of Westminster. His recent work, *Rethinking Arab Democratization: Elections without Democracy,* was published in 2009. In it, he foreshadows the events of 2011 and was the first to have investigated the link between bread protests and democratization, making a strong case for bottom-up democratic transition. He is editing the forthcoming *Routledge Handbook of the Arab Spring,* to be released in 2014. He also writes a weekly column for Al Jazeera English and is currently completing a book on the Tunisian revolution.

Silvana Toska is doctoral candidate in political science and international relations at Cornell University, with Africa and the Middle East as her regional foci. Silvana works on various topics related to revolutions, such as the causes of the spread of revolutions, reasons why some revolutionary movements succeed in overthrowing regimes when others fail, and the connection between revolutionary governments and war. She also studies the impact of media in protest mobilization, the role of emotions in social movements, and gender politics in the Islamic world.

Peter Tikuisis is a senior defense scientist in the Socio-Cognitive Systems Section at DRDC Toronto. He began his career with DCIEM (forerunner of DRDC Toronto) in 1975 and received his PhD in mechanical engineering from the University of Toronto in 1981. His earlier research covered bubble physics, decompression sickness, carbon monoxide intoxication, thermoregulation, and dismounted soldier performance. Dr. Tikuisis's expertise involves theoretical, analytical, and experimental research in conjunction with mathematical modelling. He has held associate professorships at the Universities of Toronto and Waterloo and presently holds one at the Norman Paterson School of International Affairs at Carleton University. Since joining the Socio-Cognitive Systems Section in 2006, his work has expanded into the areas of terrorism, state instability, and military operational research.